Contemporary Gulf Studies

Series Editors
Steven Wright, College of Humanities and Social Sciences, Hamad bin
Khalifa University, Doha, Qatar
Abdullah Baabood, School of International Liberal Studies, Waseda
University, Tokyo, Japan

Salient Features:

- The Gulf lies at the intersection of regional conflicts and the competing interests of global powers and therefore publications in the series reflect this complex environment.
- The series will see publication on the dynamic nature of how the Gulf region has been undergoing enormous changes attracting regional and international interests.

Aims and Scope:

This series offer a platform from which scholarly work on the most pressing issues within the Gulf region will be examined. The scope of the book series will encompass work being done on the member states of the Gulf Cooperation Council (GCC): Saudi Arabia, Oman, United Arab Emirates, Qatar, Bahrain, Kuwait in addition to Iraq, Iran and Yemen. The series will focus on three types of volumes: Single and jointly authored monograph; Thematic edited books; Course text books. The scope of the series will include publications relating to the countries of focus, in terms of the following themes which will allow for interdisciplinary and multidisciplinary inquiry on the Gulf region to flourish:

- Politics and political development
- Regional and international relations
- Regional cooperation and integration
- Defense and security
- Economics and development
- Food and water security
- Energy and environment
- Civil society and the private sector
- Identity, migration, youth, gender and employment
- Health and education
- Media, literature, arts & culture

Satoru Nakamura · Steven Wright
Editors

Japan and the Middle East

Foreign Policies and Interdependence

Editors
Satoru Nakamura
Graduate School of Intercultural
Studies
Kobe University
Kobe, Japan

Steven Wright
College Humanities and Social
Sciences
Hamad bin Khalifa University
Doha, Qatar

ISSN 2662-320X   ISSN 2662-3218   (electronic)
Contemporary Gulf Studies
ISBN 978-981-19-3458-2   ISBN 978-981-19-3459-9   (eBook)
https://doi.org/10.1007/978-981-19-3459-9

Cover design by eStudio Calamar
Cover image: Fernando Tatay, shutterstock.com

This Palgrave Macmillan imprint is published by the registered company Springer Nature Singapore Pte Ltd.
The registered company address is: 152 Beach Road, #21-01/04 Gateway East, Singapore 189721, Singapore

PREFACE

Since the United Kingdom ended its security presence east of Suez in 1971, the academic literature on the international relations and international political economy of the Middle East has understandably given significant attention to the way the United States has engaged with the Middle East region. However, case studies such as Japan offer a more intriguing insight into how international relations can evolve without reliance on a securitization narrative. Japan's GDP reached the second largest globally in 1968, and since then, Japan's international political and economic role has evolved progressively through international forums such as the United Nations and the G7, but also more broadly within Asia as a significant economic, technological, and soft-power political actor across Asia. After the end of the Cold War, Japan's economic power was at its peak and becoming the largest source of Overseas Development Assistance (ODA) during the 1990s despite this period being an era of "aid fatigue" of donors.[1]

For the Middle Eastern region, Japan was historically a "latecomer" in comparison to Western countries, in addition to those from Africa and Central Asia, yet it has been a key market for Gulf energy exports as well as being a key investor within the Middle East. Based on an overall assessment of Japan's engagement with the Middle East, it can be considered

---

[1] Mitsuya Araki, "Japan's Official Development Assistance: The Japan ODA Model That Began Life in Southeast Asia," *Asia Pacific Review* 14, no. 2 (2007).

to have played a unique role, different from that of the United States and China, and this has progressively unfolded in a complex manner. Using Japan as a case study offers the potential for wider comparative studies on the international relations and international political economy of the Middle Eastern region, in addition to feeding into the literature on Japan's foreign and economic relations. To this end, this volume seeks to examine Japan's relations with the Middle East from both interdisciplinary and multidisciplinary perspectives, by drawing on case studies in bilateral relationships in addition to thematic topics that help explain the broader evolution of relations. It also seeks to achieve this by conceptualizing Japan's engagement with the Middle East and placing it in a historical context, thereby offering a fresh perspective on this intricate and complex relationship.

There is a rich body of exceptional scholarship concerning the various aspects of what can best be termed Japan's broader "geocultural relations" with the Islamic world. Persians arrived in Japan, during the Nara Period (710–794), given that Nara was the Eastward-end of the Silk Road. This led to trading in cultural artifacts and the formation of the initial basis of a relationship between what were distant civilizations. This was further supported by the *Namban* trade, which flourished through regional trading entrepôts.

Later still, the Ottoman Empire became the first Muslim-majority state to send a diplomatic mission to Japan in 1890.[2] Undoubtedly, the imperial character of Japan helped facilitate engagement with the Ottoman Sultanate through royal linkages, which was a pattern to be later witnessed in the more contemporary era with the monarchical states of the Middle East. While the intricacies of these initial contacts are well-established and comprehensively examined within academic scholarship concerning Japan and the Islamic world, in the contemporary era, trade linkages have proven to be critical in explaining the dynamics of how the relationship has further developed. Indeed, it was well-established that Japan's relations with the Middle Eastern region grew long before oil from the Middle East became significant in Japan's overall energy consumption scenario. It should not be forgotten that Japan's trade in the first half of the twentieth century with the Middle East centered on manufactured

[2] B. Bryan Barber, *Japan's Relations with Muslim Asia* (Cham, Switzerland: Palgrave Macmillan, 2020), 35.

textiles as these had been a significant export to the Middle East since the 1920s, and the sector accounted for 49% of total Japanese exports in 1950.[3]

Since the end of the Second World War, Japan's energy security and geo-political thinking has come to consider the Middle Eastern region as strategically significant for Japan. A broad conceptualization of Japanese foreign policy towards the region is that it has consistently sought stability in the Middle East and has tried to achieve this through its diplomatic initiatives. Although Japan has been a large consumer of Middle East energy, it has maintained a dual strategy of promoting friendly relations with the energy-producing countries while transforming Japan's domestic economic base to decrease dependence on hydrocarbons.

Here, it is observable that Japan's dependence on oil declined steadily after the first oil shock of 1973 due to energy-saving efforts and a renewed perspective on industrialization and manufacturing away from energy-intensive industries. This also led to an increased focus on nuclear energy and an approach of embracing "knowledge-intensive industries" and moving away from "energy-intensive industries." Naohiro Amaya, Vice-Minister of Japan's Ministry of International Trade and Industry (MITI), remarked that "the Japanese people are accustomed to crises like earthquakes and typhoons. The energy shock was a kind of earthquake, and so even though it was a great shock, we were prepared to adjust... it was a kind of blessing, because it forced the rapid change of Japanese industry."[4] This underlines the point that the story of oil and the Middle East, is interwoven in Japan's overall economic development, which emphasizes the importance of this volume's subject matter.

As Japan was effected by instability in the Middle East, it felt compelled to aide in conflict resolution and mitigation. The Palestine Liberation Organization (PLO) was given permission to create a permanent office in Tokyo after the First Oil Shock in February 1977. Then, on its own initiative, Japan attempted to mediate the Palestine conflict. During a visit to Saudi Arabia in September 1978, Prime Minister Takeo Fukuda (December 1976–December 1978), known for the "Fukuda ideology" (see Chapter 11), emphasized Japan's view that Israel should

---

[3] Ryutaro Takahashi, "Trade Policies of the New Japan", *Foreign Affairs* 30 (1951): 290.

[4] Daniel Yergin, *The Prize: the Epic Quest for Oil, Money, and Power* (New York: Simon & Schuster, 1992), 654–55.

relinquish all occupied Arab territory, including the Arab sector in Jerusalem. Members of Japan's parliament invited Yaser Arafat, the PLO's Chairman at the time, to visit Tokyo. The United States has no justification for refusing this request. Arafat met with Prime Minister Zenkou Suzuki (in office from July 1980 to November 1982) and Foreign Minister Sunao Sonoda (May 1981–November 1981). Japan's position on Arafat was outlined by the Japanese side, who said that Japan will work for comprehensive peace via negotiation with the United States and the European Commission (EC). Arafat agreed to the Fahd proposal's eight principles, which included Israel's right to life. The United States, on the other hand, continued to support Israel's human rights violations against Palestinians. In the face of PLO politics at home, Arafat has failed to reveal his opinion on Israel recognition.[5]

Up until 1993, Japan's aid to Palestine was channeled via the United Nations Relief and Work Agency for Palestine (UNRWA). Following the First Oil Shock, the Japanese government realized that assistance to Arab non-oil-producing nations and Palestinians would be highly valued by Arab Gulf energy producers. In 1974, Japan started to expand its funding to UNRWA. From US$ 1.1 million in 1974 to US$ 34.9 billion in 1993, Japan's yearly payout to UNRWA grew by more than three times. From 1953 through 1993, Japan provided UNRWA with a total of US$ 263.2 million in assistance.[6]

Following the announcement of the Oslo Accord in 1993, Western and Middle Eastern governments created a fund in Washington, DC in February 1994 to give financial assistance for the Oslo Peace Process. Japan took part in it and pledged to provide $200 million to Palestine within two years of its signing. Following the activation of the ODA Charter in 1992, Japan started adapting its foreign assistance to disburse aid in war zones, with Cambodia and Palestine serving as the first test cases. After being branded a "free rider" and "Cash dispenser" in the United States media during the Gulf Crisis in 1990, Japan saw Palestine assistance as an opportunity to reclaim its prestige in the Middle East. The Japanese government quickly overcame legal obstacles to direct foreign assistance to Palestine, which was "an entity without sovereign

---

[5] Wakatsuki Hidekazu, *Reisen no Shuuen to Nihon Gaikou: Suzuki, Nakasone,Takeshita no Gaikou 1980–1989* (Tokyo: Chikura publishing Co., 2019), pp .73–75.

[6] Kazuo Takahashi. Chuto Wahei to Nihon. In Kohei Hashimoto ed. *Senryaku Enjo: Chuto Wahei Shien to ODA no Shourai Zou* (Tokyo: PHP Interface, 1993), 95–96.

state status or governance. The Japanese government established a task group to prepare for a rapid rise in help in programs such as hospital rebuilding, refugee camp reconstruction, infrastructure reconstruction, administrative support, higher education amongst other related fields.[7]"

After the 2011 Tōhoku earthquake and tsunami, which resulted in the Fukushima Daiichi nuclear disaster, the subsequent suspension of all of Japan's nuclear power plants for a safety review saw an increased move towards Liquefied Natural Gas (LNG) as a feedstock for electricity power stations.[8] This emphasizes that international or domestic circumstances have historically shaped Japan's energy mix and impacted its strategy for energy security. This has proven to be a driver behind Japan's focus on LNG and greater engagement with Qatar in particular, given its position as the world's largest exporter of LNG.

Energy has clearly played a significant role in Japan's engagement with the oil-rich Gulf region, and has given this region special significance, remaining a key area of interest for Japan and its energy trading companies. As both the Iranian and Arab sides of the Gulf possess the largest global reserves of oil and are stable energy suppliers, the region has come to play a significant role in Japan's energy security calculations. For Japan, the geographical location of the Gulf is attractive as an alternative source of oil, as those within Russia or Africa are further geographically for Japan. African oil fields have tended to be more unstable in constant production and exposed regional conflicts than those in the Gulf. Therefore, the Gulf region has become the rational choice for Japan given its substantial reserves-to-production ratio, refining capacity, and potential role as a swing producer through OPEC.

A well-established aspiration for the Japanese government and Japanese oil companies during the 1950s was to obtain oil concessions, given the goal of achieving energy security for Japan away from the international oil majors. Despite the international oil companies (IOCs) offering oil through the international market being a more competitive option cost-wise; yet, this underlined the goal of having autonomy and energy security. Remarkably, Saudi Arabia had set Japanese companies harsher

---

[7] Mitsugu Saito. Nihon no Tai Palestina Shien no Jittai. In In Kohei Hashimoto ed. *Senryaku Enjo: Chuto Wahei Shien to ODA no Shourai Zou* (Tokyo: PHP Interface, 1993). 155–182.

[8] Steven Wright, "Qatar's LNG: Impact of the Changing East-Asian Market," *Middle East Policy* 24, no. 1 (2017).

conditions for an oil concession to be granted and saw Japan's concession as a new standard against the IOCs. At the same time, Saudi Arabia
imposed a total 56% tax on the profit of Japan's Arabian Oil Company,
when its concession contract was concluded in 1957. This was beyond the
typical 50–50 profit share for contracts with Western developers. Asian
countries, including Japan, have paid an "Asian premium" for the price
of oil imported from the Middle East.

Non-energy relations have also been significant for Japan's relations
with the Middle East. The Middle East has also shown development as a
consuming region for Japanese manufactured goods and investments. It
is also clear that since Japan transitioned its energy policy, its engagement
with the Middle East progressively evolved and became more complex.
What is clear from this volume is how Japan's relationship with the Middle
Eastern region varies by country. While this underlines the complexity of
the relationship, it is important to appreciate that the energy trade was
the primary driver for Japan's engagement through the Gulf region.

It also reminds us that there is a need for a degree of caution in general-
izing Japan's overall engagement with the Middle Eastern region, as clear
variances exist in the character of Japan's relationship with the Middle
Eastern countries. Based on this, it is therefore important to understand
the types of interdependence Japan has developed with Middle Eastern
countries. Indeed, energy-based relations, as well as non-energy-based
relations, are both drivers behind Japan's engagement with the Middle
Eastern region.

Japan's international relations is naturally a field that has benefited
from a rich scholarship. Takashi Inoguchi, engaged with the question of
whether there are any theories of international relations in Japan, persua-
sively identified four main traditions.[9] The first identified is the German
Staatslehre tradition, which dominated international relations in Japan
from 1868 to 1945, yet remained an applied approach in scholarship in
the post-second world war era. As an approach, it is historically grounded
where particular attention was given to a rich and descriptive examination of events' personalities and their consequences and had the benefit
of yielding policy-relevant research. It primarily engaged with the fields of
law and economics, rather than politics and sociology. The second main

---

[9] Takashi Inoguchi, "Are There Any Theories of International Relations in Japan?,"
International Relations of the Asia-Pacific 7, no. 3 (2007): 371.

tradition identified is Marxism, which was used as a counter-narrative to the *Staatslehre* approach. Inoguchi observed that this stemmed from the origins of social science (*shakai kagaku*) as a discipline in Japan being synonymous with the Marxist school of thought. The third broad tradition was that of historicism, where Japanese scholars examined international relations as a branch of historical research. This can be contrasted with the *Staatslehre* tradition, as it adopted more of a constructivist epistemology that focused on an accurate presentation of the facts. The final tradition in Japanese international relations concerns the application of American and European social scientific approaches. This has lent itself to a focus on methodological design, theory formation, and empirical testing of the theory.[10]

While each of the above-mentioned traditions in Japanese international relations continues to yield scholarship based on the followed epistemologies, one can argue that the dominant approach has gravitated to the application of the final approach, which requires the application of a more positivist approach of theory construction and testing. Based on this, international relations scholarship towards Japan has become more dominated by the neorealist paradigm, given that it accounts for a mercantilist approach in foreign policy coupled with a realist security policy. While the United States has remained the cornerstone of Japan's foreign policy post-1945, it is also clear that relegating Japan's foreign policy to an "America-first" security grounded analysis often does not account for the way Japan's foreign policy and political economy have evolved. This has been reflected in a domestic policy debate on what Japan's international role and foreign policy should be.[11]

It is particularly apparent that Japan's engagement within Asia does not always converge with that of the United States. In the post-Cold War era, the changed regional and international context gave way to assessments on the process of "Asianization" and how Japan's international relations and political economy should be understood within that context of regionalization.[12] The debate surrounding this context has given way

---

[10] Takashi Inoguchi, "Japan's Role in International Affairs," *Survival* 34, no. 2 (1992): 373.

[11] Inoguchi, "Japan's Role in International Affairs," 74.

[12] Yoichi Funabashi, "Japan and the New World Order," *Foreign Affairs* 70, no. 5 (1991).

to various interpretations of Japan's foreign policy, which is important in any conceptualization of Japan's relations with the Middle Eastern region. Kent Calder advanced an influential conceptualization of Japan as a "reactive state," as he observed a reluctance in the Japanese government to take significant foreign policy initiatives.[13] Moreover, there have been other important assessments on the role of domestic politics of Japan, in addition to the influential role of Japan's bureaucracy, as being a limiting factor for the government's greater autonomy and its foreign policy conduct, which reinforce the assessment of Japan as a reactive state.

Despite this, observations have been made to the contrary that Japan's foreign policy has been progressively more active, particularly in its leadership role within Asia. Japan's economic rise was worrisome in the 1980s, and its leadership was sometimes misunderstood and warned by the United States in the 1990s. However, Japan did not challenge the United States' hegemonic leadership role after the end of the Cold War era.

Considering how to conceptualize Japan's engagement with the Middle East, the majority of studies have sought to focus on Japan's interests in natural resources as being the primary driver. One such example is that of Sugihara and Allen,[14] who gave particular focus to the essential vulnerability of Japan's dependency on oil as being the core characteristic that has shaped Japan's engagement with the Middle East. Observing the opportunities that the changing context presented to Japan, it was clear that energy politics was the dominant factor in shaping the relationship. In contrast to this, B. Bryan Barber's study on Japan's relations with Islamic Asia, insightfully identified more to the relationship, noting that several advanced factors have shaped Japan's foreign policy towards Muslim Asia.[15]

While energy resources remain a constant feature in explaining the depth of the relationship, it is also clear that other factors are important. Providing their hierarchy may prove difficult as it depends on the context and case study concerned. Nevertheless, the core question remains what

---

[13] Kent E Calder, "Japanese Foreign Economic Policy Formation: Explaining the Reactive State," *World Politics* 40, no. 4 (1988).

[14] Kaoru Sugihara and J. A. Allan, *Japan in the Contemporary Middle East* (London: Routledge, 1993).

[15] Barber, *Japan's Relations with Muslim Asia*.

would be an appropriate theoretical conceptualization for this volume's examination of Japan's relations with the Middle Eastern region.

While economic linkages through energy exports are significant, as is demonstrated in this volume, the connections that exist may be seen to transcend oil and gas interests and vary depending on the specifics of the country concerned, or indeed on the sector where cooperative relations have been achieved. Although the role of the Middle East as an energy-exporting region is a necessary and inescapable feature of both energy security and national economic security calculations, we advance the view that it has now progressed beyond the trade in energy. In other words, Japan's engagement in the Middle East is more complex and varied: it is not only about the energy sector, and this relationship has flourished beyond energy-producing countries.

It is accurate to see the oil and gas exporting countries from the Middle East region as heavily dependent on Japan as a leading import market. Yet, the way international transactions between Japan and the Middle East are now taking place, in terms of flows of people, goods, money, and expertise, has led to the form of human interconnectedness with Japan that transcends the borders within the Middle East region regardless of whether they are oil and gas exporting countries. Although the trade flows may not be symmetrical, they are important to the countries concerned, and any disruptions to those transactions can prove to be costly to all parties concerned. Importantly, such relations can go beyond the realities of economics to achieve cooperative ties in various areas and on multiple levels.

On this basis, there is a need to move beyond traditional conceptions that identify factors that may shape the relationship towards one that conceptualizes the relationship based on interconnectedness and interdependence. This volume seeks to examine the question of the nature of the complex and multifaceted nature of Japan's relations with the Middle Eastern region, coupled with the recognition of varying levels of interdependence, through its various case studies on bilateral relations and thematic issues. On this, we see it as offering a useful conceptualization of the relationship and its prospects for future growth.

Kobe, Japan   Satoru Nakamura
Doha, Qatar   Steven Wright

ACKNOWLEDGMENTS

We would like to express our sincere gratitude to Waseda University for allowing us to have a session entitled "Japan-Middle East Relations: Origins, Dynamics, and Pluralism" at their international symposium "Comparative Studies of Islamic Areas: New Actors, Fresh Angles" in September 2018 organized by Organization for Islamic Area Studies, Waseda University (WOIAS). The insights and exchanges proved to be the impetus behind this project, and it underlined that a new conceptualization was needed to serve as a basis for future scholarship on this critical subject.

We also express our thanks and appreciation to Keiko Sakurai of Waseda University, whose support and encouragement allowed this project to be achieved. We also appreciate the engagement of Shigeru Sudo, Bahadir Pehlivantür, Yeva Harutyunyan, and Koji Muto, who provided valuable engagement on aspects of this book's theme.

CONTENTS

Notes on Contributors

Matthew Brummer is an Assistant Professor at the National Graduate Institute for Policy Studies (GRIPS) and research associate at The University of Tokyo. His research interests include the international political economy of science and technology, the psychology of threat perception, and Japan–Israel diplomatic relations. He earned his M.A. from Columbia University and his Ph.D. from The University of Tokyo.

Tomoyo Chisaka is a postdoctoral research fellow of the Japan Society of Promotion of Science. She did a part of Ph.D. research in Iran as a fellow of the Graduate School of Law and Political Science at the University of Tehran from 2019 to 2020. Her research interests include electoral management under authoritarian regimes and political institutions of post-revolutionary Iran. She obtained her Ph.D. in International Public Policy from Osaka University in 2021.

Koji Horinuki is a Senior Researcher of JIME Center at the Institute of Energy Economics, Japan (IEEJ). His main research interests are contemporary Arab Gulf politics, security, and social affairs. His recent works include Asian Migrant Workers in the *Arab Gulf States: The Growing Foreign Population and Their Lives* (Co-edited with Masako Ishii, Naomi Hosoda, and Masaki Matsuo. Leiden: Brill, 2019). He obtained his Ph.D. in Area Studies from Kyoto University in 2011.

Takeru Hosoi is a Professor of Economics at Kokugakuin University, Japan. His area of research expertise is on the industrial development of the Arab Gulf countries, including the energy industries. He also studies the international management strategies of Gulf companies. He obtained his Doctor of Business Administration from Ritsumeikan University, Japan.

Satoru Nakamura is a Professor of International Relations, and a Professor at Kobe University, Japan. His career includes special assistant at Japan Embassy in Riyadh, guest researcher at Japan's Upper House of Parliament, Qatar University, King Saud University and Graduate Institute of International and Development Studies, Geneva. His area of research expertise is the international relations, security, and history of the Middle East and Islamic World with focus on the Arabian Gulf. He obtained his Ph.D. (International Cultural Studies) from Tohoku University, Japan.

Yuko Omagari is Deputy Secretary General of the Japan–Turkey Society. She is currently seconded from Itochu Corporation. Her main research interests are Japan–Turkey relations, and contemporary Turkish society, especially secularism and the veiling issue. She withdrew her doctoral program with completion of coursework without degree at the Graduate School of Social Sciences, Institute for the Study of Global Issues, Hitotsubashi University.

Eitan Oren is Lecturer at the Japan Programme/Department of War Studies, Kings College London. Previously, he was Research Associate at the National Graduate Institute for Policy Studies (Tokyo). He holds a Ph.D. in International Relations from the University of Tokyo. Oren's research interests lie at the intersection of international security and the human mind.

Jun Saito is an Associate Senior Researcher of Area Studies Center, Institute Developing Economies (IDE-JETRO), Japan. He used to be a Visiting Researcher of the United Arab Emirates University. His field of research expertise is on the Arab Gulf economy, in addition to financial development, corporate governance, corporate finance, and financial market. He received his Ph.D. in Economics from Hitotsubashi University.

Steven Wright is an Associate Professor of International Relations, and an Associate Dean at Hamad bin Khalifa University, Qatar. He previously held the positions of Associate Dean, and the Head of the Department

of International Affairs, at Qatar University. His area of research exper-
tise is on the international relations and political economy of the Arab
Gulf states, in addition to energy geopolitics. He obtained his Ph.D. in
International Relations from the University of Durham.

Makio Yamada is a Senior Adviser at King Faisal Center for Research and
Islamic Studies in Riyadh. Previously he was a Lecturer at the Institute
for Transregional Study at Princeton University, and a Teaching Fellow at
SOAS University of London. He also conducted research at University of
Tokyo and Oxford Institute for Energy Studies. He obtained his D.Phil.
in International Relations and M.Phil. in Modern Middle Eastern Studies
from the University of Oxford (St. Antony's College).

Takayuki Yokota is an Associate Professor of School of Information and
Communication at Meiji University, Tokyo. He completed the Graduate
School of Asian and African Area Studies at Kyoto University, where
he obtained a Ph.D. His specialty is Middle Eastern studies, especially
Egyptian politics and Islamic movements. He published Islam and Mass
Movements in the Contemporary Egypt (Japanese) (Kyoto: Nakanishiya,
2006) and Trend of Fundamentalism: Muslim Brotherhood (Japanese)
(Tokyo: Yamakawa Shuppansha, 2009).

Abbreviations and Acronyms

ADGAS	Abu Dhabi Gas Liquefaction Company
ADNOC	Abu Dhabi National Oil Company
ADOC	Abu Dhabi Oil Company, UAE
AKP	Justice and Development Party, Turkey
ANRE	Agency for Natural Resources and Energy, Japan
ARF	ASEAN Regional Forum
CNOOC	China National Offshore Oil Corp
Darah	King Abdulaziz Foundation for Research and Archives, Saudi Arabia
DOD	Department of Defense, United States
DOS	Department of State, United States
EJUST	Egypt-Japan University of Science and Technology, in Egypt
EPA	Economic Partnership Agreement
FDI	Foreign Direct Investment
FTA	Free Trade Agreement
GAO	General Accounting Office
GCC	Gulf Cooperation Council
GPF	Gulf Peace Fund
ICDC	Iran Chemical Development Co.
ICT	Information Communication Technology
IEA	International Energy Agency
IJPC	Iran Japan Petrochemical Company
IOC	International Oil Company
IPO	Initial Public Offering
ISF	Israel Science Foundation
JASDF	Japan Air Self-Defense Force
JBIC	Japan Bank for International Cooperation

JCCME	Japan Cooperation Center for the Middle East
JCCP	Japan Cooperation Center Petroleum
JETRO	Japan External Trade Organization
JGSDF	Japan Ground Self-Defense Force
JICA	Japan International Cooperation Agency
JICE	Japan International Cooperation Center
JIFA	Japan-Israel Friendship Association
JIIA	Japan Institute of International Affairs
JIIN	Japan-Israel Innovation Network
JMSDF	Japanese Maritime Self-Defense Force
JOCV	Japan Overseas Cooperation Volunteers
JODCO	Japan Oil Development Company
JOGMEC	Japan Oil, Gas and Metals National Corporation
JSDF	Japanese Self-Defense Forces
JSPS	Japan Society for the Promotion of Science
KAEC	King Abdullah Economic City, Saudi Arabia
KOGAS	Korea Gas Corp
LDCs	Least Developed Countries
LDP	Liberal Democratic Party of Japan
LICs	Low-Income Countries
LMICs	Lower Middle-Income Countries
LNG	Liquefied Natural Gas
MECCJ	Japanese Institute of Anatolian Archaeology of the Middle Eastern Culture Center
MENA	Middle East and North Africa
MENAP	Middle East, North Africa and Pakistan
METI	Ministry of Economy, Trade and Industry
MITI	Ministry of International Trade and Industry
MOCO	Mubarraz Oil Company, UAE
MOD	Ministry of Defense
MOFA	Ministry of Foreign Affairs
MOU	Memorandum of Understanding
Mta	Million tonnes per year
NEO	Non-Combatant Evacuation Operations
NEXI	Nippon Export and Investment Insurance, Japan
NF	National Front
NGO	Nongovernmental Organisation
NHK	Japan Broadcasting Corporation (Nihon Hoso Kyokai)
NICDP	National Industrial Cluster Development Program, Saudi Arabia
NOC	National Oil Company
NPC	National Petrochemical Company
NPO	Non-Profit Organisation
NSC	National Security Council

OAPEC	Organization for Arab Petroleum Exporting Countries
ODA	Official Development Assistance
OECD	Organization for Economic Cooperation and Development
OPEC	Organization of Petroleum Exporting Countries
PCI	Pacific Consultants International, Japan
PIF	Public Investment Fund
PLO	Palestine Liberation Organization
R&D	Research and Development
RETI	Riyadh Technical Electronics Institute, Saudi Arabia
ROE	Rule of Engagement
S&T	Science and Technology
SABIC	Saudi Basic Industry Corporation
SAGIA	Saudi Arabian General Investment Authority
SEHAI	Saudi Electronics and Home Appliances Institute
SJAHI	Saudi-Japanese Automobile High Institute
SPA	Sales and Purchase Agreement
SVF	SoftBank Vision Fund, Japan
TCF	Trillion Cubic Feet
TEPCO	Tokyo Electric Power Company, Japan
TİKA	Turkish Cooperation and Coordination Agency (Türk İşbirliği ve Koordinasyon Ajansı Başkanlığı)
TJV	Turkish Japanese Foundation (Türk- Japon Vakfi)
Tpa	Tonnes per annum
TVET	Technical and Vocational Education and Training, Saudi Arabia
UAE	United Arab Emirates
UAR	United Arab Republic
UMICs	Upper Middle-Income Countries
UN	United Nations
UNIFIL	United Nations Interim Force in Lebanon
UNMIS	United Nations Mission in Sudan
UNPKO	United Nations Peace Keeping Operations
UNRWA	United Nations Relief and Work Agency for Palestine
USSR	Union of Soviet Socialist Republics
WMD	Weapons of Mass Destruction

LIST OF FIGURES

Chapter 6

Chapter 7

Chapter 8

Chapter 10

Chapter 13

LIST OF TABLES

CHAPTER 1

A Conceptualisation of Japan's Relations with the Middle East

Satoru Nakamura and Steven Wright

1 Complex Interdependence Revisited

The way states interact along national and transnational boundaries, along with the variety of ways in which relations can evolve in an imbalanced manner, prompted the ground-breaking seminal study by Keohane and Nye, *Power and Interdependence*. The authors proposed a powerful and coherent theory of interdependence, operating at the level of the international system, which sees realism as an insufficient explanation for state conduct and the need to assess relations based on the specifics and context of the relationship concerned. At its core, Keohane and Nye advanced a theory in which states' conducts operate on a spectrum: at one extreme, it can be defined in more realist terms where the state is concerned with

S. Nakamura (✉)
Graduate School of Intercultural Studies, Kobe University, Kobe, Japan
e-mail: satnaka@kobe-u.ac.jp

S. Wright
Hamad Bin Khalifa University, Ar-Rayyan, Qatar
e-mail: stwright@hbku.edu.qa

© The Author(s), under exclusive license to Springer Nature
Singapore Pte Ltd. 2023
S. Nakamura and S. Wright (eds.), *Japan and the Middle East*,
Contemporary Gulf Studies, https://doi.org/10.1007/978-981-19-3459-9_1

1

national security and survival, and if needed, will engage in warfare to secure it. At the other end of the spectrum, they advance a conception of "complex interdependence" where linkages between states have evolved in a manner which, to greater or lesser extents, are mutually dependent. Further development is, therefore, seen to advance their national well-being in line with the national interest.

While traditional theories of international relations would reject the dichotomy proposed by Keohane and Nye and how they interact based on the particularity of the circumstances, it is proposed here that aspects of this formula most convincingly allow for a theoretical conceptualization of Japan's relations with the Middle East. Moreover. The approach allows this volume to move beyond a simple essentialising of factors that have shaped the relationship.

In terms of the components of Keohane and Nye's theory, at the one end of the spectrum lies a neoliberal theory of power politics concerning interdependence. The strength of this work rests in it being grounded in focus on the power politics of interdependence and its ability to conceptualize the way transnational actors operate and influence foreign relations. This is important in the case of Japan, given that power politics in the form of Japan's relations with the United States remains a constant influence in shaping Japanese strategy and diplomacy, as evidenced by the lasting influence of the Yoshida Doctrine. Based on the identifiable need to incorporate a liberal focus on interdependence, coupled with a realist focus on power politics, a neoliberal perspective on Japan–Middle Eastern resource politics can help explain aspects of the relationship in particular circumstances. Equally, they can also help offer a perspective on the relations between transnational actors in the form of multinational corporations and how they figure into interstate relations. This can clearly be useful in understanding the impact of Japanese multinational corporations in the bilateral relationship.

At the opposite end of the spectrum, complex interdependence theory helps explain relations that are not easily explainable through the lens of classical realism and neo-realism. Keohane and Nye acknowledged that complex interdependence is likely to better explain the realities of the international system, as the neoliberal theory of power politics of interdependence theory largely relates to what can be seen as a theoretical extreme. In essence, complex interdependence comprises three defining characteristics. First, it acknowledges that there are multiple levels to the relationship between states. It is argued here that societies are connected via a variety of means, including as official and informal foreign office arrangements, face-to-face contact between non-governmental elites, transnational organizations, and informal links between governmental elites (such as multinational banks or corporations). Interstate, trans-governmental, and transnational connections are three ways that these routes might be categorized. Realists consider interstate relationships to be the standard conduits. When we loosen the realist premise that states behave cogently as units, a transgovernmental concept applies; yet when we loosen the assumption that states are the sole units, the concept of transnational applies.[1]

Keohane and Nye's observations on the complexity and multifaceted nature of connections is a convincing form of analysis when applied to the case of Japan's relations with the Middle East. In the subsequent chapters of this volume, we argue that given the complexities of the relationships that are examined, essentialising key factors would not be satisfactory for a higher-level theoretical conceptualization of the character of the relationship and how it has progressively expanded particularly in the contemporary post-second world war era.

The characteristics of the neoliberal theory power politics as advanced within Keohane and Nye's framework indicate that asymmetrical interdependence is often characterized by an unequal relationship. The authors observed that "asymmetrical interdependence can be a source of power we are thinking of power as control over resources, or the potential to affect outcomes. A less dependent actor in a relationship often has a significant political resource, because changes in the relationship (which the actor may be able to initiate or threaten) will be less costly to that actor than to its partners."[2]

In considering the case of Japan, the 1973 oil embargo was exemplified by Keohane and Nye for the application of this framework: Japan was explained as vulnerable to the significant resources controlled by oil-producing states. Here, the concept of two dimensions of power within the concept of asymmetrical interdependence *sensitivity* and *vulnerability*

---

[1] Robert O. Keohane and Joseph S. Nye, *Power and interdependence*, 4th ed. (Boston: Longman, 2012), 20.

[2] Keohane and Nye, *Power and interdependence*, 10.

can be observed. They clarified that sensitivity involves degrees of responsiveness within a policy framework—how quickly do changes in one country bring costly changes in another, and how great are these costs. It can be measured not merely by the volume of flows across borders but also by the costly effects of changes in transactions on societies or governments."[3] Indeed, they highlighted the sensitivity that the United States, Japan, and Western Europe were affected by the oil price crisis of 1971 and in the cases of the oil price rises of 1973–74 and in 1975.

While *sensitivity* interdependence is clearly a useful concept, *vulnerability* interdependence can be defined as an actor's liability to suffer costs imposed by external events even after policies have been altered. Since it is usually difficult to change policies quickly, the immediate effects of external changes generally reflect sensitivity dependence. Vulnerability dependence can be measured only by the costliness of adjusting over a given period. They insightfully observed that "vulnerability is particularly important for understanding the political structure of interdependence relationships. In a sense, it focuses on which actors are 'the definers of the ceteris paribus clause,' or can set the rules of the game. Vulnerability is clearly more relevant than sensitivity, for example, in analyzing the politics of raw materials, such as the supposed transformation of power after 1973."[4]

In terms of the relationship between the two dimensions, Keohane and Nye's framework identifies a hierarchy of power within asymmetrical interdependence as "vulnerability interdependence includes the strategic dimension that sensitivity interdependence omits, but this does not mean that sensitivity is politically unimportant. Rapidly rising sensitivity often leads to complaints about interdependence and political efforts to alter it, particularly in countries with pluralistic political systems."[5] For Japan, this underlines that while it has inherent sensitivity to energy insecurity from Middle Eastern oil-exporting countries, it also has options to mitigate against supply insecurity or significant cost fluctuations. Indeed, the different aspects of asymmetric interdependence can be usefully applied to

[3] Keohane and Nye, *Power and interdependence*, 10.

[4] Keohane and Nye, *Power and interdependence*, 13.

[5] Keohane and Nye, *Power and interdependence*, 14.

Japan's dependence on oil and gas imports and how it shapes its relations with oil-exporting nations and in its engagement with oil-consuming countries to mitigate against the challenges posed by cartel action as highlighted by Jun'ichirō Shiratori.[6]

2 Critical Adoption of Complex Interdependence in Middle East International Relations

Keohane and Nye considered Canadian–United States relations and Australian–American relations as case studies to compare different interdependences. The case of Canadian–United States relations was seen as an "ideal case of complex interdependence" to generalize world politics. It sets Canadian–United States relations as a proximate case and Australian–American relations as a remote case. The authors selected Canada, the United States, and Australia for their study, because of their cultural and political similarities; but it is observable here that this choice fixes factors of culture and domestic politics, and enables a comparison of the effects of security and distance factors over interdependence.[7] To research interdependence, previous studies have chosen cases of advanced economies or nations with similar cultures and political institutions. This volume is unique in its approach in that the study of interdependence, between Middle Eastern countries and Japan is one where there are dissimilar cultures and political regimes.

Ray Hinnebusch combines approaches of realism, center–periphery structure, and constructivism to interpret Middle East politics.[8] His approach discussed a broad range of regional politics in the Middle East, and necessarily considered the United States as the main outside power engaging in the Middle East. Building on this was Gerd Nonneman's seminal work on European–Gulf relations. Nonneman was critical of the adoption of the center–periphery approach, suggesting that the autonomy of the Middle Eastern countries is clearly observable in both energy-producing countries and non-energy-producing countries, and also that

---

[6] Jun'ichirō Shiratori, *"Keizai taikoku" Nihon no gaikō: enerugī shigen gaikō no keisei,1967–1974-nen* (Tōkyō-to Chūō-ku: Chikura Shobō, 2015).

[7] Keohane and Nye, *Power and interdependence*, 144–45.

[8] Raymond A. Hinnebusch, *The international politics of the Middle East* (Manchester: Manchester University Press, 2003).

European diplomacy toward the Middle East can be contrasted to the United States.[9] He adopted interdependence as an alternative approach to explain the relations of the Middle East and outside powers and applied it for the first time to analyze Europe–Gulf relations.

2.1   The Role of Security in Complex Interdependence

Complex interdependence theory acknowledges that "military force is not used by governments toward other governments within the region, or on issues when complex interdependence prevails."[10] Therefore, while conflicts without force continue to occur, the use of military force between nations under interdependence will decrease.[11] It is presented as one of the main counter-proposals to the ideal type of realism in international relations theory from the standpoint of interdependence.

A further aspect of complex interdependence theory concerns the absence of hierarchy among issues. This is important in that while classical realist international relations would focus on power as the determining factor in interstate relations, Keohane and Nye recognized that the factors that dominate the agenda depending on the time and contexts concerned. Therefore, while issues relating to energy or security may have a more dominant factor in particular bilateral relations, these would not apply in other contexts or at other periods with the same state concerned. This is certainly helpful when examining a broad conceptualization of Japan's relations with the Middle Eastern region, where there are clear variances based on interests, contexts, and capacities, as outlined in this volume.

Keohane and Nye selected case studies in North America and the Pacific, areas with a low incidence of violent conflict. In comparison, the Middle East and East Asia are insecure environments. This presents a different context in which Japan's relations with the Middle East have evolved and shaped the form and extent of the Middle East's interdependence with Japan. Japan's pacifist approach, which is enshrined in the Japanese constitution, has acted as a framing agent for foreign policy construction. However, after the Cold War's conclusion, Japan started

---

[9] Gerd Nonneman, *Analysing Middle Eastern foreign policies: the relationship with Europe* (London: Frank Cass, 2005), 15, 29.

[10] Keohane and Nye, *Power and interdependence*, 21.

[11] Keohane and Nye, *Power and interdependence*, 13–23, 286–7.

considering security alternatives for dispatching the Japanese Self-Defense Force (JSDF). Overall, the ability to apply such nuances in international relations to complex case studies underline the value of applying Keohane and Nye's theoretical spectrum to the case study of this volume.

As Keohane and Nye position interdependence theory as an alternative to realism, it has a drawback in that it does not address realism theory's subcategories. Complex interdependence was uninterested in doing practical research on security issues and did not build on observations of security-related facts. One may readily recall that although nations in interdependent relationships seldom resolve international disputes via the use of force, they do not forsake weapons or military preparations in the face of threats.

After all, the government does not abandon all security measures and militaries based on a reality of strong connectivity with other states. States displaying complex interdependence see dangers arising from non-interdependent relationships and assess the likelihood that non-military disputes may develop into military conflicts. Thus, the difference between offensive and defensive realism explains how states see and behave in the context of interdependence. In reality, states with a high degree of interdependence maintain a defense-oriented security realism, while abandoning offense-oriented security perceptions. A state engaged in interdependence analysis anticipates unanticipated risks and dangers in regional politics, prioritizes defensive alternatives when calculating security, and concludes that abstaining from the use of military force is a logical and lucrative decision.

Thus, interdependence and defense oriented realism are not mutually exclusive, but are rather complimentary from this vantage point. Thus, although Japan and its ties with Middle Eastern nations may be explained via the lens of complex interdependence, their security policies can be characterized as defense-oriented realism, at least toward one another, from a theoretical perspective.

2.2   Agenda Politics

Another element of complex interdependence theory is its discussion of "agenda politics." Here, an acknowledgment is made that a national agenda may be shaped by a variety of levels and circumstances. While conventional international politics assumed that governments set their agendas mainly in response to security concerns or balance of power calculations, Keohane and Nye demonstrate that domestic politics may and do dominate the agenda and drive foreign policy. As discussed before in relation to the 1973 oil crises in the Middle East and Japan, the social unrest produced by high levels of inflation had a direct effect on how the government reacted to what became a national cause for worry. As the Middle East's interdependence with Japan grows, the scope of interaction expands beyond energy transactions and aid delivery to include the formation of partnerships, investments, advanced forms of educational cooperation, high-quality infrastructure building construction, and cultural activities.

2.3   The Role of International Actors

The function of international organizations is a last fundamental component of complex interdependence theory. From a traditional realist perspective, international organizations (IOs) are seen as small players with little influence and strength, particularly in terms of military might. In contrast, Keohane and Nye believe that international organizations are critical actors capable of developing and shaping agendas, and forming coalitions. Jun'ichir Shiratori has convincingly demonstrated how Japan's participation in the establishment of the International Energy Agency (IEA) in the aftermath of the 1973 oil embargo demonstrates how Japan collaborated with the United States and other Western powers to counterbalance the Organization for Arab Petroleum Exporting Countries (OAPEC)'s influence oversupply and price.[12] This is significant because it challenges the conventional wisdom that Japan adopted a pro-Arab stance despite its relations with the United States. A more accurate reading of Japan's behavior at the time indicates that it employed a sophisticated foreign policy strategy to maximize its national interests.

Regional organizations in the Middle East seem to have had little influence in fostering Japan's complicated interdependence with Middle Eastern nations; however, it was multinational corporations that encouraged the diversification of commercial ties, acted as sponsors of friendship organizations, and served as bridges during political crises between Middle Eastern nations and Japan.

---

[12] Jun'ichirō Shiratori, *"Keizai Taikoku" Nihon no Gaikō: Enerugī Shigen Gaikō no Keisei,1967–1974-nen* (Tōkyō-to Chūō- ku: Chikura Shobō, 2015).

Finally, by defining the connection between Japan and Middle Eastern nations as one of interdependence via the lens provided by Keohane and Nye, we can see the diverse nature of the relationships that exist throughout the Middle East area, as shown in this book. While this is true in certain instances, it is an oversimplification on the part of research focusing on this subject to reduce Japan's ties with the Middle East to be a result of energy relations. While it is undeniable that Japan's energy interests are critical for understanding its contemporary engagement with the Middle Eastern region, this does not account the way the Japanese government, or indeed transnational actors in former multinational corporations, have engaged with non-energy-producing states throughout the region. Furthermore, such an analysis obscures the complexity and richness of how Japan's bilateral relationship with each country has grown and evolved to take on a significance that either transcends the bilateral relationship or positions it for the post-oil era, which is becoming increasingly important as Japan gradually transitions to renewable energy.

In a final analysis, by conceptualizing Japan's relationship with the Middle East through an interdependence lens, we can move away from the tendency to analyze the relationship in terms of essentialising factors and toward one that can be more convincingly explained through a theoretical and empirical framework. Thus, complex interdependence theory is pushed with the knowledge that it will be updated in light of the diversification of agendas, the identification of numerous channels, the precise function of defense-oriented realism, and the accompaniment of cultural understanding.

3   Methodological Approach

This book establishes a fresh understanding of Japan's bilateral ties with Middle Eastern nations. It is intended to be the first analytical research to conceive Japan's ties with concept of adopted complex interdependence. The case studies of Japan's ties with Saudi Arabia, the United Arab Emirates, Iran, Turkey, Egypt, and Israel provide a variety of bilateral case studies. After WWII, the Middle East–Japan relationship developed in three stages. Bilateral interdependences are shown when they progress beyond energy to non-energy economic ties, strategic collaboration, and cultural exchanges. Their interconnectedness has evolved across three tiers: royal, governmental, and through people-to-people contacts.[13]

3.1   Complex Interdependence through Intercultural Communication

Japan's connections with the Middle East extend back to pre-World War II, but the steady process of dependency creation via government and public involvement began after Japan's independence in 1951. The first phase is Restart or Opening of Ties (Post-1945) (1950s–1960s), during which diplomatic relations were reestablished or opened for the first time, and private sector or citizen exchanges began. The second phase is Frictions and Stabilization (1970s–1990s), of which the First Oil shock and regional wars harmed bilateral relations, but both parties overcame them. The third phase is Diversification of Relations (post-2000s), during which multilevel and multifaceted relationships evolved. At this point, many Middle Eastern nations have formed strategic alliances with Japan.

Each instance of Japan's relations with Saudi Arabia, the United Arab Emirates, Iran, Turkey, Egypt, and Israel is unique in terms of timing and type of procedures. For example, the most of the Gulf Emirates gained full independence in 1971 (with Kuwait in 1961, and their establishment of formal ties with Japan took longer than that of other Middle Eastern nations (Fig. 1).

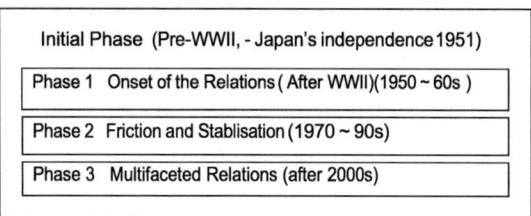

Fig. 1   Process to Deepen Interdependence

---

[13] Satoru Nakamura, "Challenges for Qatar and Japan to Build Multilayered Relations," *Gulf Monographic Series*, no. 2 (2016).

MOFA, Japan applied a concept named "multilayered relations" to describe relations with some countries in the 2000s. "Multilayered relations" connotes polysemous to apply international relations. This volume defines this as "Multifaceted relations" as being diversified to multilevel channels and agendas in multiple areas. Diversification of communication channels and expansion of agendas facilitate concurrent processes associated with the development of complex interdependence. Increasing communication channels means that specialists from a broader range of areas engage in the process of establishing interdependent relationships, which naturally expands agendas.

In January 2001, then-Foreign Minister Yohei Kono visited the Gulf States and reached an agreement with their leaders on Japan's "New Initiative toward multifaceted relations with the Gulf States" (so-called Kono Initiative). The Kono Initiative's first pillar was "Civilisational Dialogue with the Islamic World." Arab and Islamic worlds were eager for opportunities to dialogue with the world after the September 11th incident, and Japan offered them an avenue. Building cultural and religious understanding had world-class significance at the time in integrating Muslim intellectuals into the global community.

The Japanese government can be interpreted as having had a clandestine objective of restoring diplomatic and commercial ties with Saudi Arabia and Kuwait to the level they were before the failure of the Arabian Oil Company's oil concession renewal negotiations in January 2000. The "Dialogue of Civilizations" conference between the Islamic World and Japan began in March 2002 in Manama and continued annually until 2010. At the 6th "Civilisational Dialogue" in March 2008 hosted by Saudi Arabia, the Saudi King Abdullah bin Abdul Aziz Al Saud announced an initiative for world interreligious dialogue, which resulted in the World Conference on Dialogue in Madrid, Spain, in July 2008.

By April 2006, during the visit to Tokyo of then-Saudi Crown Prince Sultan bin Abdul Aziz Al Saud, he signed a joint statement titled, "Towards construction of Japan Saudi Arabia strategic multilayered relation." Saudi Arabia joined the WTO in December 2005, reaffirming its commitment to diversifying the Saudi economic structure. Japan's proclamation of a "multifaceted relationship" with Saudi Arabia underlined Japan's desire to contribute to Saudi Arabia's economic diversification.

Shinzo Abe was arguably Japan's most active prime minister in terms of diplomacy. During his second premiership (December 2012–September 2020), he traveled overseas 176 times. He fully recognized that strategic relationships and interdependence must be founded on shared values and an appreciation for the cultures of others.

The Abe government announced the Open India-Pacific Strategy in August 2007. Shinzo Abe, Japan's prime minister, paid a visit to India and delivered a speech before the Indian parliament. He argued for the dynamic coupling of the two Oceans for liberty and prosperity. He suggested establishing a strategic relationship between India and Japan based on mutual respect for each other's values, cultures, and history. He referred to Dara Shikoh (1615–1659), a prince of the Mughal Empire who embodied the era's pluralistic thinking and tolerant administration.

Abe's premiership advanced recognition of the importance of Islam in Japan's diplomacy. He made a policy speech at his visit to King Abdul Aziz University in May 2013. He stated that Saudi Arabia and Japan share common values of "Coexistence and Co-prosperity (al-taʿāish)," "Collaboration (al-taʿāun)," and "Harmony and Tolerance (al-tasāmuh in Arabic or Wa in Japanese)." This implied that the Muslim World and Japan could build interdependence over multiple agendas since he meant that "Coexistence and Co-prosperity (al-taʿaish)" is for economic value, "Collaboration (al-taʿāun)" is a value for politics and security, and "Harmony and Tolerance (al-tasāmuh)" is a cultural value. At his visit to Egypt in 2014, he stated that Japan and the Muslim World share values of "moderation (middle way, wasat)."

3.2   Interdependence through Numerous Channels and Different Agendas

Japan's Ministry of Foreign Affairs (MOFA) used the term "multilayered (multifaceted) relation" to characterize its ties with many nations in the 2000s. The term "multifaceted relationship" refers to international connections that are diverse in nature. This book defines a "multifaceted relationship" as "relationships that are diverse in terms of channels and agendas across many domains." Diversifying the agenda of interdependence beyond energy transactions to other areas such as politics, non-energy economic connections, culture, and security are examined in the context of Japan–Middle East relations.

In the case of Japan's ties with the Middle East, the channels of communication for interdependence are classified into three main categories: royals, government, and civilians. Monarchs of the Middle East exercise political authority, while the Emperor of Japan is a symbol of the state of Japan and the people's unity, since Japan is a constitutional monarchy. The disparity in power and prestige between such royals does not hinder royal ties between the Middle East and Japan, since both play significant diplomatic roles. The Emperor of Japan practice of "imperial diplomacy." Although the Emperor cannot speak on diplomatic or political matters, he serves as a conduit for Japan's dignity and cultural promotion overseas. In the Middle East, governments and people do not have the same historical animosity against Japan's Emperor as in East Asia, so the impact is positive given the monarchial character of the GCC states.

Citizens may act as conduits for interdependence in a variety of ways, including as employees of multinational corporations, members of international organizations, NGOs, artists, intellectuals, students, journalists, and athletes (Fig. 2).

The three-tiered pathways of interdependence may also be thought of as "three-tier diplomacy." Government-to-government interactions are considered "regular" diplomacy, while the royal role is referred to as "imperial diplomacy" and the citizen role as "citizen diplomacy" (Fig. 3).

Diversification of agendas between Japan and the Middle East's energy-exporting nations is described as expanding energy transactions to include political collaboration, non-energy commerce, investment promotion, Official Development Assistance (ODA), cultural exchanges, and security

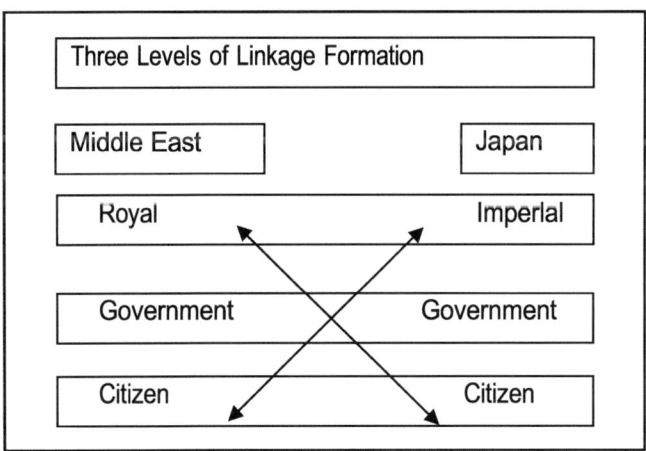

Fig. 2 Three Level of Channels between the ME and Japan

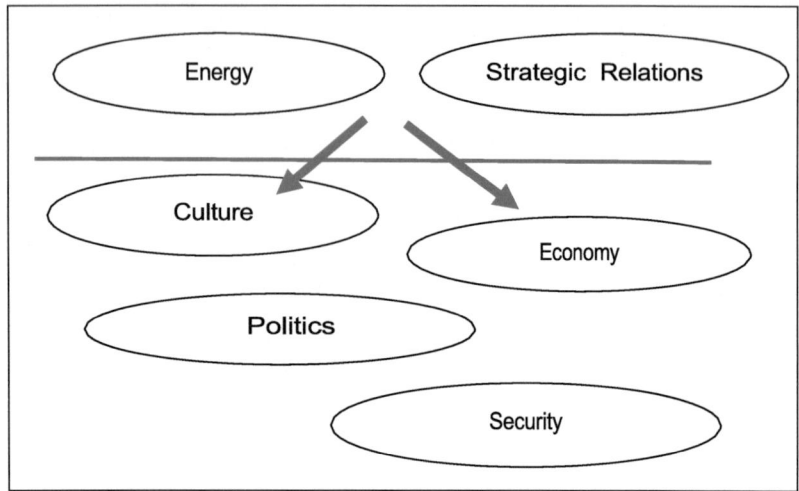

Fig. 3   Multiplying agendas that deepen interdependence

cooperation. With regards to Japan's involvement with non-energy-exporting nations in the Middle East, such as Egypt and Turkey, Japan assessed their strategic position in a broader regional context as a cross-roads for Continentals upon the resumption of ties after WWII. Their connections thereafter became more diverse in terms of ODA, bilateral relations, economics, and culture.

3.3   The Emergence of Japanese Interests and Security in the Middle East

Japan's national interests have been addressed in policy circles and in official papers, but they remain difficult to grasp unambiguously, in part because each politician, bureaucrat, scholar, and document have a different perspective on what constitutes Japan's national interests. It's difficult to think that beyond a basic grasp of energy security, Japan's national interests in the Middle East have been generally understood among Japanese citizens and intellectuals overseas.

Complex interdependence adapted to the above observations on numerous channels and different agendas serve as the foundation for this volume's examination of Japan–Middle East relations. Then, has Japan's sensitivity and fragility remained the same as they were during the First Oil Shock? Is Japan implementing effective strategies to address its vulnerability? Although the Japanese government has no territorial or military aspirations in the Middle East, how does the private sector in Japan evaluate commercial and investment possibilities there? Is the Japanese government taking adequate steps to safeguard Japanese nationals' lives and property in the Middle East? Does cultural value intersect with national interests in any way? Complex interdependence theory does not imply a particular response method to all of the above-mentioned aspects of individual situations.

3.3.1   Energy Security
Japan's energy security policy has an inherent contradiction in the aftermath of the Oil Shock; Japan views Middle East reliance as dangerous and opposes efforts to spread the risk. On the other hand, MITI and the Agency of Mineral Resources and Energy seek to improve bilateral relations with energy-producing nations to ensure supply sources and to encourage Japanese companies to invest in the development of oil resources in these countries.

The Japanese government and business sector seek low-cost energy supply, but they must also address energy conservation and expand clean energy and renewable energy facilities, which demand significant investment. Japanese policymakers continue to see renewable energy as a more challenging energy source of which production depends on climatic or technological advancements. Thus, there is cause for this book to address what path has Japan's dependency on the Middle East taken. Does energy security concern on the part of energy users and producers converge to promote energy interdependence?

3.3.2   Economic Interests
Japan's national interests regarding developing nations are stated in the ODA Charter, which was revised in 2003. It affected Japan's national interests in part because Japan's economic strength had peaked, and the Japanese government was tasked with justifying the financial burden of ODA to Japanese people. In 1992, Japan's first ODA Charter included no reference to Japan's national interests. From 1991 to 2000, Japan's ODA expenditure was the biggest in the world. In 1997, the tied aid ratio of Japan's ODA distribution reached 0%, indicating that Japan's

ODA money was allocated for the development of other countries' prosperity. However, Japan's productive age population peaked in 1995, and the financial burden of supporting an aging society compelled all financial expenditures, including ODA, to be evaluated and amended.

The ODA Charter amended in 2003 stated, "Japan proactively contributes the stability and development in developing countries through ODA," and followed with, "it is related to security and prosperity of Japan, and furtherance of Japanese nationals' interests."[14] These phrases may be construed in a variety of ways. Japan's national interests are defined in terms of interdependence with developing nations, since the declared goals of Japan's ODA are to contribute to the peace and development of developing country communities, thus assisting Japan's security and prosperity.

The Advisory Panel on the History of the 20th Century and on Japan's Role and World Order in the 21st Century, is a non-governmental organization comprised of private sector executives, academics, and former government officials that presented the idea of Japan's national interests as "common interests of the respective states."[15] In 2015, Japan's ODA Charter was renamed the International Cooperation Charter, which states, "a peaceful, stable and prosperous international community is increasingly intertwined with the national interests of Japan."[16] Again, this indicates that Japan's interdependence with emerging countries is in its national interest.

Japan's Economic White Paper issued in 2012 pointed out that Japan's trade balance deficit in 2011 was the first after 31 years. The Great East Japan Earthquake that occurred in March 2011 was the most serious and inescapable factor which damaged Japan's trade. The rising oil price and increased LNG import were the main factors to increase imports.[17]

[14] MOFA. *Seihu Kaihatsu Enjo Taikou no Kaitei ni tsuite, Heisei 15 Nenn 8 Gatsu 29 Nichi Kakugi Kettei.* https://www.mofa.go.jp/mofaj/gaiko/oda/seisaku/taikou/taiko_030829.html.

[15] Report of the Advisory Panel on the History of the 20th Century and on Japan's Role and the World Order in the 21st Century. August 6, 2015. p. 5. https://www.kan tei.go.jp › singi › pdf › report_en.

[16] MOFA, Japan. Development Cooperation Charter. November 2, 2015. https://www.mofa.go.jp/policy/oda/page_000138.html.

[17] METI, Japan. *Tsuusho Hakusho 2012 (PDF Ban)*. 233. https://www.meti.go.jp/rep ort/tsuhaku2012/2012honbun_p/index.html.

As a result, Japan's strategy in the 2010s emphasized interdependence with developing nations through ODA and corporate development in emerging markets. This volume aims to evaluate Japan's interdependence with the Middle East through the lens of energy security and non-energy economic ties. It is worth noting that the second Abe administration pursued measures to foster mutual understanding while simultaneously promoting infrastructure export to the Middle East.

3.3.3   Protection of Nationals

The Iran–Japan Petrochemical Company (IJPC) sustained the biggest loss in the Middle East for a Japanese company. It was founded in 1973 as a joint venture by Iran Chemical Development Co. (ICDC) and Iran's National Chemical Company (NPC). ICDC's biggest investor was Mitsui & Co., Ltd. However, the Islamic Revolution in Iran happened before the complex's completion, but the Japanese government pressed for its continuance and completion. Then, in September 1980, during the Iran–Iraq war, Iraq launched an air assault on it, severely destroying the project and preventing it from being finished. Mitsui & Co. agreed in 1991 to abandon its investment of 75 billion yen and loan of 125 billion yen, and paid 130 billion yen (about 1 billion US$) as settlement money. Mitsui finished its payment in 1991.[18]

The JSDF refrained from protecting Japanese citizens by evacuation from the Middle East, despite the fact that this would be detrimental to Japan's national interests there. The Arabian Oil Company Ltd. did not evacuate its Khafji oil field, which is in the neutral zone between Saudi Arabia and Kuwait, during Iraq's invasion of Kuwait in 1990, and remained there until the ground battles erupted in January 1991 to demonstrate their solidarity with Kuwait and Saudi Arabia. Later still, in 1995, Japanese business remained despite there being a coup d'état in Qatar. In January 2013, an attack by an Islamic terrorist organization kidnapped over 150 workers at a building site in Algeria for a natural gas refining facility, and ten Japanese employees were held hostage and killed.

In 2017, Japan had over 11,000 citizens residing in Middle Eastern nations. The UAE was home to the biggest Japanese population, with over 4,000 residents, followed by Turkey, Saudi Arabia, Israel, Egypt, and Qatar. Following the "Arab Spring," many countries reduced their

---

[18] Hitoshi Suzuki, "IJPC Purojekuto wo Saikou Suru," *Ajiken World Trend*, 211 (2013): 32–33.

investments in the Middle East, while the Japanese boosted their interests in the Middle East, especially in Saudi Arabia, the United Arab Emirates, and Israel. Japan's investment balance in the Middle East was 8.4 billion yen at the end of 2020, up 70.1 percent from the end of 2010. At the end of 2020, Japan's investment balance in Saudi Arabia was 4.5 billion yen, while in the UAE, it was 2.1 billion yen.[19]

3.3.4   Cultural Understanding

Cultural comprehension is a necessary condition for diplomatic and commercial ties. If two "crosscultural actors" come into conflict with one another, they will be unable to collaborate. Thus, cultural exchanges and mutual understanding may help to improve communication and provide pathways for players from other cultures to strengthen their interdependence.

Edward Said argued against the idea of "clash of civilizations" and proposed "clash of ignorance," arguing that civilizations would not clash, and that what would clash is ignorance and barbarism. For Japan, the Middle East has always been "others," but "others in connection." Since the eighth century, Middle Easterners have been a part of Japanese civilization. Since the late nineteenth century, Muslims have been a part of Japanese society.

Nonetheless, Japanese connections were limited throughout those periods, and they were forced to study and adapt Middle Eastern customs to develop a dependency on a wider scale via intimate ties. Understanding Islam may pave the way for non-Muslim Japanese diplomats and businesspeople to establish diplomatic ties, energy security, and economic success. Understanding Islam for the purpose of promoting commerce and fostering amicable connections may foster interdependence, in contrast to orientalism's aim of using knowledge and human and social sciences as a means of invasion, domination, and exploitation.

If accurate information of Islam and Muslims is communicated across cultural boundaries and trust is fostered via transcultural dialogue, business and diplomacy become viable. In light of this, the following chapters will seek to offer observations. This book will explore many cultural interactions that occurred during the early stage of Japan's complex interdependence with the Middle East.

---

[19] JETRO. *Nihon no Tyokusetu Toushi (Zangaka), 1996–2020 nenn matsu taigai.* https://www.jetro.go.jp/world/japan/stats/fdi.html.

3.3.5 Multilateralism

Japan's connection with the Middle East benefits the Middle Eastern nations' regime security and stability. Japan, on the other hand, was classified as a potential adversary during the Arab–Israeli War of 1973, because Japan had previously refrained from exporting weapons to Arab nations.[20] Japan has adhered to a policy of non-intervention and a neutral position in regional disputes. It has facilitated technology transfers. All of these efforts by Japan contribute to the improvement of regime security in the Middle East by increasing bilateral interdependence. China used this "Japan model of Middle East involvement" as a template for its own Middle East strategy.

The tangible impact of this shift toward a more sophisticated foreign policy engagement with the Middle Eastern region has allowed for a deepening of the relationship across the region and its evolution in a complex manner. Although Japan interprets safeguarding its national economic interests as an overarching objective to pursue despite balancing this with its entrenched bilateral relationship with the United States in a sophisticated manner, it can be argued here that this was to set the course of Japan's future complex relationship with the Middle Eastern region, which is the subject of this book. Based on this, it is, therefore, appropriate to provide some reflections on the characteristics of Japan's foreign policy before moving toward an overall conceptualization which will reflect the case studies on Japan's bilateral relations in addition to thematic studies that are the subject matter of this volume.

It can be argued here that 1973 proved to be an important juncture in Japan's foreign policy, as it was faced with the reality that there was an inherent incompatibility between the pursuit and advancement of national economic growth and economic security, against its bilateral support for the United States' position.

It is also worth noting that the oil crisis proved to be a shock to Japan's self-perception as a pacifist and friendly nation to others, as OAPEC did not initially classify Japan as a friendly country.

Moreover, Japan's ability to rely on the United States to safeguard its interests came into question as the United States Secretary of State Henry Kissinger could not provide guarantees that the United States would safeguard Japan's oil supplies. It is on this basis that Prime Minister Kakuei

---

[20] Katakura, Kunio and Katakura, Motko. 1991. *Japan and the Middle East*. Tokyo: Middle East Institute, 74.

Tanaka's outline of Japan's new strategy for "resource diplomacy" (*shigen gaikō*) was initiated; however, as highlighted in the above text, it should not be viewed as a binary strategy at the expense of Japan's strategic relations with the United States, but rather as the contemporary onset of Japan exercising sophisticated statecraft to further its own strategic national economic interests.

Notably, this onset of sophisticated diplomacy that Japan was able to advance interests in the Middle Eastern region facilitated the growth of its engagement regionwide, which necessarily has evolved in a complex and multifaceted manner. Nevertheless, it is also clear that the relationship can be described as one of interdependence where both Japan and energy-exporting Middle Eastern states arguably have a mutually dependent relationship.

4   PREVIEW OF CHAPTERS

Based on the above conceptualization, the challenge is for a multi-disciplinary and interdisciplinary approach to expose the complexity, multifaceted nature, and specific drivers that are specific to the context of the country or to the transnational theme. Even energy-producing countries have shifted their agenda with Japan from the energy sector toward multiple areas. These are the questions and issues that the following 11 chapters seek to engage. This book is divided into two main sections: the first examines Japan's bilateral relationship with key states across the Middle Eastern region. It engages with states where the primary relationship rests on energy; however, other country-specific case studies across the Middle Eastern region are also engaged to expose clear variations across the region. These include energy-exporting countries and strategic countries (non-energy-exporting countries or low-quantity energy producers). The second section of the volume examines thematic issues—energy-related, non-energy, political, and security issues—given that they crosscut states on a transnational basis.

In Chapter 2, "Japan's Relations with Saudi Arabia: The *Evolution* of Energy Diplomacy in Response to the Developmental Shift in the Rentier State," Makio Yamada argues that Japan's energy diplomacy with Saudi Arabia should best be understood as having evolved based on a developmental shift in Saudi Arabia. It is argued that the drivers of the relationship needs to be understood from both sides and that Saudi Arabia's drive for economic diversification has aided the complexity and depth of the relationship. This chapter also identifies the importance of applying a political economy perspective to bilateral case studies involving an oil-importing country and an oil-exporting country, and it serves to further underline the multiple levels of analysis that are needed to understand the complexity of the relationship.

In Chapter 3, "Japan – UAE Relations: Establishment of Multifaceted Interdependence Based on Energy," Koji Horinuki gives attention to a comparatively understudied, yet important bilateral relationship, which accounts for one-quarter of Japan's crude oil imports. The chapter documents the overall nature of the bilateral relationship and argues how it has evolved in multiple areas beyond the energy equation. A central argument of this chapter is Japan's complicated process of acquiring oil concessions in the UAE, and the relationship has evolved to become one that is multifaceted, multilevel, and that demonstrates clear interdependency. This serves to illustrate the need to go beyond energy relations as an essentialized factor in the bilateral relationship.

In Chapter 4, "The Three Cycles of Rise and Fall in Iran–Japan Relations: from Energy Studies to Political Causal Analysis," Tomoyo Chisaka challenges to focus the bilateral relations beyond energy relations. However, the case study establishes a variance from bilateral interdependence between the Middle East and Japan for this volume. Nevertheless, Japan is a rare country that maintains ties with Iran despite regional and international pressure to lessen or exclude relations. The chapter clearly illustrates Japan–Iranian relations has experienced three period of "rise and fall" cycles from 1929 to 2019 due to foreign intervention, war, and security issues.

In Chapter 5, "The Relations between Japan and Turkey: Three-Dimensional Diplomacy: Roles of the Imperial Family, the Government, and Citizens," Yuko Omagari argues that Japan's engagement with Turkey relies primarily on social and cultural linkages rather than purely economic relations. While this chapter establishes that Japan's relations with Turkey have a long-standing pedigree, it provides recognition that multi-dimensional diplomacy offers a more realistic understanding of the complexity, drivers, and characteristics that have allowed the bilateral relationship to develop. Recognition is given to how the Imperial Families, governments, citizens, and the commercial sector, have had an influence on both the depth of the relationship and its development into multiple areas.

In Chapter 6, "Japan–Egypt Bilateral Relations: A Main Pillar of Japanese Middle Eastern Policies," Takayuki Yokota provides an examination of the bilateral relationship beyond the oil-producing states by focusing on Egypt. Given the lack of research that has been conducted on this bilateral relationship, he focuses on how it is involved with reference to politics, official development assistance, and cultural exchanges. Although it is argued that the relationship has a long-standing history dating back to the Edo era, recognition is given to the way Egypt forms an essential pillar as part of Japan's comprehensive regional diplomacy. This underlines the strategic design of Japanese foreign policy in the Middle East and how interests vary by context.

In Chapter 7, "Beyond Power, Before Interdependence: Complex Synergy and Japan–Israel Relations," Brummer and Oren argue that the interdependent relationship needs to be understood as being the product of complex synergy, which comprises several factors that drive the relationship. The relationship is argued to have transcended energy and the role of the United States. The debate focuses on the timing of the synergy effect, which was triggered by the structural transformation of politics, economy, and security in both countries. The areas of their synergy are pointed out as parliamentary democracies, free-market economic principles, and cyber security, which better explain the full complexity of the evolving relationship.

In Chapter 8, the book moves to the second section, which focuses on thematic issues. In this chapter, "Oil Market and Supply: from the Perspective of Japan's Energy Policy," Takeru Hosoi considers how the oil sector figures into energy security, policies, and calculations by both Japan and energy-exporting countries. It is argued that although oil served as a driver of Japan's engagement with the Middle Eastern region, the context is changing based on the formation of energy policy that has finally reached the stage named 3E+S (Energy Security, Environment, Economy and Safety) and the structure of the energy industry. It is worth noting here that although it is established that Japan's trading relationship is evolving, it is also an opportunity that will lead to diversification as adaptation in foreign policy terms takes place.

In Chapter 9, "The LNG Sector in Japan's Relations with the Middle East," Steven Wright considers how the LNG sector has evolved with particular reference to Japan's relations with the UAE, Oman, and Qatar in particular. He argues that while LNG has been a primary driver of

Japan's engagement with Qatar, it has also been facilitated by multinational corporations that have enabled interdependence to be achieved the relationship. Moreover, the changing context of the global energy sector, in addition to the drive toward renewables, is recognized as being a changemaker in the relationship; notably, the LNG sector is proving to be an opportunity for a broadening of the relationship into the area of renewables. This underlines the argument of a multifaceted and multidimensional impact of the LNG sector on Japan's engagement with Qatar, in particular.

In Chapter 10, "Investment and Trade Promotion Policies: Gulf and Japan's Non-energy Sector Interdependence," Jun Saito examines the evolution of economic connections beyond trade in natural resources between GCC and Japan through statistical data. The chapter does not assume the economic potential in the energy-producing nations as fundamentally blocked by a "curse of energy" but examines their potential for economic development and transformation. Furthermore, it shows advances in trade policy agreements, joint-ventures, banking, foreign direct investment (FDI) of GCC nations and Japan. Finally, it offers several suggestions to address structural issues inherent in asymmetrical trading partners, GCC and Japan.

In Chapter 11, "Origin of Japan's Relations with Middle Eastern Countries by Practical Internationalism," Satoru Nakamura engages with the domestic debates within Japan on the purpose and direction of foreign policy. He argues that subtle shifts in Japan's engagement with the Middle Eastern region depend on the prevailing perceptions, followed by Japan's leadership. Rather than taking the view that a constant approach is adopted toward the Middle Eastern region, Nakamura identifies characteristics in Japan's foreign policy and the political trends that stemmed from the idiosyncratic outlook of the incumbent Prime Minister. This underlines the domestic level in the analysis in terms of how Japan's foreign policy materializes and challenges neo-realist assumptions that the international system and security are the primary drivers of foreign policy strategy.

In Chapter 12, "Nonmilitary Contribution by Japan in the Gulf Crisis: Funding, Intelligence Gathering, Releasing Hostages, and Minesweeping," Satoru Nakamura builds on Chapter 10 by providing an applied examination of Japan's engagement during the Iraqi invasion of Kuwait as a case study. He argues that the "reactive state" approach that was first advanced by Kent Calder is insufficient as a means of explaining Japan's conduct during this crisis. He further argues that the reality of Japan's foreign policy during this period was much more complex and based on a much more complex understanding of both of Japan's interests and the way decision-making takes place. Indeed, by debunking conventional held wisdom on the character of Japanese foreign policy, Nakamura further allows us to advance the perspective that Japan's foreign policy in the Middle Eastern region is best understood as being multi-dimensional and multifaceted, and that the concept of complex interdependence as advanced by Keohane and Nye, is a suitable theoretical lens for understanding Japan's foreign policy.

In the final chapter, co-authored by Satoru Nakamura and Steven Wright, we attempt to synthesize the volume's main lessons, areas of dispute, and points of consensus. The areas of disagreement about Japan's involvement in the Middle Eastern region center on what such engagement should look like and where it should go. In terms of convergences, the book demonstrates how Japan's relationship with the Middle East has developed into one with many dimensions, multifaced, and context-specific variables. Additionally, it has aided in the advancement of a conceptualization of multifaceted complex interdependence as a useful framework for providing a more macro perspective on the relationship; however, it is only through examining the intricacies of bilateral relationships and thematic issues on a more micro level that a broader and deeper understanding can be achieved which opens up new areas for academic enquiry.

References

Barber, B. Bryan. *Japan's Relations with Muslim Asia*. Cham, Switzerland: Palgrave Macmillan, 2020.

Calder, Kent E. "Japanese Foreign Economic Policy Formation: Explaining the Reactive State." *World Politics* 40, no. 4 (1988): 517–41.

Funabashi, Yoichi. "Japan and the New World Order." *Foreign Affairs* 70, no. 5 (1991): 58–74.

Hinnebusch, Raymond A. *The International Politics of the Middle East*. Manchester: Manchester University Press, 2003.

Inoguchi, Takashi. "Are There Any Theories of International Relations in Japan?" *International Relations of the Asia-Pacific* 7, no. 3 (2007): 369–90.

Inoguchi, Takashi. "Japan's Role in International Affairs." *Survival* 34, no. 2 (1992): 71–87.

Katakura, Kunio, and Motko Katakura. 1991. *Japan and the Middle East*. Tokyo: Middle East Institute.

Keohane, Robert O., and Joseph S. Nye. *Power and Interdependence*. 4th ed. Boston: Longman, 2012.

Nakamura, Satoru. 2016. *Challenge for Qatar and Japan to Build Multilayered Relations*. Gulf Studies Center Monographic Series, No. 2. Doha: Qatar University.

Nonneman, Gerd. *Analysing Middle Eastern Foreign Policies: The Relationship with Europe*. London: Frank Cass, 2005.

Shiratori, Jun'ichirō. *"Keizai Taikoku" Nihon No Gaikō: Enerugī Shigen Gaikō No Keisei,1967–1974-Nen*. Tōkyō-to Chūō-ku: Chikura Shobō, 2015.

Sugihara, Kaoru, and J. A. Allan. *Japan in the Contemporary Middle East*. London: Routledge, 1993.

Takahashi, Ryutaro. "Trade Policies of the New Japan." *Foreign Affairs* 30 (1951): 289.

Wright, Steven. "Qatar's LNG: Impact of the Changing East-Asian Market." *Middle East Policy* 24, no. 1 (2017): 154-65.

Yergin, Daniel. *The Prize: The Epic Quest for Oil, Money, and Power*. New York: Simon & Schuster, 1992.

CHAPTER 2

Japan's Relations with Saudi Arabia: The *Evolution* of Energy Diplomacy in Response to the Developmental Shift in the Rentier State

Makio Yamada

In January 2001, Foreign Minister Yōhei Kōno announced a new plan for Japan's relations with the Gulf states. The plan, often referred to as the Kōno Initiative, aimed at diversifying Japan's oil-based reciprocal bilateral relations with the Gulf states toward more multifaceted arrangements, which it described as a "multilayered" relationship (*jūsō-teki-na kankei*).[1]

---

[1] Yōhei Kōno, "Wangan shokoku tono jūsō-teki-na kankei ni muketa shin-kōsō," Japanese Ministry of Foreign Affairs, 9 January 2001, viewed 31 July 2020, https://www.mofa.go.jp/mofaj/press/enzetsu/13/ekn_0109.html.

M. Yamada (✉)
King Faisal Center for Research and Islamic Studies, Riyadh, Kingdom of Saudi Arabia
e-mail: makio.yamada@lincoln.oxon.org

© The Author(s), under exclusive license to Springer Nature Singapore Pte Ltd. 2023
S. Nakamura and S. Wright (eds.), *Japan and the Middle East*, Contemporary Gulf Studies, https://doi.org/10.1007/978-981-19-3459-9_2

Regarding Saudi Arabia, efforts to build such a multifaceted relationship were already seen in the 1970s, exemplified by the Japanese–Saudi Economic and Technological Cooperation Agreement in 1975, following which two joint petrochemical projects were created in the Jubail industrial city on the Gulf coast. From the 2000s onward, more diverse bilateral cooperation developed, leading to the launch of *Saudi Japan Vision 2030*, a comprehensive framework of bilateral collaboration disclosed in 2017 that corresponded with the goals of *Saudi Vision 2030*, the Saudi state's current blueprint for development. In particular, educational cooperation has substantively progressed in the current century, with three technical training colleges supported by Japanese firms and experts opening in Saudi Arabia, alongside Japanese universities accepting hundreds of Saudi scholarship students.

As the Introduction to this edited volume discusses, Japan's multilayered relations with the Gulf states can be understood as cases of *complex interdependence*, a neoliberalist concept proposed by Robert Keohane and Joseph Nye (1977) that is often contrasted with neorealist assumptions of security-oriented interstate competition—as advanced by Kenneth Waltz (1979).[2] Nevertheless, security in the context of Japanese–Saudi bilateral relations matters in forms different from that seen in the Waltzian balance of power/capabilities, such as *energy security* for Japan and *regime security* for Saudi Arabia. Therefore, the dyadic understanding of Japanese–Saudi interdependence should accompany accordingly tailored explanations which incorporate such relevant ideas in relation to security. Certain questions stand out in particular. Why did the reciprocal oil-based bilateral relationship, which simultaneously serves the energy security of Japan and the regime security of Saudi Arabia (via oil rent in the Saudi rentier state), begin to diversify in the 1970s? Why did such diversification *not* occur before despite the two states' earlier agreement to develop bilateral non-oil cooperation (such as the agreement between Prince Sultan and Foreign Minister Kosaka in 1960)? Why did particular new layers, such as investment and educational cooperation emerge, at these particular times? And how are these three main layers—energy, investment, and education—*causally* related? This chapter will answer these questions by

---

[2] Robert Keohane and Joseph Nye, *Power and Interdependence: World Politics in Transition* (Boston: Little, Brown, 1977); Kenneth Waltz, *Theory of International Politics* (Reading: Addison-Wesley, 1979).

introducing the notion of an *evolution* of energy diplomacy and developing a theoretical discussion in a methodologically integrative-pluralist manner.

1 Theoretical Framework: *Evolution* of Energy Diplomacy

Energy diplomacy generally refers to diplomacy aimed at enhancing a country's energy security,[3] while energy security is commonly understood as a stable supply of energy sources at reasonable prices.[4] One of the shortcomings of the existing literature on energy diplomacy (or similar issues), especially concerning oil, is that it is often understood only from the viewpoint of oil-importing countries. While this in itself may not be surprising given the conventional conception of energy security for oil-importing countries, such understanding is insufficient since energy diplomacy always has its counterpart—an oil-exporting country. A full understanding of energy diplomacy would require the systematic incorporation of the viewpoint of the latter.

In this chapter, I argue that energy diplomacy *evolves* in response to the developmental shift in oil-exporting countries. It does so through three stages. In the first stage, energy diplomacy is mainly about maintaining a friendly diplomatic relationship with an oil-exporting country, while in the second stage, it involves facilitating investment for economic diversification in the counterpart oil-exporting country. Finally, in the third stage, this evolved energy diplomacy includes educational cooperation. In the following, the nature of each stage will be described.

1.1 *The First Stage: Maintaining a Friendly Diplomatic Relationship*

This first stage represents a simple exchange of exporting and importing oil through the market, where energy diplomacy is largely about maintaining a friendly relationship with a counterpart state so that the inflow

---

[3] Steven Griffiths, "Energy Diplomacy in a Time of Energy Transition," *Energy Strategy Reviews* 26 (2019).

[4] United Nations, *World Energy Assessment: Energy and the Challenge of Sustainability* (New York: United Nations Development Programme, 2000).

of oil continues without interruption. Such energy diplomacy corresponds with the early phase of development in oil-exporting countries, whereby oilfields are discovered and developed and the country increasingly becomes dependent on the income it produces. A state whose fiscal foundation is reliant on oil income is often referred to as a "rentier state," particularly by experts on the political economies of oil-exporting countries in the Middle East and North Africa. A common definition of a rentier state, which was made by Giacomo Luciani (1987), is a state that relies on external revenues (rent) for over 40% of its revenues.[5] It is assumed that the political regimes of these rentier states, in many cases authoritarian ones, aim to ensure their political stability through distributing oil income to citizens, largely through public-sector employment. Therefore, as Gustav Boëthius (2011) argues, "demand security," i.e. security concerning the demand for their oil in oil-importing countries, is fiscally integral to their regime security.[6] This means that oil-exporting countries also desire to maintain friendly diplomatic relationships with oil-importing countries, as much as oil-importing countries do with them.[7]

Globally, this first stage was embedded in the division of labor between the advanced and developing worlds.[8] Oil in developing countries (which in most cases was pumped by Western firms) was exported to advanced economies at low prices, thereby helping them to produce industrial products and sell them to the world, including these developing countries. This division of labor emerged in the mid-twentieth century when oil became the main source of global energy, and combined with decolonization, it significantly changed the relationship between natural resources and development. In the traditional Western modernization paradigm,

---

[5] Giacomo Luciani, "Allocation vs. Production States: A Theoretical Framework," in Hazem Beblawi and Giacomo Luciani (eds.) *The Rentier State* (London: Croom Helm, 1987).

[6] Gustav Boëthius, "Demand Security: The GCC's Side of the Energy Security Coin," *MEI Insight* 34 (2011).

[7] Historically, however, some oil-exporting countries attempted to use oil as a political weapon in international relations. Given the demand security, this was a double-edged sword for these countries. The practice of oil embargos by Arab oil-exporting states in the Arab–Israeli War in 1973, for instance, led importers of their oil, particularly European countries, to diversify the oil supply sources; thus they had to start seeking importers elsewhere, particularly in Asia.

[8] This hierarchical division of labor was often criticized as *dependency*.

an economy's proximity to natural resources had been seen as a strong advantage for industrialization: Some economic historians attribute the *Great Divergence*—the West's rapid rise after the medieval period—to the immediate availability of coal to Western industrialists.[9] Nevertheless, oil in oil-exporting Arab countries in the early days of the Cold War did not so much fuel their own industrial growth but rather supported the economies of US allies, such as Western European countries and Japan.

1.2   The Second Stage: Facilitating Investment for Economic Diversification

Energy diplomacy, however, began to shift toward its second stage in the 1970s, to a point where it involved bilateral economic cooperation, particularly a facilitation of investment. In fact, it was a time when the concept of energy security first emerged fully, whereas the notion of security had hitherto been confined largely to military affairs. Before the 1970s, oil had almost been a normal commodity traded on the global market, but such old dynamics began to change in the late 1960s when the bargaining power of states from the Organization of Petroleum Exporting Countries (OPEC) began to grow. OPEC was created in 1960 with the ultimate goal of taking back sovereignty over natural resources from Western oil firms, but the organization was not capable of achieving this goal initially due to its fear of losing markets. Nevertheless, as the supply–demand gap in the global oil market narrowed in line with the growth of advanced economies, OPEC countries started to nationalize the assets of Western oil firms operating in their countries. This shift of ownership made it necessary for oil-importers to deal directly with OPEC states, bringing oil and energy into the domain of international relations.

OPEC states raised the price of oil and also began to use the revenue generated to fuel their own industrial growth. Although oil is sometimes viewed as a negative factor in long-term development (such as by resource curse theorists),[10] oil-exporting countries in the Gulf region

[9] Kenneth Pomeranz, *The Great Divergence: China, Europe, and the Making of the Modern World Economy* (Princeton: Princeton University Press, 2000).

[10] The literature on the resource curse is immense, but the following publication offers one of the good reviews: Paul Stevens, Glada Lahn, and Jaakko Kooroshy, *The Resource Curse Revisited* (London: Chatham House, 2015).

have achieved some degree of economic diversification, especially establishing themselves as the world's major producers of petrochemicals, thereby making use of the presence of plentiful reserves of oil and gas.[11] Gulf nations' industrialization has been slower than seen in Asia, but this is partly due to the lack of favorable initial conditions. For instance, the literacy rate in Saudi Arabia in the middle of the last century was estimated to be only 5%—one of the world's lowest.[12] However, oil-exporting countries in the Gulf have certainly been embedded in the gradual transition of the global economy away from the hierarchical division of labor, whereby the Industrial Revolution eventually spread beyond the West and select East Asian economies, as some call it the *Great Convergence* in contrast to the Great Divergence.[13]

Internally, their pursuit of economic diversification also came to be enmeshed in the concern for regime security. As discussed above, the regime security in rentier states has traditionally been maintained through the distribution of oil income exchanged with the political support (or at least the silent approval) of the regime. However, this rather static model hinges upon two core assumptions: high oil prices and a small population. As the first oil boom (1973–1983) ended and populations grew rapidly, these regimes' relative distributive power began to decline, and unemployment emerged in the 1990s. The rise of jobless youth came to be seen not only as an economic and a social problem, but also as a security concern as Islamist violence rose to prominence.[14] The Arab Spring, beginning in 2011, also pressurized regimes in oil-exporting Arab countries to deal with unemployment: although they were relatively shielded

---

[11] In this respect, oil shapes the *nature* of industrialization, promoting the development of some sectors while hindering that of others, rather than generating all-out negative or positive impacts on economies. I once coined the term "production with rentier characteristics" to describe this phenomenon.

[12] Mordechai Abir, *Saudi Arabia: Government, Society and the Gulf Crisis* (London: Routledge, 1993), 15.

[13] Leonid Grinin and Andrey Korotayev, *Great Divergence and Great Convergence: A Global Perspective* (Cham: Springer, 2015); Richard Baldwin, *The Great Convergence: Information Technology and the New Globalization* (Cambridge: Harvard University Press, 2016).

[14] Some research statistically shows the tendency of educated, jobless young individuals engaging in violent political activism due to their feeling of a sense of deprivation. See: Diego Gambetta and Steffen Hertog, *Engineers of Jihad: The Curious Connection between Violent Extremism and Education* (Princeton: Princeton University Press, 2016).

from the uprisings owing to their greater capacity to co-opt through distribution in the second oil boom (2004–2014), the end of the boom made job creation an imminent challenge. This was particularly the case for Saudi Arabia, which has a large population—over 24 million national citizens currently—and whose GDP per capita is not as high as the UAE or Qatar.

The desire for economic diversification made these oil-exporting countries seek not only demand security in their relationships with oil-importing countries, but also bilateral economic cooperation targeting the development of non-oil industries. Especially when the supply–demand gap in the global oil market is narrow, states in oil-exporting countries enjoy strong bargaining power in making such demands, as they can make the stable supply of oil and economic cooperation a quid pro quo arrangement. Such a new requirement created the need for oil-importing countries to "evolve" their energy diplomacy to include non-oil economic cooperation programs.

The scope of such evolved energy diplomacy is often greater than that of conventional aid diplomacy targeting developing countries. Indeed, major instruments in aid diplomacy do not work effectively for oil-exporting countries: Since they are already capital-abundant, they are not in any particular need of financial assistance, in-kind provision, or debt relief, which ordinary developing countries receive through aid diplomacy.[15] What they demand instead is a transfer of industrial production through foreign direct investment (FDI). This was a new challenge for oil-importing countries, as it created a need for them to facilitate private firm investment in their counterpart oil-exporting countries through setting up appropriate institutional frameworks for public–private partnerships. Such facilitation includes various supportive measures, ranging from financing through state-owned financial institutions and assisting the formation of consortiums (in order to disperse risks among multiple investors), to providing knowledge about the market to potential investors (to overcome the information asymmetry problem) and creating opportunities for bilateral business matching between firms in the two countries.

[15] Hans Morgenthau, "A Political Theory of Foreign Aid," *American Political Science Review* 56, no. 2 (1962); Carol Lancaster, *Foreign Aid: Diplomacy, Development, Domestic Politics* (Chicago: Chicago University Press, 2007).

1.3   The Third Stage: Advancing Educational Cooperation

As such investment-oriented economic cooperation fundamentally relies on market forces, the focus of the evolved energy diplomacy inevitably begins also to include bilateral cooperation for improving the investment climate of the counterpart oil-exporting country. One of the indispensable elements in investment climate is human capital,[16] which is today itself considered a major driver of economic growth.[17] Faster improvements in literacy, at least partly, explain why the West was able to benefit from the Industrial Revolution first, followed by East Asia.[18] In comparison, literacy levels in other parts of the world remained low until recently, when the world was yet to see the Great Convergence.[19]

In this respect, oil-exporting countries, particularly those in the Gulf, suffer from particular human capital barriers. Unlike other developing economies, they have sufficient financial capital to spend on public education, which in most cases is provided free of charge, and they can also offer large numbers of scholarships for citizens to study abroad and compensate for the under-development of their own higher education institutions.[20]

---

[16] Koji Miyamoto, "Human Capital Formation and Foreign Direct Investment in Developing Countries, OECD Development Centre Working Paper, 211, 2003.

[17] Richard Easterlin, "Why isn't the Whole World Developed?" *Journal of Economic History* 41 (1981); In recent years, however, institutionalists have claimed that the deeper cause of economic growth is institutions, and human capital is dependent on them, i.e. good education requires good school systems (Daron Acemoglu, Francisco Gallego, and James Robinson, "Institutions, Human Capital, and Development," *Annual Review of Economics* 6 [2014]). Nevertheless, others argue that the quality of institutions is affected by human capital, i.e. operating good school systems requires well-educated individuals. It is increasingly considered today that institutions and human capital mutually influence and progress hand in hand (Hugo Faria, Higo Montesinos-Yufa, Daniel Morales, and Carlos Navarro, "Unbundling the Roles of Human Capital and Institutions in Economic Development," *European Journal of Political Economy* 45 [2016]).

[18] James Melton, *The Rise of the Public in Enlightenment Europe* (Cambridge: Cambridge University Press, 2001); Akira Hayami, "Introduction: The Emergence of "Economic Society," in Akira Hayami, Osamu Saito, and Ronald Toby (eds.) *The Economic History of Japan, 1600–1990, Volume 1: Emergence of Economic Society in Japan, 1600–1859* (Oxford: Oxford University Press, 2004).

[19] UNESCO, *Education for All Global Monitoring Report 2006* (Paris: UNESCO, 2006).

[20] For instance, Saudi Arabia provided over 200,000 students with scholarships to study abroad between 2005 and 2015 ("Foreign Scholarship Tied to Employment," *Arab News*, 8 June 2015).

However, at the same time, their labor market often requires higher standards of human capital compared to other developing countries, because, due to their higher levels of income per capita, development models based on low-cost labor are not highly available to them, and so their citizens tend to avoid low-paid jobs which are predominantly taken by foreign workers from low-income Asian countries. Therefore, oil-exporting economies are under pressure to transition to a knowledge-based economy directly, bypassing the cheap-labor growth model that is adopted elsewhere at the early phase of development.[21] It is not very easy for educational institutions to respond swiftly to such demands.

Thus, in the third stage of energy diplomacy, educational cooperation begins to come to the fore. The methods of cooperation can be diverse. One way is to help develop curricula and assist teaching by sending experts to the counterpart oil-importing country. Another is to accept students from that country at educational institutions of the state practicing the energy diplomacy. Educational cooperation itself is often included in conventional aid diplomacy, but in many cases, it is treated as being part of cultural cooperation and is not always linked strategically to development or FDI.[22] Thus, effectively facilitating students' transitioning from education to the labor market remains a key policy agenda.

1.4 Japan and Saudi Arabia

The remainder of this chapter will empirically illustrate the above three-stage evolution of energy diplomacy, using Japan–Saudi Arabia relations as a case study.[23] Japan is currently the world's third-largest economy

[21] Makio Yamada, "Can Saudi Arabia Move beyond 'Production with Rentier Characteristics'?: Human Capital Development in the Transitional Oil Economy," *Middle East Journal* 72, no. 4 (2018).

[22] Ashok Pankaj argues that FDI and human capital are largely neglected in aid diplomacy because the origin of aid diplomacy was the Marshall Plan: European countries targeted by the Marshall Plan already had advanced industrial capacity and human capital, and therefore they did not require assistance in this regard; however, the case is different for developing countries (Ashok Pankaj, "Revisiting Foreign Aid Theories," *International Studies* 42, no. 2 (2005).

[23] The empirical findings in this chapter are largely based on the author's doctoral thesis: Makio Yamada, *Beyond Oil: The Political Economy of Saudi-East Asian Industrial Relations, 1953–2013* (University of Oxford, 2015).

(after the US and China) and the fourth-largest oil importer (after China, the US, and India). Japan provides an ideal case through which to trace the historical development of energy diplomacy, as it has been a net importer of oil throughout its history, while the US and China became net importers only in 1973 and 1994, respectively. Saudi Arabia, on the other hand, is an archetypal oil-exporting country. Its oil exports are the largest in the world, almost doubling the exports of its closest rival, Russia.[24]

Saudi Arabia has been one of the largest suppliers of oil to Japan. In recent years, over a million barrels per day (bpd) of crude oil have been supplied, which is over a third of Japan's total oil imports.[25] In recent years, Japan, the US, and China each imports slightly over a million bpd of Saudi oil, out of Saudi Arabia's total oil exports at over seven million bpd.[26] In this way, Japan and Saudi Arabia are mutually dependent: Saudi oil is irreplaceably vital to Japan's economic activities, while Japan's demand for it is integral to the fiscal health of the Saudi rentier state, which relies on oil income for the majority (67% in 2018) of its state revenues, even in the current period of low oil prices.[27]

However, although Saudi Arabia still heavily relies on oil income, its economy is more diversified than in the past. In 2018, the proportion of non-oil exports to total exports stood at 21.3%, while the figure was 9.3% in 1990 and 8.5% in 2000.[28] While the country's major non-oil sectors (such as petrochemicals, finance, and construction) are reliant on oil either in the form of feedstock or the distribution of oil revenues, the Saudi state disclosed in 2016 its blueprint for development, *Vision 2030*, aiming at promoting new economic sectors such as renewable energy and tourism/entertainment. Japan is counted as Saudi Arabia's strategic partner in achieving the goals of this blueprint. In March 2017,

---

[24] Central Intelligence Agency, The World Factbook, viewed 31 July 2020, https://www.cia.gov/library/publications/the-world-factbook/.

[25] US Energy Information Administration, "Japan," viewed July 2020, https://www.eia.gov/international/analysis/country/JPN.

[26] US Energy Information Administration, "Saudi Arabia," viewed 31 July 2020, https://www.eia.gov/international/overview/country/SAU.

[27] Saudi Arabian Monetary Authority, *55th Annual Report* (Riyadh, Saudi Arabian Monetary Authority, 2019).

[28] From Annual Reports of the Saudi Arabia Monetary Agency/Authority (various years).

upon King Salman's visit to Japan, the two states jointly launched *Saudi Japan Vision 2030*, a comprehensive framework for bilateral economic cooperation responding to the targets of *Vision 2030*.[29]

2   The First Stage: Maintaining a Friendly Diplomatic Relationship—After 1955

The Saudi oil sector was initially developed by American capital, Arabian-American Oil Company (Aramco), a consortium of four American oil firms. In the emerging Cold War structure, Aramco supplied oil at low prices to the major allies of the US, such as Western European countries and Japan.[30] Before the early 1970s, Japan's energy diplomacy toward Saudi Arabia was largely to maintain the friendly diplomatic relationship which had been established in June 1955. Economic cooperation, which characterizes the second stage of energy diplomacy, was still not evident.

This, however, does not mean that there were no initiatives to develop bilateral economic cooperation. Despite enjoying increasing oil revenues, Saudi Arabia attempted to use its natural resources to initiate non-oil industrialization—it was a lack of capacity rather than of will that barred the Kingdom from successfully achieving this ambition. Saudi Arabia's interest in economic cooperation with Japan grew following the beginning of oil production by a Japanese firm in the then-neutral zone between Saudi Arabia and Kuwait, in 1960. This investment was made by Tarō Yamashita, a nationalist entrepreneur who set up an oil business

---

[29] Saudi Ministry of Economy and Planning, "Saudi Japan Vision 2030," viewed 31 July 2020, https://www.mep.gov.sa/en/ministryinitiatives/ksa_japan.

[30] The origin of Japan's oil diplomacy toward Saudi Arabia dates back to 1939. Hearing the news of an oil discovery in Saudi Arabia the previous year, Japan sent a delegation to King Abdulaziz in March 1939 to initiate talks for a possible oil concession deal (Saudi Aramco. *Energy to the World: The Story of Saudi Aramco, Volume One* [Houston: Aramco Services Company, 2011], 97). At that time, Japan was fighting the Second Sino-Japanese War (1937–45). As its relationship with the US soured due to the war, its energy reliance on the US emerged as a major strategic concern, as over 80% of its oil imports were supplied by the country at that time (Satoshi Iwama, *Sekiyu de Yomitoku "Kanpai no Taiheiyō Sensō"* [Tokyo: Asahi Shinbun-sha, 2007], 47). This backdrop led Japan to show interest in Saudi oil. However, the talks did not progress due to the outbreak of the Second World War, in which Saudi Arabia declared war against the Axis, including Japan, in its latter stage. After the war, the US preferred the Middle East to fuel Japan and its European allies, as its own domestic oil consumption was rising and it wanted to preserve its remaining oil reserves.

after Japan's defeat in the Second World War, based on his belief that the supply of oil was an Achilles' heel for Japan's national security.[31] He was granted an oil concession in 1957 and set up Arabian Oil Company (*Arabia Sekiyu*). The Saudi state provided this concession in order to alleviate its growing dependence on Aramco.[32]

Saudi Arabia and Japan signed the first bilateral industrial cooperation agreement (the Sultan–Kosaka Agreement) in 1960.[33] However, Tokyo was not highly committed to economic cooperation with Saudi Arabia beyond the oil sector at this stage, and only the construction of a small refinery in Jeddah, by Chiyoda Corporation, took place.[34] The low level of Japan's interest in economic cooperation with Saudi Arabia was not only because of the absence of favorable conditions for investment in the Saudi economy at the time, but also due to the fact that Japan imported Saudi oil not directly from the Saudi state but through Aramco at that time. Japan thus counted the imports of Saudi oil as part of its commercial relations with the US rather than with Saudi Arabia. Under the stable supply of Saudi oil through the market, even the above investment by Arabian Oil Company in the neutral zone was criticized by Japanese economists as irrational and unnecessary.[35]

3   THE SECOND STAGE: FACILITATING INVESTMENT FOR ECONOMIC DIVERSIFICATION—AFTER THE 1970S

The environment surrounding the two countries began to change in the late 1960s when the OPEC states began to recover from Western oil firms their sovereignty over oil production. Around the same time,

---

[31] Hisahide Sugimori, *Arabia Tarō* (Tokyo: Shūei-sha, 1981), 291–292.

[32] The Saudi state first negotiated with the French, but it severed diplomatic ties with France due to France's support of Israel in the Suez Crisis in 1956. Italy's ENI was another candidate (Arabian Oil Company, *The 35-Year History of the Arabian Oil Company, 1958–1993* [Tokyo: Arabian Oil Company, 1995], 37–38).

[33] The agreement was signed upon Prince Sultan's visit to Tokyo and a meeting with Foreign Minister Zentarō Kosaka. Prince Sultan (later Crown Prince between 2005 and 2011) visited Tokyo as a transportation minister to attend an international railway conference (Zadankai, "Sengo no Waga-Kuni Chūtō Gaikō no Sokuseki," *Chūtō Kenkyū* 439 [1998], 10).

[34] Hideji Tamura, *Arabu Gaikō 55-nen, Volume One* (Tokyo: Keisō Shobō, 1983), 274.

[35] Arabian Oil Company, *The 35 Year History…*, 41–42.

Saudi Arabia also began to actively seek joint venture partners for its industrial projects. Driven by anti-imperialist nationalism, which grew among Saudi technocrats in the 1950s,[36] the Saudi state launched some early non-oil industrial projects in the 1960s through Petromin, a state-owned enterprise created in 1962 for both energy projects and industrial production using the country's natural resources. Nevertheless, its major industrial project, a fertilizer production in Jubail, was a commercial failure due to the lack of experience.[37] As a result, the Saudi state decided to absorb expertise from foreign firms by forming joint ventures. Petromin's governor, Abdulhadi Taher, visited Japan in July 1970 and called for Japanese investment in Saudi Arabia in the field of petrochemicals.[38] His visit was followed by the visit of King Faisal to Japan in May 1971.

In the early 1970s, the Japanese government was increasingly aware of the risk of relying on Western oil firms for its oil imports,[39] so it responded to the above Saudi request with a greater interest than before. Nevertheless, Tokyo developed its understanding of what Riyadh wanted from it only in an incremental manner. It first proposed to Riyadh a plan of technical cooperation, using a model similar to its conventional aid diplomacy that had been practiced with Asian developing countries. This proposal, however, was rejected by the Saudis, who believed it did not respond to its request to form joint industrial projects.[40] Meanwhile, Arabian Oil Company was also eager to push for bilateral economic cooperation. Having witnessed the beginning of Aramco's nationalization in

---

[36] Many of Saudi Arabia's early technocrats who studied at Egyptian universities were Arab nationalists inspired by Nasser. However, they faced a dilemma between their pan-Arab aspirations and their status of serving the Saudi state. One of their solutions was to practice anti-imperialist nationalism in the field of the economy, in an attempt to gradually recover sovereignty over oil and develop national industries (See Stephan Duguid, "A Biographical Approach to the Study of Social Change in the Middle East: Abdullah Tariki as a New Man," *International Journal of Middle East Studies* 1, no. 3 [1970]).

[37] SPDC, *Saudi Sekiyu-kagaku 20-nen no Ayumi: Nichi-Sa Yūkō no Kakehashi* (Tokyo: SPDC, 2001), 23.

[38] The official purpose of Taher's visit was to attend the Osaka Expo, but his real intention was to launch talks with Japanese firms on petrochemical joint ventures. He paid a visit to the Yokkaichi industrial district and suggested that the Petromin and Mitsubishi firms build a petrochemical plant in Saudi Arabia (SPDC, *Saudi Sekiyu-kagaku...*, 26).

[39] Ministry of Foreign Affairs, Japan, *70-Nendai ni okeru Shigen-Gaikō* (Tokyo: Ministry of Foreign Affairs, 1972), 189.

[40] Hideji Tamura, *Arabu Gaikō 55-nen, Volume Two* (Tokyo: Keisō Shobō, 1983), 192.

1972, the company launched its own private initiative to encourage other Japanese firms to invest in Saudi Arabia as a way to safeguard its concession. Later, the company and Japan's Ministry of International Trade and Industry (MITI) agreed to work together and set up an organization for linking energy and economic diplomacies targeting Middle Eastern countries exporting oil to Japan. The public–private partnership, namely, the Japan Cooperation Center for the Middle East (JCCME), was created in October 1973.[41]

The 1973 Oil Crisis, which emerged from new fighting in the Arab–Israeli conflict (the October War), accelerated the deployment of Japan's evolved energy diplomacy. Along with Western countries, Japan was targeted for the embargo by OAPEC, the Arab part of the OPEC (the "A" in the title stands for "Arab"). Tokyo sent (then) Vice Prime Minister Takeo Miki to the Arab states to negotiate to remove Japan from the embargo list, which happened shortly thereafter. Miki reiterated to Arab leaders Japan's plan to implement economic cooperation programs. Since the crisis, energy security had remained one of the central themes for Japan's policymakers as well as for the public,[42] supporting stronger bilateral relationships with oil-exporting countries.[43]

In March 1975, the two states signed the Japanese–Saudi Economic and Technological Cooperation Agreement, which involved an annual minister-level joint committee. Bilateral negotiations for launching petrochemical projects in Saudi Arabia also progressed. Meanwhile, the Saudi side underwent a substantive restructuring of governmental organizations following the assassination of King Faisal. Petromin was downsized and given responsibility only for oil and gas projects (and was further marginalized by Aramco's full nationalization, which completed

[41] Arabian Oil Company, *The 35 Year History...*, 121; Former Arabian Oil Company staff, interviewed by the author, Tokyo, June 2012.

[42] In the Oil Crisis, the Japanese public experienced a period of confusion as they rushed to shops to hoard toilet rolls, believing the rumor that they would run out (See Kunio Yanagida, *Ōkami ga Yattekita Hi* [Tokyo: Bungei Shunjū, 1982]).

[43] It is also worth mentioning that the Oil Crisis also led to the creation of the International Energy Agency as a cooperation framework for oil-importing countries to prevent hoarding and keep the circulation of oil in the market (See Junichirō Shiratori, *"Keizai Taikoku" Nihon no Gaikō: Enerugī Shigen Gaikō no Keisei, 1967–1974 nen* [Tokyo: Chikura Shobō, 2015]).

in 1980).[44] The Kingdom's economic diversification efforts were undertaken by a new state-owned enterprise, Saudi Arabian Basic Industries Corporation (SABIC), which was created in 1976 and supervised by the newly established Ministry of Industry and Electricity.

In the early 1980s, two Saudi–Japanese petrochemical joint ventures (JVs) came on stream. Both were located in Jubail on the Gulf coast, a new industrial city developed during the oil boom. One, launched in 1983, produced methanol; it was named "Al-Razi" after a prominent Muslim chemist in the ninth and tenth centuries, Muhammad Al-Razi, and was a JV between SABIC and Japan Saudi Arabia Methanol Company, a consortium led by Mitsubishi Gas Chemical and Itochu Corporation. The other, launched in 1985, was set up to produce ethylene-based products; it was named "SHARQ" (meaning "East" in Arabic) and was a JV between SABIC and SPDC, a Japanese consortium led by Mitsubishi Group. The Japanese government called both JVs "national projects" (*nashonaru purojekuto*) and provided partial funding through the state-owned Overseas Economic Cooperation Fund (today's Japan Bank for International Cooperation) and assisted in the formation of consortia.[45]

These two large petrochemical projects were initially considered to be bellwethers of the greater industrial cooperation between Japan and Saudi Arabia. However, bilateral industrial cooperation stagnated thereafter due to multiple factors. On the Saudi side, as the first oil boom ended, the Kingdom entered a long period of budget deficits, and its capacity to invest in industrial expansion declined. The focus of Saudi policymakers also shifted to coping with security challenges in the region such as the rise of radical Islamists, represented by the Mecca Grand Mosque seizure

[44] Steffen Hertog, "Petromin: The Slow Death of Statist Oil Development in Saudi Arabia," *Business History* 50, no. 5 (2008).

[45] Japan Saudi Arabia Methanol Company, *Nichi-Sa Gōben Jigyō, Shiren to Kandō no Ayumi: Nihon–Sauji Arabia Metanōru Kabushiki-Gaisha 10-nen Shōshi* (Tokyo: Japan Saudi Arabia Methanol Company, 1992); SPDC, *Saudi Sekiyu-kagaku...*; Japan was not the only country to develop such a technology-for-oil exchange with Saudi Arabia. SABIC also formed petrochemical JVs with Western oil firms such as Exxon, Mobil, Shell, and Italy's ENI. Following the nationalization of Aramco, these firms aimed to maintain a good relationship with the Saudi state and hence access its oil by collaborating in the development of the Saudi petrochemical industry (Saudi Arabian Basic Industries Corporation, *The SABIC Story: Twenty-Five Years of Achievement, 1976–2001* [Houston: SABIC Americas, Inc., 2001], 39).

incident in 1979, and the Iran–Iraq War (1980–88) following the Iran Islamic Revolution in 1979.

On the Japanese side, the end of the oil boom meant that the situation surrounding its energy security became relatively relaxed. Greater amounts of oil were available in the market, as global oil production once again comfortably outstripped demand due to stagnating demand as a result of the recession caused by the oil crisis and oil-importing countries' energy diversification efforts, as well as rising production owing to investment supported by high oil prices in new oilfields such as those in the North Sea. Thus, the strong driver for the Japanese government's commitment to bilateral economic cooperation with oil-exporting countries faded.

Moreover, the long Iran–Iraq War changed the perception of many Japanese investors about the risk of investing in the Gulf region. Especially, the affairs of the Iran–Japan Petrochemical Company (IJPC) had a non-negligible impact on their perception.[46] IJPC was a JV between Iran's National Petrochemical Company and a Japanese consortium led by Mitsui & Co. The JV was also earmarked as a national project by the Japanese government. The construction of the petrochemical plant began before the Islamic Revolution. During the Iran–Iraq War, the plant while under construction was attacked by the Iraqi army, resulting in the Japanese consortium eventually withdrawing from the project and paying compensation. Such risk perception about the region was further aggravated by the Gulf War (1990–91), in which Japanese citizens were taken hostage by Saddam Hussein, and Khafji where Arabian Oil Company produced oil became a battleground.[47]

Furthermore, the Japanese economy entered a long downturn following the collapse of the real estate bubble in 1991, which forced firms to restructure their business portfolio: Many reconsidered their global investment strategy and began to focus on investment destinations that were in the ascendancy at that time, especially those in Southeast Asian countries such as Malaysia and Thailand. Thus, after the end of the Gulf War, Saudi policymakers began to turn their attention back to the

[46] Zadankai, "Sengo no Waga-Kuni…," 29.

[47] Tarō Shōji, *Arabia Tarō to Hinomaru Gen'yu* (Tokyo: Enerugī Fōramu, 2007), 170–171.

economy, but they found a little appetite by Japanese firms for investing in Saudi Arabia.[48]

The Japanese state, however, was enthusiastic about facilitating investment in Saudi Arabia in the 1990s despite the continuing low oil prices because the oil concession held by Arabian Oil Company was set to expire in 2000, and the Japanese government hoped for its extension, as oil from Khafji accounted for 5–10% of its total oil imports. The alliance between Arabian Oil Company and the MITI, which had created the JCCME in the early 1970s, was reinvigorated for this purpose, and a number of new institutional frameworks for bilateral cooperation were established.[49] These frameworks included: The opening of the Saudi office of the Japan External Trade Organization (JETRO) in Riyadh in 1994; the creation of the Organization for the Promotion of Japanese Investment in Saudi Arabia as a joint initiative between the JCCME and the Keidanren, Japan's largest business organization, in 1995; and the creation of the GCC-Japan Industrial Investment Company, funded by the Japan International Development Organization (JAIDO), in 1996.[50] The alliance's efforts gained political backing in the late 1990s. In November 1997, Prime Minister Ryūtaro Hashimoto visited Riyadh and proclaimed a "Comprehensive Partnership toward the Twenty-First Century" between the two countries. In return, Saudi Arabia's Crown Prince Abdullah, a de facto leader of the Kingdom on behalf of the ailing King Fahd, visited Tokyo in October 1998 and signed the Japanese–Saudi Cooperation Agenda, to ratify and commence the above partnership.

Investment outcomes, however, were not highly positive, as Japanese investors were still traumatized by insecurity in the Gulf region, their financial situation was not great, and they saw better investment opportunities in Southeast Asia, at least until the Asian Financial Crisis (1997–98), which spurred a further decline in the price of oil. This in turn made it harder for the alliance to win support within the government and among the public to spend further public resources on efforts to extend the

---

[48] Ahmed Kandil, "The Political Economy of International Cooperation between Japan and Saudi Arabia," *Annals of Japan Association for Middle East Studies* 22, no. 1 (2006), 48.

[49] Tarō Shōji, *Arabia Tarō...*, 182–183.

[50] The JAIDO was co-funded by the Japanese government and Japanese private firms. It existed between 1989 and 2002 and aimed to contribute to industrialization in developing countries by promoting investment in them.

concession. Oil was cheap and plentifully available in the market, and thus it was now seen as a normal commodity rather than as a strategic resource integral to national security. Perceiving that an increase in Japanese investment was unlikely to happen, the Saudi state at the last moment shifted its negotiation strategy to demanding that Arabian Oil Company builds a railway in Northern Saudi Arabia to support the development of the local mining industry. Such a public infrastructure project was beyond the financial capacity of the company, so the company asked the government for help. Nevertheless, given the above situation in the global oil market, the Japanese government did not find a rationale strong enough to justify spending on such a new project.[51] The concession was subsequently lost in February 2000.

3.1   The Resurgence of Investments

Somewhat ironically, Japanese investment in Saudi Arabia began to improve after the expiration of the concession. In the early 2000s, the global oil market, which had been in the period of glut for two decades, began shifting again to a narrow supply–demand gap. The global oil demand increased fast again due to the growth of emerging economies, particularly China and India, thus making energy security once again a priority agenda for policymakers in oil-importing countries. Japan's energy dependence on Middle Eastern oil increased again, particularly following a slowdown in the increase of the use of nuclear energy after the nuclear accident in Tōkai village in 1999 (and the use of nuclear energy itself was halted following the Fukushima Nuclear Crisis in 2011).[52] Witnessing rising oil prices, the Japanese government embarked on reinforcing energy diplomacy. Taking the loss of the concession as a somewhat painful lesson, it announced in 2001 a new policy aimed at building multilayered relationships with the Gulf states, as mentioned at the beginning of this chapter.

[51] Shōji, *Arabia Tarō...*, 184–186; Waki Yūzō, *Chūtō Daihenbō no Jokyoku* (Tokyo: Nihon Keizai Shinbun-sha, 2002), 286–289.

[52] Paul Midford, "The Impact of 3–11 on Japanese Public Opinion and Policy toward Energy Security," in Espen Moe and Paul Midford (eds.) *The Political Economy of Renewable Energy and Energy Security: Common Challenges and National Responses in Japan, China and Northern Europe* (New York: Palgrave Macmillan, 2004), 73.

On the Saudi side, a reform initiated to improve the country's investment climate progressed.[53] As the low oil price continued in the 1990s, Saudi Arabia suffered from a long period of budget deficits and growing debt. As the country's population increased at the same time, youth unemployment emerged as a social problem. Crown Prince Abdullah (King after August 2005) took steps to accelerate the Saudi state's efforts to diversify the economy to create jobs for its young citizens. In 2000, the Saudi Arabian General Investment Authority (SAGIA) was launched to invite foreign investment by cutting red tape and creating a one-stop procedural shop for foreign investors. Crown Prince Abdullah also doubled the Saudi state's endeavors to join the World Trade Organization by implementing stipulated reforms: The accession eventually took place in December 2005.

There were also sector-specific factors that pushed for new Japanese investments in Saudi Arabia. In the petrochemical industry, more Japanese producers began to invest abroad, as they faced harder competition from emerging producers in Asian countries and found themselves in need of restructuring their business portfolio, focusing mostly on high-tech products in their plants in Japan and moving the production of basic products overseas. While many redeployed their operations to Southeast Asia, the Gulf region—where labor costs were not necessarily low, but feedstock costs were overwhelming at times of high oil prices—also came to be seen as a promising destination.[54]

A harbinger of new Japanese investment in this sector was the participation of Mitsui & Co. in a methanol plant project in Jubail in 2003 through a JV (Japan–Arabia Methanol Company) with Sipchem, a private Saudi petrochemical firm affiliated with Zamil Group. Sipchem was one of the first private investors in the Saudi petrochemical sector, which had been monopolized by SABIC previously but opened up to private investors in 1995. This decision by Mitsui & Co., which had suffered major losses from the IJPC incident in the 1980s, helped shift Japanese

---

[53] Tim Niblock with Monica Malik, *The Political Economy of Saudi Arabia* (London: Routledge, 2007), Chapters 6 and 7.

[54] This is because petrochemical production in Gulf countries uses associated gas as feedstock. Associated gas is a by-product of oil production. It used to be burned in the oilfields, but it began to be used for petrochemical production in the 1980s. In contrast, petrochemical producers in oil-importing countries use naphtha as feedstock. As naphtha is distilled from crude oil, production is costlier than when using associated gas, particularly in times of high oil prices.

investors' perceptions of the Gulf region.[55] Moreover, Saudi Aramco also entered this sector (Saudi Aramco later absorbed SABIC in 2019), and it chose Japan's Sumitomo Chemical as a partner for its first JV, Petro Rabigh, after its initial negotiations with Dow Chemical had been shelved after Dow's withdrawal from the table following the 9/11 incident (Dow later came back and launched a JV, Sadara Chemical, with Saudi Aramco). The plant, built in Rabigh on the Red Sea coast, began its operation in 2009.

The second oil boom continued for around a decade (2004–14) and brought about another round of industrial expansion in Saudi Arabia. In addition to the existing industrial cities in Jubail and Yanbu, the construction of new industrial cities began, most prominently King Abdullah Economic City (KAEC) in Thwal on the Red Sea coast, close to Jeddah and Rabigh. To develop new non-oil sectors by attracting FDI, the National Industrial Cluster Development Program (NICDP) was launched, targeting several strategic sectors such as automobiles, renewable energy, and plastics.

These developments led to the expansion of bilateral economic cooperation between Japan and Saudi Arabia. In 2007, following Prime Minister Shinzō Abe's visit to Saudi Arabia, the Japan–Saudi Arabia Industrial Cooperation Taskforce was launched. The taskforce, which was administered by the JCCME on the Japanese side and the NICDP on the Saudi side, facilitated Japanese industrial investment in Saudi Arabia beyond the petrochemical sector, and it created 11 new investments with the participation of 13 Japanese firms in total through informing Japanese firms about the Saudi market and assisting their market surveys and business matching in the Kingdom (two projects/firms later withdrew).[56] Most investments occurred in the manufacturing sector in areas such as the production of industrial equipment for the oil and gas industries and for desalination plants. It also facilitated Isuzu Motors opening a truck

---

[55] There was in-firm opposition to the idea of returning to the Gulf, but the consideration of the market won (Japan–Arabia Methanol Company, interviewed by the author, Tokyo, May 2014).

[56] Japan Cooperation Center for the Middle East, interviewed by the author through email, August 2020.

assembly plant in Dammam in 2012.[57] The initial five-year program of the Taskforce was renewed in 2012 and continued until 2017. The second oil boom came to an end with the collapse of oil prices in 2014, thus exerting strong pressure on Saudi state coffers again and making economic diversification and job creation ever-urgent policy agendas. King Salman, who succeeded his brother Abdullah in January 2015, left the task of economic reform to his son Mohammed, who rose to the position of Deputy Crown Prince in April 2015, and then Crown Prince in June 2017. Under the leadership of Prince Mohammed, a new blueprint for development, namely, *Vision 2030*, was disclosed in April 2016 and targeted the development of new non-oil sectors, including tourism and entertainment, in addition to renewable energy and industrial equipment for the oil and gas sectors.[58]

Saudi Arabia counts the world's major economies, such as the US, China, and Japan, as key strategic partners for achieving the goals of *Vision 2030*. Following the announcement of the Vision, Prince Mohammed visited Japan in August/September 2016. Following this visit, the two states set up a joint group to re-establish the framework for bilateral economic cooperation.[59] The new framework, "Saudi Japan Vision 2030," was announced in March 2017 when King Salman paid a visit to Tokyo (an updated version (2.0) was disclosed in June 2019), and it aimed to align bilateral cooperation with the agendas and goals of *Vision 2030*.[60] To supervise bilateral cooperation under the framework, its Riyadh office, jointly run by the JETRO and the JCCME, was created in January 2018, taking over the office of the Taskforce.

One of the major non-oil sectors targeted by *Vision 2030* is renewable energy. As mentioned above, this sector began to be targeted in

---

[57] Japan-Saudi Arabia Industrial Cooperation Taskforce, viewed 31 July 2020, http://www.saudiarabia-jccme.jp/.

[58] *Saudi Vision 2030* is available at its website: https://vision2030.gov.sa/.

[59] Makio Yamada, "Vision 2030 and the Transformation of Saudi-Japanese Economic Relations," King Faisal Center for Research and Islamic Studies Special Report, 2017.

[60] Saudi Japan Vision 2030 (2.0) is available at the website of the Japanese Ministry of Economy, Trade, and Industry: https://www.meti.go.jp/press/2019/10/20191024005/20191024005.html.

the late 2000s. Saudi Arabia had traditionally abhorred the development of renewable energy, which threatens its long-term oil exports.[61] Nevertheless, an incentive to develop non-hydrocarbon energy domestically emerged as the rise in domestic oil consumption began to constrain the country's oil export capacity.[62] Japan's Solar Frontier, a subsidiary of a Japanese downstream oil company Showa Shell, in which Saudi Aramco invests, assisted Saudi Arabia's early small-scale solar projects, such as Saudi Aramco's carpark project in Dhahran and Saudi Electricity Company's pilot solar project on Farasan Island.[63] In March 2018, Soft-Bank Vision Fund (SVF) announced that it would invest in the Saudi solar sector to develop 200 gigawatts (GW) by 2030.[64] The target figure sounded extremely high, given that the total global solar capacity at that time was around 400GW. SVF is a $100 billion fund set up by Soft-Bank, a conglomerate based in Japan, in May 2017 as a mega venture capital fund investing in futuristic technologies and businesses. Saudi Arabia's sovereign wealth fund, Public Investment Fund (PIF), was the largest investor in this fund, investing $45 billion. SVF initially aimed to launch two solar plants in Saudi Arabia, collectively generating 7.2GW, in 2019.[65] However, at the time of writing this chapter (August 2020), this has not materialized, and the PIF's 2GW solar project planned in Makkah may be its first project in the Kingdom.[66]

Entertainment is another targeted sector. Following the creation of the Saudi General Entertainment Authority in May 2016, the Kingdom began to develop this sector. Cinemas, which had been banned for 35 years, began to re-open in April 2018.[67] In this field, the Prince

---

[61] Joanna Depledge, "Striving for No: Saudi Arabia in the Climate Change Regime," *Global Environmental Politics* 8, no. 4 (2008).

[62] Glada Lahn and Paul Stevens, *Burning Oil to Keep Cool: The Hidden Energy Crisis in Saudi Arabia* (London: Chatham House, 2011).

[63] Makio Yamada "GCC–East Asia Relations in the Fields of Nuclear and Renewable Energy: Opportunities and Barriers" Oxford Institute for Energy Studies Paper MEP14, 2016, 25.

[64] "SoftBank Vision Fund, Saudi Arabia to create world's biggest solar power firm," *Reuters*, 28 March 2018.

[65] "Saudi Crown Prince Signs MoU with SoftBank to Set up World's Largest Solar Project", *Arab News*, 28 March 2018.

[66] "2,600 MW Solar Project for Makkah," *Saudi Gazette*, 24 March 2019.

[67] "Cinema returns to Saudi Arabia," *Saudi Gazette*, 18 April 2018.

Mohammed bin Salman bin Abdulaziz Foundation (MiSK Foundation), under the patronage of Crown Prince Mohammed, has been particularly active in promoting cooperation with Japanese entities. The foundation set up an arm for producing animations, Manga Productions, which signed a cooperation agreement with Japan's Toei Animation in November 2017.[68] Its first production, "The Woodcutters' Treasure" (*Kanz al-Hattab/Kikori to Takaramono*), was aired by Tokyo TV in May 2018.[69] In early 2020, it completed its first anime series, "Future's Folktales" (*Asātīr/Mirai no Mukashi Banashi*),[70] as well as its first animation film, "The Journey" (*Al-Rihla/Jānī*).[71] The stories of these animations are based on the history and folklore of the Arabian Peninsula. In December 2019, Manga Productions also signed an agreement with the King Abdulaziz Foundation for Research and Archives (Darah) to produce comics and animations to illustrate Saudi history.[72] It also offered opportunities for young Saudis to receive training at Japan's Digital Hollywood University.[73]

Moreover, a number of MoUs have been signed for potential Japanese investments in other fields in the Kingdom, such as desalination, automobiles (conventional and electronic), construction, media, and healthcare.[74] Japanese banks and the Tokyo Stock Exchange also eye financial opportunities created by Saudi Aramco's potential initial public offering (IPO) abroad,[75] the first step of which took place in late 2019 with its

---

[68] "Major Boost for Saudi Creative Industries at MiSK Global Forum," *Arab News*, 17 November 2017.

[69] "For the First Time, Tokyo TV to Air Saudi Anime 'Woodcutter's Treasure'," *Arab News*, 20 May 2018.

[70] "Saudi Anime Series Ready to Liftoff," *Arab News*, 23 January 2020.

[71] "Manga Productions to Show First Saudi Movie Using DX4 Technology," *Saudi Gazette*, 25 February 2020.

[72] "Misk to Illustrate Saudi History through Animation," *Saudi Gazette*, 4 December 2019.

[73] MiSK Foundation, "Misk/Digital Hollywood University Internship Program," https://misk.org.sa/fellowship/services/digital-hollywood-university/.

[74] "Abdul Latif Jameel, Toyota & NICDP Plan Car Production in Saudi Arabia," *Saudi Gazette*, 15 March 2017; "Japanese Reap Rewards as Three Firms Win Operational License at Business Forum in Riyadh," *Arab News*, 15 January 2018; "Saudi Arabia, Japan Seek to Bolster Enduring Partnership," *Saudi Gazette*, 23 October 2019.

[75] "Japanese Banks Secure Slots as Saudi Aramco Underwriters," *Nikkei Asian Review*, 28 September 2019.

1.7% domestic listing at the Saudi Stock Exchange (Tadawul).[76] Whether these agreements and negotiations will progress to actual investments, however, remains to be seen.

4   THE THIRD STAGE: EDUCATIONAL COOPERATION—AFTER THE 2000S

It is still too early to evaluate fully the outcomes of the new Saudi Japan Vision 2030 framework. However, given low oil prices, too heavy a commitment to bilateral economic cooperation with Saudi Arabia which would require high levels of spending is unlikely to win support either within the Japanese government or from the Japanese public. The focus of the cooperation is therefore likely to continue to fall on fostering private exchanges in the market, with the state playing a facilitative role rather than being a direct player. This indicates that the investment climate is key to the success of Saudi–Japanese economic cooperation. In particular, human capital is a major element in the investment climate. Investors can recruit workers from Asian countries, as the Saudi private sector has traditionally been open to foreign workers, who account for the majority (around 80% currently) in the private sector.[77] However, due to the worsening unemployment problem, the Saudi government recently tightened labor localization requirements.[78] For employers, local workforces tend to create higher costs than imported labor due to the wage expectations of local citizens who demand similar levels of wages to those in the public sector (which is financed by oil income).[79]

This conundrum for investors necessitates improvement in the country's technical and vocational education and training (TVET): Without production-prepared human capital, investors will choose investment destinations elsewhere, either in lower-cost economies (for low-skilled

---

[76] "Taps Open for Saudi Listings after Aramco's Record IPO," *Reuters*, 4 February 2020.

[77] Saudi General Authority for Statistics, Labor Force Survey, First Quarter 2020.

[78] Steffen Hertog, "A Comparative Assessment of Labor Market Nationalization Policies in the GCC," in Steffen Hertog (ed.) *National Employment, Migration and Education in the GCC* (Berlin: Gerlach Press, 2012).

[79] Makio Yamada, "Can a Rentier State Evolve to a Production State?: An 'Institutional Upgrading' Approach," *British Journal of Middle Eastern Studies* 47, no. 1 (2020).

production) or economies with higher human capital (for knowledge-based production). On the one hand, this understanding has resulted in the Saudi government's effort to empower its TVET programs, which have long been marginalized in the Saudi education system due to the economy's long reliance on foreign labor and Saudi citizens' preference for working in the public sector.[80] On the other hand, it has led to the rise of educational cooperation as a new pillar of Saudi–Japanese bilateral collaboration, as raising human capital has increasingly been seen by policymakers of both countries as a prerequisite for successful investment-based economic cooperation.

Saudi–Japanese educational cooperation itself is not new, as it has been part of Japan's conventional aid diplomacy for many years. In the early 1970s, at the request of the Saudi government, the Japan International Cooperation Agency (JICA) proposed to set up an industrial school in Riyadh through bilateral cooperation.[81] This proposal was shelved for years due to the restructuring of government organizations in Saudi Arabia after the death of King Faisal, but re-planning took place in the late 1980s, leading to the opening of the Riyadh Technical Electronics Institute (RETI) in 1993. This secondary-level institute was staffed by Japanese technical experts dispatched through the JICA, and its Saudi staff received training in Japan.[82] The JICA also contributed to the establishment of the Saudi–Japanese Automobile High Institute (discussed below) and a college to instruct technical trainers in Riyadh (a precursor of today's Applied Engineering College). However, as Saudi Arabia's GDP per capita came to exceed $20,000 and the country was removed from the OECD Development Assistance Committee's list of recipients of

---

[80] Another reason why TVET did not stand center stage in the Saudi education system is that it was administered not by the education ministry but by the labor ministry between 1980 and 2016.

[81] Japan International Cooperation Agency, *Saudi Arabia Ōkoku Riyado Denshi Kōgyō Kōkō Secchi ni Kakawaru Sōgō Hōkoku* (Tokyo: Japan International Cooperation Agency, 1977).

[82] Japan International Cooperation Agency, *Saudi Arabia Ōkoku Riyado Denshi Gijutsu Gakuin: Syūryō-ji Hyōka Hōkoku-sho* (Tokyo: Japan International Cooperation Agency, 1996).

official development assistance, the JICA's full operation in Saudi Arabia ended in 2010.[83]

In the 2000s, however, the Saudi–Japanese TVET cooperation witnessed a leap under the new framework. Three TVET colleges supported by Japanese firms opened across the Kingdom. These two-year colleges are run by the Saudi TVET authority and Japanese firms operating in Saudi Arabia, as well as their Saudi partners. They are part of the Saudi TVET authority's "strategic partnership" scheme, in which major firms support the curriculum development of sector-specific TEVT colleges, often employing their graduates as well. Other strategic partners include Saudi state-owned firms (such as Saudi Aramco and Saudi Telecom Company) and large private businesses (such as Saudi Oger and ACWA Power).[84]

Many Japanese firms operating in Saudi Arabia had already developed their own programs for training Saudi employees, both on and off the job, and they applied this know-how to a formal TVET curriculum. The first college was the Saudi–Japanese Automobile High Institute (SJAHI), which opened in Jeddah in 2002. Toyota, as well as Nissan and Honda, developed the college's curriculum and provided instructors. The second was the Higher Institute for Plastics Fabrication (HIPF), which opened in Riyadh in 2007. This college was developed by SHARQ, the Japanese–Saudi petrochemical JV. The third was the Saudi Electronics and Home Appliances Institute (SEHAI), which opened in Dir 'iya in 2009. This college was supported by Japanese home appliance firms selling products in Saudi Arabia (such as Panasonic, SHARP, Toshiba, and SONY—although many of them later withdrew as they began to exit the home alliances market due to South Korean and Chinese firms rapidly growing in strength) and the Nihon Kōgakuin College.

Moreover, Japanese universities began to accept larger numbers of Saudi students, who were supported by the Saudi state scholarship program (the Custodian of the Two Holy Mosques Overseas Scholarship Program, previously known as the King Abdullah Scholarship Program,

---

[83] Japan International Cooperation Agency, "Kenkatsu-koku Sauji Arabia heno kyōryoku naiyō," viewed on 31 July 2020, https://www.jica.go.jp/egypt/office/activi ties/saudiarabia.html.

[84] Technical and Vocational Training Corporation, "Strategic Partnership Institutes," viewed on 31 July 2020, https://www.tvtc.gov.sa/English/Departments/Departments/ SC/SPI/.

which was launched in 2005 by King Abdullah). Under this program, at least over 600 Saudi students pursued degrees at universities in Japan,[85] although the scale of the initiative shrank after 2016, due to the decline in oil prices and the criticism that the returnees had not been absorbed well into the Saudi labor market because of the gap between education gained abroad and the local market.[86] In fact, facilitating young Saudis' transition from education to employment is one of the key agendas in Saudi education reform,[87] and it remains a challenge to both Saudi Arabia's economic diversification and Saudi–Japanese educational cooperation.

5 Conclusions

In this chapter, I argued that Japan's energy diplomacy toward Saudi Arabia has evolved through three stages in response to the developmental shift in the latter. In the initial stage, when the Saudi oil industry was fully controlled by American capital, energy diplomacy was largely about maintaining a friendly relationship, while oil trade was left to the market. For Saudi Arabia, demand security was integral to regime security, but it was met as long as Aramco steadily exported Saudi oil to the US' Cold War allies. At the macro level, Japan and Saudi Arabia were embedded in the global division of labor, whereby developing economies export natural resources, and advanced economies manufacture industrial products using these natural resources.

Energy diplomacy in the second stage, which emerged after the early 1970s, came to involve active economic cooperation, exchanging investment for the stable supply of oil. Japan and Saudi Arabia signed the bilateral Economic and Technological Cooperation Agreement in 1975, and it was recently upgraded to the more comprehensive *Saudi Japan Vision 2030* framework. This bilateral relationship appeared after oil-exporting countries recovered the control of oil production and exports from Western capital. This made energy security a major concern, with energy diplomacy becoming about directly dealing with these states for the supply of oil. Around the same time, the Saudi economy began

---

[85] "Japan: Fast becoming Saudi students' favorite destination," *Arab News*, January 30, 2019.

[86] The then-Saudi education minister Ahmed Al-Issa (2015–18) had been a critic of the scholarship program.

[87] Yamada, "Can Saudi Arabia Move beyond...".

to diversify gradually. While diversification, driven by nationalism, had already been intended in the first stage, the rise in financial and human capital after the 1970s enabled Saudi Arabia to realize this intention. At the macro level, such a shift was embedded in the transition of the order of the global economy from the division of labor to the Great Convergence—the global diffusion of industrialization. Then, as the Saudi state's relative distributive capacity started to decline after the 1990s, creating jobs and opportunities outside the public sector via economic diversification became integral to the long-term regime security of the kingdom. However, because investment is largely carried out by private firms, what the state can do in promoting economic cooperation in this field is often limited to facilitative roles. Thus, if Japanese private firms do not find the investment climate in Saudi Arabia attractive enough, they invest elsewhere, even if institutional frameworks encouraging investment are created through interstate cooperation. This happened in the 1990s when the Japanese state tried to increase its investment in Saudi Arabia in order to extend the concession held by Arabian Oil Company, but failed due to the inaction of private firms.

This led to the third stage of energy diplomacy, in which bilateral educational cooperation emerged as its new pillar. The beginning of educational cooperation was based on the realization that human capital was integral to the investment climate. Human capital remains one of the challenges to the Saudi economy's further diversification, given that a common development model based on low-cost labor does not work well in a nation whose income per capita is much higher than other developing economies, thereby requiring a leap to the knowledge economy. Thus, educational cooperation became integral to Japanese–Saudi relations in the 2000s, leading to the institutionalization of technical training provided by Japanese firms and experts for Saudi youth.

Finally, from a theoretical perspective, my argument is new in two regards. First, it systematically incorporated the political-economy perspective of a counterpart oil-exporting country to an understanding of the evolution of energy diplomacy. Second, by doing so, it provided a framework with which to analyze the dynamics of how complex interdependence develops between an oil-importing country and an oil-exporting one. This framework enables us to find how major elements of interdependence, or "layers" in a "multilayered relationship"—energy, investment, and education—are *causally* related, thereby overcoming a mere descriptive and over-factualist approach to this matter. Furthermore, it is likely to aid researchers of rentier state, as well as the resource curse, in understanding the process of economic diversification by highlighting the international aspects of such a process.[88]

Acknowledgements I am grateful to the Japan Cooperation Center for the Middle East and the King Faisal Center for Research and Islamic Studies for helping my doctoral research which forms the empirical foundation of this chapter. I also extend my gratitude to the following individuals for their support: Philip Robins, Michael Willis, Tim Niblock, Bassam Fattouh, Masayuki Yamauchi, Haruo Endo, Munehiro Mishima, Takashi Mitsuka, Makoto Mizutani, Essam Bukhary, Mashi Al-Shammari, Matteo Legrenzi, Bernard Haykel, Eliza Gheorghe, and Asher Orkaby, as well as the editors of this volume, Satoru Nakamura and Steven Wright.

[88] For the latest discussions on rentier states, see the special issue of the *British Journal of Middle Eastern Studies*, Vol. 47, Issue 1, "Revisiting Rentierism: The Changing Political Economy of Resource-Dependent States in the Gulf and Arabian Peninsula," which I co-edited with Steffen Hertog.

CHAPTER 3

Japan–UAE Relations: Establishment of Multifaceted Interdependence Based on Energy

Koji Horinuki

What do the people of the UAE think of Japan, and what do the Japanese think of the UAE in their minds? This is where the intensity of cultural exchange between the two countries will be measured. (The preface, "Thoughts on International Cultural Exchange," UAE-Japan Society *UAE*, No. 1, 1975 Summer)

1 INTRODUCTION

This chapter discusses the development of bilateral relations between Japan and the UAE. The relationship between the two countries began in the late 1960s and developed through oil development, import, and export. Fifty years have passed since then, and although the bilateral relationship has become very diversified, energy remains the foundation

K. Horinuki (✉)
JIME Center, The Institute of Energy Economics, Japan, Tokyo, Japan
e-mail: koji.horinuki@jime.ieej.or.jp

© The Author(s), under exclusive license to Springer Nature
Singapore Pte Ltd. 2023
S. Nakamura and S. Wright (eds.), *Japan and the Middle East*,
Contemporary Gulf Studies, https://doi.org/10.1007/978-981-19-3459-9_3

of the two countries' relationship today. Japan continues to import oil and natural gas from the UAE and is involved in its development and production. Even by 2020, about 30% of Japan's crude oil imports come from the UAE. Correspondingly, Japan is an energy market for the UAE and has also been a recipient of various technologies and ideas from Japan. Today, the two countries have a multifaceted interdependence that constitutes an indispensable relationship for both sides.

Despite the importance of the relationship between Japan and the UAE, only a few studies have comprehensively discussed it. The journal of the UAE-Japan Society, *UAE*, records events related to bilateral exchanges and is considered a valuable source for further analysis. In addition, UAE governmental organizations provide overviews of bilateral relations, mainly describing the diplomatic, political, economic, energy-related, and cultural fields from the UAE perspective (Zayed Center for Coordination and Follow Up 2002; UAE Deputy Prime Minister's Office, n.d.). Nishizaki also examined Japan–UAE relations in the context of Japan–Middle East–U.S. relations and pointed out that although bilateral relations have developed and diversified, especially in the areas of economy and energy, they have not fully realized their potential (Nishizaki 2011). In addition, bilateral relations have been comprehensively described in each field of exchange, including diplomacy, culture, and economy (Akimoto 2018; Hosoi ed. 2011; Kamo 2015; Hamada 2011). It is clear from all these discussions that Japan–UAE relations have developed significantly and diversified over the past five decades.

This chapter serves two purposes: the first is to illustrate the overall picture of the diversifying Japan–UAE relationship. The second is to highlight the process and the central actors involved in how the bilateral relationship, which began with energy as its starting point, has created exchanges between citizens. The role of energy actors will be re-evaluated, including oil companies and government agencies, to show how these actors have supported bilateral relations in non-energy areas in addition to their role in providing a stable supply of energy. The role of energy actors has not been sufficiently examined in previous studies, despite their importance in bilateral relations. This point will reveal an expanding and deepening relationship between the people of Japan and the UAE. Through the above discussion, this chapter attempts to clarify the establishment and deepening of a multifaceted, interdependent relationship between Japan and the UAE, rather than simply viewing the relationship as one of oil imports and exports.

This chapter begins with an overview of the development process of Japan–UAE relations, roughly divided into three 20-year periods: (1) the emergence period (1960–1979), (2) the development period (1980–1999), and (3) the transformation period (2000–2020). Next, it will summarize the process of entry into the UAE by Japanese oil companies, which have been central actors in forming bilateral relations, followed by an analysis of the approaches of these companies toward the UAE. Furthermore, the historical role of the UAE-Japan Society in cultural and citizen exchanges will be examined.

2 OVERVIEW OF JAPAN–UAE RELATIONS

2.1 The Emergence Period (1960–1979)—Bilateral Relations Driven by the Business Community

The beginnings of the Japan–UAE relationship remain unclear. In 1943, a book entitled *The Chiefdoms of the Arabian East: Kuwait, Bahrain Island, Trucial Oman, and Oman* was published in Tokyo (Tōakeizai Kenkyūsho: 1943). It indicates that Japan had been interested in the energy resources of the Gulf States since that time. After the Second World War, the Ministry of Foreign Affairs (MOFA) of Japan sent an economic mission so-called "The Japanese Government Economic Research Mission to the Arabian Peninsula" to the Trucial States in 1961. A second survey group visited Abu Dhabi, Dubai, Sharjah, and Ra's al-Khaimah in 1966 (MOFA 1962, 1967; UAE-Japan Society 1975: 6). Although Japan and the UAE did not formally establish diplomatic relations until May 1972, the private business community drove bilateral relations until the late 1970s.

In the late 1960s, several Japanese companies seemed to have already started operations in the Trucial States. It is said that Pacific Consultants International (PCI), a construction and civil engineering consulting company, was the first company to enter the UAE in 1967. PCI provided construction management and urban development consulting services mainly in Abu Dhabi, and Mr. Katsuhiko Takahashi of PCI was appointed Director-General of the Abu Dhabi Urban Planning Department (Abu Dhabi-Japan Society 1973: 24–25). Then, when Japanese oil companies entered the UAE to acquire oil concessions in Abu Dhabi, bilateral relations between the two countries began in earnest. In 1967, the oil companies signed a concession agreement to explore and develop offshore oil blocks in Abu Dhabi. Subsequently, the Abu Dhabi Oil Company (ADOC) was established as the operating company of the blocks. When the Abu Dhabi-Japan Society (later the UAE-Japan Society) was established in 1970 to promote friendship and goodwill, ADOC assumed the secretariat.

Although there were no official diplomatic relations between Japan and the UAE by 1972, government officials carried out some bilateral visits. In 1969, Masayuki Fujio, the parliamentary vice-minister for trade and industry, became the first Japanese government official to visit Abu Dhabi. In 1970, when Abu Dhabi exhibited at the Osaka Expo, Sheikh Khalifa bin Zayed Al Nahyan (the then Crown Prince of Abu Dhabi) and Minister of Petroleum Mana Otaiba visited Japan. When the UAE was established in December 1971, the Japanese government immediately afforded it diplomatic recognition, and the two countries formally established diplomatic relations in May 1972. In 1973, the Embassy of the UAE was established in Tokyo, and then in 1974, the Embassy of Japan was formed in Abu Dhabi. In 1973, Yasuhiro Nakasone, the minister of international trade and industry, became the first Japanese cabinet minister to visit the UAE. When the oil crisis occurred in 1973, Deputy Prime Minister Takeo Miki visited the UAE and other Middle Eastern countries as a special envoy to explain Japan's position on the Palestinian issue. Then, in September 1978, Takeo Fukuda became the first Japanese prime minister to visit the UAE. In this way, Japan was able to build closer diplomatic ties in the very short term since the founding of the UAE.

Japanese companies played an active role in state construction in the UAE, such as urban infrastructure development projects and the construction of oil-related facilities. For example, Chiyoda Corporation, Ishikawajima-Harima Heavy Industries, Toyo Kanetsu, and others were involved in constructing the liquefied petroleum gas facility on Das Island. Takenaka Corporation and Kumagai Gumi co. participated in constructing the Abu Dhabi International Airport as a joint venture. In addition, Sumitomo Corporation, Mitsubishi Corporation, Nissho Iwai Corporation, Marubeni Corporation, and other leading Japanese trading companies were all involved in the business with the UAE, delivering Japanese products such as construction materials, machinery, and automobiles (Table 1). At that time, Japanese products such as home appliances and fabrics were already popular in the local market (Abu Dhabi-Japan Society 1974: 3).

Table 1 Major Japanese companies in the UAE (1960–1970s)

Company name	Year of the office/branch establishments in the UAE
Pacific Consultants International	1967
Abu Dhabi Oil Company	1968 (Abu Dhabi Office)
Sumitomo Corporation	1968 (Abu Dhabi Office), 1977 (Dubai Office)
Mitsubishi Corporation	1969 (Abu Dhabi Office), 1970 (Dubai Office)
Nissho Iwai Corporation	1969
Marubeni Corporation	1972 (Abu Dhabi Office), 1977 (Dubai Office)
Japan Oil Development Company	1974 (Abu Dhabi Branch)
Idemitsu Kosan Co., Ltd.	1975
Itochu Corporation	1975 (Dubai Office), 1976 (Abu Dhabi Office)
Nichimen Corporation	1975
Tokai Marine and Fire Insurance Company	1976
Mitsui & Co., Ltd.	1976 (Abu Dhabi Office), 1977 (Dubai Office)
TOA Corporation	1977
Japan Airlines	1979

Source UAE-Japan Society and corporate information of each company

Human and cultural exchanges also underpinned bilateral relations from the early days. In terms of human interaction, Japan Airlines commenced flights to Abu Dhabi in 1978. The number of Japanese residents in the UAE increased from 137 in 1973 to more than 1000 in 1977. The Japanese Association of the UAE was established in February 1975, laying the foundation for exchange among the Japanese community in the UAE. In 1977, the Japanese School in Ajman (later the Japanese School in Dubai) was established, and in April 1978, the Japanese School in Abu Dhabi was opened. In this way, a Japanese community began to take root in the UAE. Conversely, the UAE's approach toward Japan during this period is limited. One unique initiative is the involvement in the traditional Japanese sport of sumo. Since 1979, the UAE has been awarding the "United Arab Emirates Friendship Trophy" and a prize of gasoline for one year to the champion sumo wrestler, and this award continues today.

Thus, in the early days of Japan–UAE relations, private companies had already entered the UAE before the establishment of diplomatic relations. The acquisition of oil concessions in 1968 became the cornerstone of the bilateral relationship. In addition, exchanges between the people of Japan and the UAE began gradually during the emergence period.

2.2   The Development Period (1980–1999)—Progress in Diplomatic, Economic, and Technological Cooperation Relations

When the Islamic Revolution in Iran took place in 1979, the situation in the Gulf began to descend into chaos. In 1980, the Iran–Iraq War broke out, and the Gulf region continued in a state of instability. However, despite this instability, the relationship between Japan and the UAE continued to grow steadily. The 1980s and 1990s saw the strengthening of inter-governmental and inter-business relations.

Diplomatic relations between the two countries have grown, along with the active exchange of high-level officials. In May 1990, President Sheikh Zayed bin Sultan Al Nahyan visited Japan as a state guest. Furthermore, the then Crown Prince Naruhito and his wife Princess Masako visited the UAE in January 1995. This was a significant event in Royal Family relations between the two countries. In 1995, the Consulate-General of Japan in Dubai was established, with responsibility for Dubai and the Northern Emirates. During the development period, Japan and the UAE signed an aviation agreement, the first bilateral agreement between the two countries.[1]

In addition, Japan expanded its technical cooperation with the UAE. The Japan International Cooperation Agency (JICA) researched various fields within the UAE, including agriculture and fisheries, desert greening, power generation, desalination, water resources, and marine affairs, and reported the results to the Japanese and UAE governments. In 1984, JICA supported establishing a mariculture research center in the Emirate of Umm al-Quwain to undertake aquaculture research and technology transfer. The Japan Cooperation Center, Petroleum (JCCP), established

---

[1] Subsequent bilateral agreements, Nuclear Agreement (2014), Tax Treaty (2014), and Investment Agreement (2020), have been signed between the two countries.

in 1981, has been responsible for cooperation in human resource development in the oil sector by accepting many trainees from oil-producing countries, including the UAE.

The economic institutions of both countries established their offices in each other's countries from the 1980s to 1990s. To provide business support to Japanese companies, the Japan External Trade Organization (JETRO) established its office in Dubai in 1981. The Japan Oil Corporation (now renamed Japan Organization for Metals and Energy Security, JOGMEC) moved its office from Bahrain to Abu Dhabi in 1996.[2] The development of the UAE, especially Dubai's growing status as a global business hub, also led to increasing economic relations between the two countries. On the UAE side, Dubai's Department of Tourism and Commerce Marketing established its office in Japan in 1990 and began promoting Dubai's tourism and businesses. The establishment of economic organization offices is an important indicator of the economic interdependence between the two countries.

Academic exchange between the two countries also began at that time. In 1980, Keio University conferred an honorary doctorate on Mana Otaiba, the UAE Minister of Petroleum and Mineral Resources. Otaiba then donated USD50,000 to Keio University, which was used to purchase thousands of Arabic books to create the "Arabic Book Collection of the Faculty of Law" (Tomita 2016: 66–67). In the cultural field, events showcasing Japanese traditional culture, including "Japan Week," were held in the UAE from the late 1980s. In addition, the mutual dispatch of journalists and museum officials from both countries through the UAE-Japan Society in the 1990s began to expand the scope of multifaceted understanding between the two countries.

In this way, Japanese companies established a base of economic activities in the UAE, and the Japanese government began to provide full-scale support to Japanese companies. In addition, the bilateral relationship achieved full-scale development, including mutual visits between the leaders of the two countries.

---

[2] Japanese economic organizations continued to establish their offices in the UAE: JCCP set up its Middle East office in Abu Dhabi in 2002, the Japan Bank for International Cooperation (JBIC) set up a Dubai representative office in 2006, and the Japan Cooperation Center for the Middle East (JCCME) set up a UAE-Japan desk in Abu Dhabi in 2009.

2.3   The Transformation Period (2000–2020)—The Qualitative Change in Bilateral Relations and the Coming of a New Era

In the twenty-first century, Japan–UAE relations have diversified from the traditional energy and economic-centered relationship. While energy and economic ties remain at the center of the relationship, mutual visits and exchanges of citizens have increased, and relations in non-energy and economic fields have expanded.

Regarding diplomatic relations, the number of visits by ministers and senior officials of the two countries has increased. In 2002, the Japan-UAE Parliamentary Friendship Association was established to promote communication between both countries' parliaments. When President Sheikh Zayed bin Sultan Al Nahyan, the founding father of the UAE, passed away in November 2004, Japan sent former foreign minister Yoriko Kawaguchi to the UAE as a special envoy of the prime minister. As will be discussed later, in the 2000s, the deadline for the renewal of oil field working interests held by Japanese oil companies in Abu Dhabi was approaching, and the Japanese government was pushing for negotiations on the concessions.

Therefore, Prime Minister Shinzo Abe visited the UAE in 2007, the first visit by a Japanese prime minister in 29 years, and met with President Sheikh Khalifa bin Zayed Al Nahyan and other officials (MOFA 2007a). In the same year, Sheikh Mohammed bin Zayed Al Nahyan, Crown Prince of Abu Dhabi, visited Japan at the invitation of the Japanese. Sheikh Mohammed bin Zayed paid a courtesy call to the Emperor of Japan and held bilateral talks with Prime Minister Yasuo Fukuda (MOFA 2007b). Since his second administration, Abe has visited the UAE three times and has been responsible for top-level negotiations to maintain oil field interests. During his second visit to the UAE in May 2013, Japan and the UAE issued the "Joint Statement on the Strengthening of the Comprehensive Partnership between Japan and the United Arab Emirates towards Stability and Prosperity" (MOFA 2013) to strengthen bilateral relations in various fields. In 2014, Sheikh Mohammed bin Zayed revisited Japan. The increase in mutual visits by the leaders of both countries indicates strong diplomatic relations between them.[3]

---

[3] The countries' friendly diplomatic relations are also reflected in the ambassadorial appointments. Ambassador Khalid al-Amiri (2016–2020) is a Japanophile who graduated from Tokai University in Japan in 2002 and obtained a Master of Science in Engineering

During this period, economic relations in non-energy sectors also became more active, and many Japanese companies made inroads into the UAE market. For example, as the domestic market shrinks, Japan's major general contractors look for overseas business opportunities, especially in Gulf countries experiencing a construction boom. Infrastructure export was also in line with the Japanese government's policy. The Dubai Metro, which opened in 2009, was built by a consortium of Japanese companies, including Mitsubishi Corporation, Mitsubishi Heavy Industries, Obayashi Corporation, and Kajima Corporation, together with Turkish companies. In addition, Kinki Sharyo delivered 395 railcars for the Dubai Metro (Horinuki 2019: 20).[4] Japan also aimed to export nuclear power plants to the UAE. However, in the bidding for the Abu Dhabi nuclear power plant in 2009, Japanese companies were defeated by a consortium of South Korean companies, and the 2011 Fukushima nuclear accident forced Japan to reconsider its nuclear export strategy.

Meanwhile, the economic relationship between the two countries has continued to diversify. Japan's exports to the UAE have expanded beyond the traditional heavy industry sector, automobiles, home appliances, and machinery to agricultural and food products, as well as Japanese-style services. In 2011, the Japan Cooperation Center for the Middle East (JCCME) launched the Abu Dhabi-Japan Economic Council, which regularly supports mutual investment and improves the environment for this purpose. What is also noteworthy is that Japan's presence in the UAE was not limited to the central government and large corporate level but also extended to the local governments and small regional enterprises. In particular, local governments recognize the high purchasing power of UAE residents and are proactively marketing high-quality, premium agricultural and marine products to the UAE market.

At the request of the UAE, Japan is also promoting human resource development and technical cooperation for the next generation, which will drive the UAE's post-oil economy. Within the Japan-Abu Dhabi Business Council framework, the Japan International Cooperation Center (JICE) has been encouraging UAE students to study in Japan. More than

from Shonan Institute of Technology. The current UAE ambassador to Japan, Shihab al-Faheem (2021–), is also a Japanese speaker, having studied in Japan. Ambassador al-Faheem has been tweeting in Japanese since his arrival in Japan.

[4] However, the Dubai Debt Crisis of 2009 led to debt collection problems for Japanese companies that participated in the construction of the Dubai Metro.

500 students have come to Japan through this scheme to study at universities, engage in training, or participate in internships (Kanamori 2019). Another area of cooperation that has been growing in recent years is space exploration. The two countries agreed in 2016 to promote cooperation in the space sector. As a result, the UAE-made Mars probe *al-Amal* (Hope) was successfully launched from the Tanegashima Space Center in Japan by a Japanese-made H-IIA rocket in July 2020 (MHI 2020). It is important to recognize that cooperation in the space sector is the opening of a new era.

The two countries have become more familiar with each other since the 2000s. Dubai became a popular tourist destination for the Japanese when Emirates Airlines launched its service to Osaka in 2002, which led to an increase in popularity and public awareness of Dubai and the UAE in Japan. Today, the UAE hosts the largest Japanese community in the Middle East, with more than 4200 Japanese residents (Fig. 1). With the increase in the Japanese population in the UAE, restaurants, clinics, and beauty salons opened, offering their services to the Japanese residents. During this period, the UAE became a more attractive place for Japanese people to live and work. In addition, grassroots exchanges within the private sector have also emerged during this period. In the UAE, Naoko Kishida, a Japanese national living in the country, established the Japan-UAE Cultural Center in 2008, which introduces UAE culture to Japanese people living in the UAE and offers Japanese language classes to expatriates living in the UAE (Kishida 2009).

Residents from both Japan and the UAE began to visit each other's countries more casually. In addition to visits for business and tourism, students studying Japanese at the UAE University and Zayed University, for example, have visited Japan on study tours, and opportunities for Japanese students learning English and Arabic to visit the UAE have increased. With the development of the internet, Japanese anime, and pop culture have also become popular among the UAE youth; when Books Kinokuniya, a major Japanese bookstore chain, opened in Dubai in November 2008, it attracted crowds of local young people. Following the success of the Dubai store, Books Kinokuniya opened its branch in Abu Dhabi in 2019. Today, the Books Kinokuniya bookstore has become a hub for Japanese pop culture in the UAE and the Gulf countries. During this period, the Japanese government realized that pop culture is a soft power that is very influential and pervasive in the world. In 2017, MOFA appointed Hideaki Takizawa, a celebrity in Japanese pop culture, as a

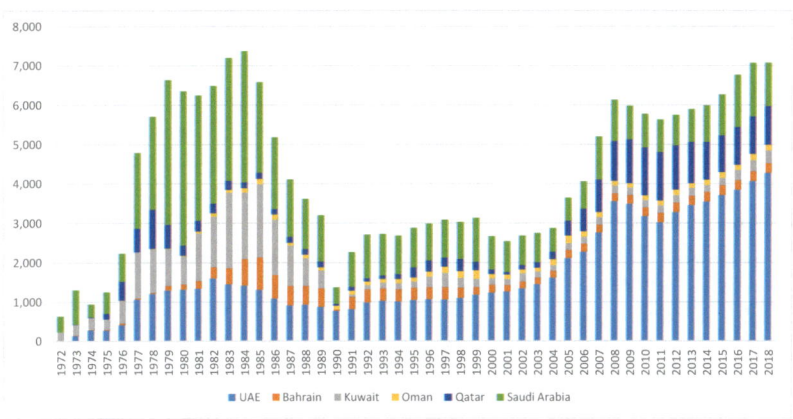

Fig. 1 Overseas Japanese residents in the Gulf Countries (1972–2018)

Japan–UAE goodwill ambassador, aiming to expand its soft power and promote its diverse attractions (MOFA 2017). This cultural exchange is reciprocative, and in 2008, the first Japan–UAE manga collaboration, *Siwār al-Dhahab* (The Gold Ring), was born. This work results from the cooperation between UAE and Japanese artists, in which the UAE's traditional culture of falconry has been transformed into a story of Japanese manga. It symbolizes a milestone in cultural exchange between the two countries.

In short, the transformation period has seen an expanded bilateral relationship that differs in both quality and quantity from the emergence and development periods. The two countries have become closer to each other and deepened their interdependence in all areas.

3 Development of Bilateral Relations and Citizen Exchanges Fostered by Energy Security

3.1 *The Birth of the Abu Dhabi Oil Company (ADOC)*

The bilateral relationship between Japan and the UAE has been based on energy transactions, and even today, when the relationship is diversified and multi-layered, the structure remains the same. The origin of the energy relationship between the two countries is ADOC. In 1967, the Abu Dhabi Marine Area (ADMA), which BP and CFP (now Total Energies) established to conduct exploration in offshore blocks, returned some of its blocks to the Abu Dhabi government, leading to new international bidding for the concessions. Three Japanese companies, Maruzen Petroleum, Daikyo Oil, and Nippon Mining, jointly bid and won the offshore A and B blocks. In December 1967, the Abu Dhabi government and the three companies signed a concession agreement. In January 1968, the three companies established the ADOC to promote the project, transferred the concession to the company, and immediately set up an office in Abu Dhabi, commencing exploration in May 1968 (ADOC 1998: 24–25). In May 1969, the company began exploratory drilling that was successfully developed, named the Mubarraz oil field, and full-scale development started in July 1971. Production from the field began in May 1973, and the first shipment to Japan was made in June the following year (ADOC 1998: 24–41).

There are various theories regarding how ADOC acquired its concession in Abu Dhabi. According to the corporate history of ADOC, in the summer of 1965, an employee of a Japanese trading company visited Abu Dhabi for market research and met with Sheikh Shahbout bin Sultan Al Nahyan, the then Emir of Abu Dhabi, although the meeting was unsuccessful. During the same visit, he also met with an Iraqi who lived in Abu Dhabi, Ziyad al-Askari, and signed a one-year agent contract with him in July 1966. Later, Askari reportedly informed him about bidding for the returned ADMA fields. He also met with Nadim al-Pachachi, who served as an oil advisor for Sheikh Zayed bin Sultan Al Nahyan, the founding father of the UAE (ADOC 2018: 46–54). Later, this information was brought to Sohei Nakayama, president of the Industrial Bank of Japan, via Pacific Consultants, operating in Abu Dhabi. Nakayama approached three companies, Maruzen Petroleum, Daikyo Oil (now integrated as Cosmo Energy Holdings), and Nippon Mining (now JX Nippon Oil & Gas Exploration). The three companies embarked on a joint effort to acquire an interest in the returned ADMA concession, with Shigeru Sugimoto, former vice president of Maruzen Oil, as the negotiator. Sugimoto conducted four months of negotiations with the Abu Dhabi government, starting in August 1967. Then, in December of the same year, Sheikh Zayed and the three companies signed the concession agreement (ADOC 2018: 48–54).

Since the dawn of Japan–UAE relations, ADOC has played a significant role in developing bilateral relations. According to corporate history, the Abu Dhabi government treated ADOC like a representative of Japan until the establishment of the Japanese Embassy. In 1970, when the Osaka Expo was held, Abu Dhabi Oil was requested by the secretariat of the Japanese Expo Preparatory Committee to invite the Emirate of Abu Dhabi to participate in the event. After which, ADOC continued to assist in setting up and operating the exhibition site. Then, in commemoration of the then Crown Prince Sheikh Khalifa bin Zayed Al Nahyan's visit to the exposition, the Abu Dhabi-Japan Society was established in December 1970, with Abu Dhabi Oil serving as the secretariat (ADOC 2018: 79–81). The Abu Dhabi-Japan Society was later reorganized into the UAE-Japan Society in 1974 to support exchanges between the two countries.

3.2   Japanese Oil Companies Acquired Additional Oil Concessions in Abu Dhabi

Japan sought to acquire oil concessions worldwide to meet the high demand for energy during rapid economic growth. Led by ADOC, Japanese oil companies continued to obtain concessions in Abu Dhabi and were involved in exploration, development, and production. In addition, the Japanese electric power companies and trading companies also became deeply involved in the UAE's energy sector through investments and joint participation in oil companies.

After acquiring the ADMA concession, ADOC continued to obtain concessions in Abu Dhabi. In November 1970, ADOC established United Petroleum Development Co. (UPD) with Qatar Petroleum, North Slope Oil, and Alaska Petroleum Development. UPD took over half of the Bunduq Co. shares held by BP and participated in the development project with ADMA as the operating company. The company began exploratory drilling in 1971, and commercial production began in 1975 (Iwasa 1995: 41). ADOC also acquired an interest in the Mubarraz oil field in 1979 and transferred it to a newly established operating company, Mubarraz Oil Company (MOCO), which began developing the field (Iwasa 1995: 49). Subsequently, ADOC started production at the Umm al-Anber oil field, and, in 1995, also began production at the Neewat al-Ghalan oil field.

Japan Oil Development Company (JODCO) is one of the major Japanese oil companies operating in Abu Dhabi, together with ADOC. The origin of JODCO dates back to November 1970, when BP offered to sell a part of its ADMA interests to Japan. In 1971, Japan Overseas Petroleum Development Corporation (renamed from North Slope Oil) began negotiations and agreed to purchase the ADMA interests for USD780 million in December 1972 (Iwasa 1995: 42). The Japanese government viewed the ADMA concession as a stable source of crude oil supply to Japan, and the cabinet agreed to provide support from the standpoint of national interest (Inpex 2019a: 19; JNOC 1987: 79). Therefore, Japanese private companies invested in the ADMA project to promote it and established JODCO in 1973.

Initially, JODCO's participation in the development and production of the ADMA field was limited to indirect participation through a joint venture with BP (BP-JODCO). JODCO lobbied the Abu Dhabi government to participate in direct operations, and in 1977, the company participated in the establishment of ADMA-OPCO with Abu Dhabi National Oil Company (ADNOC), BP, and Total, enabling direct operation of the oil field (Inpex 2019a: 19). The following year, 1978, JODCO acquired a 12% stake in the Umm al-Dalkh oil field and established the Umm al-Dalkh Development Co. In the same year, JODCO participated in the Upper Zakum oil field project with ADNOC and took a 12% stake. The Upper Zakum oil field has been operated by ZADCO, a fifty-fifty joint venture between ADNOC and Total. JODCO has been substantially involved in the operation through the secondment of its staff through UDECO (Inpex 2019a: 19). In addition, JODCO signed an agreement with ADNOC in 1980 for exploration, development, and production of the undeveloped Satah, Jarnain, and Dalma structures in the ADMA field and UDECO took over operations (Iwasa 1995: 50). Regarding the Satah oil field, JODCO holds a 40% share.

Japan's acquisition of oil concessions in the UAE, however, has not always been a success story. During the same period that ADOC acquired interests in offshore blocks in Abu Dhabi, other Japanese companies were also seeking to enter onshore blocks. In 1968, the five Mitsubishi Group companies (Mitsubishi Corporation, Mitsubishi Heavy Industries, Mitsubishi Mining, Mitsubishi Oil, and Mitsubishi Petrochemical) participated in the international competitive bidding for the onshore blocks of E, F, and G that had been returned by Abu Dhabi Petroleum Company (ADPC). As a result, the five companies of the Mitsubishi Group won the bidding for these concessions and signed the concession agreement with the Emir of Abu Dhabi in May 1968. The company then established

Middle East Oil Co. Ltd to promote exploration and development activities in the blocks and transferred the concessions to the new company. Middle East Oil then acquired additional concessions for onshore blocks of H, I, and J in 1970. Middle East Oil conducted exploration and exploratory drilling of the concession from March 1970 to February 1974 but failed. As a result, the company returned the concession to the Abu Dhabi government and was liquidated in 1976 (JNOC 1987: 73–74). Also, in 1980, Mitsubishi Oil Corporation decided to participate in the Fujairah offshore concession, and in July of the same year established Fujairah Oil Exploration and Development Co. However, the company concluded after the exploration that the potential for the existence of an oil field was low and abandoned the block and returned it to Fujairah (JNOC 1987: 134–135).

3.3   Japan's Import of UAE Crude Oil and the Challenge of Renewing Oil Concessions

As mentioned above, ADOC and JODCO have acquired several oil field concessions in Abu Dhabi. Through the operating companies they established, the two companies have been involved in developing and producing oil from the 1970s until today. The volume of UAE crude oil traded by Japan continued to increase through 1997, reaching a peak of 70 million kiloliters per day in that year. After that, as the demand for oil in Japan declined, the import volume of UAE crude oil also decreased. However, the share of UAE crude oil in total crude oil imports still exceeds 30% (Fig. 2). Just as the UAE is a major oil supplier to Japan, Japan is also a significant oil consumer for the UAE. Today, the volume of crude oil exports from the UAE to emerging Asian countries such as China, South Korea, and India are increasing, but at its peak, the UAE exported nearly 70% of its crude oil to Japan (Fig. 3). It is important to note that even during the oil glut of the 1980s, when the supply and demand for oil eased, Japan received, on average, nearly 50% of the UAE's crude oil. In other words, Japan has supported stable oil production in the UAE.[5]

---

[5] For example, JODCO has been supporting ADNOC's sales of crude oil; since the mid-1980s, ADNOC has struggled to secure markets for its Zakum crude oil. In order to help, JODCO took on a share of the crude oil sold by ADNOC and encouraged

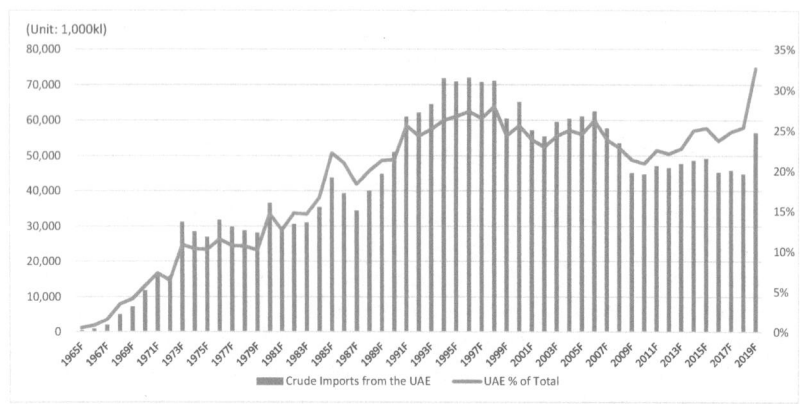

Fig. 2   Crude oil imports from the UAE (*Source* IEEJ-EDMC Data Bank)

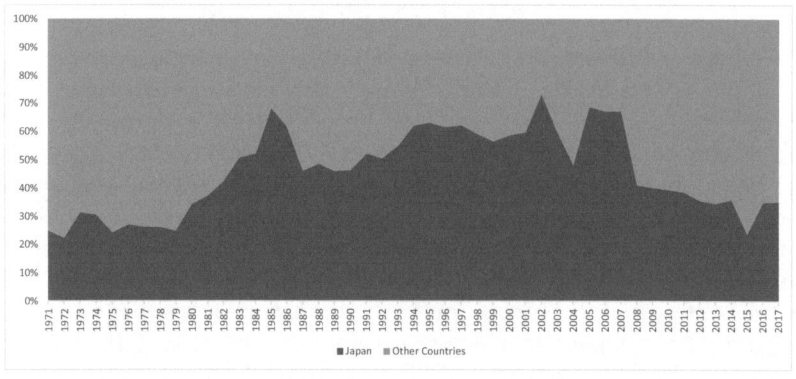

Fig. 3   UAE's crude oil export market (1971–2017) (*Source* OPEC Annual Statistical Bulletin [1971–2008] and UN Energy Statistics Yearbook [2009–2017])

In the 2000s, the deadline for renewing the oil field concessions held by ADOC and JODCO was approaching. The two companies made preparations for the renewal of their concessions, and the Japanese

the Japanese government to stockpile it, thereby contributing to the expansion of Zakum crude oil production and export volume (Inpex 2019a, b: 20).

government's support for them began in earnest. As will be discussed in detail in the next section, ADOC, JODCO, and the Japanese government promoted support for the economic diversification and human resource development that the UAE was seeking. In 2006, the Japanese government launched the "New National Energy Strategy" and began full-scale resource diplomacy. Following the failure of the Arabian Oil Company's negotiations to extend its concession in the Khafji oil field in Saudi Arabia in 2000 and Kuwait in 2003, the Japanese government reaffirmed the importance of the government working together with the public and private sectors to secure natural resources. To achieve this, MOFA, the Ministry of Economy, Trade and Industry (METI), and the Agency for Natural Resources and Energy (ANRE) became the leading players in resource diplomacy at the ministry level. In addition, JOGMEC, the Japan Bank for International Cooperation (JBIC), Nippon Export and Investment Insurance (NEXI), and JCCP provided the necessary support for resource diplomacy.[6] Summit diplomacy has also been actively undertaken. Prime Minister Abe (September 2006–August 2007, December 2012–September 2020) visited the UAE four times to expand the strategic partnership, which included requests to extend oil concessions. As part of the bilateral cooperation in the oil field, the two countries launched the Joint Oil Storage Project between Japan and Abu Dhabi to strengthen bilateral relations in 2009.

Public- and private-sector efforts to lobby the UAE were successful. In February 2011, ADOC successfully renewed its 30-year concessions in three existing oil fields and acquired additional concessions in the Hail field (Cosmo Oil 2011). In January 2014, JODCO also successfully extended its concession in the Upper Zakum field with the Supreme Petroleum Council (INPEX 2014). In 2015, INPEX, the parent company of JODCO, acquired a 5% participating interest in the ADCO Onshore field (INPEX 2015). And in February 2018, INPEX successfully extended

---

[6] In 2013, JOGMEC signed an MoU with ADNOC on technical cooperation in the oil and natural gas sector, stating that they would cooperate in terms of introducing advanced technologies to oil and gas fields and human resource development. In addition, JOGMEC has been accepting trainees from the UAE since the days of the Japan National Oil Corporation (JNOC) and providing training courses on oil and natural gas development (Inohara 2013: 46–47). In 2007, JBIC signed a loan agreement with ADNOC for up to $3 billion, and the two companies signed a business cooperation agreement in 2010. In 2013, JBIC extended a $2.1 billion loan to ADNOC. JBIC is also providing Abu Dhabi Oil with a loan to cover the cost of renewing its concession.

its concessions in the Satah and Umm al-Dalkh oil fields for a further 25 years. It also secured an additional 28% stake in the Satah oil field through JODCO. INPEX also acquired a 40-year concession in the Lower Zakum field with a 10% working interest (INPEX 2018). In 2019, INPEX also won a bid for Onshore Block 4 through its subsidiary JODCO Exploration Limited (INPEX 2019b). Table 2 shows the concessions and the percentage held by Japanese oil companies and equity investors in Abu Dhabi today.

Japan is also engaged in producing and importing liquefied natural gas (LNG) in the UAE. In 1969, Tokyo Electric Power Company (TEPCO) and Tokyo Gas began importing LNG from Alaska to meet the growing demand for electricity in Japan. At the time, TEPCO was also seeking to import LNG from the Middle East, and in 1972, TEPCO signed a heads of agreement with Abu Dhabi Gas Liquefaction Limited (ADGAS) for a long-term LNG contract (Dargin and Flower 2011: 453–454). TEPCO signed a long-term contract with ADGAS to purchase 2.06 million tons of LNG and liquefied petroleum gas (LPG) per year for 20 years. The ADGAS project involved ADNOC, BP, Total, and two Japanese companies, Mitsui and Bridgestone Liquified Gas. The following year, in March 1973, the construction of the liquefaction facility on Das Island was awarded to a joint venture between Bechtel of the United States and Chiyoda Corporation of Japan (Dargin and Flower 2011: 457). ADGAS made its first shipment of LNG to Japan in April 1977, making the UAE the first exporter of LNG in the Middle East, most of which was exported to Japan. At its peak in 1982, UAE LNG accounted for 12% of Japan's total imports (Fig. 4).

3.4 Multifaceted Development of Non-energy Relationships Supported by Oil Companies

The role played by oil companies in Japan–UAE relations is not limited to developing oil fields and importing oil. Oil companies have also supported the multifaceted development of bilateral relations in non-energy fields. The UAE has pursued the transfer of new technologies in the non-energy sector as part of its state-building process, and Japanese oil companies have assisted in their process. Until today, oil companies are directly or indirectly involved in human resource development, environmental protection, and cultural exchange in the UAE.

Table 2   Oil concessions held by Japanese oil companies in Abu Dhabi

Oil filed/Block	Ownership interest	Operator	Production year
Abu al-Bukhoosh (–2018)	Total Abu al-Bukhoosh Oil Company 75%	Total Abu al-Bukhoosh Oil Company	1974
	INPEX 25%		
ADCO Onshore Consession (2015–)	ADNOC 60%	ADNOC Onshore	1963
	TOTAL 10%		
	BP 10%		
	CNPC 8%		
	INPEX (JODCO Onshore Limited) 5%		
	NPIC 4%		
	GS 3%		
al-Bunduq (1970–)	BP 3%	al-Bunduq Oil Company	1975
	Union Petroleum Company 97%		
Hail (2012–)	ADOC 100%	ADOC	2017
Mubarraz (1968/2012–)	ADOC 100%	Mubarraz Oil Company (MOCO)	1973
Neewat al-Ghalan (1983/2012–)	ADOC 100%	ADOC	1995
Onshore Block 4 (2019–)	INPEX (JODCO Exploration Limited) 100%	INPEX (JODCO Exploration Limited)	–
Satah (1980–)	ADNCC 60%	ADNOC Offshore	1987
	JODCO 40%		
Umm al-Anbar (1982/2012–)	ADOC 100%	Mubarraz Oil Company (MOCO)	1989
Umm al-Dalkh (1978–)	ADNOC 60%	ADNOC Offshore	1985
	JODCO 40%		

(continued)

Table 2 (continued)

Oil filed/Block	Ownership interest	Operator	Production year
Zakum(Upper) (1978–)	ADNOC 60% ExxonMobil 28% JODCO 12%	Zadco	1982
Zakum (Lower) (2018–)	ADNOC 60% INPEX (JODCO Lower Zakum Limited) 10% ONGC Videsh-led Consortium 10% CNPC 10% TOTAL 5% Eni 5%	ADNOC Offshore	1967

Source Inohara (2013) and the press releases of oil companies

Fig. 4 LNG Imports from the UAE (*Source* IEEJ-EDMC Data Bank)

For example, Kashima Oil implemented the Abu Dhabi Government Technical Cooperation Agricultural Project (Kashima Abu Dhabi Farm) in Al Ain in November 1981. Kashima Oil installed a cooled cultivation room and conducted experimental cultivation of vegetables (UAE-Japan Society 1983: 29–30; 1985: 23). Environmental initiatives are also crucial in oil-producing countries. Oil companies are likely to emit CO_2 and other pollutants through the development, production, and consumption of oil, thereby affecting the local environment. For this reason, ADOC and JODCO have been working on environmental protection activities such as mangrove planting and flaring and CO_2 emission reduction through the recovery of associated gases, which has been evaluated highly by the UAE. In the field of cultural cooperation, the Gulf region was historically an area of pearl extraction, and JODCO has been sending experts in pearl cultivation technology to support technology transfer since 2006 (Inpex 2019a, b: 79).

The UAE, founded in 1971, has been focusing on education to develop the human resources that will lead the nation in the future. Since the labor market in the UAE has long been dependent on foreign experts and workers, it is critical to promote the Emiratization of the labor force and secure employment for young Emiratis. For example, in geology, which is closely related to the oil industry, JODCO and ADOC have jointly invited ten students from the Department of Geology, UAE University to participate in practical training in Japan every year since 1993. Since 2007, students from the Petroleum Institute have also been invited for practical training (Kawaguchi 2009: 82). Furthermore, the development of highly skilled human resources was also an area of concern for the future establishment of a post-oil economy. The UAE recognized that Japan, which does not have natural resources, had achieved rapid economic growth after the Second World War and anticipated that Japan would support human resource development. In order to support education, JODCO introduced the Kumon Method of education to public schools in the region as the "JODCO-KUMON Activity" in 1998, which was expected to improve the basic academic skills of UAE students (Asada 2006: 7–8).

The acceptance of UAE national children into the Japanese School and kindergartens in Abu Dhabi is a particularly symbolic event in human resource development cooperation between the two countries. In 2004, Crown Prince of Abu Dhabi Sheikh Mohammed bin Zayed Al Nahyan, through the embassies of Japan, France, Germany, and China, requested that local schools in Abu Dhabi accept UAE national children. After discussions between the Embassy of Japan in the UAE and the Japanese Association in Abu Dhabi, two children have been received every year at the kindergarten attached to the Japanese School in Abu Dhabi since 2006. As a support organization for this project, the UAE-Japan Association for Youth Development and Exchange was established in 2007 by ten companies, including oil companies and trading companies. Two local children who entered the kindergarten in 2006 went on to a Japanese school in April 2009, and four local children have been admitted every year since 2012 (Kawaguchi 2009: 82–83).[7] This program indicates that the UAE regards Japanese-style education very highly and is looking to expand human exchange opportunities with Japan.

The cultural interest of Japan in the UAE has also been increasing. In particular, Japanese animation and manga are popular among young people in the UAE, and there is a certain demand for learning Japanese. However, opportunities to learn Japanese in the UAE are limited. The Embassy of Japan in Abu Dhabi has held only small-scale language classes and speech contests in the past. To provide opportunities for Japanese language education and promote understanding of Japanese culture in

---

[7] As of July 2020, there are 12 UAE children in Japanese kindergartens (out of a total of 34 children) and 25 UAE children (out of a total of 61 children) in Japanese schools (elementary and junior high) (UAE 2020: 20).

the UAE, Cosmo Oil launched a Japanese language education program in 2007. In May 2011, Cosmo Oil, ADOC, and the Ritsumeikan Trust launched the "COSMO-ADOC-RITSUMEIKAN Japanese Language Teaching Program" to dispatch Japanese language teachers to high schools in the UAE (Ritsumeikan, n.d.). Another remarkable cultural exchange is that JODCO dispatched Dr. Sen Genshitsu, the 15th Grand Master of the Urasenke Tea Ceremony, to Abu Dhabi to deepen exchanges with local dignitaries and cultural figures. In 2009, Dr. Sen Genshitsu presented a tea ceremony room to Sheikh Mohammed bin Zayed Al Nahyan, which he named "Ryokusui-an" (the room of green and water). Tea ceremonies were held at the Ryokusui-an Tea Room at the Emirates Palace Hotel in Abu Dhabi, leaving a significant mark of traditional Japanese culture in Abu Dhabi (Urasenke, n.d.).

In this manner, oil companies are actively engaged in non-energy fields that are not directly related to their core business of aiming to acquire and maintain oil field concessions. At the same time, they are also trying to contribute to the local community, based on their corporate social responsibility (CSR) as companies operating in the UAE.

4   The Role of the UAE-Japan Society

4.1   Activity Summary

The United Arab Emirates Japan Society (hereafter referred to as the UAE-Japan Society) has its origins in the Abu Dhabi-Japan Society established in December 1970 and reorganized as the UAE-Japan Society in April 1974. According to the society, it was the third friendship society established between Japan and the Gulf states, following the Japan-Saudi Arabia Society in 1960 and the Japan-Kuwait Society in 1965. Its mission is "to deepen friendly relations between Japan and the UAE and contribute to economic cooperation and cultural exchange." The society's principal activities are the biannual publication of the society's magazine, *UAE*, lectures for members, and public relations activities.[8] In addition, the society uses the profits from the Zayed Friendship Fund to expand human and cultural exchanges between Japan and the UAE.

ADOC manages the general secretariat of the society, and corporate and individual members support its activities. The Abu Dhabi-Japan

---

[8] UAE-Japan Society "Activity Summary", http://www.uaesociety.jp/about.html.

Society started with 68 member companies, including mining, electrical power, construction, manufacturing, and insurance companies, and 99 companies were members in 1978, the society's peak year. As of March 2021, the association consists of 53 corporate members and 59 individual members. Although the number of corporate members of the UAE-Japan Society has halved compared to the oil boom period when there remains a strong demand for information on the UAE, and it has maintained a certain number of members. Therefore, it can be said that the UAE-Japan Society is still the core organization of Japan's network with the UAE, even today.

4.2   Development of the UAE-Japan Society As a Hub for Bilateral Exchange

As stated in its regulations, the UAE-Japan Society has promoted friendship and goodwill between the two countries. Today, a people's exchange is relatively easy, but in its early days, an organization like the UAE-Japan Society needed to play a central role in raising funds for activities, coordination, and invitation programs.

Sohei Nakayama (1906–2005) supported the activities of the UAE-Japan Society since its establishment. Nakayama was a businessperson who had served as president and chairman of the Industrial Bank of Japan and was known as the "*Kurama Tengu* (a famous hero in Samurai literature) of the business world." He had a strong awareness of Japan's energy security and was also involved in the launch of the Arabian Oil Company, which developed the Khafji oil field straddling Saudi Arabia and Kuwait, the first oil field in which Japan acquired an overseas concession. Regarding Nakayama's involvement with the UAE, he played a coordinating role when the three Japanese oil companies sought to acquire oil concessions in Abu Dhabi in 1968. Nakayama became president of the Abu Dhabi-Japan Society in 1970, when it was established, and served as president of the UAE-Japan Society until 1988, continuing to support its activities as an advisor. Since January 1971, when he visited Abu Dhabi, Dubai, and Sharjah for the first time as the head of the Gulf Economic Mission, he has visited the UAE many times as a representative of the business community and as the president of the UAE-Japan Society. Nakayama developed a close relationship with President Sheikh Zayed and other UAE government officials during his visit. So why was Nakayama so deeply involved with the UAE and oil development? First, as a business leader, Nakayama believes that energy security is the most crucial issue for economic growth in Japan. Therefore, he requested the business community supply funds to oil companies to acknowledge the high business risks associated with the industry despite its economic importance. Second, he stressed the necessity of mutual understanding for the further development of bilateral relations. For example, Nakayama actively introduced Japanese culture to the Middle East (UAE 1989: 16–21). Thus, it is not an exaggeration to say that Nakayama was a central actor in bilateral relations from the emergence to the development period.

The UAE-Japan Society, following Nakayama's philosophy, supported bilateral exchanges in the fields of culture and sports. For example, in sports, the volleyball and table tennis teams of the Al Ain Sports Club visited Japan in 1978 and held training camps in Japan for seven weeks. This project was supported by the Ministry of Foreign Affairs of Japan, the Japan Foundation, the Japan Volleyball Association, and the Japan Table Tennis Association. In addition, the UAE-Japan Society received the support of 24 million yen (about USD114 thousands at the 1978 rate) from 59 companies, including members of the society (UAE 1978: 12–17). In addition, the society frequently held events to introduce Japanese culture and promote understanding of Japan in the UAE. In 1977, the UAE-Japan Society established its branch in Abu Dhabi to support goodwill and cultural exchange in the UAE. In 1978, the society reportedly distributed a guidebook on Japan in Arabic (UAE 1978: 33).

During his visit to Japan in 1990, President Shaikh Zayed bin Sultan Al Nahyan donated USD500 thousands to the UAE-Japan Society to expand human and cultural exchange between the two countries. In addition, members of the UAE-Japan Society who supported this purpose also donated. With Shaikh Zayed's donation, the Zayed Fund for UAE–Japan Friendship was established with a fund of 191 million yen. In the 1990s, the UAE-Japan Society used its funds to send journalists from both countries to each other, Japanese museum personnel to the UAE, and Japanese students to the UAE University. In the twenty-first century, it has become much easier to travel and obtain information about the two countries, but society still supports grassroots communication. The UAE-Japan Society supports travel to the UAE by the Japan-GCC Association of Students and the Japan-Middle East Student Conference, student organizations that promote exchanges with the Middle East (Togashi 2018: 10).

4.3   The Society's Magazine Produced by Citizens and Its Historical Role

One of the main activities of the UAE-Japan Society is the publication of the society's magazine, *UAE*. Since the first issue was published in 1975, 68 issues had been published by 2020.[9] The magazine is published in Japanese, but an abridged version in Arabic is also issued. The articles cover political, economic, and social developments in the UAE, trends of Japanese companies operating in the region, personal memoirs involved in the UAE, the introduction of Arab and Islamic culture, and the news of local dignitaries and developments in Japan–UAE relations. The magazine's contributors are incredibly diverse, including Japanese residents, embassy staff, researchers, educators, and individuals involved in the UAE.

Articles in the magazine are unique to each period, and the editions of the 1970s contained valuable local information from the UAE. Today, local information reaches Japan in real-time through the internet, personal blogs, and social networking platforms; however, during the 1970s, the magazine's information was considered extremely valuable. For example, the magazine provided helpful information on expatriate life, such as obtaining a visa (1976, No. 2; 1984, No. 10; 1994, No. 20) and hotel conditions (1978, No. 5; 1995, No. 21). In addition, from the 1970s to the 1980s, there were articles on roundtable discussions by Japanese expatriates and members of Japanese women's groups. The articles provide insight into the local situation and hardships of life in the UAE. For this reason, the magazine is an interesting resource for understanding UAE society and the lives of Japanese residents in the UAE at that time. Since around 2000, the society's magazine has begun introducing reports from local newspapers in the UAE, helping readers to feel more familiar with the UAE. In this manner, the magazine's contents reflect the changing times and the relationship between Japan and the UAE. Therefore, the images and impressions that both Japanese and UAE people have of each other's country continue to change with time.

---

[9] During the period of the Abu Dhabi-Japan Society, the society published the third issue of its magazine.

5 Conclusion

This chapter has discussed the evolution of Japan–UAE relations from the 1960s to 2020. In short, the bilateral relationship between Japan and the UAE has evolved from the development and import/export of oil resources. Even today, the essential link between the two countries is mediated by energy resources. For many years, Japan has sought oil and natural gas from the UAE, and the UAE has also sought to emphasize its relationship with Japan as an energy market. Led by two companies, ADOC and JODCO, Japan has been working to acquire, develop, and maintain oil field concessions in the UAE. In addition, the Japanese government and related organizations have developed direct and indirect support for oil companies to achieve the national interest of securing energy resources.

Since the emergence of the relationship between the two countries, the business community, and oil companies have been the driving force. In addition, the UAE-Japan Society has served as a nexus for private-sector exchange, and the society has supported such interactions. As the age of globalization began, bilateral relations between the two countries naturally expanded. As the exchange of people and information between the two countries increased, the psychological distance between them became much closer. Today, it can be said that a multifaceted interdependence has been forged between Japan and the UAE. As the world moves toward an era of decarbonization, the Japan–UAE relationship will likely have to change. In other words, the relationship over energy imports and exports, which has been at the core of the bilateral relationship, will inevitably evolve. Both countries have already begun to work together toward a new era. In particular, technological cooperation in renewable energy and hydrogen fields and promoting cooperation in space development symbolizes a new generation of Japan–UAE relations. The multifaceted interdependence between the two countries is about to enter a new phase.

Acknowledgements In writing this article, I received much support from people involved in Japan and the UAE. In particular, the UAE-Japan Society, ADOC, and JODCO provided me with valuable materials and comments. In addition, I received valuable comments from Mr. Sho Inokuchi of METI and my colleague Prof. Shuji Hosaka of the Institute of Energy Economics, Japan. I would like to express my gratitude to them again.

Bibliography

Abu Dhabi-Japan Society. 1973. *Abu Dhabi* (2): 24–25.

———. 1974. *Abu Dhabi* (3).

Abu Dhabi Oil Company (ADOC). 1998. *30 Years Offshore Abu Dhabi 1968–1998*. Osaka: Shimpu Shobo.

———. 2018. *Abu Dhabi Sekiyu Souritsu 50 Syūnen: Chōsen wo Tsuduketa Hanseiki* (Abu Dhabi Oil Co., Ltd.: 50th Anniversary of Foundation). Tokyo: Nikkei Business Publications.

Akimoto, M. 2018. "Sengo Nihon no Tai Chūtō Bunka Kōuryū Katsudō: KBS/Kokusai Kouryū Kikin no Jigyō wo Chushin ni (Japan's Postwar Cultural Exchange Policy toward the Middle East: The Case Study of the Society for International Cultural Relations (KBS) and the Japan Foundation)," *Kokusai Seiji* 192: 17–32.

Asada, Naomi. 2006. "Abu Dhabi Kumon Shiki Gakusyū: JODCO ga Kodomo Tachito Sugoshita 8 Nen (The Kumon Method in Abu Dhabi: 8 Years JODCO Spent with Children)," *UAE* 40: 7–8.

Cosmo Oil. 2011. ADOC Sign a New Concession Agreement. https://ceh.cosmo-oil.co.jp/eng/press/110203/index.html. Accessed 26 November 2020.

Dargin, J. and A. Flower. 2011. "The UAE Gas Sector: Challenges and Solutions for the Twenty-First Century," in Bassam Fattouh and Jonathan P. Stern eds. *Natural Gas Markets in the Middle East and North Africa*. Oxford and New York: Oxford University Press, pp. 429–485.

Ministry of Foreign Affairs, Japan (MOFA). 1962. *Diplomatic Bluebook Vol. 6*.

———. 1967. *Diplomatic Bluebook Vol. 11*.

———. 2007a. Abe Sōridaijin no Arab Shuchōkoku Renpō Houmon ni Tsuite (Regarding the Prime Minister Abe's visit to the UAE). https://www.mofa.go.jp/mofaj/kaidan/s_abe/usa_me_07/uae_gai.html. Accessed 26 November 2020.

———. 2007b. Muhammad Abu Dhabi Kōtaishi no Hounichi (Crown Prince Mohammad's Visit to Japan). https://www.mofa.go.jp/mofaj/area/uae/visit/0712_gh.html. Accessed 26 November 2020.

———. 2013. Joint Statement on the Strengthening of the Comprehensive Partnership between Japan and the United Arab Emirates towards Stability and Prosperity. https://www.mofa.go.jp/mofaj/files/000004138.pdf. Accessed 26 November 2020.

———. 2017. Kōno Gaimu Daijin niyoru Takizawa Hideaki-shi ni Taisuru Nichi UAE Shinzen Taishi Isyokujyō Kōfu (Minister of Foreign Affairs Kono Appointed Mr. Hideaki Takizawa as a Goodwill Ambassador to the UAE). https://www.mofa.go.jp/mofaj/press/release/press4_004960.html. Accessed 26 November 2020.

Hamada, H. 2011. "Asia Gaikō: Kokunai Indo Power no kensei to Nicchūkan tono Keizai Kōryū (Asia Diplomacy: Checking Domestic Indian Power and Economic Exchange with Japan, China and Korea)," in T. Hosoi ed. *UAE o Shirutame no 60 Shou.* Tokyo: Akashi Shoten, pp. 299–302.

Horinuki, K. 2019. Dubai Shuchōkoku no Keizai Hatten wo Sasaeru Shakaikiban: Kōkyō Kōtsūkikan wo Jireini (Social Infrastructure and Economic Development in Dubai: The Case of Public Transportation). *Energy Review* June 2019: 19–20.

Hosoi, T. ed. 2011. *UAE wo Shirutame no 60 Shou* (60 Chapters to Know the UAE). Tokyo: Akashi Shoten.

Inohara, W. 2013. "Abu Dhabi no Sekiyu Tennen Gas Kaihatsu wo Meguru Genkyō (Current Oil and Natural Gas Development in Abu Dhabi)," *Oil and Gas Review* 47 (6): 55–68.

Inpex. 2014. Extension of the Concession Agreement for the Upper Zakum Oil Field Offshore Abu Dhabi, United Arab Emirates. https://www.inpex.co.jp/english/assets/pdf/e20140121.pdf. Accessed 26 November 2020.

———. 2015. INPEX Acquires Participating Interest in ADCO Onshore Concession, Abu Dhabi, United Arab Emirates. https://www.inpex.co.jp/english/assets/pdf/e20150427.pdf. Accessed 26 November 2020.

———. 2018. INPEX Acquires Stake in Lower Zakum Concession, Extension of Satah and Umm Al Dalkh Concession Offshore Abu Dhabi, United Arab Emirates. https://www.inpex.co.jp/english/assets/pdf/e20180226.pdf. Accessed 26 November 2020.

———. 2019a. *Kokusai Sekiyu Kaihatsu Teiseki 10 Nen no Ayumi: Yūgou, Chōsen, Soshite Mirai e* (10 Years History of the INPEX: Integration, Challenges, and the Future).

———. 2019b. INPEX Awarded Onshore Block 4 in Abu Dhabi Licensing Block Bid 2018. https://www.inpex.co.jp/english/news/assets/pdf/e20190318.pdf.

Iwasa, S. 1995. "Abu Dhabi no Sekiyu Shi 2 (Abu Dhabi's Oil History 2)," *Sekiyu Kaihatsu to Bichiku* 28(4): 29–57.

Japan National Oil Corp. (JNOC). 1987. *Sekiyu Kodan 20 Nen Shi* (20 Years History of the Japan National Oil Corp).

Kamo, Y. 2015. "Nichi-UAE Kankei to Saikin no UAE Jyōsei (Japan-UAE Relations and Recent Development of the UAE)," *Chūtō Kenkyū* 524: 3–6.

Kanamori, T. 2019. "Abu Dhabi Shuchōkoku ni Okeru Nihon Ryūgaku Sokushin Jigyō (Promotion of Study in Japan in the Emirates of Abu Dhabi)," *UAE* 65: 13–17.

Kawaguchi, K. 2009. "Abu Dhabi Tono Eizokuteki Kankei wo Mezashite (Toward an Enduring Relationship with Abu Dhabi)," *Oil and Natural Gas Review* 43 (3): 77–84.

Kishida, N. 2009. "Nihon-UAE Bunka Center Sousetsu (Establishment of the Japan-UAE Cultural Center)," *UAE* 45: 7–12.

Mitsubishi Heavy Industries (MHI). 2020. MHI Successfully Launches the Emirates Mars Mission, HOPE Spacecraft. https://www.mhi.com/news/202 00720.html. Accessed 26 November 2020.

Nishizaki, S. 2011. "The United Arab Emirates and Japan: Diversifying Bilateral Relationships and Challenges in the Context of Japan's New Foreign Policy Focus and US-Japan Relation," *Comparative Islamic Studies* 7 (1–2): 269–294.

Ritsumeikan. n.d. COSMO-ADOC-RITSUMEIKAN Japanese Language Program. http://en.ritsumei.ac.jp/intl/program/abdhabi/.

Tōakeizai Kenkyūjyo. 1943. *Arabia Tougan Shuchō Shuyokoku: Kōweito, Bārein Tou, Torūshyaru Ōman, Ōman* (Eastern Coast of Arabian Emirates: Kuwait, Island of Bahrain, Trucial Oman, and Oman).

Togashi, Masato. 2018. "UAE Kenbunroku: Enerugi Shigen to Keizai wo Fumaete (Report of the UAE Study Tour: Based on Energy Resources and Economy)." *UAE* 64: 5–10.

Tomita, Hiroshi. 2016. "Gijyuku wo Otozureta Gaikokujin 8: Otaiba (Foreigners Visiting Keio University 8: Otaiba)," *Mita Hyōron* 1203: 64–67.

UAE Japan Society. 1975. *Arab Shuchokoku Renpou to Nihon no Kouryu: Renpou Kessei 5 Shunen wo Kinenshite* (Bilateral Exchange between the UAE and Japan: In Commemoration of 5 years Anniversary of the Formation of Federation).

———. 1978. *UAE* 5: 12–17, 33.

———. 1983. *UAE* 9: 29–30.

———. 1985. *UAE* 11.

———. 1989. "Kyōkai Katsudō 18 Nen wo Furikaette: Kyōsei no Jidai ni Ikiru. Nakayama Sohei Tou Kyōkai Sōdanyaku ni Kiku (Looking Back on 18 Years of UAE-Japan Society: Living in the "Age of Coexistence". Interview with Sohei Nakayama, Advisor of the Society)," *UAE* 15: 16–21.

———. 2020. "NPO Hōjin Nihon UAE Seisyōnen Jidō Ikusei Kōryū Kyōkai Katsudō Houkoku (Report on the Activities of the UAE-JAPAN Association for Youth Development and Exchange)," *UAE* 68: 20.

UAE Deputy Prime Minister Office. n.d. *The UAE-Japan Relations.*

Urasenke. n.d. Daisoushō Abu Dhabi wo Gohōmon: "Ryokusui An" Chashitsu Biraki (The Master visited Abu Dhabi: Open the Tea Room Ryokusui An). http://www.urasenke.or.jp/textm/headq/soke/visit/visit069/visit069.html.

Zayed Center for Coordination and Follow-Up. 2002. *The UAE-Japan Relations.*

CHAPTER 4

The Three Cycles of Rise and Fall in Iran–Japan Relations: From Energy Studies to Political Causal Analysis

Tomoyo Chisaka

1 Introduction

This research examines the process of how Iran–Japan relations have developed over the last 90 years (1929–2019). These processes demonstrate that real efforts were made by both Iranian and Japanese politicians and private enterprises, especially when Iran–Japan relations were on the verge of establishing diplomatic ties (1929–1945), and when they experienced development after two political challenges: World War II and the Iran–Iraq War. However, scholars pay little attention to the dynamics and the factors behind the turning points of Iran–Japan relations. This article is among the first to empirically examine the process of the changing cycle

T. Chisaka (✉)
College of Arts and Sciences, The University of Tokyo Graduate School, Tokyo, Japan
e-mail: t-chisaka@g.ecc.u-tokyo.ac.jp

© The Author(s), under exclusive license to Springer Nature Singapore Pte Ltd. 2023
S. Nakamura and S. Wright (eds.), *Japan and the Middle East*, Contemporary Gulf Studies, https://doi.org/10.1007/978-981-19-3459-9_4

of Iran–Japan relations, and explain the turning points of these relations, by studying international political impacts on Iran–Japan relations.[1]

Previous research on Iran–Japan relations can be divided into two streams. The first group of scholars follow the process of establishing diplomatic relations between Iran and Japan, which originated in 1878 with a meeting between the Japanese minister in Russia, Takeaki Enomoto, and the fourth Iranian king of the Qājār dynasty, Nāser al-Din Shāh, in St. Petersburg.[2] Thereafter, Japan's first official delegation was dispatched to Iran in 1880.[3] However, World War I (1914–1918) was a trigger event that motivated Japan to expand its economic market to Iran, whereas before this war, Japan was interested in Iran simply to observe the activities of three major European countries which had already a presence in Iran: the United Kingdom (UK), the Union of Soviet Socialist Republics (USSR) and German.[4] Meanwhile, the second group of scholars discusses energy issues between Iran and Japan; in particular, Iran–Japan oil transactions in the 1950s, and Japanese development investments in Iranian petrochemical industries in the 1970s, are frequently studied.[5]

Still, the existing research has three problems. First, there is no research that examines Iran–Japan relations in the long term (1929–2019); therefore, no research has been done to explain certain cycles that appear in Iran–Japan relations. Second, it is necessary to review issues other than energy issues, because these two countries' relations also experienced a rise and fall in political affairs. Third, the triggers behind the turning points of Iran–Japan relations should be analysed; because causal analysis tells not only when but also why Iran–Japan relations changed.

This article argues that Iran–Japan relations developed over energy affairs, but such relations have hinged on international political impacts; consequently, Iran–Japan relations experienced three 'rise and fall' cycles from 1929 to 2019. To reveal this argument, this research looks into

[1] While this paper provides an original analysis on political factors affected Iran–Japan relations, economic factors are also important in explaining the development of the relationship between these two countries.

[2] Kuroda, "Pioneering Iranian Studies in Meiji Japan," 652.

[3] Okazaki, "Japan and Iran in the Meiji Era," 72.

[4] Hinata, "Kindai Nihon to Perusha" [Modern Japan and Persia], 121.

[5] Abdoly, "Energy and Japan-Iran Relations," 152–53; Umeno, "The Historical Analysis," 133; Takahashi, "The Iran-Japan Petrochemical Project," 83–84.

how Iranian and Japanese actors have been interdependent on each other, as well as their views towards international political environments. This study utilises primary sources, including Japanese diplomatic documents, and secondary sources, such as Japanese newspapers and the website of the Japanese Ministry of Foreign Affairs. Additionally, it collects statistical data from the Japan External Trade Organization (JETRO) and the Ministry of Economy, Trade and Industry (METI), and previous research published in Persian. Of note, in the context of this chapter, international political impacts include the Second World War, regional wars in the Middle East and international economic sanctions imposed on Iran, and Iran–Japan economic relations refer to oil transactions and Japanese development investments in Iran.

This chapter is organised as follows: the second section reviews the first rise and fall cycle (1929–1953), in which Iran and Japan became close upon their establishment of diplomatic relations, but came apart during World War II (WWII). The third section presents the second rise and fall cycle (1953–1988), when although Iran–Japan economic relations improved in the beginning of this period, they faced a sudden end, due to the Iranian revolution in 1979 and the Iran–Iraq War in the 1980s. The fourth section demonstrates the third rise and fall cycle (1988–2019), covering how Iran–Japan relations saw progress at first, yet declined once more following international economic sanctions against Iran, especially in the mid-2000s.

2 First Cycle (1929–1952): From the Opening of Diplomatic Ties to World War II

This section explains the first rise and fall cycle of Iran–Japan relations, from their establishment in 1929 to their decline during WWII. Iran is the second earliest country, after Turkey, in which a Japanese legation was established in the Near East; therefore, this event drew attention from Japanese media as an important step for Japanese economic promotion in the Near East.[6] Given the efforts made by the Japanese government to expand its economic activities to Iran, the relationship between Iran and Japan rapidly broke down during WWII. It is important to note that

---

[6] *Yomiuri Newspaper*, "Iyoiyo Kaisetsu sareru Perusha Kōshikan" [The Japanese Legation in Persia Is to Be Opened], July 30, 1929.

Japanese diplomats thought that this disintegration was caused by neither Iran nor Japan's true will; rather, they thought of WWII as the decisive factor.

2.1   Rapprochement: Seeking New Economic Arenas

Since the establishment of diplomatic relations in August 1929, the relationship between Iran and Japan made significant progress, mainly because both states had strategically sought to expand their power through new international economic markets. Particularly, Japan wanted access to Iranian markets, including oil. In the 1920s, the Japanese government conducted research about domestic oil production capabilities and realised how limited they were. To overcome this lack of oil, the Japanese government started to explore foreign, resource-rich lands.[7]

As a result, in October 1932, Japan and Iran ratified the Japan-Persia Treaty of Amity and Commerce, in which amity, dwelling and free trade were accorded.[8] Based on this treaty, the Iranian government asked the Japanese government for technical support in several areas, including railroad construction and the sericulture industry. In response to such requests, the Japanese government dispatched railroad engineers and sericultural industry manuals to industrial experiment stations in Tehran.[9]

Additionally, Japan made efforts to negotiate cotton transactions with Iran. The following is an excerpt of a telegram sent from the Japanese minister in Tehran, Shouichi Nakayama, to the Japanese Minister of Foreign Affairs, Kazushige Ugaki, on 27 July 1938.

[…] The new Iranian Foreign Minister regarded promoting Iran-Japan trades by selling raw Iranian cotton with great favour. But, in the meantime, the Foreign Minister demanded Japan export cotton cloths; though, he suggested, if negotiations over cotton cloths should fail, exporting raw cotton would be difficult to permit. If a fundamental problem of this

---

[7] Hinata, "Modern Japan and Persia," 2016.

[8] "Nihon to Perusha/Iran" [Japan and Persia-Iran], *Ministry of Foreign Affairs of Japan*, May 18, 2008.

[9] Ibid.; *Yomiuri Newspaper*, "Perusha Seifu Yōsangyō ni Chūmoku" [Persian Government Paid Attention to A Sericulture Industry], October 19, 1930.

negotiation is the transaction of cotton cloths, competition with third countries may emerge. Thus, I would like to humbly request the central government's sincere consideration of this matter.[10]

This telegram provides a better understanding of Japanese economic policy towards Iran: promoting trade with Iran based on negotiations and demands by Iranians.

In the meantime, Iran's oil market at the beginning of the 1920s was almost completely controlled by the UK and their cotton market by the USSR. To diminish economic dependency on these two countries, Reżā Shāh, the first Iranian king of the Pahlavi dynasty, became close to a state that was relatively strong and unfriendly towards these two countries: Germany. While Iran's rapprochement with Germany was motivated mainly by political incentives, Iran also sought economic benefits from Japan, because Iran knew that Japan was trying to expand its cotton market in Iran, after the USSR failed to renew its economic treaty with Iran in 1939.[11] In fact, imports from the UK and the USSR dropped by 32% and 18.2%, respectively from 1928 to 1929, when Iran and Japan established diplomatic ties. By contrast, Iranian imports from Japan significantly increased by 81.7%.[12] Figure 1 shows increases in both Iran's import and export trade with Japan, especially after Iran and Japan ratified the Treaty of Amity and Commerce in 1939.[13]

2.2 The Rupturing of Iran–Japan Diplomatic Relations: The Impact of WWII

To understand the connection between WWII and Iran–Japan relations, it is important to note the conflict structure: the Axis powers, including Germany and Japan, versus the Allied powers, including the UK and the USSR. This structure brought diplomatic relations between Iran

---

[10] "Imperial Trade Policy toward Iran," *JCAHR*, picture no. 59. Translated by author.

[11] "Imperial Trade Policy toward Iran," *JCAHR*, picture no. 64.

[12] Ibid., picture no. 44.

[13] "Imperial Trade Policy toward Iran," *JCAHR*, picture no. 68. The main Iranian import to Japan was cotton fabric, and the main export opium, with the latter in Japanese colonies in Southeast Asia. The total opium sales reached 720,000 pounds. Although it is a small amount compared to the British patent on Iranian oil, Japan thought of opium transactions as one of the key policies towards Iran.

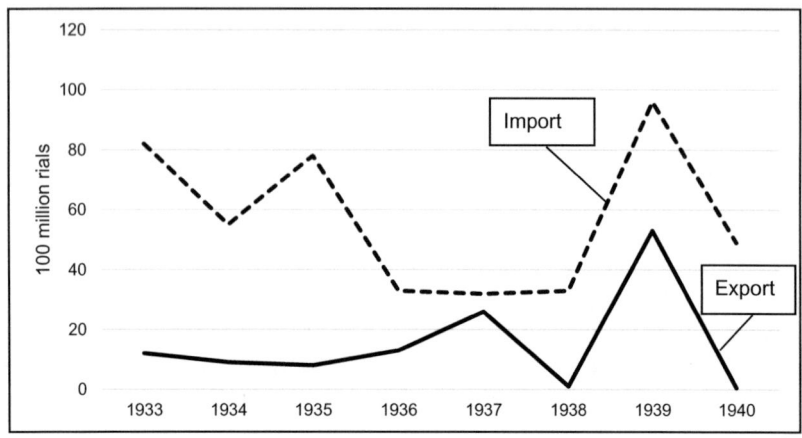

Fig. 1 Iran's trade with Japan before WWII (1933–1940) (*Source* Shokrzadeh and Abadian [2017: 54]. *Note* This graph shows the change in the amount of Iranian export to and import from Japan before WWII)

and Japan to a temporary end, as Iran and Japan did not intend direct militarised dispute.

Rather, at the outbreak of the WWII in September 1939, Iran declared its neutrality, in order to distance itself from the conflict. However, soon after, Iran received a note sent from the British and the Soviets, in which they demanded the Iranian government expel Germans from Iran. When Reżā Shāh delayed his response, on 25 August 1941 British and Soviet troops entered Iran.[14] Under Allied military occupation, Iran had no choice but to pull away from Japan, which was an Axis power. Similarly, pressure from the British and Soviets made Iran change their policy towards Japan. In the end, Iran declared separation from Japan in April 1942.

Interestingly, however, when Iran changed their position towards Japan, Japanese diplomats recognised that such Iranian behaviour was not made willingly. For instance, a Japanese minister in Tehran, Santarō Ichikawa, said, 'Iran had completely lost its autonomy as an independent state, due to the military intervention from the British and Soviets. Thus, Iranian foreign policy was not decided by Iranian will. Now, Iran behaves

[14] Keddi, *Modern Iran*, 105.

under British and Soviet orders'.[15] This report indicates that although on the surface Iran–Japan relations broke during WWII, Japanese diplomats believed that Iran's real intentions were different: Iran wanted to keep their relations with Japan.

In summary, the first turning point of Iran–Japan relations from positive to negative was caused by WWII, as the war (an international political factor) cast a shadow over the economic associations between Iran and Japan. Two other rise and fall cycles of Iran–Japan relationships, featured below, followed this first cycle. Similarly, they too suggest that international political expediency determines the closeness of two countries' economic relations.

3   SECOND CYCLE (1953–1988): FROM SURGE TO DECLINE

The second rise of Iran–Japan relations begins with restoration in 1953 and ends with the outbreak of the Iran–Iraq War in 1988. The years from 1953 to 1979 saw the astonishing growth of economic relations between Iran and Japan. However, the Iranian revolution in 1979 ended such development, and the Iran–Iraq War further worsened Iran–Japan relations. After the Iranian revolution in 1979, while a breakup of Iran–US relations brought some challenges to Iran–Japan relations, it is worth paying attention to Japanese struggles for seeking autonomy, not completely following US policy towards Iran, when Japan decided foreign policy towards Iran after the revolution.

3.1   Golden Age of Iran–Japan Economic Relations

3.1.1   Oil Transactions

Signs of recovering Iran–Japan relations can be seen earlier than when Iran and Japan re-established their diplomatic ties in 1953, dating back to Iran's oil nationalisation policy. In 1951, the Iranian government decided to nationalise the Anglo-Iranian Oil Company (AIOC), to which the British, who were a main shareholder of the AIOC, were strongly opposed, calling for a global boycott of Iranian oil involving their allies

---

[15] "The Greater East Asia War," *JCAHR*, picture no. 3.

and other countries.[16] This event explains why Iran desired to find new customers for their oil, in which Japan was included.

Also at this time, Japan's main energy gradually shifted from coal to oil. With the demand for domestic oil consumption rising, Japan eyed the rich Iranian oil reserves, like they had before WWII. Especially after the restoration of diplomatic relations in 1953, the Japanese government supported private Japanese oil firms, such as Idemitsu, which had already begun negotiating with their Iranian counterparts, prior to diplomatic restoration.

These situations suggest how Iran and Japan became interdependent over oil: Iran saw Japan as an indispensable oil importer, while Japan recognised Iran as a significant oil exporter. As such, since Japan relied on Iranian crude oil to meet its domestic oil consumption, maintaining a sustainable and trustworthy oil flow from Iran was crucial. This Japanese attitude towards Iran is evident from Japan's response to Iran's criticism on the trade gap: Since the Iranian government did not consider Japanese oil imports, which were included under foreign investment oil firms in Iran, as part of trade between Iran and Japan, Iran criticised Japan for export surplus.[17] Thus, Iran requested Japan purchase oil produced by the Iranian National Oil Company, not by international oil firms.[18] Iran warned that, if Japan failed to respond to this request, they would increase tariffs on Japanese goods.[19] Indeed, Iran declined the renewal of a commerce treaty with Japan in July 1966.

Even though Japan faced such criticism from Iran, the Japanese government patiently negotiated with Iran to maintain its oil supply. For instance, in a meeting with the Iranian Minister of Economics and Minister of Finance held in Tehran in April 1973, the Japanese Minister of Commerce, Hirofumi Nakasone, said, 'Iranian oil shares 40%

---

[16] Keddi, *Modern Iran*, 127.

[17] "The Diplomatic Bluebook 1967," *Japanese Ministry of Foreign Affairs*. International oil firms were composed of foreign investments from the UK, the US, the Netherlands and France. They shared more than 90% of Iranian oil production. Additionally, although the actual oil imports from Iran shared the biggest ratio of Japanese oil imports in the early 1970s, the Japanese export amount to Iran was about $72 billion, while Japanese imports of primary products from Iran were only about $8 million in 1966.

[18] Ibid.

[19] *Yomiuri Newspaper*, "25 Pāsento Hikiage Iran no Tainichi Yunyū Kanzei" [25% Increase of Iranian tariff on Japanese goods], January 8, 1959.

of Japanese oil consumption, and we desire to continue importing Iranian oil in the future. Also, Japan will sincerely commit economic cooperation with Iran'.[20] That is, Japan offered economic investment into Iran, to compensate for the trade gap.

3.1.2 Iranian Development Policy and Japanese Economic Cooperation

It is necessary to remember the importance of development investments, both from the Japanese government and Japanese private enterprises, in response to Iranian demands. For example, Iran wanted to maintain a telecommunications network as part of its modernisation politics during the 1960s. Targeting such needs, the Japanese government offered a $17 million loan for constructing a microwave system in 1965.[21] In addition, Japan provided another $8 million loan for oil field development in Iran's Lorestān Province in 1971.[22]

Regarding this Lorestān Province oil field development project, Japanese private companies played significant roles, taking the initiative to negotiate with the Iranian government, and succeeding in strengthening Iran–Japan inter-government economic relations. In fact, after meeting with the Iranian government, the Deputy Chief of Mitsui & Co., Ltd. sent a letter to the Japanese Minister of Commerce as follows:

In Iran's opinion, the Japanese government's cooperation in generating commerce in Iran's petrol-chemical industry is a crucial condition of Japan winning the right to invest in Lorestān's oil field. Especially, as for $230 million among the total sum of $350 million of this oil field development project, the Iranians demanded our company supply a low-interest government fund for a long-term.[23]

Later, the Japanese government agreed to this request.

[20] *Yomiuri Newspaper*, "Sekiyu Shohikoku Renmei Nihon ha Husanka" [Japanese Absent in Oil Consumption Countries' Associations], April 30, 1973.

[21] *Yomiuri Newspaper*, "Iran ni Enshakkan" [Yen Loans for Iran], May 19, 1965.

[22] *Yomiuri Newspaper*, "Iran Sekiyu Hossoku" [Establishment of Iran Oil], September 23, 1971.

[23] Umeno, "The Historical Analysis," 141.

Moreover, Japanese private companies' interests in Iran were not only investing in oil fields but also in training Iranian skilled workers. This attempt was made based on the fifth economic five-year plan proposed by the Iranian government. According to the Chairman of Keidanren (the Japan Business Federation), Kougoro Uemura, Iran requested that 3000–5000 Iranian workers complete technical training in Japanese factories. Keidanren positively considered Iranian demands; therefore, Uemura announced that Keidanren would establish special committees, divided into petrochemical, heavy, electronics, fibre, mining and agriculture industries.[24]

To summarise, through oil transactions and economic cooperation for Iran's development, the years between 1953 and 1979 saw the peak of Iran–Japan relations. What we should remember is that both oil transactions and economic cooperation were promoted by mutual interests between Iran and Japan. The positive effects of such good economic relations were seen in the cultural exchange between Iran and Japan during this period.[25]

3.2   Iran's Regime Change and the Japanese Struggle to Stay On

The Iranian revolution on 11 February 1979 changed the Iranian political regime from a monarchy to an Islamic republic. Since regime change by mass movement was a drastic event, Iran's domestic as well as foreign policies also changed entirely. Even so, the Japanese government made surprising efforts to maintain good relations with Iran's new regime; however, Japan was forced to withdraw from Iran, due to the start of the Iran–Iraq War and the rising conflict between Iran and the US.

[24] *Yomiuri Newspaper*, "Iran Kenshūsei Ukeire" [Accepting Trainees from Iran], September 3, 1972.

[25] "Nihon to Perusha/Iran" [Japan and Persia/Iran], *Ministry of Foreign Affairs of Japan*, May 18, 2008. In 1957, the Japan-Iran Cultural Agreement was concluded as the first formal bilateral pact since the countries' restoration of relations on 1 November 1953. This cultural treaty accorded the promotion of academic exchange (both scholars and students), as well as the exchange of cultural activities, such as movies and art.

3.2.1   Revolution and War: Japanese Private Companies Withdraw from Iran

The first and most noticeable change in this period was the Japanese private enterprise withdrawal from Iran, due to the instability of the new Iranian domestic politics. In the late 1970s, anti-Shah mass demonstrations spread across Iran.[26] Subsequently, Japanese companies' business activities in the country faced serious threats, such as local worker strikes, gas supply cuts and arson by protesters. As such, the cost of business for Japanese enterprises in the Iranian market increased, and most Japanese companies withdrew from Iran.[27]

Some Japanese companies, including those within the oil and natural gas industries, that had already invested huge amounts of money in constructing oil and gas fields in Iran, waited for conditions to become stable. Yet, a year after the revolution, Iraq invaded Iran, and the ensuing war devastated Japanese factories in Iran, as well as tankers that navigated the Persian Gulf. As a result, almost all Japanese enterprises ordered their employees to leave Iran. Figure 2 demonstrates how sharply trade between Iran and Japan declined during the Iran–Iraq War.

3.2.2   Iranian Political Factionalism: The Japanese Government's Patience

Unlike their private companies, which began leaving Iran during the uprising, Japan tried to hold economic relations with Iran during and even after the revolution. Such a position is evident from how Japan maintained economic negotiations with Iranian political elites, despite their frequent and shifting changes during the regime's transitional periods.[28]

After the Shah fled Iran, Shāpūr Bakhtiyār, the head of the National Front (NF), one of the stronger nationalist political parties from the monarchical era, seized power. Bakhtiyār was appointed by the Shah as Iran's prime minister on 29 December 1978, under the condition that he reign rather than rule while the Shah took an extended vacation abroad.[29] Like Western governments, Japan expressed their support of Bakhtiyār's

---

[26] Rasler, "Concessions, Repression, and Political Protest," 132.

[27] *Nihon Keizai Shimbun* [*Nikkei*], "Teijin Iran Sekiyu kara Tettai" [Teijin Withdrew from Iranian Oil], May 26, 1978.

[28] This paper defines the regime transitional period from the beginning of Bakhtiyār's administration, to the end of the Bāzarqān provisional government.

[29] Abrahimian, *Radical Islam*, 39.

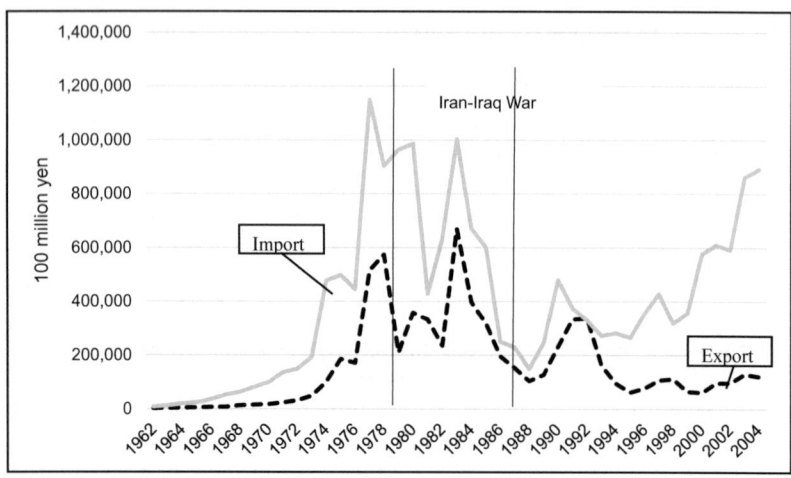

Fig. 2 Japanese trade with Iran (1962–2004) (*Source* Statistic Bureau, Japanese Ministry of International Affairs and Communication. *Note* Export includes Iranian oil produced by international oil farms)

administration and sent a telegram, reading, 'Japan will not break off oil development plans'.[30] The Japanese government's cooperative attitude towards Bakhtiyār's administration contrasted with that of the country's private enterprises that had left Iran over business costs. This cooperation probably resulted from 85% of Japanese oil plant construction in Lorestān having already been accomplished, and accordingly, cancellation of this oil project would be a huge cost for Japan.[31]

However, Bakhtiyār's administration did not last long, because of his failure to ease tensions with Rūh Allāh Mūsavī Khomeinī, who was exiled to Paris, and who would later become the first Supreme Leader in the

[30] *Yomiuri Newspaper*, "Ippouteki ni Chudan senu" [No Unilateral Disrupt], January 27, 1979.

[31] *Yomiuri Newspaper*, "Iran Sekika Shien Zokkou" [Continuing Assistance for Iran Oil Project], January 10, 1979. The Ministry of Commerce requested Mituibussan to continue the project, based on initial guidelines.

newly established Islamic Republic of Iran.[32] Thus, the Japanese government lost a new negotiation partner, Bakhtiyār's administration only a few weeks and had to find an alternative partner.

After the exile of Bakhtiyār, the Japanese faced difficulty in continuing negotiations with Iran over the oil project. This is because a strong Iranian political party, the Islamic Republic Party (IRP), played a major role in writing the constitution, in which the new Iranian regime accorded the nationalisation of industries. The main nationalised industries include oil, gas, main and heavy industries, which had been dominated by foreign investment during the monarchical era. This new constitution aimed for independence from great powers such as the US and the UK. Such a policy frightened Japan, which had committed to oil field construction in Lorestān.

What was good for Japan was that Supreme Leader Khomeinī appointed Mehdī Bāzarqān, one of the leaders of the NF and not of the IRP, as the first prime minister of Iran's Islamic Republic. Thus, pushing against the IRP-led nationalisation of the oil field development project in Lorestān, the Japanese government negotiated with the Bāzarqān provisional government and received permission to continue its construction.[33] Moreover, the Japanese government upgraded the Iranian oil development project to a national project, to prove their commitment[34] right before their official delegation visited Tehran in September 1979. These positive Japanese attitudes were highly valued by the Iranian government, as many foreign investors, including the US and the UK, left Iran after the revolution.[35] In other words, Japan seriously invested in maintaining economic relations with Iran.

---

[32] Although Bakhtiyār continued militarised resistance against Khomeinī as he and his clerical followers attempted to gain state power. Yet, soon after the Iranian national army declared their neutral position, Bakhtiyār was exiled from Iran. Abrahimian, *Radical Islam*, 41.

[33] On 22 February 1979, the Japanese government agreed to pay 750 billion yen out of the Iranian government's charges, to construct the Lorestān oil field. *Yomiuri Newspaper*, "Iran Sekiyu Kagaku Konbinato Keikaku Seifu ga Zenmen Shien" [Government Supported Iran's Petrochemical Complex Project Thoroughly], February 23, 1979.

[34] *Yomiuri Newspaper*, "Iran Sekiyu Kagaku Konbinato Keikaku Kokkateki Jigyo ni Kakuage" [Iran Petrochemical Complex Project Was Upgraded to National Project], August 31, 1979.

[35] Amuzegar, *Iran's Economy*, 168.

However, the Japanese investment faced a problem once again when the Bāzarqān resigned in December 1979, because of deepening the divide between them and the IRP over decision-making about the hostage crisis at the American Embassy in Tehran (November 1979–January 1981). In the end, the Japanese government lost another important negotiation partner after the revolution. Soon after, supporters of the nationalisation of industries cemented their dominant position over Iranian politics, and the Iranian parliament declined a supplementary accord suggested by Japan in April 1985. The possibility of Japan continuing negations with Iran was now over.

These processes demonstrate how the Japanese government strongly desired to retain friendly relations with Iran, even after the latter's revolution. By contrast, due to Iran's political fragmentation, the Japanese government was unable to find a trustworthy or reliable negotiating counterpart, causing the cancellation of their oil development projects.

3.2.3   The Iran–Iraq War: Japanese Initiatives for a Ceasefire Pact

In addition to changes in domestic politics, Iran's foreign policy towards America altered with the final regime change. The most critical event is the hostage crisis at the American embassy in Tehran, which began in November 1979 and lasted 444 days.[36] After this event, American president Jimmy Carter's administration imposed economic sanctions on Iranian oil exports and froze Iranian assets in the US. More importantly, the Carter administration asked their allies, including Japan, to cooperate with their policies. Consequently, Japan faced a serious dilemma; that is, while Japan wished to continue oil transactions with Iran, it was also necessary to accommodate their American ally. Growing pressures from the US diminished Japanese investment in constructing Iran's petrochemical complex.

It is important to note that meanwhile, the Japanese government was seeking initiative for a ceasefire of the Iran–Iraq War.[37] During the war,

[36] On 4 November 1979, the Jimmy Carter administration permitted the Shah to enter the US for medical treatment. Protesting this decision, many Iranian youths attacked the American embassy in Tehran and took hostages.

[37] Tanaka, "Japanese Diplomacy," 18. In the 1980s, while Western countries closed diplomatic relations with Iran, Japan consistently tried to maintain good relations with Iran. Thus, the Japanese ability to gain information about Iran received high reputation from the West; *Asahi Newspaper*, "Kuranari Gaisyo I-I Senso Shuketsu Ketsugian

Japanese prime minister Shintaro Abe officially visited Iran in 1983 and met with Iranian prime minister Mīr Ḥoseyn Mūsavī. They discussed a peace pact to end the Iran–Iraq War, as well as a large economic cooperation with Iran. Abe also visited Iraq during the war. Two years later, the chairman of the Iranian parliament, ʿAlī Akbar Hāshemī Rafsanjānī, and Iranian Foreign Minister ʿAlī Akbar Velāyati visited Japan for further discussion on the Iran–Iraq War peace pact, along with oil transactions. These visits by high-ranking politicians indicate that Iran and Japan retained a good relationship, even when Iran–US relations significantly declined.

Overall, at a glance the second cycle of Iran–Japan relations is similar to the first cycle, as rising and falling is a characteristic of the first cycle, too. However, they are different in the following two aspects. First, the cost both for Japan and Iran of declining relations was larger than the cost that these two countries experienced during the first cycle of falling. This is because for Japan Iran became an indispensable oil supplier, and for Iran Japan became an important foreign investment. Second, during the second cycle, the rising and falling of Iran–Japan relations hinged on the Iran–US relations as is different from the first cycle when relationship between Iran and the European countries played major roll to determine the Iran–Japan relationship.

4 THIRD CYCLE (1989–2015): FROM RESTART TO DEADLOCK

This section discusses the third cycle of Iran Japan relations, which covers the period from the end of the Iran–Iraq War, to the Iran nuclear agreement in 2015. Despite the constraints and challenges that Iran–Japan relations faced during WWII, and in the Iran Iraq War, both coun tries gave efforts to strengthen their ties again. The first feature of this third period is that these countries' relations improved through economic

no Shuseian wo Beikoku Taishi ni Teiji" [Foreign Minister Kuranari Suggested American Ambassador to The United Nations with A Revised Draft of Resolution on The End of The Iran-Iraq War], July 10, 1987. One of the possible reasons that Japan wanted to promote a ceasefire was to facilitate between the UNSC and Iran. In fact, the Japanese Foreign Minister, Tadashi Kuranari, met with the US ambassador of the UN and said, "[…]we need considerations not to force one country involved in war to accept concession".

cooperation. The second point is that Iran–Japan relations still diminished once more, due to fluctuating international politics surrounding Iran, including those on nuclear weapons and economic sanctions.

4.1   Rising Pragmatists in Iran: The Achievements of Japanese Patience

The years after the end of the Iran–Iraq War saw the recovery of Iran–Japan relations, as Japan was able to seize Iran's political moderation in a post-war opportunity. During the Rafsanjānī administration (July 1989–April 1997), to proceed with economic reconstruction after the war, Iran tried to change their revolutionary image. In response to this policy, Japan began investing in economic development projects in Iran once again.

However, in the 1990s, Japan was still exposed to US pressure on economic cooperation towards Iran. For example, in 1996, the US ratified the Iran-Libya Sanction Act, warning that they would impose sanctions on foreign enterprises that invested in Iran. Still, the Japanese government did not change its policy towards Iran. One of the reasons for this stance is that Japan believed that isolating Iran from international society would not contribute to stabilising the region or the world, but rather make Iran more radical and worsen the situation.[38]

Furthermore, Japan was able to pay off its steady efforts towards keeping economic relations with Iran during the Moḥammad Khātamī administration (May 1997–April 2005), in which Iran's foreign policy became more moderate. For instance, soon after the presidential election in 1997, Khātamī asked to have a conversation with the US, which led a global expectation that Iran's foreign policy towards the US may change. Khātamī also declared 'dialogue between civilisations' in the United Nations General Assembly in September 2001, which also received positive response worldwide. Thus, in spite of US pressure on Japanese economic investment in Iran, the Japanese government had few difficulties in doing so.

There are several examples that suggest that Iran–Japan relations had become closer during the Khātamī administration. First, the Japanese Foreign Minister, Masahiko Komura, met with President Khatami in August 1999 in Tehran. In this meeting, Iran and Japan agreed to

---

[38] *Yomiuri Newspaper*, "Tai Iran Seisai de Nihon ha Dōchōsezu" [Japan Disagree with Sanction against Iran], June 9, 1995.

construct a dam in the Kārūn River, located in southwest Iran, to increase Iran's hydroelectric power supply.[39] Second, during Khātamī's visit to Japan in November 2000, Japanese public and private organisations gained the privilege of negotiating with Iran over the construction of the Āzādegān oil field, one of the largest oil fields in the Middle East.[40] Third, the Japanese International Cooperation Bank ratified the protocol to invest 319 billion yen in the Iranian government's development plan.[41]

Considering these events, it is easy to recognise that the recovery of Iran–Japan relations was promoted from the 1990s to the beginning of the 2000s. This does not only account for Iran's pragmatic and reformative policies, but also for Japan's continuous ambition to enhance economic relations with Iran. These developments, however, reduced after the Iranian nuclear controversy, and the strengthening of multilateral economic sanctions on Iran.

4.2 Iran Nuclear Controversy and the Third Decline of Iran–Japan Relations

The trigger event of the current Iran nuclear controversy goes back to August 2002.[42] Since then, the US and other Western countries have doubted Iran for making nuclear weapons, while Iran has argued a right to develop nuclear technology for peaceful purpose. During the years when Iran committed to negotiations with European countries and suspended their nuclear activity from 2003 to 2004, Japan once again opposed the American economic sanctions on Iran, saying that isolating Iran was not preferable for international society; rather, it made the situation worse.[43]

---

[39] Japan International Cooperation Agency (JICA).

[40] Yomiuri Newspaper, "Iran ni Chokusetsu Shakkan" [Direct Yen Loan for Iran], November 3, 2000.

[41] Ibid.

[42] In 2002, the Iranian anti-regime organisation acting in the US revealed that Iran had been developing nuclear technology without notifying the International Atomic Energy Agency (IAEA).

[43] For example, based on the Tehran declaration ratified with Germany, France and the UK in October 2003, Iran voluntarily suspended their nuclear activity. In December 2004, Iran ratified additional protocol from the IAEA, which allowed the IAEA to expand inspection authority over Iran's nuclear activity.

However, as a result of Iran's 2004 parliamentary election, and its 2005 presidential election, conservative politicians tightened their hold on power. Hence, Iran revoked their suspension of nuclear activity, and instead expanded its nuclear capabilities. In the end, the United Nations Security Council (UNSC) adopted the first economic sanctions on Iran in 2005 and the first financial sanctions on Iran in 2010. To cooperate with the UNSC resolutions, Japan finally began to cut oil exports and investments in Iran (Fig. 3). These processes during the nuclear negotiations in the 2000s suggest that Japan decided to diminish economic relations with Iran, not directly because of US pressure, but because of their cooperation with the multilateral decision-making undertaken by the UNSC.

The Iran nuclear controversy weakened Japanese leverage for Iran's economy, while China and South Korea increased their presence in Iran's economy. In the above two sections, I described how Japan had ranked almost at the top in terms of trade partners with Iran. Japan retained its high presence, with Japanese exports to Iran at 1.5–2 times that of China and South Korea, until the end of the 1990s. In contrast, as international society began to follow the Iranian nuclear controversy in the 2000s, the amount of Japanese exports to Iran was overtaken by China and South Korea. In fact, in 2005, the total amount of Chinese exports to Iran doubled that of Japan, and the total amount of South Korean exports to Iran became about 1.5 times than that of Japanese (Fig. 4). Additionally,

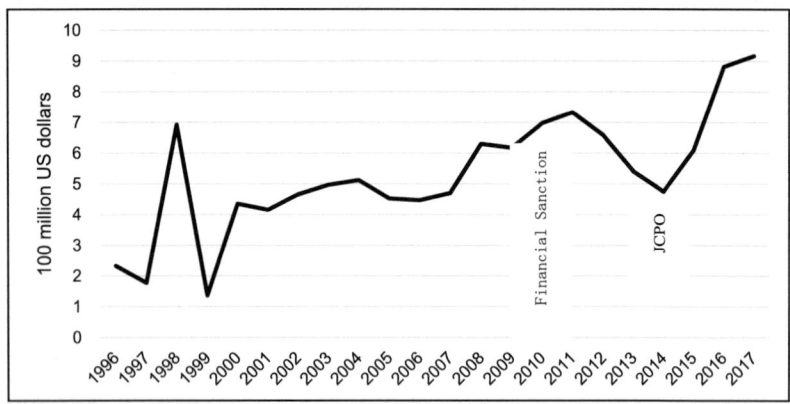

Fig. 3 Japanese development investment stocks toward Iran (1996–2017) (*Source* JETRO, Statistics of Foreign Direct Investment)

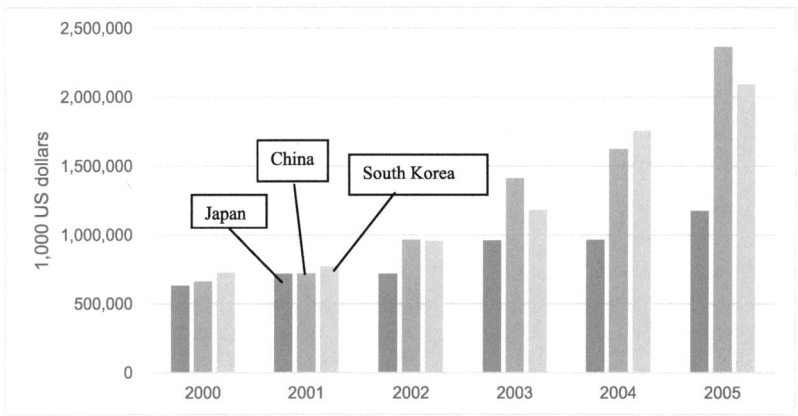

Fig. 4 Import to Iran from Japan, China and South Korea (2000–2005) (*Source* World Bank, World Integrated Trade Solution. *Note* This figure indicates a comparison of export to Iran from Japan, China and South Korea. The left graph is Japan, the middle graph is China and the right graph is South Korea)

in comparing oil imports from Iran, while Japan reduced their oil imports by approximately 40% from 2007 to 2011, China's figure increased by 30% and South Korea's by 20%. These data show that, whereas Japanese status in Iran had reduced, South Korea and China have increased their own; Chinese presence in Iranian oil imports especially grew after financial sanctions on Iran were adopted by the UNSC in 2010.

In summary, the turning of the third cycle was caused by the Iranian nuclear controversy, and economic sanctions imposed on Iran by multilateral countries. At the beginning of this period, due to Japan's approach to continuing economic relations with Iran, they were temporarily able to grasp an opportunity while pragmatic Iranian politicians held power. However, such an attempt faced barriers once again, because of one significant international political factor: the economic sanctions from the UNSC.[44]

---

[44] Iran ratified the nuclear agreement with P5 + 1 (permanent members of the UNSC, plus Germany), in which Iran agreed to voluntarily suspend nuclear activity, and P5 + 1 lift economic sanctions on Iran; however, it seems to be difficult to expect the Iran-Japan gradual rapprochement after the start of the Donald Trump administration.

5   CONCLUSION

This chapter revealed the three rise and fall cycles of Iran–Japan relations from 1929 to 2019.

The first cycle covers the establishment of Iran–Japan diplomatic ties in 1929, to WWII in the 1940s. Whereas Iran and Japan smoothly started trade at first, they had to reluctantly end such economic relations, upon the outbreak of WWII.

The second cycle follows the re-establishment of Iran–Japan diplomatic ties in the early 1950s, to the Iranian revolution in 1979 and the Iran–Iraq War (1980–1988). While Iran–Japan economic relations enjoyed a golden age from the 1950s to the 1970s, they once again faced a deadlock, triggered by the Iranian revolution and the Iran–Iraq War. However, while it is true that Japan lost its leverage to some extent after the revolution and start of the war, Japan did not change its economic ambition in oil transactions with Iran, even after the revolution. Rather, they tried to maintain relations with Iran during the Iran–Iraq War.

The third cycle consists of the end of the Iran–Iraq War in 1988, to the rise of Iran's nuclear controversy in the 2000s. At the beginning of this period, continuous Japanese trade negotiations with Iran were realised, when Iranian foreign policy gradually shifted from revolutionary to pragmatic. However, the two countries faced constraints once again, due to the nuclear controversy and international economic sanctions imposed on Iran.

Overall, while the 90-year history of Iran–Japan relations faced several challenges, including WWII, the Iran–Iraq War and nuclear controversies, both countries always tried to seek sustainable political and economic relations. Thus, after such difficult periods, Iran–Japan relations found refreshment or even promotion, such as summit meetings and economic cooperation. Lessons learned from the three cycles may apply to future relations between Iran and Japan.

REFERENCES

ENGLISH

Abrahamian, Ervand. *Radical Islam: The Iranian Mojahedin.* New York: I. B. Tauris, 1989.

Amuzegar, Jahangir. *Iran's Economy Under the Islamic Republic.* New York: T. B. Tauris, 1993.

Keddi, Nikki. *Modern Iran—Roots and Results of Revolution.* New Haven: Yell University Press, 2006.

Kuroda, Kenji. "Pioneering Iranian Studies in Meiji Japan: Between Modern Academic and International Strategy." *Iranian Studies* 50, no. 2 (2017): 651–70.

Rasler, Karen. "Concessions, Repression, and Political Protest in the Iranian Revolution." *American Sociological Review* 61, no. 1 (1996): 132–52.

Takahashi, Kazuo. "The Iran-Japan Petrochemical Project: A Complex Issue." In *Japan in the Contemporary Middle East*, edited by Kaoru Sugihara and J.A. Allan, 83–93. New York: Routledge, 1993.

PERSIAN

Shokrzadeh, Hasan and Hossein Abadian. "Iran-Japan Trade Relationship in the Reza Shah Era." *Journal of Historical Researches* 9, no. 33 (2017): 58–71.

JAPANESE

Abdoly, Keivan. "Idemitsu Sekiyukyotei ni miru 1950 nendai no Nihon to Iran no Enerugī Gaikō" [Energy and Japan-Iran Relations in the 1950s: Reassessing the Idemitsu's Oil Deal with Iran]. *Middle East Review*, no. 5 (2018): 152–60.

"Daitoa Sensō" [The Greater East Asia War]. *Japan Centre for Asian Historical Records (JCAHR)* (November 11, 1941): picture no. 3.

"Gaikō Seisho" [The Diplomatic Bluebook]. *Japanese Ministry of Foreign Affairs.* 1967.

Hinata, Leo. (2016) "Kindai Nihon to Perusha" [Modern Japan and Persia: The Backgrounds of the Establishment of Diplomatic Relations]. *Gaikō Shiryō Kanhō* [Journal of the Diplomatic Archives] 29, (2016): 107–26.

Japan International Cooperation Agency (JICA), https://www.jica.go.jp/oda/project/IN-P1/index.html. Accessed April 4, 2019.

"Nihon to Perusha - Iran" [Japan and Persia-Iran], *Ministry of Foreign Affairs of Japan.* https://www.mofa.go.jp/mofaj/ms/da/page25_000040.html. Accessed April 4, 2019.

Okazaki, Shoko. "Meiji no Iran to Nihon –Yoshida Masaharu Shisetsudan (1880) ni tsuite" [The First Japanese Mission to Qajar Persia]. *Journal of Osaka University of Foreign Studies* 70, no. 3 (1985): 71–86.

Tanaka, Koichiro. "Daméji Contorōru ni Keichu subeki Nihon Gaikō" [Japanese Diplomacy Should Focus on Damage Control]. *Diplomacy Forum* 10, (2006): 18–20.

"Teikoku Bōeki Seisaku tai Iran Koku" [Imperial Trade Policy toward Iran]. *JCAHR* (September 4, 1932): picture no. 44.

———. *JCAHR* (July 27, 1938): picture no. 59.

———. *JCAHR* (June 12, 1939): picture no. 68.

———. *JCAHR* (May 28, 1939): picture no. 64.

Umeno, Naotoshi. "Iran-Japan Sekiyu Kagaku Purojekuto Tanjōkatei no Shiteki Bunseki" [The Historical Analysis of the Process of Starting the Iran-Japan Petrochemical Project]. *Japan Academy of International Business Studies* 1, no. 2 (2009): 133–45.

CHAPTER 5

The Relations Between Japan and Turkey: Three-Dimensional Diplomacy—Roles of the Imperial Family, the Government, and Citizens

Yuko Omagari

1 INTRODUCTION: TURKEY—THE IMAGE OF A PRO-JAPAN COUNTRY AND REALITY

The friendly relations between Japan and Turkey have recently resurfaced thanks to the fictional movie, based on real-life events, titled *Ertuğrul 1890 (Kainan 1890).*[1] The movie shows that ties between Japan and

[1] The *Ertuğrul* incident is recognized as the start of the Japan–Turkey relations. The Ottoman Empire sent the frigate *Ertuğrul* to Japan on a goodwill visit in 1890. It stayed in Japan and accomplished its mission. However, on setting sail from Yokohama on its return voyage to Turkey, the *Ertuğrul* encountered a typhoon which caused severe damage, (vapor explosion), it broke up at the Kashino Peninsula in Oshima (currently Kushimoto) in Wakayama.

Y. Omagari (✉)
The Japan-Turkey Society, Tokyo, Japan
e-mail: omagari.yuko@itochu.co.jp

© The Author(s), under exclusive license to Springer Nature Singapore Pte Ltd. 2023
S. Nakamura and S. Wright (eds.), *Japan and the Middle East*, Contemporary Gulf Studies, https://doi.org/10.1007/978-981-19-3459-9_5

Turkey don't rely solely on economic relations but on social and cultural friendships. The movie shows that ties between Japan and Turkey don't rely solely on economic relations but on social and cultural friendships. In fact, the multi-layered compounds that continue to shape the relationship between the two countries are lesser known and include cultural exchanges, academic connections, and collaboration on disaster prevention, among others. This work is motivated by this very gap of mutual understanding that continues to shape the actual relations between Japan and Turkey; it provides insights from a professional who has been working for the Japan-Turkey Society—a bilateral friendship association—for more than two decades.

This paper describes and discusses the roles of 'the three dimensions of diplomacy' on bilateral relations, including royal, governmental, and citizen-led. While there is a significant amount of research on the origins of the Japanese–Turkish relationship, there is far less relating to more recent decades. This paper adopts Nakamura's (2016)[2] approach to multi-dimensional diplomacy and seeks evidence among the essays, writings, lectures, and speeches of the diplomats from the *Diplomatic Blue Books* published by the Japanese Ministry of Foreign Affairs. The bilateral relationship between the two countries began in the late nineteenth century before diplomatic relations were established and developed during four subsequent phases: pre-World War II, post-World War II, the post-Cold War era, and the 2000s. By assessing the activities of the Japanese Institute of Anatolian Archaeology, which articulates the three aforementioned dimensions of diplomacy, this paper addresses how each dimension continues to shape the relationship between Japan and Turkey.

1.1   Sources for the Paper

Sources relating to the bilateral relations between Japan and Turkey are limited. The Japanese bureaucrat of the Ministry of Foreign Affairs,

It is said that some 532 passengers died (this number is provided by the Turkish Ministry of Foreign Affairs, and the Turkish Navy. The correct number is still unknown). Thanks to the efforts of people from the island, 69 crewmembers were saved, and a fundraising campaign spread across Japan. Related ceremonies and activities will be described in this chapter.

[2] Nakamura (2016) argues that the three-dimensional actors of the relations between the Middle Eastern countries and Japan are the royal families, the governments, and the citizens.

Mr. Hironao Matsutani, who served as the Consul General of Japan in Istanbul from 2006–2008, endeavored to collect materials and documents on diplomacy, economy, and culture and published them as papers and books (1999, 2005) and by historical era (1986, 2016). Ward and Rustow (1970) contribute a comparative analysis of the modernization process during Japan's Meiji Revolution and Turkey's Republic-founding period. Mr. Tatsuo Takeda, the former Consul General of Japan in Istanbul from 1985 to 1989, identifies both countries' relationships with Russia as a common feature (1987). Mr. Yoichi Yamaguchi, former Ambassador to Turkey (1990–1992), stresses that Japan should have its own understanding of and views toward Turkey (1991). Ms. Atsuko Toyama, the former ambassador to Turkey (1996–1999), notes in her essays (2001, 2013) that the exchanges between two countries vary remarkably, from economy and culture to disaster prevention.[3]

The Ottoman Navy frigate *Ertuğrul* incident in 1890 is recognized as the beginning of Japan–Turkey relations, and many studies discuss various aspects of its significance. Hatano (1999) points out that the tragic *Ertuğrul* incident resulted in closer ties between the two countries. Misawa (2005a, 2008) discusses the implications of the *Ertuğrul* tragedy for diplomacy in the Ottoman Empire and what the incident has meant for the Japanese in terms of historical disaster management. He also points out that, over time, the *Ertuğrul* incident has been misinterpreted in relation to the changing situation between Japan and Turkey. Misawa stresses the need to discuss whether Turkey really is a pro-Japan country and looks for evidence to support this belief. Nagaba (2005) and Takahashi (2008), on the other hand, explain that commercial and intelligence activities commenced prior to the establishment of diplomatic relations. The 70 years chronical book published by the Japan-Turkey Society records its activities since its foundation in 1926, including citizen exchanges that took place until 1995.[4] The newsletters of the society include many original materials, such as essays on bilateral relations written by members of the society, academics, diplomats, and businesspersons.[5]

---

[3] See lectures and essays by the former ambassadors to Turkey and to Japan.

[4] *Nihon Toruko Kyokai 70 Nenshi*, (a historical book of the Japan-Turkey Society) was mainly written by Mr. Shoichi Takahashi, who used to work as a specialist of Turkey at the Ministry of Foreign Affairs.

[5] *Nihon Toruko Kyokai Kaiho* (1–26. The first edition was issued in June 1971. It continued until March 1987 when it combined with the newsletter *Anatolia News*)

Research papers on bilateral relations have also been published in Turkey and other countries outside Japan. Firstly, Ward and Rustow (1970), Tuncok (1996), and Dündar (2016) studied the comparison of the modernization process of the two countries and the beginning of their bilateral relations.[6] Former Ambassador to Japan Mr. Umut Arık (1991), in his investigation of the hundred-year history of the two countries, and Apatay Çetinkaya (2008), retired admiral of the Turkish Navy, both note the significance of the *Ertuğrul* incident in forming bilateral ties and establishing the naval relations as a basis for the two countries to cooperate. Bahadır Pehlivantürk (2012) mentions that the bilateral relations are not based on pragmatism but on the feeling of romanticism, since the two countries have never suffered from serious diplomatic issues and have maintained positive relations from the beginning to the present day. In contrast, Ali Çolakoğlu (2017) discusses how the alliance between Japan and the USA may have a negative impact on Japan–Turkey relations.

Given the limited material on Japan–Turkey relations, I will discuss the countries' bilateral relations based on the primary sources in this paper. Some, who may have overlooked certain facts, predict that the two countries' relationship could be influenced by the relations with superpowers. However, in reality, the bilateral relations have been developing with roles of 'the three dimensions of diplomacy' (royal, governmental, and citizen-led) on politics, economy, and culture, steadily and with continuous efforts. Thus, proving that they recognize the significance of their bilateral relations' and place great value on their diplomatic policy.

1.2   Economic Relations: A Reflection on the Bilateral Relations

The scope of economic cooperation reflects the importance of the bilateral relations. The economic relationship between Japan and Turkey began after Turkey announced its open-door policy in 1981, which was strengthened by the then Prime Minister (later 8th President) Turgut Özal's visit to Japan in 1985. When Turkey's Justice and Development Party (AKP)

---

and *Anatolia News* (1–146. The first edition was published in January 1973). Prior to World War II, Nichi Do Kyokai published *Nichi Do Kyokai Kaiho* vol. 1 on December 12, 1926, and Misawa collected data from vols. 1–28 (CD-ROM Ver. 1, supervised by Nobuo Misawa, 2009, Toyo University Institute of Asian Culture).

[6] Dündar (2016) points out that there are many misunderstandings regarding the beginning of the bilateral relations.

became the leading political party in November 2002, its economic policies contributed to progress within the Turkish economy and highlighted it as one of the promising emerging countries. Japan started to recognize Turkey as an emerging country, with the number of Japanese enterprises in Turkey increasing to 200 in 2015, with Japan listed among the top ten countries investing in Turkey in 2016. However, the share of Japan's investment and trade toward Turkey is just 1–2% of the Japanese economy (Araki 2014: 7), and only a few Turkish companies are currently operating in Japan. As Turkey started to increase its economic relations with China and South Korea within the East-Asian geopolitical area in 2002, its economic relations with Japan began to decline (Akkemik 2016, 2017).

When evaluating the relationship between the two countries, the economic scale is not enough to explain the real bilateral relations. The process of developing economic relations doesn't always reflect the domestic economic conditions in Japan and Turkey. The interaction between political, economic, and cultural factors appears to strengthen the bilateral relationship in every aspect. In other words, the various exchanges between the governments, businesses, and citizens deepen relations between Japan and Turkey. Furthermore, the Imperial Family played a unique yet important role in establishing bilateral relations. The second section of this paper will investigate the timeline before and after World War II and the Cold War period. The third section will discuss how the strategic partnership and the exchange between civil society have been strengthened and developed. The fourth section will consider cultural, civilian, and 'the royal diplomacy,' leading to the conclusion, which includes implications for the future relations of the two countries.

2   The History—The Dawn of the Bilateral Relations

2.1   The Dawn: The First Contact with the Ottoman Empire

The *Ertuğrul* tragedy is widely believed to have initiated Japan–Turkey relations. However, the Japanese people acknowledged the strategic importance of Turkey's geographical locations in the center of the Middle East, Europe, and Central Asia, even before this tragic accident. The first contact between Japan and Turkey was during the Iwakura mission to Europe in 1873 (Shiraiwa 1999: 12; Matsutani and Matsutani 2014: 7). At that time, the Japanese government was forced to sign an unfair treaty with European countries. The purpose of the Iwakura mission was to conclude a treaty of friendship (amity) with the Ottoman Empire, despite it being on the decline.

The first action for building relations was the visit of T.I.H. Prince and Princess Akihito of Komatsu to Turkey in 1887 (Before this visit, the Japanese frigate *Seiki* visited Istanbul in 1878). As Japan changed its policy from national isolation to newly opening up the country to the world at that time, the high status of the Imperial Families was readily accepted during their first contact with the European countries. In fact, the *Ertuğrul* was dispatched to Japan as a return salute for Prince Komatsu's visit from the then Ottoman Emperor, Abdülhamid II.[7]

Japan's victory over Russia in the Japan–Russia War made a significant impact on Turkey for several decades, and it encouraged Turkey to develop close relations with Japan following Japan's victory in the conflict. Admirals Togo and Nogi gained popularity in Turkey, and the leather goods store Togo can still be found today (Ikei 2003: 8–9). Recognizing Turkey was of strategic importance, Japan sent military attachés to Turkey to analyze European politics. From 1875, both governments tried to establish a diplomatic relationship but failed at the time despite major efforts by both sides. The Ottoman Empire was replaced by the Republic of Turkey after WWI; the official treaty was signed in 1924. Just one year later, after the establishment of the Republic of Turkey, both embassies were opened, and in the following year, 1925, 'Nichi-Do Boeki Kyokai' (the Japan-Turkey Trade Association) was established in Japan. The Japanese products store 'Nihon Shohinkan' was opened in Turkey, and several joint ventures commenced their operations, leading to the signing of the Japan-Turkey Trade Agreement in 1937.

To meet the need for an institution to promote bilateral relations (Ikei 1999: 152), the former body of the Japan-Turkey Society (Nichi-do Kyokai, currently Nihon Toruko Kyokai) was established in 1926 by Sadatsuchi Uchida, the first Japanese Ambassador to Turkey (Uchida

---

[7] Regarding the details of the *Ertuğrul* tragedy, refer to Shiraiwa (1999), Hatano (1999), and Misawa (2005a, 2005b, 2005c). The Emperor Meiji ordered an escort of 69 Turkish crewmembers by two Japanese naval ships *Hiei* and *Kongo*. The voyage served as training for Japanese naval members. However, its main purpose was as a demonstration to enhance national prestige (Misawa 2005a: 90) Japanese Disposal Acts of Financial Donations for the Ottoman Empire (1890–1892): Terminus of the Disaster of the Ottoman Battleship *Ertuğrul* for the Japanese society (The Bulletin of the Faculty of Sociology, Toyo University No. 41–1, 2003: pp. 57–91).

served as a minister and was later appointed as an ambassador, however, the Turkish Government recognized Uchida as a having the rank of minister). The main activities of the society were publishing newsletters and Japanese-Turkish and Turkish-Japanese dictionaries, organizing exhibitions on Turkey, and holding receptions to promote further understanding of the country. In 1929, H.I.H. Prince Nobuhito of Takamatsu was inducted as a patron of the society, bringing three-dimensional diplomacy—by the royalty, the government, and the citizens—together.

2.2 The Reopening of Diplomatic Relations After WWII

After Turkey declared war against Japan in 1945 during WWII, Japan and Turkey broke off their diplomatic relations. However, they did not engage in conflict with each other and the two countries reinstated their diplomatic relations after Japan restored sovereignty in 1953. Before that, during the Korean War, many Turkish soldiers, who participated in the war as part of the United Nations Command, were transported to the logistics support point in Japan to rest and receive medical treatment. The Turkish soldiers who stayed in Japan formed a good impression of the country, which was passed down to their families after they returned to their homeland (Naito 1971: 8–9).

As the normalization process continued, the Turkish Embassy in Tokyo reopened in 1952, and the Japanese Embassy reopened in Ankara in 1953. Both governments started to consult on treaties and agreements; the Commerce and Navigation Treaty was reactivated in 1953, the Agreement on Payment of Trade in 1955, and the Visa Exemption Agreement in 1958. These treaties promoted the movement and exchange of people and goods. Compared with those between other countries, restoring diplomatic relations with Turkey was a swift process (Imai 2017: 273). In particular, the Visa Exemption Agreement, which was realized early, with Turkey being the 14th country to sign the agreement with Japan. At that time, Japanese enterprises started to make inroads into Turkish markets. However, Japan's trade deficit led Japanese trading companies to withdraw from Turkey in the late 1950s (Kawabe 2016: 95–96).[8]

---

[8] Japanese trading company Mitsubishi Corporation established its liaison office in Turkey in 1954, followed by Mitsui & Co. Ltd., in 1955. Kawabe (2015) and Kawabe (2016) explain the details of the activities of Japanese companies, including investments, through seminars on Turkish economy.

The Japanese government's priority, post-WWII, was to return and re-position itself within the international community. Turkey, as a non-permanent member of the UN Security Council, acted as a joint proposal country in support of Japan's resolution to become a member of the UN in 1954. Japan was accepted as a member of the United Nations in 1956.

The bilateral visits were initiated by the Turkish side, with a visit by Turkish members of parliament taking place in 1954. The then Prime Minister Mr. Adnan Menderes' visit in 1958[9] prompted bilateral relations as well as economic and technical cooperation.[10] On his departure from Japan, Menderes gave an impressive speech, stating that deepening the Japan–Turkey relations would contribute to world peace (Matsutani 1986: 162). The Prime Minister's visit provided an opportunity to hold an exhibition on Turkey's ancient civilization. As a result of such prominent events, the Japanese people started to take an interest in Turkey.

After WWII, the Imperial Family made an official visit to Turkey, with T.I.H. Prince and Princess Takahito of Mikasa visiting in 1963, thus showing that the members of the Imperial Families have played an important role in maintaining bilateral relations.[11]

Reopening the diplomatic relationship between Japan and Turkey was demonstrated to the international community—it was not of the scale of the past but fit for the new era. It reflected the will of the Turkish side, the role of the royal families, and the high expectations from the business world.

---

[9] Prime Minister Mr. Menderes visited Japan accompanied by the then Foreign Minister Zorlu and Vice Minister of Foreign Affairs Esembel (Mr. Esembel later became the Turkish Ambassador to Japan and Minister of Foreign Affairs. His daughter, Prof. Dr. Selçuk Esembel, became a prominent academic in Japan).

[10] Technical cooperation between Japan and Turkey started in 1959 after the Turkish Fishery Survey group visited Japan.

[11] H.I.H. Prince Takahito of Mikasa wrote the essays "Toruko wo Tazunete" in Sankei Shimbun's evening paper on May 4, 25, and 27, 1963.

2.3   1970s–1980s: Realization of the Exchanges in Politics, Economy, and Culture

After the 1970s, Japanese diplomatic policy toward Turkey could be characterized by a combination of high-level officials' visits within the business circle. It should be noted that after the Japanese 'Keidanren' (Japan Federation of Economic Organizations) dispatched a delegation to Turkey, the Japan-Turkey Society was reactivated in 1971, prompting exchanges between both countries.

Japan recognized there was much business potential for Japan in Turkey because Turkey required higher-level industry and infrastructure projects for its development. The Japanese government provided ODA (Official Development Aid) for some infrastructure projects, such as the construction of dams and bridges. The Japanese government continued to do its best to increase economic cooperation with Turkey, though it failed in the tender for the first Bosphorus Bridge construction project, which was built by British firms. At the same time, the Japanese were interested in investing in the industrial field. However, the Turkish government had a strict rule for applying foreign capital, and the Turkish economy collapsed in the late 1970s, so it was not achieved at that time (Kawabe 2016: 96). The delay in establishing stronger economic ties irritated the then Japanese ambassador to Turkey, Mr. Mitsuo Tanaka, who, in an essay, stated, 'Our side should see the situation of the international community, and judge with not a prejudicial view but a fresh point of view' (Tanaka 1972: 29). This suggests that the bilateral relations should be seen as a medium–long-term strategy.

As the Turkish economy experienced a fiscal crisis in the late 1970s, Japan supported Turkey with 340 million dollars following other OECD member countries, the USA, West Germany, and France. It demonstrated Japan's view toward Turkey, as Mr. Hironao Matsutani stated, 'The traditionally friendly relations with Turkey and Turkey's strategical importance in the Middle East led to Japan's decision for supporting Turkey'[12] (Matsutani and Matsutani 2014: 182). Meaning that Japan recognized Turkey's importance as a stable country among the Middle Eastern countries (Matsutani and Matsutani 2014: 182). Japan had acknowledged

---

[12] Quoted by *Anatolia News* Special Issue No. 21 (July 18, 1979), which was extracted by the articles of Information and Culture Section of the Turkish Ministry of Foreign Affairs in on May 30, 1979.

Turkey as a key country since the Iwakura mission to Europe, and refreshed its perception in 1980s. In diplomacy, Japan took a neutral position on the Cyprus issue at the UN's general assembly. Turkey appreciated Japan's loyalty to the country (Arık 1991: 226; Matsutani and Matsutani 2014: 175).

The 1980s was an important period, with frequent bilateral visits and many investment projects being realized. The first high-level visit by the Japanese side was from the then foreign minister, Shintaro Abe, in 1983. Turgut Özal, known to be a pro-Japan prime minister, paid his first visit to Japan after he took office in 1983. Özal's vision was that Japan would become the model for Turkey, introducing the slogans, 'Let's learn from the Japanese' and 'Make Turkey the Japan of the Middle East.' In response, Japan strengthened relations with Turkey through cultural activities, citizen exchange opportunities, and business transactions (Sugihara 1987: 3–5). In 1985, the *Turkish Airlines*' rescue flights for Japanese residents in Tehran during the Iran-Iraq War marked an important moment between the two countries. Above all, royal diplomacy played a significant role in the diplomatic relations between Japan and Turkey. T.I.H. Prince and Princess Takahito of Mikasa made a second visit to Turkey in 1986.[13] In the post-Ottoman era, they became the symbol of Japan's diplomacy toward Turkey in the post-Cold War period. Turkey's various political approaches, the war, and the Imperial Family's visit to Turkey encouraged bilateral relations to deepen in the 1980s.

In the 1980s, bilateral economic relations were also strengthening. The Japan-Turkey Economic Committee was established in Keidanren, fueling industrial investments from Japan to Turkey. The first joint venture between Japan and Turkey after WWII was established by Japanese automobile manufacturer Isuzu, supported by the ITOCHU Corporation 'Anadolu Isuzu' with Turkish Conglomarate group Anadolu in 1985, with Toyota and Honda following. The automobile industry was Turkey's main industry during that time. Most notably 'sogo-shosha' companies (Japanese trading and investment companies) were particularly active in Turkey, with food, electrical, banking, insurance, tourism, and construction sectors also starting to invest in the country. High-quality Japanese products were introduced in Turkey, gradually attracting Turkish people to the Japanese market. The bid for the second Bosphorus Bridge, a major

---

[13] H.I.H. Prince Takahito of Mikasa wrote the essays "Toruko Saihouki" in Asahi Shimbun paper on July 15, 16, 17, 18, 21, 22, and 23, 1986.

project connecting two continents, was obtained by Japanese, Turkish, and Italian companies in 1985, with the project completed in July 1988. Since the Japanese and Turkish are hardworking people, in general, the bridge was completed six months earlier than planned. The huge opening ceremony[14] and the issue of special postage stamps in Turkey signified the country's will to build stronger ties with Japan in various fields (Nishiwaki 1999: 7). Energized by the agreement between Japan and Turkey for Air Services in 1989, Japanese investments in Turkey steadily increased. While Japan's economic relations with other Middle Eastern countries focused mainly on the energy trade, its relations with Turkey remained an exception, with an emphasis on industrial and infrastructure investments.

3 THE POST-COLD WAR PERIOD: THE STRATEGIC PARTNERSHIP AND THE STRENGTHENING OF CITIZEN EXCHANGES

3.1 The End of the Cold War: The Strengthening of Bilateral Relations with Turkey

In the 1990s, Turkey was affected by various global crises, including the ending of the Cold War, the Gulf War, etc. At the same time, Turkey found its own strategical importance, which covered European and Central Asian countries. The Japanese government also acknowledged attention to Turkey as an important, stable regional power and tried to promote more active relations with the country (Gaikoseisho 1991). The Japanese business community's attention was drawn to Turkey due to its unique relationship with the Turkic countries of Central Asia after the dissolution of the Soviet Union[15] and its free tax agreement with the EU

---

[14] Then Prime Minister Mr. Özal mentioned that the second Bosphorus Bridge (Fatih Sultan Mehmet Köprüsü) is the monument of Japanese and Turkish cooperation. 'It is a symbolic ODA project of Japanese corporation to Turkey.' IHI Corporation, Mitsubishi Heavy Industries, Ltd., Nihon Kokan (NKK) Corporation, and ITOCHU Corporation were involved in the project. This bridge is a sister bridge of the Great Seto Bridge (Seto Ohashi). (Nihon Toruko Kyokai, *Anatolia News*, No. 56, p. 26, 1988).

[15] About 100 Japanese and Turkish businesspersons joined the delegation for CIS countries in 1993 organized by Keidanren and DEİK. It is recognized as a very impressive visit among both sides. Some accounts of exchanges between Turkish and Japanese businesspersons could be found in the famous Turkish businessman the late Şarık Tara's autobiographical reminiscences *Şarık Tara Anlatıyor* (Tüzün 2016).

in 1996. These factors were incentives for Japanese companies, driving them to increase business with Turkey.[16]

At the end of the Cold War, relations between Japan and Turkey progressed and became more stable through contracts such as the Agreement between Japan and Turkey on Air Services on July 20, 1989; the Agreement Concerning the Reciprocal Promotion and Protection of Investment on March 12, 1993; and the Convention between Japan and Turkey for the Avoidance of Double Taxation and the Prevention of Fiscal Evasion with Respect to Income Taxes on December 28, 1994. These led to the expansion of bilateral economic relations, business travel, and tourism visits between Japan and Turkey.

Certainly, diplomatic relations supported and strengthened the economic relations mentioned above. High-level visits continued in the 1990s, starting with the first visit to Turkey by the Japanese Prime Minister, Mr. Toshiki Kaifu, in 1990.[17] From Turkey, Prime Minister Süleyman Demirel visited Japan in 1992 followed by Tansu Çiller in 1995. The 9th president, Mr. Süleyman Demirel continued the late Mr. Turgut Özal's pro-Japan policy. As Turkey faced serious domestic political instability in the late 1990s, high-level political visits became less frequent. However, it didn't affect bilateral relations.

The exchanges in diplomacy and economy during the 1980s had strengthened cultural exchanges by the 1990s. In Japan, the activated exchanges in diplomacy and economy in the 1980s strengthened cultural exchanges. In Japan, the Department of Turcology established two universities, and the number of Turkish students studying in Japan with scholarships from the Japanese Ministry of Education and Science increased (see details in the next section). Turkey's state-owned airline, *Turkish Airlines*, resumed its scheduled flights in 1989, attracting Japanese tourists to Turkey.

---

[16] Japanese investments in Turkey in various sectors such as the manufacturing industry, tourism, insurance, banking, and trade. The manufacturing industry companies such as Toyota, YKK, Yazaki, and Honda started to produce their products in Turkey, and insurance companies followed. As years passed by, many Japanese companies invested in Turkey with full-scale constructions, such as the electric power plants by BOT, hotel developments, and banking sectors.

[17] The second visit to Turkey by the Japanese foreign minister was made by Taro Nakayama in 1990. The friendship association of the Japan-Turkey parliament members was re-established in 1994.

The *Ertuğrul* incident marked its 100th anniversary in 1990, and cere-monies and commemorative cultural events were held in both Japan and Turkey. T.I.H. Prince and Princess Tomohito of Mikasa visited Turkey for the first time to attend the ceremony in Mersin. After the cere-mony, the late H.I.H. Prince Tomohito of Mikasa visited the inside of the memorial tower and found bottles containing soil and water from Oshima (Kushimoto). He later commented that the Japanese and Turkish shared common values.[18] In the same year, the Turkish naval frigate *TCG Turgutreis* paid its first friendly visit to Japan, and the top naval commander, Karabulut, attended the ceremony.

Relations between Japan and Turkey stabilized in the 1980s, and on this basis, Japan again recognized the strategic importance of Turkey into the 1990s. The bilateral relations were reinforced through exchanges in diplomacy, economy, and culture.

3.2   Turkey Begins Cooperating with Japan to Provide Foreign Aid: TIKA and JICA

The development and stability of Turkey is a key factor affecting the stability of the countries surrounding Turkey. The stability of the Middle East is particularly important for Japan since Japan has depended primarily on energy resources from Middle Eastern countries. From this perspec-tive, Turkey is regarded as a stabilizer in the Middle East. With this in mind, the Japanese government proposed a two-phase strategy. The first phase was to support the development of Turkey, which would have a positive knock-on effect for Japan and the countries around Turkey.

The first Japanese governmental support to Turkey was a training program for Turkish trainees in Japan. There are 29 cases, 687.2 billion yen of loan assistance, 4.1 billion yen by exchange of notes from bilateral government loans up to the 2015 fiscal year, and, technological coopera-tion of JICA was 47.5 billion yen in 2015. A total of 1560 experts offered official development assistance and 5222 Turkish participants joined the training programs.[19]

---

[18] 'Tomohito Shinnou Denka Special Interview' in *Anatolia News*, No. 106 (2002), pp. 4–10.

[19] Activities and projects by JICA refer to 'ODA' on Turkey the Japanese Ministry of Foreign Affairs website, the essays contributed by the JICA in the Turkey Office. See 4th

After the establishment of TİKA (Türk İşbirliği ve Koordinasyon Ajansı Başkanlığı: The Turkish Cooperation and Coordination Agency) in Turkey in 1991, JICA and TİKA accelerated assistance for third countries and now TİKA is a very important partner for JICA (Imai 2017: 281). Turkey used to be an aid recipient. However, after the establishment of TİKA, Turkey became Japan's multi-lateral corporate partner.

With the cooperation of TİKA, JICA started to provide training programs in Turkey for third countries in 1997. Twenty programs and 76 courses with 1083 participants from 34 countries had been delivered by January 2018. Courses in Turkey included aquaculture technology, energy efficiency, disaster management (in general), disaster management (for factories), investigation of mineral resources, and a security training program for Afghan police being one example of the security training carried out.

Among the various projects in Turkey was support for the improvement of municipal plumbing and the disposal of waste in various cities, in support of 3.6 million Syrian refugees residing in Turkey. Without Turkey's cooperation, Japan's projects mentioned above wouldn't have been implemented.[20]

3.3   Cooperation on Disaster Prevention Management: Overcoming the Earthquakes

JICA has provided support to Turkey by improving disaster prevention management. As Turkey is an earthquake-prone country, like Japan, various projects relating to disaster prevention management were introduced, such as the establishment of prediction systems, the strengthening of main infrastructures, and disaster prevention education for schoolteachers.[21]

Turkey Seminar (lecturer Mr. Takahiro Yasui, JICA Turkey Representative) organized by the Japan-Turkey Society.

[20] The Japanese NGO *AAR Japan* has also been providing humanitarian assistance to *Syrian refugees* in Turkey.

[21] The first cooperation with Turkey on seismology dates back to 1952 (or 1953), when UNESCO's dispatched expert, Takahiro Hagiwara, worked at Istanbul Technical University for two years. The bilateral relations were strengthened by the establishment of the Disaster and Emergency Management Authority (T.C. Başbakanlık Afet ve Acil Durum Yönetimi Başkanlığı: AFAD) in Turkey in 2009. Tokyo Bunkyo City and Istanbul Beyoğlu Municipality cooperated for the disaster management programs with

The Marmara earthquake, which occurred in August 1999 in the northwest region of Turkey, caused tremendous damage, including 20,000 casualties. Soon after the earthquake, the then Japanese Foreign Minister, Mr. Masahiko Komura, visited Turkey, and emergency support was rapidly provided by Japan. This strengthened bilateral cooperation for disaster management, which became one of the defining factors in the two countries' bilateral relations.

A relatively lesser known event is the Japan Maritime Self-Defense Force's (JMSDF) 'Blue Phoenix Operation'. Japanese naval ships carried prefabrication houses, which had been initially used by the people affected by the Hanshin Awaji Earthquake in 1995—an example of the cooperation between Japan and Turkey's continuous bilateral defense cooperation for security. In addition, it was an important milestone for JMSDF, as it successfully completed its first humanitarian disaster support mission abroad. The prefabrication houses were settled in 'Türk-Japon Köy' (Turkish–Japanese Village) and many Turkish victims of the earthquake lived there for several years. At that time, some Japanese NGOs traveled to Turkey to provide emergent humanitarian support, and JICA senior volunteers worked in women's self-support and disaster prevention education. These are some examples of the Turkish public's reliance on Japan. Kobe's city municipal staff, who were sent to Turkey as an emergency rescue team, later founded the Friendship Association with Turkey in Kobe in 2007 and have been continuing activities, such as organizing football matches with the Turkish junior football team and supporting disaster prevention education.[22]

In 2011, Great East Japan Earthquake hit east Japan. At that time, a Turkish rescue team carried out the rescue activities in Shichiga-hama of Miyagi prefecture, staying longer than any other rescue team bar the US. In addition, many Turkish residents in Japan, including the Turkish ambassador to Japan, voluntarily traveled to the northeast region to deliver food and necessities to the local people. Turkish citizens also

support and collaboration from JICA and AFAD. This has also enhanced the citizen's exchanges.

[22] Japanese communities relating to Turkey organized many supporting activities for the disasters. Some Japanese friendship associations organized charity events in Japan. A Japanese businessman, whose life was saved by the *Turkish Airlines* special flight from Tehran to Istanbul in 1985, delivered relief supplies to sufferers, and many groups and individuals engaged in supporting activities.

showed their heartfelt support for the victims. For instance, Turkish children sent messages, letters, and pictures extending their sympathy for the affected Japanese children. This kind of emotional support has not been forgotten. In the same year, eastern Turkey was hit with a big earthquake and one of the Japanese NGO volunteers was killed by a second quake. Turkey showed great sympathy toward him, and his body was repatriated to Japan with great respect[23] (Naito 2014: 334).

The bilateral relations have been strengthened by cooperation during difficult times such as the *Ertuğrul* tragedy, wars, and earthquakes. One may say that the common values shared by both countries, and the support given to each other, contributed to the strengthening of relations.

3.4   The Twenty-First Century: The Era of the Strategical Partnership

Bilateral relations became even more productive in the 2000s through different events. Japan's attention toward Turkey seemed to increase when the Japanese and Turkish national football teams met at the Football Association World Cup in 2002. This was followed by the 'Year of Turkey in Japan', which launched in January 2003 and continued until May 2004. Around one hundred sixty events relating to Turkey were organized across Japan. Among these events, the exhibition 'The Three Civilizations of Turkey- Hittites, Byzantine and the Ottoman Empire' attracted several hundred thousand Japanese. The Year of Turkey was planned by the Turkish government and was supported by the Japanese government, with organizations, municipalities, enterprises, and friendly associations supporting these events.[24] The then Prime Minister Recep Tayyip Erdoğan paid an official working visit to Japan in 2004 with 300 members of the Turkish delegation, including eight ministers, members of parliament, and business persons, with other high-level visits following. Japanese companies continued to invest in Turkey with remarkable success. For example, Toyota was marked as the best exporting company

---

[23] The *AAR Japan*'s member was killed by the earthquake. The Turkish government held a remembrance ceremony for him, which was the equivalent of a state funeral. Many parks and institutions in Turkey are named after him.

[24] The Japanese Cabinet Office implemented international youth exchange program in Turkey.

in Turkey in the early 2000s, and the Marmaray project by the Taisei Corporation and Turkish companies began in 2003.

In 2006, the then Japanese Prime Minister, Junichiro Koizumi, visited Turkey for the first time in 16 years. As a guest of the state, President Abdullah Gül paid the first bilateral visit as the Turkish President in 2008. The honorary consulate of the Republic of Turkey in Fukuoka and Osaka opened in 2007, and both honorary consul generals made great efforts to stimulate bilateral relations, toward the economy in particular. To celebrate the 120th year of friendly relations that started with the *Ertuğrul* tragedy, the commemorative 'Japan Year 2010 in Turkey' was organized with the slogan 'Japan and Turkey can be closer'. It was also the 35th year since the rescue of Japanese people by a *Turkish Airlines* plane during the Iran-Iraq War in 1985. One hundred and eighty-six events, varying from traditional Japanese culture to more modern activities such as animation, were organized throughout the year, contributing to a greater understanding about Japan for the Turkish people.[25]

The then Prime Minister Shinzo Abe's visit to Turkey in 2013 accelerated the high-level visits. During Abe's visit in May 2013, the 'Joint Declaration of the Establishment of Strategic Partnership between Japan and the Republic of Turkey' was signed to further expand cooperation between the two countries in regional and international politics, economy, culture and science, and defense, at official and citizen levels.[26] Prime Minister Abe recognized Turkey as an important country. This was in contrast to the ministers of other nations who may have gained a different

---

[25] *Anatolia News* of the Japan-Turkey Society (No. 127–129). After Japan Year 2010 in Turkey conducted a survey: 'Opinion Poll: Turkish Image of Japan' in Turkey. The results reported that about 80% of Turkish thought that Japan–Turkey relations were 'friendly relations' or 'almost friendly relations.' (https://www.mofa.go.jp/mofaj/press/release/24/5/052201.html, accessed February 5, 2017; https://www.mofa.go.jp/mofaj/area/turkey/2010/index.html, accessed September 22, 2017).

[26] After 2013, bilateral agreements followed: the agreement between the government of Japan and the government of the Republic of Turkey for Co-operation in the Use of Nuclear Energy for Peaceful Purposes (signed in 2013, effectuated in June 29, 2014), the agreement between the government of Japan and the government to the Republic of Turkey for Co-operation for Development of Nuclear Power Industry in the Republic of Turkey (signed in 2013, effectuated in July 31, 2015), and the agreement on the Establishment of the Turkish-Japanese Science and Technology University (signed in 2016, effectuated November 11, 2016).

understanding of Turkey. In the same year, Abe carried out a second visit to Turkey to attend the opening ceremony of Marmaray, which is a joint Japan–Turkey project with ODA. Since then, they have continued with bilateral visits and regular meetings—six visits in addition to the continuous exchange of messages and more than ten meetings on occasions of the international congress such as the UN and G20. In May 2020, Abe attended, by video link, the opening ceremony of a hospital built by Japanese and Turkish companies despite it being a challenging time for not only Japan and Turkey but the world due to the Covid-19 pandemic, thus symbolizing the close relationship between the two leaders.

High-level visits demonstrate the best diplomatic relations and are the most efficient way of accelerating bilateral relations (Nitch 2007). For example, under Prime Minister Abe's leadership, the Japanese established the Council for Promoting Exchanges in Economy and Culture with Government and Citizen in 2014.[27] This council contributed to adjusting the government and private sectors in Japan, and by organizing various projects in Turkey and training programs for young people, using facilities relating to Japan in Turkey. These strengthened and deepened the bilateral relations. The Japan–Turkey relationship is a bilateral one but it also enhance Japan's multilateral relations with European and Central Asian countries.

---

[27] The committee was organized with eight ministries (Ministry of Foreign Affairs; Financial Services Agency; Ministry of Internal Affairs and Communications; Ministry of Education and Science; Health, Labour and Welfare; Ministry of Agriculture Forestry and Fisheries; Ministry of Economy, Trade and Industry; and Ministry of Land, Infrastructure, Transport and Tourism) and 38 private entities to promote bilateral understanding through organizing symposiums and seminars, student exchanges for human resource development by public–private partnership, strengthening local governmental exchanges by Japanese gardens or sister cities, and effectively using facilities such as the Turkish Japanese Foundation (TJV). The purpose of the committee was to strengthen bilateral relations with public–private partnerships since Turkey was the host country of the G20 in 2015 and Expo 2016 'Flowers and Children', and many more events were expected to be held. As with exchanges of local governments, the Baltalimanı Japanese Garden in Istanbul was renewed with technical cooperation of its sister city, Shimonoseki, and Japanese companies. During PM Abe's visit to Turkey for the G20 in 2015, the renewal ceremony of the garden was held. For details, see http://www.mofa.go.jp/mofaj/press/release/press4_001574.html.

4 CULTURAL AND ACADEMIC EXCHANGE: 'DIPLOMACY' BY THE IMPERIAL FAMILIES, GOVERNMENTS, AND CITIZENS

4.1 Ceremonies of Ertuğrul: Effects on the Bilateral Relations

Soon after the *Ertuğrul* frigate tragedy, many Japanese people showed great compassion for the casualties, which led to activities of support such as raising donations for the bereaved families. However, over time, the tragedy gradually became recognized as merely a local incident, and it started to be forgotten. Those who had ties with Turkey continued to hold ceremonies in remembrance of the *Ertuğrul* to raise awareness of the incident. Each time, the ceremony was held with a different style of program, attendees, and scale, but regardless of style, each ceremony created a ripple effect on Japan–Turkey relations.[28]

The first phase of changing the style of the ceremony appeared during the first half of the twentieth century. The *Ertuğrul* frigate disaster had been remembered for its rescue activities and disaster prevention measures. Then, associations such as the Japan-Turkey Society and the Japan-Turkey Trade Association started to regard the incident as the origin of the Japan–Turkey friendship. A massive-scale memorial ceremony was held in 1928, co-organized by the Japan-Turkey Trade Association and Oshima village. Emperor Showa (Hirohito)'s memorial visit to Oshima on June 3, 1929, raised the profile of the incident further.[29] The Emperor's visit also meant the formality of relations between the two countries increased. Turkey started to recognize the importance of the tragedy after the visit by the Showa Emperor, and Ambassador Gelede proposed to rebuild the cemetery and monuments of the *Ertuğrul* tragedy in Oshima. The current monument was built in June 1937, and its opening ceremony was held by the Near East Trade Association, the Japan-Turkey Trade Association, and the Japan-Turkey Society, with Oshima village leading the ceremony. This made the ceremony unique, as it brought clergies of Buddhism, Shinto, and Islam together

---

[28] Regarding the details of the memorial ceremonies of the *Ertuğrul* tragedy, see Misawa (2005c: 125–139), Matsutani and Matsutani (2014: 23–39), and Apatay (2008: 253–280).

[29] The large-scale ceremonies, organized every 5 years, were often scheduled on June 3, the day that Emperor Showa   had visited Oshima.

for the prayer, which was captured in a photograph. The following year, 1938, the Turkish Embassy in Tokyo published the book *Türk -Nippon Dostluğunun Sonsuz Hatıraları, Ertuğrul* both in Japanese and Turkish. The Commander of the Turkish Naval Force, Admiral Celal Eycioğlu, visited Kushimoto in 1971 and ordered a same-shaped monument be built in Mersin.[30] Then, Kushimoto and Mersin agreed to be sister cities in 1975, signing the agreement in 1994. The Memorial Museum of Turkey was opened at the *Ertuğrul*'s 85th memorial ceremony in 1974, which was redesigned and reopened in 2015 to introduce the tragedy and the bilateral relations with exhibitions of documents and relics. As such, memories and ceremonies in remembrance of *Ertuğrul* promoted exchanges between local governments and citizens.

At the 110th ceremony, held in 2000 in Oshima, H.I.H. Prince Tomohito of Mikasa made the first Imperial Family's attendance, and the ceremony changed its title from 'The Memorial Ceremony' to 'The Celebration of the Bilateral Friendship.' In fact, the *Ertuğrul* tragedy became a symbol of the friendship formed between Japan and Turkey. H.E. Mr. Abdullah Gül, the 11th President of Turkey, visited Oshima for the first time as a Turkish president in 2008, and Turkish ministers started to visit Oshima during their visits to Japan.

In 2010, H.I.H. Prince Tomohito of Mikasa, the then patron of the Japan-Turkey Society, attended the 120th ceremony in Kushimoto with his eldest daughter, H.I.H. Princess Akiko of Mikasa. The 'Japan Year 2010 in Turkey' had been held in Turkey, and the training ships of the Japan Maritime Self-Defense Force paid a goodwill visit to Mersin to celebrate the commemorative year. In 2015, on the occasion's 125th year, the Turkish naval ship *TCG Gediz* paid a goodwill visit to Japan. H.I.H. Princess Akiko of Mikasa, the patron of the Japan-Turkey Society, attended the ceremony with the then speaker of the Turkish Parliament Mr. Cemil Çiçek. Several cultural events, such as concerts, exhibitions, and symposiums were held both in Japan and Turkey, and the film *Ertuğrul 1890 (Kainan 1890)*, a Japanese–Turkish co-production, was released in both countries, demonstrating the maturation of their bilateral relations.

As time passed, the ceremony of the *Ertuğrul* incident changed its format. Before WWII, trading organizations and friendship associations

---

[30] The monument also commemorates the cargo ship *Refah* which was sank by a submarine attack during World War II, around the coast of Mersin.

held ceremonies on a large scale. The visit by Emperor Showa emphasized the incident's significance. Interestingly, books published in both countries showed that the religious authorities of Buddhism and Shinto in Japan and Islam in Turkey attended the ceremonies several times. After WWII, bilateral relations were promoted through sports, local governments, sister cities, businesses, the film industry, and naval forces. Since 2000, the ceremony of *Ertuğrul* has been held every five years and has started to have a dual meaning: it became a memorial ceremony and a celebration of the friendly relations between Japan and Tukey, making the scale of the events larger and richer.[31]

4.2   Three-Dimensional Diplomacy Between Japan and Turkey: The Japanese Institute of Anatolian Archaeology of the Middle Eastern Culture Center and Imperial 'Diplomacy'

Looking back at the history of bilateral relations, the members of the Imperial Family played a significant role. Before WWI, the first high-level visitor from Japan to Turkey after the Iwakura mission to Europe was H.I.H. Prince Akihito of Komatsu, and after WWII, the first VIP visit to Turkey was also made by the Imperial Family. In the 1960s, when bilateral relations became more substantial, the Mikasa family played an important role in establishing the two countries' friendship. Activities by the friendship associations, the Institute of Middle East Studies in Japan and their cultural endeavors, and the Imperial Families all supported the bilateral relations. The Japan-Turkey Society being one example. H.I.H. Prince Nobuhito of Takamatsu was its patron before WWII, and H.I.H. Prince Takahito of Mikasa was its honorary patron from 1991 until 2017. After the 1990s, the Imperial Family members' visits to Turkey became more frequent than before.[32]

---

[31] The ceremony for the *Ertuğrul* incident provided an opportunity to open exchanges between Japanese and Turkish navies. The Japanese Maritime Self Defense Force dispatches the Oversea Training Cruise Force to Turkey every several years. In addition, MSDFF has stationed a defense attaché since 1960. The Turkish Navy organized international symposiums, on only Turkey and Japan, in Istanbul in 2010 and 2015. These were quite exceptional since the Turkish Navy had not previously organized a bilateral conference.

[32] 1990 marked 100 years of friendly relations between Japan and Turkey, and the two governments organized a large-scale ceremony. T.I.H. Prince and Princess Tomohito of Mikasa were invited by the Turkish government to attend the memorial ceremony

During the Imperial Family's visit to Turkey, several important events were organized. For example, the opening ceremony of the Department of the Japanese Language Education at Çanakkale 18 Mart University, the ceremony of the laying of the stone of the Turkish-Japanese Foundation (Türk-Japon Vakfı), and the opening ceremony of the Mikasa Memorial Garden in Kaman were organized on the T.I.H. Prince and Princess Takahito of Mikasa's third visit to Turkey in 1993. Later, during H.I.H. Prince Tomohito of Mikasa's visit to Turkey in 1998, the Turkish-Japanese Foundation and the Institute of Anatolian Archaeological Studies were opened.

Activities by the Japanese Institute of Anatolian Archaeology of the Middle Eastern Culture Center (MECCJ) provide an example of how members of the Japanese Imperial Family contributed to the bilateral relations.[33] MECCJ was established in 1975 in Tokyo, and it started preliminary research at the site of in Kırşehir in the Middle Anatolian region in 1985 for one of its excavation and research programs. The aim of this research was to create the world's first original Japanese timeline. As the research progressed, and to achieve wider goals, there was a need for a permanent facility to carry out further research. The institute decided to build a facility in Kaman since it is illegal to take research findings outside of Turkey.

This project has several distinguishing features. Firstly, it started as a bilateral research collaboration. Then, by partnering with foreign specialists, it became an international research project. Secondly, it provides training courses for the specialists, preserves findings onsite, and contributes to tourism, adding to the local value. Thirdly, hiring local villagers and students helps contribute to the local economy. Fourthly, the project offers a scholarship for the local youth, and, finally, the museum that exhibits the findings, built with the support of a Japanese ODA, the

---

of the *Ertuğrul* in Mersin. Furthermore, Turkish Naval ship TCG *Turgutreis* was sent to Kushimoto to attend the ceremony. As for the Imperial families, T.I.H. Prince and Princess Takahito of Mikasa visited Turkey in 1994 for the third time, T.I.H. Prince and Princess Tomohito of Mikasa carried out a second visit to Turkey in 1998 and thereafter, H.I.H Prince Tomohito of Mikasa visited several times. His first daughter, H.I.H. Princess Akiko of Mikasa, also visited to Turkey for several times. In 2009, then the Crown Prince Naruhito visited Turkey to attend the 5th World Water Forum.

[33] Regarding the details of the Japanese Institute of Anatolian Archeologey, see: Omura (2018), 'Anatolia Kokogaku Hakkutsuki' (pp. 1–16), 'Anatolia Kokogakukenkyujo kara no Hokoku', *Anatolia News*, 101–117, 121–present (The latest issue is 152).

Kaman-Kalehöyük Archaeological Museum, was donated to the Ministry of Culture and Tourism of Turkey in 2010. The first excavation began in 1986. At that time, there were only eight members and 17 local workers. However, as the archeological research progressed successfully, the number of local workers increased up to 140–150 per year. The institute hires some local villagers every summer, offering benefits such as health insurance and a pension—many villagers are used to applying for these posts, which is a great help to the Çağırkan village whose official population is 2000 and has, otherwise, a poor local economy. The director of the Japanese Institute of Anatolian Archeology, Dr. Sachihiro Omura, employs workers with consideration given to the situation of each family.

The institute not only supports the lives of the villagers, but it provides educational opportunities to the youth. It hires junior-high and high-school students for part-time jobs and provides scholarships for the distinguished students at junior colleges or universities who support the research and preserve the findings. The fund for the scholarship was offered by H.I.H. Prince Tomohito of Mikasa and started in 1990. Later, with H.I.H. Prince Takahito of Mikasa's contribution, the scholarship named after Mikasa, the 'Mikasa Scholarship Fund,' started in 1998 and offers scholarships to several students every year.[34] Despite the fact that the students don't study archeology, their contribution to society exemplifies the institute's positive impact on Turkish society. Classes are also organized for the local workers, with lectures for the local women and children, to let them know that all the archeological sites and findings are their property and to be passed down to the next generation. In addition, the institute hosts and trains foreign academics and curators.

Former Turkish Minister of Culture and Tourism, Mr. Ertuğrul Günay, appreciated the various projects of the institute and said that the institute would be the model of Turkey's cultural policy (Omura 2018: 6). However, the institute had to overcome many difficulties. When founded in 1998, the building consisted of a group of rather small, prefabricated buildings, which was very different from the permanent usage facility. To

---

[34] The Soroptimist International Kyoto established the Kaman Kale Höyük Scholarship for Girls in 2004, and has provided a scholarship to several students every year. The Prince Mikasa Foundation offers a nine-months scholarship for six male students, and Soloptimist International Kyoto provides a scholarship for seven students, for nine months every year.

improve the research facilities, the Japanese Institute of Anatolian Archaeology Construction Fund was established, with H.I.H. Prince Takahito of Mikasa appointed as an honorary patron and H.I.H. Prince Tomohito of Mikasa as chairman. Through organizing some activities, such as lectures and cultural events all over Japan and tours for Turkey, they completed raising funds to build the complex in September 2005. In March 2017, the Prince Mikasa Memorial Foundation was established to support various institute initiatives in Turkey. The board members of the foundation are not only retired ambassadors and academics but also prominent Japanese and Turkish businesspersons. The institute is a symbol of the three-dimensional diplomacy of Turkey and Japan.

In recent years, the institute has become a popular tourist attraction in Turkey, hosting about 100,000 visitors a year, recorded 130,000 visitors in 2019. The Prince Mikasa Memorial Garden, which is one of the biggest Japanese style garden abroad, is especially popular, not only among local visitors but also serving as a hot spot for wedding photo shoots, thus further supporting the local economy.

The institute is an example of how cooperation and exchanges among the Imperial Family, governments, and citizens have strengthened bilateral relations. Turkey showed further understanding and appreciation for the contributions of the Mikasa family by leading the development of 'Prens Mikasa Caddesi (Prince Mikasa Street)' in Kaman, named after H.I.H. Prince Takahito of Mikasa. In addition, the Turkish government expressed its condolences to H.I.H. Prince Tomohito of Mikasa by setting up a board of condolence in the downtown area of the capital, Ankara. Moreover, the Ministry of Tourism and Culture organized a memorial concert for Prince Tomohito of Mikasa in Ankara in 2014, which was attended by H.I.H. Princess Akiko of Mikasa. While bilateral relations don't change overnight, progress continues to be shown with each connection.

4.3   The Exchange Between Citizens: Widening the Inter-Exchange in Academic, Education, Local Governments, and Friendship Associations

The exchange between citizens was introduced by the sister-city agreement between Shimonoseki and Istanbul in 1972. Shimonoseki and Istanbul both face major straits (Kanmon and Bosphorus, respectively), the function and landscape of both cities have similarities, and they have been continuing sister-city exchanges over the years by hosting students and cultural exchanges.

The Turkish government started a scholarship program for Japanese students in 1965 and made a significant contribution to current Turkish studies in Japan.[35] In the 1970s, the initiatives of the Japan-Turkey Society and some other friendship associations became more active.[36] In the 1980s, exhibitions, such as those on Turkish civilization in 1985 and the treasures of the Topkapı Palace in 1988, took place in Japan, many TV programs broadcast them in Japan, films were shown on screen, and lectures were organized. Through these activities, the Japanese people started to gain interest in Turkey. Similarly, the Turkish people reciprocated interest in Japan. Ankara University established the Japanese Language and Literature Department in the Faculty of Languages, History, and Geography in 1986. Japanese language programs were launched by the History Department of Boğaziçi University in 1988 and by the Department in its Faculty of Languages at the Middle East Technical University in 1989. Currently, there are six universities with Japanese language or Japanese studies programs, in addition to some high schools offering Japanese language courses.

In the first half of the 1990s, the economic exchanges extended to cultural exchanges, which led to more frequent citizen exchanges. At the time, Turkey was not a well-known country among the Japanese. However, when *Turkish Airlines* launched its direct flight to Japan in 1992, it provided opportunities for people to explore, which led to much greater coverage of Turkey in the media.

There were many high-level exchanges in the first half of the 1990s, as mentioned above. The then Prime Minister, Mr. Süleyman Demirel, decided to establish the Turkish-Japanese Foundation (Türk- Japon Vakfi: TJV in Ankara) after attending the welcome reception organized by the Turkish Embassy and the Japan-Turkey Society during his visit to Japan. TJV is a unique institute with the function of introducing Japan to the host country. Turkey's two high schools, *Ankara Radyo Televizyon Anadolu Teknik High School* and *Istanbul Kağıthane Ticaret ve Sanayi*

[35] See 'Turkology in Japan' by Nagata (1996).

[36] There are many bilateral associations such as the Tokyo Japan-Turkey Women's Association, Japan Turkey Cultural Exchange Association founded by citizen, academicians, sister cities locate in Japan. It is not easy to get full information on all of them.

Odası Anadolu Ticaret High School teach lessons in Japanese, and departments for Japanese language education and studies have been set up at two Turkish universities, Çanakkale On Sekiz Mart University and Kayseri University.

In Japan, the Tokyo University of Foreign Studies and Osaka University of Foreign Studies (now Osaka University) established faculties of Turkish studies in 1992. Student exchange programs began along with the Japan-Turkey Students Conference in 1993. Turkish students studying in Japan founded the Association of Turkish Students in Japan (Japonya Türk Öğrenciler Derneği) in 1999.[37]

Citizen exchanges increased in the 2000s. 'The Year of Turkey in Japan 2003' and 'Japan Year 2010 in Turkey' widened exchange opportunities for junior high and high schools. As such, the three-dimensional diplomacy which started and took shape in the 1990s continued to deepen and widen in the 2000s.

5   Conclusion: Past, Present, and Future

As discussed in this paper, the bilateral relations between Japan and Turkey are multi-dimensional, both in scope and in terms of the actors involved, ranging from the   Imperial Families, the government, and citizens to the business sector.

Among the many key features of the bilateral relationship, this chapter focuses on a few. The two countries have always maintained good relations despite internal and external pressures at times, and the governments, the Imperial Families, and citizens continue to play different types of roles, creating spill-over effects for each other at every phase. Ikei (2003) points out that to maintain good relations, two countries should share some common factors, such as domestic matters or adversaries; they should continue exchanges between their people, culture, and economics, and express positive sentiments toward each other. On the other hand, the factors for confrontation include not sharing a common enemy, domestic concerns caused by diplomatic issues, and discontinuation of the exchanges of people, culture, and economics. Ikei's arguments apply to the relations between Japan and Turkey. Both countries shared a historic goal—to leave Asia and enter Europe, and they have had common

---

[37] At the time of the Marmara earthquake in 1999, the ties between the two countries stepped into a new phase.

enemies. The Soviet Union provided a shared threat until the end of the Cold War. However, following the Cold War, there seem to be no relevant common enemy. Japan and Turkey have been developing their bilateral relations for more than 130 years. During WWII, their diplomatic relations ceased for a while. However, after their relations were re-established, the government, the Imperial Families, and citizens started exchanges again, showing remarkable progress during the Cold War period. In the 2000s, Turkey was recognized as an emerging economy, thus giving rise to economic relations. In 2013, the strategic partnership was signed by the two countries' leaders, demonstrating their determination to deepen and strengthen bilateral relations further. The current generation continues to build on this long-standing and strong foundation.

For the Japanese people, Turkey has evolved from a country that needed Japan's support to a partner in support of third-country development and international communities. Turkey's support is essential for Japan to continue international relations. The Japanese Institute for Anatolian Archaeology is a product of the three-dimensional diplomacy, exchanges, and collaboration. The role of the friendship associations, such as the Japan-Turkey Society, are also significant actors in maintaining the bilateral relations. Cooperation in economy and technology has nurtured academic and cultural exchanges.

The stories of two incidents, the *Ertuğrul* tragedy in 1890 and the *Turkish Airlines'* rescue flight in 1985, continue to capture and symbolize the spirit of the two countries' ability to collaborate during a difficult situation. The Japanese *Diplomatic Blue Book 2017* attributes the term 'pro-Japanese country' only to Turkey. The present positive relationship is, no doubt, a result of the achievements of the Imperial Families, the government, and the citizens of the two countries.

The task for the future of bilateral relations is quite clear. Turkish people still possess limited knowledge about Japan, despite a predisposition to be pro-Japanese, and the same can be said for the Japanese people. The importance of the *Ertuğrul* tragedy should serve as a principal asset in maintaining friendly bilateral relations. However, it is time to foster a deeper, pragmatic relationship. Japan and Turkey have built a strong foundation, developed through continuous exchanges within three-dimensional diplomacy involving the Imperial Families, the governments, and the citizens.

REFERENCES

Akkemik, K. Ali. 2016. Is Turkey Turning Its Face Away from Japan to China and Korea? Evidence from Trade Relations. *Perceptions* 21 (1): 45–62.

Akkemik, K. Ali, 2017. On Turkish-Japanese Economic Relations. *Japan-Turkey Dialogue on Global Affairs, ORSAM Report* 207: 45–56.

Amiral (e) Çetinkaya, Apatay. 2008. *Türk Japon İlişkileri ve Ertuğrul Fırkateyni'nin Öyküsü*. İstanbul: Deniz Basımevi Müdürlüğü.

Araki, Kiyoshi. 2014. Toruko Genkyou to Nichido Kankei. *Chuto Kenkyu* 519: 8–13.

Arık, Umut. 1991. *A Century of Turkish-Japanese Relations: A Special Partnership*. Tokyo: Japan-Turkey Friendship Centenary Program Committee.

Çolakoğlu, Selçuk. 2017. Türkiye'nin Kuzeydoğu Asya'daki Rolü. In Deniz Kuvvetleri Komutanlığı, ed. *Uluslararası Ertuğrul'un İzinde Deniz Kuvvetleri ve Diplomasi Sempozyum*. İstanbul: Deniz Basımevi Müdürlüğü.

Chuunichi Toruko koku Taishikan. 1935. *Toruko koku gunkan Erutogururu gou*. Tokyo: Kaigai Insatsujo.

Dündar, Merthan Ali. 2016. Atatürk ve Japonya. In *Deniz Kuvvetleri Komutanlığı. Uluslararası Ertuğrul'un İzinde Deniz Kuvvetleri ve Diplomasi Sempozyum*. İstanbul: Deniz Basımevi Müdürlüğü.

Gaikoseisho. 1991. http://www.mofa.go.jp/mofaj/gaiko/bluebook/1991/h03-4-6.htm (accessed on July 14, 2017).

Hatano, Masaru. 1999. Erutuururugou Jiken wo Meguru Nichido Kankei. In (Ikei and Sakamoto 1999).

Ikei, Yu. 1999. 1926 nen Kinto Boeki Kaigi- Nihon-Toruko Kankeishi no Ichidanmen. In (Ikei and Sakamoto 1999).

Ikei, Yu and Tsutomu Sakamoto, eds. 1999. *Kindai Nihon to Toruko Sekai*. Tokyo: Keiso Shobo.

Ikei, Yu. 2003. Nihon to Toruko no Gaikou Kankei. *Anatolia News* 109: 9.

Imai, Kohei. 2017. *Toruko Gendaishi- Osuman Teikoku Hokai kara Erudoan no Jidai made*. Tokyo: Chuo Koron Sha.

Kawabe, Junko. 2015. Toruko no Keizai Hatten to Nihon Kigyou. *Jousai Daigaku Keiei Kiyou* 11 (9): 1–26.

Kawabe, Nobuo. 2016. Nikkei Kigyou no Toruko Shinshutsu. In *Toruko to Nihon no Keizai Keiei Kankei*. Tokyo: Bunkyo Gakuin Daigaku Sougou Kenkyuujo.

Matsutani, Hironao. 1986. *Nihon to Toruko—Nihon Toruko Kankeishi*. Tokyo: Chuutouchousakai.

Matsutani, Hironao. 1999. *Nihon Toruko Koushoushi—Kaisetsu to Shiryou*. Tokyo: Okazaki Kenkyuujo.

Matsutani, Hironao. 2005. *Nihon Toruko Koushoushi (zoku)—Kaisetsu to Shiryou*. Tokyo: Okazaki Kenkyuujo.

Matsutani, Hironao and Matsutani, Isao. 2014. *Nihon Toruko Kankei no Keisei to Hatten- Reimeiki kara Tsuzuku Yuukou Shinzen no Kaiko.* Tokyo: Gendai Toruko Kenkyuukai.

Misawa, Nobuo. 2005a. Erutuururugou Jiken. Naikakufu Chuuou Bousai Kaigi Saigai Kyoukun no Keishou ni Kansuru Senmon Chousakai. In *1890 Erutuururugou Jiken Houkokusho.*

Misawa, Nobuo. 2005b. Erutuururugou to Shimbun Medhia. Naikakufu Chuuou Bousai Kaigi Saigai Kyoukun no Keishou ni Kansuru Senmon Chousakai. In *1890 Erutuururugou Jiken Houkokusho.*

Misawa, Nobuo. 2005c. Erutuururugou no Bousai Taisei to Saigai Kyoukun Denshou.

Misawa, Nobuo. 2008. Nihon Toruko Kankei Shoushi. *Toruko towa Nanika. Bessatsu Kan* 14, 164−173.

Nagaba, Hiroshi. 2005. *Kaisou no Isutanburu- Kaikyou Toshi no Henbou.* Tokyo: Mana shobou.

Nagata, Yuzo. 1996. Nihon ni Okeru Toruko Kenkyuu Shoushi. *Anatlia News* 86: 10−18.

Naito, Chishu. 1971. Nichi-Do Kyoukai ni tsuite no Omoide. *Nihon Toruko Kyoukai Kaihou* 1: 8−9.

Naikakufu Chuuou Bousai Kaigi Saigai Kyoukun no Keishou ni Kansuru Senmon Chousakai. In *1890 Erutuururugou Jiken Houkokusho.*

Naito, Masanori. 2012. Nihon to Toruko- 21 seiki no aratana yuukou ye no Tenbou. In Omura, Sachihiro, Yuzo Nagata, and Masanori Naito, eds. *Toruko wo Shirutame no 53 shou.* Tokyo: Akashi shoten.

Nakamura, Satoru. 2016. *Challenge for Qatar and Japan to Build Multilayered Relations.* Gulf Studies Center Monographic Series, No. 2. Doha: Qatar University.

Nihon Toruko Kyokai Nanajuunenshi Henshuuiinkai. 1996. *Nihon Toruko Kyokai 70 Nenshi.* Tokyo: Keisou Shobou.

Nihon Toruko Kyoukai. 2007. *Nihon Toruko Kyokai Tsuiho- 1996 Nen − 2006 Nen.* Toyko: Dakichi Hoki.

Nishiwaki, Yasuyuki. 1999. *Toruko no Mikata- Kokusai Rikai to shite no Chishi.* Tokyo: Ninomiya shoten.

Nitch, Volker. 2007. State Visits and International Trade. *The World Economy* 30 (12): 1798−1816.

Omura, Sachihiro. 2018. *Anatoria no Kaze Koukogaku to Kokusai Kouken.* Tokyo: Liton.

Shiraiwa, Kazuhiko. 1999. Meijiki no Bunken ni Miru Nihonnjin no Torukokan. In (Ikei and Sakamoto 1999).

Pehlivantürk, Bahadır. 2012. Turkish Japanese Relations: Turning Romanticism into Rationality. *International Journal* 67 (1): 101−117.

Sugihara, Shinichi. 1987. Toruko kara Kikoku Shite. In *Anatolia News* 52: 3−5.

Takahashi Tadahisa. 2008. Isutanburu no Nihon Shouten. *Toruko towa Nanika*. *Bessatsu Kan* 14: 174–175.

Takeda, Tatsuo. 1987. *Shin Gekki no Kuni Toruko: Sono Rekishi to Genzai*. Tokyo: Saimaru shuppankai.

Tanaka Mitsuo. 1972. Toruko no Genjou. *Nihon Toruko Kyokai Kaihou* 2: 17–29.

Toyama, Atsuko. 2001. *Toruo Seiki no Hazama de*. Tokyo: NHK shuppan.

Toyama, Atsuko. 2013. *Koshikata no ki*. Kamakura: Kamakura shunjusha.

Tuncok, Mete. 1996. *Toruko to Nihon no Kindaika- Gaikokujin no Yakuwari*. Tokyo: Saimaru shuppankai.

Tüzün, Çiğdem. 2016. *Şarık Tara in his own words*. Istanbul: NMC Television ve Reklamcılık Tic.A.Ş.

Yamaguchi, Yoichi. 1991. *Toruko ga Mietekuru- Kono Shinnichi koku no Juuyusei*. Tokyo: Saimaru shuppankai.

Ward, Robert E., and Dankwart A. Rustow, eds. 1970. *Political Modernization in Japan and Turkey*. New Jersey: Princeton University Press.

Historical Records

Cidal, Abdülkerim and Bahadır Pehlivantürk, eds. 2014. *Japan and Turkey in the International Community: Cooperation and Potential*. Ankara: Center for Middle Eastern Strategic Studies.

Hasebe, Yoshihiko, Nobuo Misawa, and Sinan Levent, eds. 2018. *Osuman Teikoku to Nihon Toruko Kyowakoku shushofu Osuman Monjokan Shozobunsho ni motozuku Ryokokukankankei (Waseda Daigaku Shiryotenjikai 2017)*. Asian Cultures Research Institute of Toyo University.

Kobayashi, Kujo, and Nobuo Misawa, eds. 2017. *Shukou bon Nihon Gikyo Homare no Kai – Erutuururugou Jiken Kanren Shiryou (1) [The handwritten manuscript, "the Japanese chivalry as the pioneer of the honor": Source materials about the tragedy of Ottoman frigate Ertuğrul (1)]*. Tokyo: Toyo University.

Naito, Masanori, İdiris Danışmaz, Bahadır Pehlivantürk, and Mustafa Serdar Palabıyık, eds. 2015. *Orta Doğu Barış için Türk Japon İşbirliği*. Kyoto: Doshisha University.

Pehlivantürk, Bahadır, ed. 2017. *Japan-Turkey Dialogue on Global Affairs*. ORSAM Report 207.

Web Pages

The Japanese Ministry of Foreign Affairs
https://www.mofa.go.jp/mofaj/gaiko/bluebook/
https://www.mofa.go.jp/mofaj/press/release/24/5/pdfs/0522_01_01.pdf
(accessed on June 6, 2018).

CHAPTER 6

Japan–Egypt Bilateral Relations: A Main Pillar of Japanese Middle Eastern Policy

Takayuki Yokota

1 Introduction: Neglected Bilateral Relations between Japan and Egypt

In Japan, mainstream scholars of diplomatic history and the Middle Eastern area studies almost neglect Japan–Egypt bilateral relation. Iokibe Makoto, one of the most prominent scholars on Japanese diplomacy, discusses the Middle East Wars, such as Gulf War (1991), Afghan War (2001), and Iraq War (2003), from the perspective of Japanese security policy transition and US-Japan relations, but there is no mention to Egypt (Iokibe 2014). Most of the Middle Eastern studies, humane studies, and social science studies in Japan have made observations and analyses on the issues and events in the Middle East, but they have not focused on the bilateral relations between the Middle Eastern countries and Japan; this applies to the bilateral relation between Japan and Egypt with a few valuable exceptions such as (Tsuchiya 2012; Sakai 2016). One of the reasons

T. Yokota (✉)
School of Information and Communication, Meiji University, Tokyo, Japan
e-mail: yokotaka@meiji.ac.jp

© The Author(s), under exclusive license to Springer Nature
Singapore Pte Ltd. 2023
S. Nakamura and S. Wright (eds.), *Japan and the Middle East*,
Contemporary Gulf Studies, https://doi.org/10.1007/978-981-19-3459-9_6

139

for the lack of research on the bilateral relation is lack of Egypt's role in the three principles of Japanese diplomacy; "United Nations-centralism," "Cooperation with liberal states," and "maintaining the position as a member of Asia."[1] Egypt is not regarded as a critical factor of the three principles by academics in Japan.

However, Japan and Egypt have maintained a friendly relationship and recognized each other as a significant partner since the nineteenth century. Egypt has been a bridgehead and hub for Japan's Middle Eastern policy, especially since 1950s. Both countries developed multi-faced bilateral relation in economic cooperation, diplomacy, and cultural ties. This is because Egypt is the leading country in the Middle East, which means its strategic and diplomatic value is more important than other countries. Although Egypt exports only small amount of oil and gas, Egypt is regarded in Japan as key to the stability of whole of the Middle East, of which role in security in the region and its security is concerned seriously in Japan. Moreover, Egypt's role as the center of Arab culture and the highest authority of Islamic study in the world have attracted Japanese intellectuals. Egypt's movies, music, and religions have been rich sources of bilateral relations. Thus, the experts of Egypt in Japan, and their counterparts in Egypt in various fields of diplomacy, foreign aid, and culture, recognize the significance of the bilateral relations passionately. This contrasts sharply with the neglects mentioned in the above paragraph.

Therefore, this chapter discusses the unique multi-faced bilateral relation between Japan and Egypt in the fields of economy and trade, diplomacy, and culture. These three aspects form the main pillars underpinning the bilateral relations and are to be examined in detail. This chapter can describe the realities of the relation beyond a narrow perception of academic specialties, and also can point out that new pluralism in Japan's diplomacy "finds" Egypt anew in the twenty-first century.

---

[1] See *Showa 32 Nen Ban Waga Gaikou no Kinkyo [Diplomatic Bluebook for 1957]* (in Japanese), http://www.mofa.go.jp/mofaj/gaiko/bluebook/1957/s32-1-2.htm#a, accessed on June 15, 2021.

2 PRE-WWII JAPAN–EGYPT RELATION: ENCOUNTER BETWEEN JAPAN AND EGYPT

The first encounter between Japan and Egypt dates back to the end of the *Edo* period. Egypt is one of the oldest partners for Japan among the Middle East countries. This section reviews the pre-WWII bilateral relations between Japan and Egypt, which formed foundation of diplomatic, strategic, and cultural perception of Egypt in Japan after the World War II. They are the civilization of pyramid, common strategic position against the West, and food cultural marriage "Koshary."

Figure 1 shows a group of Japanese warriors (*samurai*) wearing traditional clothes (*kimono*) with Japanese swords (*katana*) in front of a statue of the Sphinx adjacent to the three major pyramids of Giza in Egypt. The group was the Second Japanese Embassy to Europe, a delegation from the Edo Shogunate, which left Japan in 1864. They visited Egypt on the way to Europe by sea. Since the Suez Canal was not yet open at that time, they used the railroad, which had been laid as part of the modernization under Muhammad Ali's dynasty, to go to Alexandria, the starting port of the Mediterranean Sea route (Fig. 2). On their way, they stopped in Cairo and this photograph was taken by the Italian photographer Antonio Beato. From the end of the Edo period to the beginning of the *Meiji* era, totally five delegations traveled to Europe via Egypt.[2]

After the encounter with Egypt after the Edo period, Japan became more interested in more concrete issues rather than a "surprise" or a "discovery" of cross-cultural exchange. Namely, Japan researched Egypt's mixed court system in relation to treaty revisions with the Western countries and sympathized with the Ahmad Urabi Movement[3] (1881–1882) as the same oppressed people (Sugita 1995: 112–126). However, after Japan's victory in the Sino-Japanese and Russo-Japanese wars, this interest and sympathy gradually waned and Japan became more interested in British domination of Egypt as a model of colonial management (Sugita

---

[2] The participants of these missions did not necessarily have a positive view on Egypt. For example, Fukuzawa Yukichi, who joined the first embassy as an interpreter, disgusted Egyptian society as poor and filthy, and attributed its "backwardness" to the "lazy" nature of the people and the "rigid" Islamic legal system in his book "Western Voyages (Seikou-ki)" [Sakai 2016: 126].

[3] A national movement that claims liberation from the rule by European powers, led by Egyptian military officer Colonel Ahmad Urabi, who advocated that "Egypt for the Egyptians."

Fig. 1   The Second Japanese Embassy to Europe in front of the statue of the Sphinx[4]

1995: 126–129; Katayama 2014). The imperialist policies were employed by the Japanese government until the end of WWII.

During the Meiji and *Taisho* periods, Japan's relations with Egypt deepened, while Egypt was under the British control. Japan opened a consulate in Port Said in 1919 and recognized the independent Kingdom of Egypt from Great Britain in 1922. In the 1920s, the bilateral relations developed as several Japanese companies began business activities in Alexandria to purchase Egyptian cotton and to sell Japanese cotton products (Tsuchiya 2012: 369). Japanese companies regarded Egypt with Suez Canal as a central transit hub for Japanese cotton products to Europe and the Middle East. The Japanese legation was established in Cairo in 1936.

One of the most notable bilateral exchanges between Japan and Egypt during this period is the agricultural crop of rice. *Koshary*, which is one

---

[4] Source: National Diet Library, Japan. https://www.ndl.go.jp/kaleido/entry/14/1. html#anchor1.

Fig. 2 Steam locomotives in Egypt from Yuhei Takashima's *Travels to Europe and the West* [5]

of the national foods for modern Egyptians, uses Japonica rice, which is commonly consumed in Japan. According to statistical data from the Food and Agriculture Organization of the United Nations (FAO), Egypt harvested approximately 5.5 million tons of rice in 2014.[6] According to an article on the webpage of the Japan International Cooperation Agency (JICA), about 80% of rice production in Egypt is Japonica rice, which is mainly consumed within the country. In Egypt, breeding improvements were made in 1917 based on a Japanese Japonica rice variety named *Yabani* (Arabic for "Japan"), and Giza 171 and Giza 172, which were bred from the *Yabani*, have been the main rice varieties.[7] Many people

[5] Source: National Diet Library, Japan, https://www.ndl.go.jp/kaleido/entry/14/1.html#anchor1.

[6] See FAO's "Food and Agriculture Data," http://www.fao.org/faostat/en/#home, accessed on June 15, 2021.

[7] JICA, "Ejiputo no Kome ha Nihon kara: Ejiputo Nougyou to Inasaku Nihon no Kyouryoku (Sono 2)" [Egyptian Rice Came from Japan: Agriculture and Rice Farming,

in Egypt today know that most of the rice they eat is of Japanese origin, and the length and depth of the history of bilateral relations can be seen through the food culture of *Koshary*.

The bilateral relation developed during the Meiji and Taisho periods. However, due to the war between Japan and Britain in WWII, the relations were temporarily ruptured. Because Egypt was under the de facto control of Britain, the Japanese legation in Cairo was closed after Japan entered the war with the Axis powers. At the end of WWII, when Japan was likely defeated, Egypt declared war on Japan as a member of the Allied Powers. The exchanges between Japan and Egypt were interrupted by WWII, but the experience in the period contributed to reconstruct the bilateral relation between the two countries after WWII.

3   Economic Relation: Japan's Essential Hub in the Middle East

The economic relationship between Japan and Egypt was resumed in the 1950s and developed especially during Japan's period of rapid economic growth. Egypt was the hub of the Middle East when Japanese companies re-entered the global trade and business. Egypt was the main entrance to the region for the Japanese private sector. Figure 3 shows the number of Japanese residing in Egypt since 1972. The number drastically increased in mid-1970s and the maximum number so far is 1478 in 1978. This is because other trade and business hubs in the region, such as Beirut and Tehran, were in political turmoil then, and a great number of companies and business persons moved to relatively stable Cairo. The number of Japanese residents in Egypt increased and decreased in 1980s and has been around 800 to 1100 since 1990s. The number is one of the highest in the Middle East and Africa. Furthermore, as discussed later, treaties or agreements were concluded between Japan and Egypt, which improved the environment for the economy, trade, and investment. In fact, Japan's tax treaty network as of June 2021 includes only eight countries in the Middle East, including Egypt, and similarly only three countries in the

and Japanese Cooperation Vol. 2] (in Japanese), October 22, 2008. https://www.jica.go.jp/project/egypt/0702252/news/column/081022.html, accessed on June 15, 2021.

Fig. 3 The number of Japanese residents in Egypt (1972–2016), Population Number

African Continent.[8] Japan and Egypt signed the Treaty for the Avoidance of Double Taxation in 1969, and it is clear that Japan considered Egypt as an indispensable partner from the earliest stage.

The volume of trade and foreign direct investment (FDI) are also helpful indicators when considering the economic relationship between Japan and Egypt. Figure 4 shows the trend in the value of bilateral trade from 1970 to 2016. Japanese exports to Egypt grew significantly in the 1980s and have been on the rise again since 2000. While neighboring European and Arab countries account for a large share of Egypt's trade, due to the geographical reasons, Japan has accounted for a large share of trade among Asian countries over the years. Egypt has also become an important trading partner accounting for more than ten percent of Japan's exports to the African Continent. Japan's main exports to Egypt

[8] MOFA, "Waga Kuni no Sozei Jouyaku Nettowaku" [Japan's Tax Treaty Network] (in Japanese), June 1, 2021. http://www.mof.go.jp/tax_policy/summary/international/182.pdf, accessed on June 15, 2021.

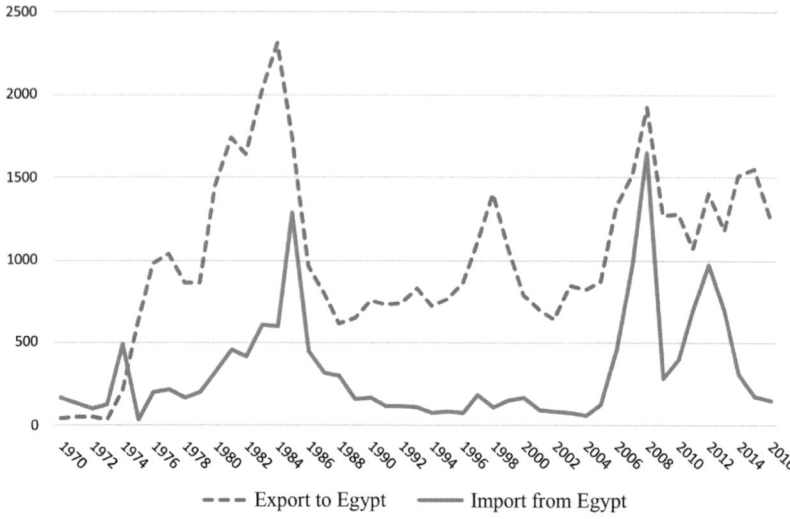

Fig. 4   Value of trade between Japan and Egypt (1970–2016, JPY 100 mn)

are automobiles and machineries, while Egypt's main exports are fossil fuels and clothing.

Figure 5 shows the trend in the amount of FDI by Japan in Egypt from the Egyptian Fiscal Year 2001/2002 (from July 2001 to June 2002) to Egyptian FY2016/2017. While the percentage of the figures in the total amount of FDI for both Japan and Egypt have been low (1–2% for Egypt and less than 1% for Japan), there have been a steady growth since the 2010s. In fact, the al-Sisi administration has made attracting FDI a pillar of its development and economic policies, and he discussed investment as one of the main topics of summit talks with Japanese Prime Minister in 2015 and 2016. It is expected that FDI will increase in the future.

In recent years, the rapid economic development of Gulf countries has led to Japanese companies setting up regional branches in cities such as Dubai and Doha. However, 51 Japanese companies still operate in Egypt as of December 2016,[9] since the Japanese private sector regards Egypt

[9] The Japanese embassy in Egypt shows basic information of the bilateral relation on its website. As for the number of Japanese companies in Egypt, see the following webpage, http://www.eg.emb-japan.go.jp/j/egypt_info/basic/egypt_japan.htm, accessed on June 15, 2021.

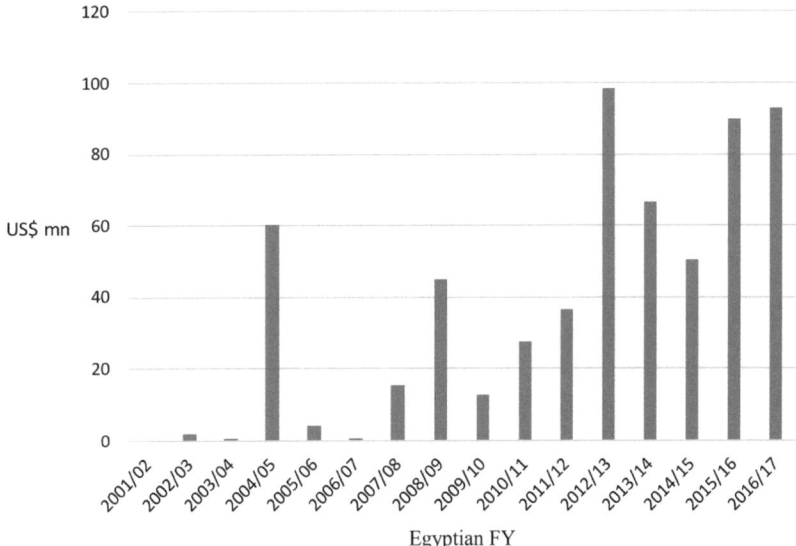

Fig. 5 FDI from Japan to Egypt (2001/02–2016/17)

as a huge market with 100 million population which is still growing fast pace. Japan expects that Egypt's economic power will rise with support of Japan's ODA and educational-cultural partnership.

Egypt has been an essential hub for Japanese business and trade in the Middle East since the 1950s, which was supported by the conclusion of necessary treaties and agreements between the two countries. The number of Japanese residents in Egypt and the volume of trade and FDI have been one of the largest in the region. Japanese companies still regard Egypt as a main hub amid the economic rise of Gulf countries because of its huge market and economic potential for the near future.

4   DIPLOMATIC RELATION: STRATEGIC IMPORTANCE

After the defeat in WWII, Japan had to formulate its new diplomatic policy almost from the beginning. Japan regarded Egypt as its bridgehead in the Middle East and succeeded in establishing close diplomatic relation. The bilateral relation has contributed as a main pillar of Japanese

Middle East Policy. This section discusses the reconstruction of the bilateral relation in 1950s–1970s firstly, and the strategic development after 1980s secondly.

4.1   Bilateral Relation in 1950s–1970s: Egypt as Bridgehead of Japanese Middle East Diplomacy

Japan and Egypt maintained a friendly relation in 1950s–1970s, when Egypt was faced with diplomatic difficulties: some Western countries regarded Gamal Abd al-Nasser (Nasser) as pro-Soviet socialist leader, and to some Arab countries Anwar Sadat was a treachery after Camp David accords in 1978. Japan placed Egypt as an entrance or a bridgehead to the Middle East, and bilateral relation was the main pillar of its diplomacy.

As a defeated nation in World War II, Japan was placed under occupation by the US-led General Headquarters. The occupation was ended by the San Francisco Peace Treaty between Japan and the Allied nations in 1951. Egypt was one of the signatories to the treaty and ratified it in December of the following year, and the state of war between Japan and Egypt came to an end.

With the entry of the Peace Treaty into force in April 1952, Japan restored its sovereignty and reopened its legation in Cairo in December of the same year. The fact that the legation was reopened in the same month as the ratification of the Peace Treaty by Egyptian government shows that the Japanese government considered Egypt as the high priority country in the region. The Egyptian government also opened an embassy in Tokyo in 1953. The Japanese legation in Cairo was upgraded to the status of an embassy in 1954. Yosano Shigeru, the second son of Japanese famous poets Yosano Tekkan and Yosano Akiko, became the first ambassador. Yosano was later to serve as the Secretary General of the Organizing Committee of the 1964 Tokyo Olympics. The appointment of Yosano, a "big-name diplomat," showed the importance of Egypt in Japan's diplomacy. In fact, the Japanese government regarded Egypt as a major partner in its Middle Eastern policy. The above-mentioned "Diplomatic Bluebook for 1957" has a section of "Diplomatic Relations with Middle Eastern Countries" and refers to Egypt with regard to the importance of free navigation in face of the Suez Crisis of 1956.

It was during the Cold War when President Nasser was in power in Egypt from 1956 to 1970. Egypt employed a policy that leaned toward the Soviet Union after the conflict with the US over the construction of Aswan High Dam. While Japan's foreign policy at that time was strongly defined by the Cold War structure, Japan–Egypt relations developed steadily. This is because Japan regarded Egypt as a leader in the Third World and found a friendly relation with Egypt was in the national interest. For example, at the first Asian-African Conference in Bandung in 1955, led by President Nasser with Indian Prime Minister Jawaharlal Nehru, Chinese Premier Zhou Enlai and Indonesian President Sukarno, a Japanese delegation led by Takasaki Tatsunosuke, commissioner of the Economic Council Agency, participated. President Nasser also had a strong presence at the Non-Aligned Countries Conference (the first Belgrade Summit in 1961), and the Japanese government treated him as a leading figure in the Third World.

In addition, several practical treaties and agreements were concluded to consolidate the bilateral relationship: the Cultural Agreement (1957), the Trade and Payment Arrangement (1958), the Aviation Agreement (1963), and the Treaty for the Avoidance of Double Taxation (1969). In particular, the Trade and Payments Arrangement and the Treaty for the Avoidance of Double Taxation formed the basis for investment, trade, and economic exchanges between the two countries. These treaties and agreements were signed at the earliest stage in the Middle East, which shows that Japan regarded Egypt as a main trade partner in the region. One of the reasons for the early restoration and development is that Egypt is the global hub with Suez Canal.

During the Anwar Sadat presidency from 1970 to 1981, the friendly relationship between Japan and Egypt continued. It was particularly true after the 1973 Arab–Israeli War (October War). The first oil crisis that was caused by the war forced the Japanese government to reconsider its policy in the Middle East and to aim at strengthening relations with the Arab countries, including Egypt.[10] In Japan's diplomacy, the presence of Egypt, which has been at war with Israel since 1948, has increased suddenly and drastically since the first oil shock in 1973. The Japanese government's special envoy led by Deputy Prime Minister Miki

---

[10] "Diplomatic Bluebook for 1976" stated that "In recent years, the Near and Middle East, a significant source of petroleum and export market for Japan, has been exercising an increasingly important influence on international politics and economics," and "Economically, approximately 80% of Japan's petroleum imports in 1976 came from [...] the Middle East. [...]. it is anticipated that their economic relations with Japan will become increasingly broad and deep," https://www.mofa.go.jp/policy/other/bluebook/1976/1976-3-1.htm, accessed on June 15, 2021.

Takeo visited Arabian oil exporting countries and also Egypt. Japanese government regarded Egypt as key to stabilize the region amid the Israel-Arab War and calm down the anger of the Arabian Gulf countries. The two sides agreed to further strengthen bilateral relations and promised Japan's financial support for the Suez Canal expansion project as a loan of 38 billion yen, equivalent to the cost of the first phase of construction. In 1978, the Investment Protection Agreement came into force, contributing to the development of the investment circumstances and economic exchanges. There was also a visit by Prince Mikasa to Egypt in 1975, and a visit by the wife of President Sadat to Japan in 1976.

During 1950s–1970s, Japan regarded Egypt as a significant diplomatic and trade partner in the Middle East, and the bilateral relation was steadily developed and deepened amid international and regional political changes. Considering the presence of Egypt in the regional and international politics, Japan established its Middle East diplomacy by placing Egypt as a critical bridgehead.

4.2   Consolidation of Partnership After the End of the Cold War

The feature of Japan–Egypt relation moved to a new stage after the late 1980s: it developed into strategic and security-oriented. Japan and Egypt, under the early presidency of Hosni Mubarak, inherited the previous bilateral relation. However, the collapse of the Cold War regime brought about a change to it. Japanese diplomacy has faced a new situation; the development of globalization, the restructuring of US–Japan relations, the rise of regionalism around the world, and the confrontation of non-state actors such as terrorist organizations. The pluralization of Japanese diplomacy accelerated amidst these changes in the new international affairs (Kuriyama 2016: 21).

The establishment of the Japanese Parliamentary Association for the Friendship between Japan and Egypt in 1991, the year of the Gulf War, partly represented Japanese politicians' view that Egypt is the indispensable stabilizing actor in the Arabian/Persian Gulf. The Egyptian Parliamentary Association for the Friendship between Egypt and Japan was also established in 1994. Both associations grew up opportunities to deepen and broaden politicians' relations in later years. It was Mubarak who visited Japan for the first time as the president of Egypt in 1999. The delay of the Egyptian president's visit to Japan was not because the relationship had not been good, but because Nasser and Sadat could not do due to regional turmoil they had managed to deal with. During the official visit to Japan, Mubarak met the Emperor and Empress and held a summit meeting with Prime Minister Obuchi Keizo. The joint Japan–Egypt statement of the two leaders referred not only to bilateral relations but also to the Middle East peace process. Japan also regards Egypt as the key to the solution of the Palestinian problem, which is the source of "all conflict and terrorism" in the Middle East.[11] On the other hand, an attack by jihadists in Luxor in 1997, in which ten Japanese tourists were killed, caused security concerns among the Japanese about Egypt.

During the Mubarak presidency, Japan evaluated Egypt to stabilize the whole Middle East after the Iraq War, too. In 2003, Koizumi Junichiro visited Egypt for the first time as the prime minister of Japan and held a summit meeting with Mubarak. During the meeting, they agreed economic cooperation with more than $200 million especially in the fields of water supply, irrigation, and infrastructure development in Egypt.[12] They also discussed cooperation to promote peace process in the Middle East and support for reconstruction in Iraq after the war in 2003,[13] which Japan and Egypt would cooperate with the World Health Organization (WHO) in providing urgent medical assistance to Iraq.

Japan hoped to gain the understanding of Egypt, a major power in the region, about Japan's Middle East policy including the deployment of Japanese Self Defense Forces (JSDF) to Iraq. Furthermore, it was announced that Japan, Egypt, and Saudi Arabia would launch a trilateral meeting of experts, "the Japan-Arab Dialogue Forum," and the first meeting chaired by former Japanese Prime Minister Hashimoto Ryutaro was held in Tokyo in 2003.[14]

---

[11] For more information about Mubarak's visit to Japan, see the following webpage: MOFA, "Hosuni Mubaraku Daitouryou Hounichi nisaishiteno Nihon Ejiputo Kyodo Seimei" [Join Statement on the Occation of President Hosni Mubarak's Visit to Japan] (in Japanese), April 12, 1999. https://www.mofa.go.jp/mofaj/kaidan/yojin/arc_99/m_s eimei.html, accessed on June 15, 2021.

[12] Prime Minister Koizumi's visit to Egypt is summarized on MOFA's webpage: MOFA, "Koizumi Souridaijin no Ejiputo oyobi Saujiarabia Houmon" [Prime Minister Koizumi' Visit to Egypt and Saudi Arabia] (in Japanese), May 25, 2003. https://www.mofa.go.jp/ mofaj/kaidan/s_koi/us-me_03/es_gh.html, accessed on June 10, 2021.

[13] See the Japanese Cabinet's website, http://www.kantei.go.jp/jp/koizumispeech/ 2003/05/24press.html, accessed on May 25, 2019.

[14] MOFA, "Nihon Arabu Taiwa Foramu" [Japan-Arab Dialogue Forum] (in Japanese), http://www.mofa.go.jp/mofaj/area/middleeast/jaf_gh.html, accessed on June 19, 2021.

In 2006, Foreign Minister Aso Taro announced his concept of "Arc of Freedom and Prosperity" in a speech at the Japan Institute of International Affairs (JIIA) in Tokyo, advocating "value-oriented diplomacy."[15] In the same year, he also announced Japan's Concept for Creating the "Corridor for Peace and Prosperity."[16] In both cases, Egypt was regarded as a major regional partner essential to the realization of the plans. In fact, Prime Minister Abe Shinzo visited Egypt in 2007, held a summit meeting with Mubarak, and requested Egypt's cooperation in the "Corridor of Peace and Prosperity." At the meeting, they agreed and announced that a Japan-Arab Conference would be held with the aim of building multi-layered relations with Arab countries in the political, economic, and cultural fields. In the same year, the first meeting was held in Alexandria, attended by about 100 participants from Japan, including former Foreign Minister Nakayama Taro, and about 150 participants from the Arab world. However, the new diplomatic efforts came to a virtual halt with the change of government from the Liberal Democratic Party to the Democratic Party of Japan in 2009.

In face of the upheaval in Egypt in the wake of the Arab Spring, the Japanese government essentially took an "ex-post approval" stance on the outcome of the power struggle and regime change in Egypt, while calling for a halt to the violence. As a result, this stance minimized the changes in bilateral relations following the political upheaval. In fact, Japan succeeded in maintaining good relation with Abd al-Fattah al-Sisi

---

[15] "Arc of Freedom and Prosperity" and "value oriented diplomacy" were new pillars of Japanese diplomacy placing emphasis on universal values such as freedom, democracy, fundamental human rights, the rule of law, and the market economy. The Arc would start from Northern Europe and traverse the Baltic states, Central and South Eastern Europe, Central Asia and the Caucasus, the Middle East, and the Indian subcontinent, then cross Southeast Asia finally to reach Northeast Asia. For more information, see the MOFA's webpages: "Speech by Mr. Taro Aso, Minister for Foreign Affairs on the Occasion of the Japan Institute of International Affairs Seminar 'Arc of Freedom and Prosperity: Japan's Expanding Diplomatic Horizons,'" https://www.mofa.go.jp/announce/fm/aso/speech0611.html, and *Diplomatic Bluebook for 2007*, https://www.mofa.go.jp/policy/other/bluebook/2007/html/h1/h1_01.html, both accessed on May 28, 2021.

[16] "Corridor for Peace and Prosperity" aimed to achieve sustainable peace in the Middle East, which is essential for the peoples in the region to enjoy a peace dividend and for Arabs and Israelis to promote confidence among them, especially for Palestinians and Israelis. For more detailed information of the concept: MOFA, "Japan's Concept for Creating the Corridor for Peace and Prosperity" July, 2006, https://www.mofa.go.jp/region/middle_e/palestine/concept0607.html, accessed on June 18, 2021.

administration that was formed in 2014. Prime Minister Abe visited Egypt in 2015 and held a summit meeting with President al-Sisi. The joint statement by the two leaders confirmed the further development of bilateral strategic relations, the promotion of regional and international peace and stability, and the strengthening of economic cooperation by the public and private sectors.[17] The main aim of the statement was to consolidate the security cooperation in the context of combating against jihadist terrorist organizations such as al-Qaeda and "Islamic State."

In 2016, al-Sisi was invited and visited Japan. He received first-class hospitality during his stay in Japan. In addition to the summit meeting with Abe, he visited the emperor at his palace and attended an imperial palace dinner. He also addressed at the Japanese Diet and met senior Japanese business figures.[18] Consolidating the close relation with Egypt was one of the main pillars of Abe administration's comprehensive policy, "Diplomacy That Takes a Panoramic Perspective of the World Map."[19] He evaluated Egypt with strategic importance because of Egypt's counterterrorism capability as well as global trade presence with Suez Canal.

Since the end of the Cold War, the close relation between Japan and Egypt has been one of the pillars supporting Japan's pluralistic foreign policy. It is going into strategic and focusing on security issues today. The Japanese government has proposed several comprehensive and plural diplomacies toward the Middle East, and Egypt was always regarded as an essential partner of Japan. As a major regional power in the Middle East, Egypt's role and presence in Japan's diplomacy are expected to continue to enhance in the future.

[17] MOFA, "Japan-Egypt Joint Statement," January 18, 2015. http://www.mofa.go.jp/mofaj/me_a/me1/eg/page23_001314.html, accessed on June 17, 2021.

[18] MOFA, "Japan-Egypt Summit Meeting," February 29, 2016. http://www.mofa.go.jp/mofaj/me_a/me1/eg/page4_001826.html, accessed on June 17, 2021.

[19] Since his inauguration, Prime Minister Abe pursued a strategic foreign policy that "Takes a Panoramic Perspective of the World Map," upholding universal values such as freedom, democracy, respect of fundamental human rights, and the rule of law. For detailed information of the perspective: MOFA, *Diplomatic Bluebook for 2014*, https://www.mofa.go.jp/policy/other/bluebook/2014/html/chapter1/japans diplomacy.html, accessed on May 1, 2021.

5   Official Development Assistance:
One of the Most Important Tools
for Reinforcing the Bilateral Relations

Official Development Assistance (ODA) has played a crucial role in Japanese diplomacy with developing countries. According to "Cabinet decision on the Development Cooperation Charter" formulated in 2015, "it is necessary to fully recognize that development cooperation is one of the most important tools of Japan's foreign policy."[20] The total amount of Japanese assistance expenditure in 1954–2019 is USD 550.5 billion, around 80% of which is bilateral ODA, and 190 countries/areas have received it.[21] Egypt became a major recipient of Japanese ODA since 1970s. Faced with the first oil crisis, Japan sought to strengthen relations with Egypt, a major regional power in the Middle East, and ODA was an important pillar of this effort (Tsuchiya 2012: 369). According to the Japanese Foreign Ministry's report, "Egypt has some position like a center of Arabic diplomacy and plays an important role in regional issues such as the Middle East peace process or peace-building in Iraq and Sudan" and "Thus Japan regards Egypt as a diplomatically important country which plays a constructive and crucial role concerning the peace and stability in the Middle East."[22]

This view is shared by the Japan International Cooperation Agency (JICA), which handles Japan's bilateral assistance projects based on ODA in the world, and has provided bilateral aid with Egypt in the forms of technical cooperation, ODA loans, and grant aid. The contribution of Japanese ODA to Egypt can be reviewed through JICA's activities. Japan provided various schemes of assistance with Egypt from early period as Japan regarded Egypt as a pilot model in the Middle East. According to the Japanese Ministry Foreign Affairs (MOFA), Japan has provided Egypt

[20] MOFA, "Cabinet Decision on the Development Cooperation Charter," February 10, 2015. https://www.mofa.go.jp/mofaj/gaiko/oda/files/000067701.pdf, accessed on April 10, 2021.

[21] MOFA, "Nihon no Kaihatsu Kyoryoku" [Japan's Development Cooperation] (in Japanese), https://www.mofa.go.jp/mofaj/gaiko/oda/files/100161697.pdf, accessed on June 12, 2021.

[22] MOFA, "Country Assistance Evaluation of Egypt: Summary," March, 2011. https://www.mofa.go.jp/policy/oda/evaluation/FY2010/text-pdf/egypt.pdf, accessed on March 29, 2021.

Table 1 ODA provided to Egypt (USD mn)

	1960s	1970s	1980s	1990s	2000s	2010–2016
US	903	2023	10,090	11,965	4973	▲463
Japan	1	410	931	2080	163	▲291
G7 without Japan	222	755	2468	7369	2679	1838
Others	90	11,381	2181	8801	4451	15,432
Total	1215	14,569	15,671	30,215	12,265	16,516

with ODA totally amounted to USD 70.8 billion in 2017.[23] Egypt is the second largest recipient in the Middle East after Iraq, which received a huge amount of ODA for reconstruction after the Iraq War; that is, Egypt had been the first for a long time before Iraq War.

According to JICA's website, "Egypt is a great nation, which locates in geopolitically important position, linking the Middle East, Africa and Europe. Given this, strengthening Egypt's stability and development as well as its constructive role in the region is important for the regional peace and stability." It clearly shows that JICA sees Egypt as one of its main partners. Based on the policy, ODA has been provided to Egypt (see Table 1).[24] Japan's assistance to Egypt dates to the technical cooperation in 1954. In 1973, the Japanese government provided grant aid (240 million yen) for emergency disaster relief (relief of war-damage sufferers), followed by a yen loan in 1974 (7.5 billion yen for the first commodity credit), and a technical cooperation agreement was signed in 1983, which stipulated the dispatch of experts and research teams to Egypt and the acceptance of Egyptian trainees. In 1995, the Japan Overseas Cooperation Volunteers (JOCV) dispatch agreement was signed, and two of the JOCV members left for Egypt for the first time in the following year.[25]

---

[23] The Data is from the following website: MOFA, "Kuni Betsu Kaihatsu Jisseki" [Develop Cooperation by Country] (in Japanese), June 25, 2019. https://www.mofa. go.jp/mofaj/gaiko/oda/shiryo/jisseki/kuni/index_kaihatsu.html, accessed on June 12, 2021.

[24] https://www.stats.oecd.org/qwids/The reason for the decline in the amount of ODA provided to Egypt after the 2000s is that the amount of yen loans repaid has exceeded the amount of ODA expenditure [Tsuchiya 2012: 371].

[25] For more information, see JICA's website: https://www.jica.go.jp/volunteer/out line/publication/results/contracts.html, accessed on June 19, 2021.

The Japanese ODA was used to construct social infrastructures in Egypt. For example, the Opera House (National Cultural Center), located in the center of Cairo, is a building familiar to many Cairo residents. It was built with Japanese grant aid (about 6.5 billion yen) in 1988 and is used to hold Egypt's most renowned national concerts and performances such as a popular Egyptian opera "Aida." The Peace Bridge (Japan–Egypt Friendship Bridge) over the Suez Canal in Qantara in Ismailia governate is also a symbol of Japan's ODA project. The bridge was built with the support of ODA (approximately 14 billion yen totally) and opened to traffic in 2001. The opening of the bridge facilitated the access from the west bank of the Canal to the Sinai Peninsula on the east bank of the Canal and is aimed to drive the development of the Sinai Peninsula in line with the Sinai Peninsula Development Plan formulated by the Egyptian government in 1994.

In 2012, a yen loan contract (approximately 33 billion yen) was signed for the Cairo Metro Line, a means of daily public transportation for Cairo residents, for the first phase of Line 4 development project. While Lines 1, 2, and 3 of the Cairo Metro subway system have been opened and operated based on construction plans by the French consultant SOFRETU, Japanese subway construction technology is introduced to Line 4 for the first time (Mishima 2011). The population growth in Cairo and its surrounding areas has led to an urgent need for expanding public transportation capabilities, especially for a subway network that is not affected by road congestion and is expected to meet the increasing transportation demand there.

Japan's ODA also plays an active role in the field of tourism, a vital source of foreign currency revenue for Egypt. The Grand Egyptian Museum was constructed in the area adjacent to the three major pyramids of Giza, for which a yen loan has been provided; about 35 billion yen in 2006 and about 49 billion yen in 2016. The Museum is not only of academic value as a repository of valuable archaeological materials but is also expected to promote Egyptian tourism industry, suffered by the instability following the "25 January Revolution" and the damage caused by the COVID-19.

It is true that Japan is not in the first rank of ODA provider to Egypt, but Japan has been usually among top five donors.[26] On the other hand,

---

[26] MOFA, "Japan's ODA Data by Country," June 27, 2018. https://www.mofa.go.jp/mofaj/gaiko/oda/files/000142577.pdf, accessed on June 19, 2021.

Egypt is the second recipient in the Middle East. Although Egypt is not at the level of top receivers such as India or Indonesia, ODA for Egypt is still a huge amount. Yen loan is provided with a very lucrative condition, in comparison to the financial market. But Japan does not make the borrower including Egypt to over loaned or spoiled. Japan's ODA is also aimed to implement cooperation that caters to the needs and characteristics of each region.[27] Japan's ODA for Egypt was provided on the principle and contributed to development projects and infrastructure constructions in Egypt. ODA has been one of the important tools to reinforce the relations, and its achievements show Japan's presence in Egypt.

6   Cultural Exchange: Foundation of Mutual Understanding

Culture, as well as politics and economy, is an important field of Japanese diplomacy. Cultural exchange is critical to attain the understanding of foreign governments and promotes mutual understanding with foreign nationals. Japan emphasizes its culture as a source of soft power, which can be found in several government-led initiatives, such as *Cool Japan* strategy.[28]

Egypt has been one of Japan's main hubs for cultural exchanges in the Middle East, especially after the World War II. Japanese government founded kinds of cultural institutions in Egypt, which it regarded as an essential bridgehead to the Middle East. In 1965, the Japanese Embassy in Cairo established a Cultural Center, which was reorganized as the Information and Culture Center in 1988, to expand cultural exchange. In 1986, the Japan Society for the Promotion of Science (JSPS) established the Cairo Research Station. The stations have been established in 11 cities around the world as a center for academic research activities. The

---

[27] MOFA, "Cabinet Decision on the Development Cooperation Charter," February 10, 2015. https://www.mofa.go.jp/mofaj/gaiko/oda/files/000067701.pdf, accessed on April 10, 2021.

[28] The strategy was started by Japanese Ministry of Economy, Trade and Industry in 2010. Cool Japan Foundation has been in charge of the whole strategy since the establishment in 2013. The aim is to develop Japan's soft power by enhancing Japan's brand power and increasing the number of foreigners who have love for Japan through gaining sympathy from the world. For more information, see the Foundation's website, https://www.cj-fund.co.jp/, accessed on June 18, 2021.

Cairo station is the only one in the Middle East, and there are only two stations, Cairo and Nairobi, in the African Continent. It shows Egypt as a hub for the Japanese academic researches.

In 1995, the Japan Foundation established a branch in Cairo, which was the only one in the Middle East and Africa. The foundation aims to introduce and publicize Japanese culture, including demonstrations of tea ceremony (*sado*) and flower arrangement (*kado*), and screenings of Japanese movies. Many Egyptians have studied in the Japanese language courses at the center, and some of the graduates have used their Japanese language skills to work for Japanese companies there or become Japanese language tour guides. The foundation is at the forefront of cultural exchange between grassroots. "Japanese Culture Week 2000" and "Japan Festival 2001" were held in Cairo to promote Japanese culture and were ended successfully. In recent years, Japanese subcultures such as animation and pop culture have been more popular in Egypt especially among young people. Japanese animation films, such as "Dragon Ball," "Captain Tsubasa," and "Pocket Monsters," were broadcast on television and became a huge boom among children.

The pioneer in Japanese language education and Japanese studies in Egypt is the Department of Japanese Language in the Faculty of Arts at Cairo University, founded in 1974. The department has produced many graduates well-versed in Japan, including professors Issam Hamza and Karam Khalil, who served as Cultural Councilor at the Egyptian Embassy in Tokyo from 2005 to 2008, both are erudite scholars in Japanese language and studies and are well-known for it.

In 2017, the department established the Center for Japanese Studies to advance its research activities.[29] Other departments of Japanese language were also established; at Ain Shams University in 2000, the Egyptian Technology University in 2005, Aswan University in 2013, and Benha University in 2016. The establishment of these Japanese language departments reflects the growing interest in Japan among Egyptians and is the basis of cultural exchange.

President al-Sisi is most ambitious to enhance educational and cultural exchanges. He eagerly pushed to conclude the agreement on the Egypt–Japan Education Partnership (EJEP) on the occasion of his first official

---

[29] Cairo University, "Cairo University Establishes Center for Japanese Studies with Japan," March 2, 2017. https://cu.edu.eg/Cairo-University-News-11893.html, accessed on June 19, 2021.

visit to Tokyo. The agreement aims to improve primary and secondary education in Egypt; introduction of Japanese education system including *Tokkatsu*, spontaneous extracurricular activities by students in the educational curriculum, establishment of model schools to apply it, and dispatch at least 2500 Egyptian researchers, teachers, and students to Japan over the next five years.[30] In particular, Egypt is the pilot model to export Tokkatsu system in the Middle East. It shows the mutual intimacy and trust between the two countries.

The Egypt–Japan University of Science and Technology (EJUST) was also established in the city of Borg Arab in Alexandria governorate in cooperation with Japanese industry, government, and academia. EJUST started accepting graduate students in 2010, and the inauguration ceremony was held in 2020 in the presence of al-Sisi and other ministers. The university accepted undergraduate students and would expand its educational activities. The university is expected to contribute to develop higher education in the field of science and technology.

Regarding sports exchanges, Japanese experts in *judo* and *karate* were dispatched to Egypt since the late 1970s and laid the foundation for the Japanese traditional sports in Egypt. Mohamed Rashwan is a legendary player who showed true sportsmanship in the final match with Japanese famous *judoka* Yamashita Yasuhiro at the 1984 Los Angeles Olympics. He is a well-known judoka in both countries. In 2013, Egyptian-born *sumo* (Japanese traditional wrestling) wrestler *Osuna-Arashi* (Big Sandstorm), whose real name is Abd al-Rahman Sharan, became the first sumo wrestler from the Middle East and Africa to rise to the top division of sumo tournament. Osuna-Arashi caught the attention of sumo fans at the July tournament in 2013, held during Ramadan, where he showed good results despite refraining from eating and drinking. After the tournament, he was invited to an *iftar* (the evening meal eaten by Muslims after sunset during Ramadan) dinner party at the Prime Minister's Office with the ambassadors from Islamic countries. He represented a fusion of two traditional values, Sumo and Islam.

---

[30] MOFA, "Ejiputo Nihon kyouiku Patonashippu: Ejiputo no Wakamono no Nouryoku Kyouka, Nihon-shiki Kyouiku no Dounyu" [Egypt-Japan Education Partnership (EJEP): Capability Enhancement of Egyptian Youth and Introduction of Japanese Education System] (in Japanese). http://www.mofa.go.jp/mofaj/files/000136266.pdf, accessed on June 19, 2021.

These sports exchanges have raised interest in Egypt among the Japanese. It is true that the role of cultural and sports exchanges in the bilateral relations between Japan and Egypt has not been always noticeable. However, it has developed mutual understanding and friendship at the grassroots in both countries. The cultural and sports exchanges have been regarded as a diplomatic tool between Japan and Egypt, but it is not only that but it unites the heart and respect of the two nations.

7   Conclusion

The bilateral relation between Japan and Egypt began in the late Edo period. Although the long history between Japan and Egypt was interrupted by World War II, the relationship has been friendly in general. Since the 1950s, Japan regarded Egypt as a main bridgehead or hub for its Middle Eastern policies. Japan and Egypt have developed a good relationship in various fields. Economic, trade, and business exchanges between Japan and Egypt are the largest volumes in the region, and steadily increasing FDI promotes them. In the field of diplomacy, Japan regarded Egypt as its essential partner and concluded necessary treaties and agreements at the earliest stage in the Middle East. The close bilateral relationship has been consolidated by more comprehensive partnership agreements. In recent years, Japan and Egypt focused on security and anti-terrorism cooperation. ODA underpins the bilateral relation. Egypt had been the first among Japan's ODA recipient countries in the Middle East for a long time, and Japan has been usually among the top 5 donors to Egypt. Cultural exchanges are also the driving factors to promote mutual understanding at the level of grassroots and deepen the bilateral relations based on friendship among Japanese and Egyptian nationals. Under al-Sisi's presidency, educational cooperation is rapidly expanding in particular. Considering the fact that the close bilateral relation with Egypt is substantially the critical core of Japan's Middle Eastern Policy, the bilateral relation should be studied more adequately and accurately. Development of the studies on the relationship between the two countries will surely underpin mutual understanding and cooperation and promote bilateral relations in all fields.

References

Books and Articles

Iokibe, Makoto. ed. 2014. *Sengo Nihon Gaikoshi [History of Post-War Japanese Diplomacy]*. Tokyo: Yuhikaku (in Japanese).

Katayama, Yoshitaka. 2014. "Japan-United Kingdom Relations in the Process of Colonization of Korea: A Study Focusing on United Kingdom's Policy toward Korea." *Journal of Inquiry and Research* 100: 167–182 (in Japanese).

Kuriyama, Takakazu. 2016. *Sengo Nihon Gaikoushi: Kiseki to Kadai [Post-War Japanese Diplomacy: Tracks and Challenges]*. Tokyo: Iwanami Shoten (in Japanese).

Mishima, Teruki. 2011. "Ejiputo Kairo Chikatetsu 4 Gousen Seibi Jigyou [Constructing Project of Line 4 of Cairo Metro in Egypt]." *JREA* 54 (2): 35768–35771 (in Japanese).

Sakai, Keiko. 2016. *Usturou Chutou, Kawaru Nihon: 2012–15 [Changing Middle East, and Changing Japan: 2012–15]*. Tokyo: Misuzu Shobo (in Japanese).

Sugita, Hideaki. 1995. *Nihonjin no Chutou Hakken: Gyaku Enkinhou nonakano Hikaku Bunkashi [Discovery of the Middle East by Japanese: History of Comparative Culture from the Reversed Perspective]*. Tokyo: University of Tokyo Press (in Japanese).

Tsuchiya, Ichiki. 2012. "ODA wo Chushin to Suru Nikokukan Kankei: Nihon to Ejiputo [The Bilateral Relations Focusing on ODA: Japan and Egypt]." In *Gendai Ejiputo wo Shirutameno 60 Shou [60 Chapters to Know the Contemporary Egypt]*, ed. Suzuki Emi, 369–373. Tokyo: Akashi Shoten (in Japanese).

Website/URL

Cairo Research Station, Japan Society for the Promotion of Science. https://jsp scairo.com/en/.

Cairo University. https://cu.edu.eg/Home.

Food and Agriculture Organization of the United States (FAO), "Food and Agriculture Data." http://www.fao.org/faostat/en/#home.

Prime Minister of Japan and his Cabinet. http://japan.kantei.go.jpf.

The Embassy of Japan in Egypt. https://www.eg.emb-japan.go.jp/itprtop_en/index.html.

The Japan Foundation, Cairo. https://www.facebook.com/jfcairo.

The Japan International Cooperation Agency (JICA). https://www.jica.go.jp/index.html.

The Ministry of Foreign Affairs of Japan (MOFA). https://www.mofa.go.jp/index.html.

CHAPTER 7

Beyond Power, Before Interdependence: Complex Synergy and Japan–Israel Relations

Matthew Brummer and Eitan Oren

1 Introduction to Japan–Israel Relations in the Post-War Period

Japan and Israel share much in common. Both are parliamentary democracies, both adhere to free-market economic principles and both count the United States as a strategic alliance partner and security patron. Given the shared institutional systems across political, economic, and security affairs, one might assume—and much International Relations theory would predict—a robust bilateral relationship spanning government, industry, and citizen affairs. Yet, for most of the post-WWII period, relations

M. Brummer (✉)
GRIPS Innovation, Science and Technology Policy Program (GIST), Tokyo, Japan
e-mail: m-brummer@grips.ac.jp

E. Oren
Department of War Studies, King's College London, London, UK
e-mail: eitan.oren@kcl.ac.uk

© The Author(s), under exclusive license to Springer Nature   163
Singapore Pte Ltd. 2023
S. Nakamura and S. Wright (eds.), *Japan and the Middle East*,
Contemporary Gulf Studies, https://doi.org/10.1007/978-981-19-3459-9_7

between Japan and Israel have remained remarkably undeveloped, with feeble trade and investment, non-committal political engagement, and a void where there would otherwise be strategic-military cooperation. Why?

After over half a century of distant and guarded relations, however, Japan and Israel have recently moved to significantly upgrade ties in a break from the status quo past. The countries have entered into a number of important security and trade agreements since 2012, remaking the once sparse bilateral institutional and policy environment into one more characteristic of allied partners. From a series of high-level dialogues on national and cyber security to their first bilateral investment agreement and to prestigious awards bestowed on Israeli nationals by Japan's Imperial Household, Japan–Israel relations are thriving.[1] Again, why?

Scholarship seeking answers to these questions has focused almost exclusively on two factors: Japan's dependence on OPEC—comprised of states hostile to Israel—for oil and gas imports, and Japan's dependence on the United States for security, a state intimately aligned with Israel.[2] These two often contending dynamics "push and pull" Japan's foreign policy as it relates to Israel, and thus they dictate the bilateral relationship, or so the orthodoxy goes.[3] To be sure, both the "oil factor" and the "Washington factor" are necessary for understanding Japan–Israel relations, but they are not sufficient.

The relationship is more complex and nuanced than these two factors alone can hope to capture, and it is driven by forces operating at different levels of analysis—from security concerns to market and economic structure and to agency in national leadership. Additionally, the relative importance of these diverse factors fluctuates over time, further complicating a blunt two-factor analysis moored to Realist power explanations of strategic resource dependence and alliance politics. And the balance of what has driven Japanese relations toward Israel, and Israeli relations toward Japan, is not necessarily common across factors and time.

---

[1] For an introduction to this relationship, see: Matthew Brummer and Eitan Oren. "Israel and Japan's Rising Sun Relations," *Foreign Affairs*, 28 July 2017, https://www.foreignaffairs.com/articles/japan/2017-07-28/israel-and-japans-rising-sun-relations.

[2] See, for example: Raquel Shaoul, "Japan and Israel: An Evaluation of Relationship-Building in the Context of Japan's Middle East Policy," *Israel Affairs 10*, nos. 1–2 (2004): 273–97.

[3] See, for example: Yaacov Cohen, "Japanese-Israeli Relations, the United States, and Oil," *Jewish Political Studies Review 17*, nos. 1/2 (2005): 135–55.

1.1   Japan's Relations with Israel

Japan's relations with Israel must be understood across myriad inter-related forces that influence its foreign policy in general and bilateral relations with Israel in particular. Japan's energy insecurity and close strategic alliance with Washington both influence the relationship in important ways, but the strength of their explanatory significance varies over time and across levels of diplomacy. Early in the bilateral relationship, for example, neither oil nor Washington factors appeared to greatly affect government or citizen relations between the two nations. From the early 1970s to the late 1980s, however, the influence of both oil and Washington on the bilateral relationship grew significantly. Today, in contrast, Japan's dependence on OPEC oil has never been higher, and Japanese perceptions of Washington as a reliable alliance partner have never been weaker; nevertheless, Japan–Israel relations are currently flourishing.[4]

Beyond oil and alliances, security and geopolitical considerations, more broadly in the Middle East and the Asia Pacific region, also influence Japan's interest in pursuing or eschewing relations with Israel, for the security concerns of the Gulf region also concern Tokyo elites, and the reemergence of China's great power consciousness weighs heavily on Japanese foreign policymaking decisions. It is worth remembering, for example, that the "oil factor" is simply a result of the conflict between Israel and her OPEC neighbors. That is, oil as a matter of causal concern to Japan–Israel relations must be couched in a broader security understanding of the Middle East and Gulf region, for without tension between Israel and OPEC, the oil factor ceases to exist. Additionally, the geopolitical climate in Japan's own backyard plays importantly to its foreign policy and diplomatic relations generally, and with Israel (and countries in the

---

[4] For long-run summary statistics on Japan's dependence on OPEC oil imports, see: Agency for Natural Resources and Energy, "FY 2017 Japan's Independent Development Ratio of Oil and Natural Gas," Press release, Ministry of Economy, Trade and Industry, 27 July 2018. For an analysis of how the US-Japan relationship has weakened, see Nicholas D. Anderson, "Anarchic Threats and Hegemonic Assurances: Japan's Security Production in the Post-war Era," *International Relations of the Asia-Pacific* 17, no. 1 (2016): 101–35. For a recent survey of Japan's threat environment and perceptions, see: Eitan Oren, "Japan's Evolving Threat Perception: Data from Diet Deliberations 1946–2017," *International Relations of the Asia-Pacific*, Published electronically 16 July 2019. https://academic.oup.com/irap/article-abstract/doi/10.1093/irap/lcz016/5533104. See also: Oren, Eitan. *Japan's Threat Perception during the Cold War: A psychological account.* (New York: Routledge, 2023).

broader Middle East) in particular, because as China reemerges onto the world stage and begins to play a more active role in shaping outcomes in the international system, Japan must respond in turn.[5] Japan–China relations are fraught with discord and historical misgivings, and for many Japanese elites, China's more active international presence is viewed as a direct challenge to national interest in both the security and economic realms.[6] Thus, national security and geopolitical conditions in both the Middle East and Asia strongly influence Japanese foreign policy and bilateral relations with Israel.

Economic interests led by Japan's powerful Keidanren (Federation of Economic Organizations) business lobby have also shaped Japan's diplomatic relations with Israel. Comprised of Japan's most influential corporations and associations, this institution wields substantial influence over the country's diplomatic affairs. For much of the post-War era, Keidanren actively eschewed relations with Israel, considering it a country with whom doing business carried unacceptable risks. As a natural resource-poor nation, heavily reliant on imports of oil and gas to fuel production and manufacturing, Japanese industrialists favored non-investment in and non-engagement with Israel as a means to appease Middle East nations and protect the vital energy trade with OPEC. Additionally, until Israel rapidly developed economically in the late 1980s, Keidanren saw little benefit in doing business with Israel, which could not afford many of Japan's major exports, including electronics, automobiles, and heavy machinery, and could not contribute valuable inputs to Japan's production machine, which required energy, human resources, high-tech facilities, and beyond. Thus, due to unacceptable risks and unattractive rewards, Keidanren long preferred not to engage with Israeli counterparts and even actively lobbied for arms-length diplomatic relations.

Taken together, then, Japan's relations with Israel are not simply pushed and pulled by oil and Washington; rather, and more precisely, they are formed by security and geopolitical concerns, and by domestic vested interest groups and business lobbies. All of these factors—security,

---

[5] Eric Heginbotham and Richard J. Samuels, "Active Denial: Redesigning Japan's Response to China's Military Challenge," *International Security* 42, no. 4 (2018): 128–69.

[6] See: Sheila A. Smith, *Japan Rearmed: The Politics of Military Power* (Cambridge: Harvard University Press, 2019); Matthew Brummer and Eitan Oren, "We Must Protect This Peace with Our Hands: Strategic Culture and Japan's Use of Force in International Disputes," *Journal of Advanced Military Studies* 13 (2022): 88–111.

economic, and political—have recently undergone considerable change. Traditional fault lines in the Middle East have shifted, accompanied by a relative improvement in relations between Israel and several oil-producing countries in the Gulf, while China's reemergence has taken on expansionist elements. Energy markets have diversified, weakening cartel influence, and global production systems and technology have evolved rapidly, with Keidanren now far more focused on the knowledge economy than on domestic heavy industry production. Finally, Shinzo Abe emerged as Japan's most outward-looking prime minister in the post-War era, championing a newly assertive foreign policy doctrine.[7] All of these changes across security, economics, and politics benefit from enhanced diplomacy with Israel.

1.2   Israel's Relations with Japan

Israel's relationship with Japan must be understood in light of Israeli interests as they relate to foreign policy in general and to Japan in particular. Failing to do so, and relying solely on Japan-centered explanations (such as oil dependence), would mean neglecting to capture important drivers of continuity and change in bilateral diplomatic affairs.

Two broadly conceived forces that define national interest have shaped Israel's approach to its bilateral relationship with Japan. The first is security. Surrounded by rivals, Israel long staked its survival on maintaining close relations with Western Europe and, later, the United States.[8] The many and varied international tensions between the West and East during the Cold War meant that Israeli commitment to building stronger ties with the Asian powers was subordinate to deepening relations with the West. From the early 1990s and coinciding with the launch of Israeli-Palestinian/Arab peace talks (Madrid Conference, Autumn 1991),

---

[7] Eitan Oren and Matthew Brummer, "Threat Perception, Government Centralization, and Political Instrumentality in Abe Shinzo's Japan," *Australian Journal of International Affairs* 74, no. 6 (2020), https://doi.org/10.1080/10357718.2020.1782345. Eitan Oren and Matthew Brummer, "How Japan Talks About Security Threats," *The Diplomat*, August 14, 2020. https://thediplomat.com/2020/08/how-japan-talks-about-security-thr eats.

[8] Between 2013 and 2017, Israel imported 60% of its arms from the US, and 40% from the EU. See Pieter D. Wezeman, Aude Fleurant, Alexandra Kuimova, Nan Tian, and Siemon T. Wezeman, "Trends in International Arms Transfer, 2017," *SIPRI Fact Sheet*, March 2018, 6.

Japan's foreign policy stance on the Israeli-Arab conflict became more neutral in what paved the way for Israeli elites to view the bilateral relationship more positively. More recently, as a result of growing discord with Western governments surrounding issues such as Iran's nuclear program and the Israeli-Palestinian conflict (mostly with Western European/EU but also with the US during the Obama Administration 2009–2017), the Israeli government has begun to "look East" in an attempt to diversify its pool of friends in the international arena. Thus, its security considerations—including the threats it perceives and its relations with its Arab neighbors—shape its balancing act between the West and East, and it is within this context that Israeli attitudes toward bilateral relations with Japan should be viewed.

Second, Israel's economic union with the US and Western Europe has also taken precedence over developing relations in Asia. This has resulted in an extreme trade bias toward the Western hemisphere, whereby the European Union is currently Israel's largest trading partner and the US is its largest single-country trading partner. But the apparent disparity between Israel's economic relations with the West, on the one hand, and its relations with the East, on the other, has also been a result of more nuanced economic conditions. To begin with, throughout much of the post-War period, the Israeli and Japanese markets had little to offer to each other. Japan's early post-War economic policy placed primary emphasis on securing the supply of resources, which Israel lacked. Similarly, before Japanese car manufacturers came to dominate the Israeli market in the late 1980s, Japan had little to offer Israel. Partly the result of the lack of compatibility in their economic systems and partly the result of the sheer geographical distance between them (triple the distance between Israel and Western Europe), in economic as much as in geopolitical terms, Israel's gaze was fixated toward the West.

These factors shaping Israel's views toward Japan have registered significant changes in recent years. Since the 2010s, for instance, Israel's security, trade, and political affairs with East-Asian powers, including Japan, have begun to boom. This upgraded engagement has been driven by a shift in Israel's security calculus, the rapid development of its high-tech industries and their resulting compatibility with Asian markets, and a desire, backed by a strong leader and emerging lobby groups, of Israeli elites to expand the nation's network of partners beyond the West and toward East Asia.

2 Royal, Government, and Citizen Diplomacy

For the purpose of this study, diplomatic relations are categorized into three separate spheres: Royal, government, and citizen. Royal relations are symbolic acts and practices that exhibit goodwill and shared understanding between nations. These gestures, rituals, ceremonies, and the like rarely attempt to solve problems directly, formulate interests, or make policies; rather, they help to construct the standards of normality that shape expectations, conduct, and levels of harmony and discord. As such, they legitimize some relations and delegitimize others, either by their presence or a lack thereof.[9] Royal relations pertain largely to the Imperial Family of Japan, and are measured by such variables as royal visits, royal audiences, and royal awards granted in demonstrating weak, moderate, or strong symbolic-ceremonial relations between Japan and Israel.

Government relations relate to national government policies and programs covering political, economic, and security affairs. They are operationalized as patterns of interaction and communication between national government bodies and organs. Thus, government diplomacy as defined herein contributes to standardizing the conduct between states, thereby legitimizing or delegitimizing diplomatic affairs at the government level. In this way, and in a manner similar to royal diplomacy, government relations can indicate "who are our friends and who are not." In this study, we trace such government relations across Japanese-Israeli economic and security spheres, including formal pacts, agreements, policies, institutions, and mutually defined and communicated interests in demonstrating weak, moderate, or strong bilateral government relations.

Finally, citizen relations pertain to a broad sweep of non-royal, non-government diplomacy between states and incorporate the private sector, NGOs, and people-to-people cooperation and exchange. Fundamentally, they are transnational links among individuals or collective citizen actors originating in private society. Citizen relations can be measured by such variables as industrial cooperation and trade, foreign direct investment (FDI), humanitarian and educational initiatives, tourism, and immigration flows exemplified by expatriate workers and foreign residency rates. In this study, we cast a broad net in capturing these diverse variables in

---

[9] For this framing and a review of symbolic acts in international relations, see: Ulrich Krotz, *Flying Tiger: International Relations Theory and the Politics of Advanced Weapons* (New York: Oxford University Press, 2011).

demonstrating weak, moderate, or strong citizen relations between Japan and Israel.

3   THE LONG FREEZE AND SLOW THAW

In the following section, we briefly trace the history of Japan–Israel relations over three periods: 1952 to the mid-1960s; the mid-1960s to the late 1980s; and the late 1980s through the first decade of the twenty-first century. Each period demonstrates distinct differences from the others in terms of our dependent variable—diplomatic relations—as well as significant changes in our causal factors of international security and economic interest. Thus, the periods are defined by changes in our dependent and independent variables, i.e., they are "data-driven." The subsequent section, titled "The Diplomatic Turn," examines in more depth the second decade of the twenty-first century and the significant rapprochement underway between the two countries. As these case sections demonstrate, a more nuanced interpretation of the bilateral relationship illuminates four distinct periods: Cool but diplomatically correct; cold and at times openly hostile; warm and yet uncommitted; and, ultimately, today's hot, rising sun relations.[10]

3.1   Cool but Diplomatically Correct, 1952–Mid-1960s

3.1.1   Security
The security environments facing Japan and Israel at the outset of formal relations in the 1950s were tense. Both countries encountered uncertainty as to which states were dependable allies and which were threatening rivals. The "Security Treaty Between the United States and Japan" was signed in 1951 and remained in effect throughout the 1950s, but it left much to be desired in Tokyo, where it was viewed by political conservatives as unequal and, more importantly, unreliable, as it both restricted Japan's ability to defend itself and yet did not explicitly guarantee its

---

[10] This division into four distinct periods differs from most studies on Japan-Israel relations, which tend to analyze only two periods: Before and after the dissolution of the Soviet Union, and the conclusion of the Madrid Talks in 1991.

sovereignty.[11] At the same time, Japan faced security and political threats from the Soviet Union: This dual-pronged Soviet threat, one military, the other ideological, weighed heavily on Japanese defense planners.[12]

Israel, too, faced external security threats during the period, as well as the menace of Communism as a destabilizing force in domestic politics. Moreover, similar to the sentiment in Japan, Israeli elites did not view Washington as a highly dependable security partner during the 1950s.[13] The Suez Crisis of 1956 saw the invasion of Egypt, which had nationalized the strategically important Suez Canal, by Israeli and then British and French forces.[14] Additionally, Israeli perceptions of the Soviet Union and the threats posed by communism to the Zionist enterprise differed across the political spectrum. After an initial period of adherence to non-alignment in its foreign policy—partly taken in order to avoid domestic upheaval from pro-communist forces—the leading party Mapai's pro-Western stance ultimately prevailed.[15] Israeli-Soviet relations grew tense as a result, and they were even temporarily suspended in 1953.

Thus, both Japan and Israel faced international security threats and unreliable security alliances throughout the 1950s and into the early 1960s. In addition, they also confronted the nuclear question, with Japan exploring the option to acquire nuclear weapons after China had done so in October 1964 (but deciding against it), as did Israel, which by the second half of the 1960s employed a deterrent strategy of "strategic ambiguity" with a nuclear weapons program and several nuclear devices.[16] At the same time, both countries openly lamented the unreliability of the

---

[11] Prime Minister Hatoyama Ichiro was one prominent advocate of this view. See: Makoto Iokibe, Caroline Rose, Junko Tomaru, and John Weste, eds., *Japanese Diplomacy in the 1950s: From Isolation to Integration* (New York: Routledge, 2008), 3–5.

[12] Eitan Oren and Matthew Brummer, "Reexamining Threat Perceptions in Early Cold-War Japan," *Journal of Cold War Studies* 22, no. 4 (2020).

[13] See: Uri Bialer, *Between East and West: Israel's Foreign Policy Orientation 1948–1956* (New York: Cambridge University Press, 1990), 267.

[14] Derek Varble, *The Suez Crisis* (New York: Rosen Publishing, 2008).

[15] Louise Fischer, ed., *Moshe Sharett: The Second Prime Minister, Selected Documents (1894–1965)* (Jerusalem: Israel State Archives, 2009), 422–26.

[16] For Japan's consideration of the nuclear option, see: Nobumasa Akiyama, "Disarmament and the Non-Proliferation Policy of Japan," in *The Routledge Handbook of Japanese Foreign Policy*, ed. Mary M. McCarthy (New York: Routledge, 2018), 173–87. For Israel's nuclear program, see: Avner Cohen, *Israel and the Bomb* (New York: Columbia University Press, 1998).

US alliance partnership, and they were confronted with a shared danger from pro-Communist ideological movements emanating from the Soviet propaganda machine.

3.1.2   Economy

While Japan and Israel shared similarities in their security calculi during this period, the two countries had very little in common in terms of economic interests. Japan had quickly recovered from the devastation of WWII, and by 1960 it had become a major international economic power grounded in heavy industry and manufacturing with a GDP 350% higher than pre-war levels.[17] Furthermore, it embraced a national project of technological advancement by encouraging the introduction of innovative technologies from overseas and strengthening domestic capabilities for research and development (R&D). Imports and direct investment from abroad were managed with the aim of forcing foreign firms to sell their technologies to Japanese companies, rather than to enter into the Japanese market directly. In absorbing, assimilating, and iterating on the technologies introduced from abroad, the nation's technological and human infrastructure boomed, and in order to fuel its economic recovery and growth, it transitioned away from a coal-based energy system to oil, and then gas, and began to prioritize these energy imports as a matter of national strategy.[18]

Israel, too, saw its economy take off during this period. The essentially agrarian- and textile-based economy forged ahead, growing by 13% each year between 1950 and 1955, and by approximately 10% each year for the decade between 1955 and 1965.[19] This expansion was driven by a combination of two factors: Population growth, due largely to immigration,[20] and large capital inflows comprised of US aid in the forms of unilateral transfers and loans, reparations from Germany, and the sale

---

[17] Ichirō Nakayama, *Industrialization of Japan* (Tokyo: Centre for East Asian Cultural Studies, 1963), 7.

[18] See: Masaru Yarime, "Integrated Solutions to Complex Problems: Transforming Japanese Science and Technology," in *Japan: The Precarious Future*, ed. Frank Baldwin and Anne Allison (New York: New York University Press, 2015), 213–35.

[19] Dan Senor and Saul Singer, *Start-up Nation: The Story of Israel's Economic Miracle* (New York: Hatchette Book Group, 2009).

[20] Meron Medzini, "From Alienation to Partnership: Israel-Japan Relation," *Contemporary Review of the Middle East* 5, no. 3 (2018): 232–40.

of State of Israel Bonds.[21] Yet, while relative growth was considerable, economic fundamentals were weak and the government took a highly interventionist approach to managing the economy, even implementing a rationing program for staple foods and energy. Golda Meir once described Israel during this period as a community "coping—not always well—with all sorts of economic, political, and social discontents."[22]

Thus, while both economies experienced strong economic growth during this period, the embodiment of their growth had little in common. Japan's heavy production and increasingly high-technology-focused economy required energy, investment, and a highly skilled labor force, while Israel could offer little in the way of these inputs, as it lacked energy, financial, and S&T human resources. Likewise, the latter could not afford to purchase Japan's new and expensive exports of automobiles and electronics equipment, and Japan had little demand for Israeli textiles and could offer little to its economy, which sought food imports and agricultural sector FDI.

3.1.3   Diplomacy

As outlined above, the 1952 to mid-1960s period of Japan-Israeli relations exhibited relatively strong synergy in security affairs but relatively weak synergy in economic systems. Amidst common security challenges but fragile economic compatibility, diplomatic relations got off to a moderately strong start, led by political actors and government bureaucracies. In January 1952, Israel's Foreign Minister, Moshe Sharett, proposed mutual recognition and the establishment of diplomatic missions with Japan.[23] After considerable deliberation within Japan's industry-bureaucracy-political organs, the Japanese government agreed to

---

[21] Nadav Halevi and Ruth Klinov-Malul, *The Economic Development of Israel* (New York: Praeger, 1968).

[22] Golda Meir, quoted in: Michael C. Desch, *Power and Military Effectiveness: The Fallacy of Democratic Triumphalism* (Baltimore: John Hopkins University Press, 2008), 129.

[23] Sharett, as Medzini notes, had initially objected to the Japanese declaration of intent to enter diplomatic relations, due to its cooperation with Nazi Germany, but later changed his mind. See: Meron Medzini, "Reflections on Israel's Policy Toward Japan Since 1952," in *Japanese Studies in Israel as a Micro-cosmos of Japanese Studies in the World: Lectures Delivered at the Israel-Japan Symposium*, ed. Helena Grinschpun, Shalmit Bejarano, and Nissim Otmazgin (Jerusalem: Hebrew University of Jerusalem, 2012), http://japan-stu dies-org.stackstaging.com/wp-content/uploads/2019/04/medzini-fulltext.pdf.

mutual recognition and to host an Israeli minister in Tokyo. As John de Boer has pointed out, this agreement represented a breakthrough for Israel's diplomatic efforts, for although it had gained recognition from several Asian states (such as India and Burma) by that time, it had yet to secure diplomatic relations with any of them.[24] Japan's acceptance of Israel's overture opened the door for the latter's first formal mission in Asia and made it the first Middle Eastern country to open diplomatic operations in Tokyo. In turn, Japan appointed a resident minister to Israel in 1955, and it later established a full embassy in 1963, the first Asian state to do so. Although cautious in approach and intermittent in practice, official diplomatic visits began in 1956 when Moshe Sharett visited Japan, later followed by economic and political envoys in 1958, 1962, 1966, and 1967.[25]

Yet, despite relatively rosy government relations, citizen and royal relations showed little signs of life. Transnational links among individuals or collective citizen actors originating in private society remained undeveloped throughout the period, there was no tourism to speak of, and NGO networks were virtually non-existent.[26] A small, bright spot in citizen affairs was the establishment of Japanese studies programs at three universities in Israel: In 1964 at the Hebrew University, and in 1965 at Tel Aviv and Haifa universities. Trade, however, consisting of primarily polished diamonds, wool, and yarn from Israel, and ship hulls, machinery, and parts from Japan averaged a meager total volume of $26.6 million per year during the period between 1962 and 1967, thus reflecting the low level of economic synergy between the countries.[27] Royal relations, too, were slow to develop. The Japanese Emperor granted only a single audience to an Israeli national during this period (FM Golda Meir, 1962), a rigid and brief meeting that "lacked warmth."[28] The bilateral relationship at the time was largely barren of such high-level symbolic acts of goodwill and shared understanding.

---

[24] John de Boer, "Before Oil: Japan and the Question of Israel/Palestine, 1917–1956," *The Asia–Pacific Journal 3*, no. 3 (2005): 2159.

[25] For details, see the Ministry of Foreign Affairs website: www.mofa.go.jp/.

[26] Visa Exemption Arrangements between both countries were only signed in 1971.

[27] Data from The Observatory of Economic Complexity, MIT: https://atlas.media.mit.edu/en.

[28] Meron Medzini, *Golda Meir: A Political Biography* (Berlin: De Gruyter, 2017), 321.

Taken together, Japan and Israel shared common security challenges and experienced relatively productive government-driven relations at this time, while the compatibility of economic systems and interests remained far apart, as did the development of royal and citizen diplomacy. Meron Medzini described the bilateral relationship during this period as "cool but diplomatically correct," a phrasing particularly illustrative in capturing the Japan–Israel diplomatic milieu of the time.[29]

3.2   Cold and at Times Openly Hostile: 1967–Late 1980s

3.2.1   Security

Unlike the relatively compatible security concerns at the outset of formal relations, the security environments facing Japan and Israel from the late 1960s to the late 1980s shared little in common. Japan and the United States had signed the new Treaty of Mutual Cooperation and Security, confirming the US commitment to protect Japan against all international military threats to territory and sovereignty, and the contentious issue of land use and ownership was effectively settled with the return of Okinawa in 1972. The new and improved security alliance with the US, coupled with the strong personal bond between President Ronald Reagan and Prime Minister Yasuhiko Nakasone (1982–1987), greatly ameliorated engagement and abandonment fears in Japan.[30] At the same time, the security environment facing Japan worsened: The Soviet Union had increased its Far East military capabilities, and China had detonated several nuclear and hydrogen bombs throughout the second half of the 1960s.[31] Thus, Japan's security environment turned from one largely hinging on ideological confrontation in the 1950s and early 1960s to one largely rooted in "brute material" capabilities from the late 1960s.

While Japan's security environment "hardened" during the period, the country remained at peace. In contrast to this stable security environment, Israel was at war. The Six-Day War in 1967, the War of Attrition between 1967 and 1970, and the Yom Kippur War in 1973 all meant that Israel faced a constant threat to its survival. It found itself fighting not only

---

[29] Medzini, "From Alienation to Partnership," 234.

[30] Victor D. Cha, "Abandonment, Entrapment, and Neoclassical Realism in Asia: The United States, Japan, and Korea." *International Studies Quarterly 44*, no. 2 (2000): 261–91.

[31] Oren and Brummer, "Reexamining Threat Perception."

against its Arab neighbors but also against the formidable Soviet military, which contributed men and weapons to the battlefields.[32] Alignment with the United States strengthened during this period, as Israel found itself caught in the middle of the two superpowers wrestling for hegemony in a war-torn Middle East at the height of Cold War hostilities.[33]

Japan's security interests at this time were primarily focused on maintaining regional stability through deepening its alliance with Washington and incremental, "comprehensive security" policies of providing foreign aid to countries it deemed important to securing a stable supply of energy, while at the same time diversifying its sources of energy.[34] Additionally, now facing the reality of being surrounded by nuclear-equipped rivals (China and the USSR), Tokyo moved to embrace the international nonproliferation regime, adopting the "Three Non-Nuclear Principles" in 1968.[35] Israeli security interests required importing military weaponry, engaging in brutal and near-constant combat operations, and building alliances with like-minded states. Japan could offer Israel nothing on these fronts, as it was still committed to its "pacifist Constitution" which forbade the use of military capabilities in international dispute settlements and was bound by its "Three Principles of Arms Exports," ratified in 1967, that essentially prohibited the export of military weaponry abroad. Thus, what Japan needed most for security, Israel could not provide, and what Israel needed most, Japan could not provide. Finally, exacerbating these already incompatible security interests was the unprecedented attack by the Japanese Red Army, a terrorist group aligned with the Popular Front of the Liberation of Palestine (PFLP), on Israeli soil, which killed twenty-six people and wounded seventy more.[36] In some

---

[32] Isabella Ginor and Gideon Remez, *Foxbats over Dimona: The Soviets' Nuclear Gamble in the Six-Day War* (New Haven: Yale University Press, 2008).

[33] US military aid to Israel reached its peak during the Yom Kippur War with Operation Nickel Grass—a strategic airlift that provided the Israeli army with more than 23,000 tons of essential military equipment—leading the way.

[34] For a discussion on comprehensive security, see: Cha, "Abandonment, Entrapment, and Neoclassical Realism."

[35] In 1968, Prime Minister Sato commissioned a secret study (which leaked in 1994) to examine the costs and benefits of developing nuclear weapons. The study concluded that the costs of developing nuclear weapons would outweigh the benefits and thus have an aggregate net-negative effect on Japanese security.

[36] Patricia G. Steinhoff, "Portrait of a Terrorist: An Interview with Kozo Okamoto," *Asian Survey 16*, no. 9 (1976): 830–45.

non-inconsequential ways, Japan and Israel not only differed greatly in their security interests during the period, but they were also in direct opposition to each other.

3.2.2 Economy

Similar to incompatible security interests, the Japanese and Israeli economies shared little congruity. Japan's economy underwent a significant change from the early 1970s through the late 1980s. The 1973 oil crisis, caused by OPEC's oil embargo against nations it perceived as supporting Israel during the Yom Kippur War (including Japan), and the second oil shock in 1979, initiated by the Iranian Revolution and prolonged by the Iran-Iraq War (1980–1988), profoundly affected Japanese policymakers and business leaders. Shocked by the degree of vulnerability in which it found itself, due to its reliance on Middle East oil, Japan began an extensive reorganization of its economic structure, moving from heavy manufacturing in such sectors as shipbuilding and automobiles, steel and chemicals, to more efficient, services-focused tertiary sectors from the mid-1970s, including finance, insurance, retailing, and communications.[37] This move from "ships to computer chips" was driven by an ever-more advanced education system, a skilled workforce, and increased investment in R&D. The economy surged ahead, and by the late 1980s, the Tokyo Stock Exchange had become the world's largest, accounting for over 60% of global market capitalization.[38]

Israel, conversely, was bankrupt. The constant warfare took its toll on public finances, trade, and investment, and from 1973, it fell into a decade-long economic crisis. GDP growth slowed from an average of 10% in the mid-1960s, to below 3%, inflation soared 450%, unemployment spiked by double digits, and foreign debt skyrocketed.[39] Economic hardship came to a head in 1983 when the nation's four largest banks collapsed and, with them, the banking system. While crisis countermeasures, including billions in financial and lending support from the United

---

[37] By the late 1980s, this tertiary sector employed more than half of the entire national workforce. See: Yarime, *Japan: The Precarious Future*.

[38] For a review, see: Jeff Kingston, *Japan in Transformation, 1945–2010*, 2nd ed. (New York: Routledge, 2014).

[39] Dan Breznitz, *Innovation and the State: Political Choice and Strategies for Growth in Israel, Taiwan, and Ireland* (New Haven: Yale University Press, 2007).

States, ultimately managed to avert the worst of potential outcomes, Israel found itself in the unique position of having to deal with, for the first time in its post-War history, comparable economic threats to survival as foreign military threats to sovereignty. By the mid-1980s, the country was bordering on complete economic failure.

There was thus little to no economic compatibility between Japan and Israel during this period, because while Japan boomed, Israeli busted. In response to the constant conflict in the Middle East and the Arab boycott of Israel and her allies, Tokyo elites reshaped the country's industrial structure by diversifying its energy mix, investing in education, and expanding incentives for high-technology R&D. Inherent in this adjustment was a deep skepticism of Israel as an economic partner. Israelis generally refrained from or were unable to participate in foreign commerce, while Japanese investors looked into large and wealthy markets. Economic synergies by which both countries could deepen trade and investment ties were weak, and those that did exist were limited in scope to "diamonds for automobiles."

3.2.3   Diplomacy

In such an environment, whereby the two nations shared little in the way of security and economic interests, and in some respects were at loggerheads with each other on both fronts, the "cool but correct" diplomatic relations of the 1950s and 1960s dissipated. What transpired instead was a bilateral relationship that Meron Medzini has described as "chilly and at times openly hostile."[40] The relatively brisk government relations of the previous period vanished, and between 1967 and 1988, Japan paid zero high-level visits to Israel. From 1967 to 1984, Israel, too, sent no diplomatic missions to Japan, and no formal bilateral economic or security agreements were discussed, much less adopted. In multilateral and international organizations also, relations soured. Japan regularly took positions against Israel in the United Nations General Assembly and at UN specialized agencies, voting against or abstaining on the many anti-Israel resolutions deliberated after the war in 1967.[41] In 1975, Japan was

---

[40] Medzini, "From Alienation to Partnership," 235.

[41] Meron Medzini, "Asian Voting Patterns on the Middle East in the UN General Assembly," in *Israel in the Third World*, ed. Michael Curtis and Susan A. Gitelson (New Brunswick: Transaction Books, 1976), 318–24.

the only industrialized democracy to abstain from Resolution 3379 in the UN General Assembly that likened Zionism with racism.

Royal relations were non-existent, in that the imperial house of Japan granted no Israeli national an audience or award over the entire period. Furthermore, citizen diplomacy remained feeble at best and hostile at worst. Following the first oil crisis of 1973, various private institutions and NGOs were established in Japan that espoused goals that were fundamentally at odds with Israel, including the Japan Oil Development Company, which sought to deepen relations with Arab countries. High-ranking Japanese elites were appointed to helm pro-Arab institutions, with Foreign Minister Toshio Kimura chairing the Japan-PLO Friendship League, and MITI Minister Yasuhiro Nakasone chairing the Arab Friend-ship League. Later, Nakasone would continue to hold this position, even after being elected prime minister.

Toward the end of the period, following the Israeli-Egyptian peace agreement (1979), the cold diplomatic relations began to warm—slowly. In 1985, the Israeli FM visited Tokyo for the first time since 1967, and in 1988, Foreign Minister Uno Sōsuke became the first cabinet minister to visit Israel. The latter's visit, however, was deemed a diplomatic failure by some in Israel who viewed the short visit (twelve hours, four of which were spent in a Palestinian refugee camp) as insulting.[42] Still, it paved the way for the next period of bilateral relations.

3.3 Warm Yet Uncommitted: 1989–Early 2000s

3.3.1 Security

The security environments facing Japan and Israel in the 1990s and 2000s continued to evolve in many ways. In East Asia, the dissolution of the Soviet Union undermined the logic of the US–Japan alliance[43] and reoriented tensions concerning the main fault lines of the region, namely, the Korean Peninsula and the Taiwan Straits. The first nuclear crisis involving North Korea (1993–1994), and the *Nodong* 1 missile test over the Sea of Japan (1993), brought North Korea's nuclear and missile programs to the acute attention of Japanese defense planners.

---

[42] Medzini, "Reflections on Israel's Policy."

[43] Japanese abandonment fears rose as US troops in East Asia rose from over 100,000 in 1989 to approximately 60,000 in 2005, with an over 30% decline in personnel stationed in Japan.

This would persist throughout the period, as North Korea continued to saber-rattle. However, while North Korea did indeed represent a clear and present danger, it was the rise of China that vexed Japanese security planners the most. China's dozen nuclear tests between 1992 and 1996, the Taiwan Straits Crisis (1996), and the Senkaku Islands disagreement (2005) in particular generated concerns in Tokyo about the intentions of the Chinese leadership.

In the Middle East, Israel's security environment was also undergoing significant changes as a result of the demise of the Soviet Union, the First Gulf War (1990–1991), and the relative improvement in Israel's relations with several neighboring countries.[44] In addition to the launch of the peace talks with the Palestinians, Israel had signed a peace agreement with Jordan (1994) and upgraded its strategic cooperation with Turkey (1996). Although the peace process with the Palestinians stalled and later collapsed in 2000, and relations with the Arab world have waxed and waned ever since Israel came to be less preoccupied with the threat of a large-scale war fought simultaneously on several fronts. Its ongoing peace agreements with Egypt and Jordan meant that its primary vulnerability in its "inner ring" was now confined to its northern border, where Syria and Hezbollah were sources of growing concern.[45] Threats of the proliferation of WMD from Israel's "outer ring," and of terrorism, became acute during this period, as by the late 1990s Iran's nuclear and missile programs had advanced significantly, and non-state actors, including Hamas, escalated their attacks on Israeli civilian centers. Finally, Israel's relations with the US remained strong, as the strategic cooperation, security coordination, and joint development of weapons between both countries continued to be robust.[46]

Throughout the 1990s and well into the 2000s, certain aspects of Japan–Israel national security considerations began to align, and yet they shied away from cooperation. Advances in nuclear and missile programs made by North Korea and Iran underscored the growing intensity of

---

[44] These changes were mainly beneficial to Israel. See: Efraim Inbar, "Israel's Strategic Environment in the 1990s," *Journal of Strategic Studies* 25, no. 1 (2002): 21–38.

[45] Israeli defense planners emphasized in the 1990s a two-concentric perspective, an inner and an outer ring, in assessing regional security threats. The "first ring" included the neighboring countries sharing a common border with Israel, and "the outer ring" referred to the more distant countries in the Middle East. See: ibid., 26.

[46] Ibid., 22–23.

these regional dangers in Tokyo and Jerusalem, with long-range missiles in particular resulting in both countries investing increasingly higher budgets in ballistic missile defense systems, albeit this investment was not coordinated and instead was made bilaterally with the United States. Likewise, by the early 2000s, the strategic partnerships both Japan and Israel enjoyed with the US, now the world's sole superpower, had survived the dramatic change in the international system brought about by the end of the Cold War. Both countries began exploring complementary strategic alignments with like-minded countries in their respective regions: Japan with South Korea, Australia, and India, while Israel talked with Turkey and Jordan. Thus, despite growing alignment in their threat environments during this period, the two countries did not coordinate—let alone cooperate—in their national security efforts.[47]

3.3.2 Economy
The Japanese and Israeli economies became increasingly complementary during this period.[48] After Japan's "bubble economy" burst (the stock market in 1990 and the land market in 1991), its economy entered into a long period of recession, registering low growth in terms of both real and nominal GDP as well as in terms of industrial production.[49] Although growth indicators and especially the export sector registered improvement between 2002 and 2007, this was most likely a result of the expansion of the global economy over the same period; structural hurdles, including price deflation, a shrinking labor force, and high fiscal deficits, remained throughout the period, and the global financial crisis of 2008–2009 had negative implications for the Japanese economy, which in 2009 contracted more than any other major advanced nation.[50] Subsequently,

---

[47] This lack of cooperative behavior can also be seen in terms of preferred approaches to non-state actors, with Japan favoring "soft" economic aid, humanitarian assistance, and the development of international legal frameworks, while Israel preferred a "hard" boots-on-the-ground approach to thwarting terrorist and militant attacks.

[48] For a similar argument, see Shaoul, "Japan and Israel," 281.

[49] The average annual growth rate of per capita GDP in Japan was 0.5% in the 1991–2000 period, compared with 2.6% for the US. See: Fumio Hayashi and Edward C. Prescott, "The 1990s in Japan: A Lost Decade," *Review of Economic Dynamics* 5, no. 1 (2002): 206–35.

[50] In 2009, the Japanese economy contracted by 5.2%. See: Masahiro Kawai and Shinji Takagi, "Why Was Japan Hit So Hard by the Global Financial Crisis?" in *The Impact of*

the Government of Japan employed various measures in order to enhance potential growth, including the promotion of information technology (thought to lead to improved productivity); deregulation and the removal of various structural impediments in the goods, services, and capital markets; encouragement of venture businesses; and the enhancement of a national innovation system.[51]

Israel survived the severe challenges of economic stagnation and hyperinflation of the 1980s and embarked on a wide-ranging economic liberalization plan of market-orientated structural reforms that included relaxing its trade and foreign currency policies, privatization, deregulation, reduced government spending, and tax cuts under the Economic Stabilization Plan.[52] During the 1990s, the economy registered strong growth rates, an upward trend in its trade volume, and qualitative change in its exports, namely, less military-centered, European-dependent trade, and more high-tech-centered trade with markets in Eastern Europe and Asia. A large-scale immigration wave of nearly one million people, many of whom were highly educated engineers and scientists from the former Soviet Union, had strongly positive implications for the country's economy.[53] Moreover, by the late 1990s, Israel had become for the first time a target of substantial FDI, which had previously been the limited purview of Jewish investors.[54]

Overall, between the late 1980s and 2010, economic synergies by which both countries found value in deepening trade and investment ties increased compared to previous periods. With the end of the old boycott and the emergence of the IT and service sectors, they thus began to find common ground for trade and commerce where none had existed before.

the Economic Crisis on East Asia: Policy Responses from Four Economies, ed. Daigee Shaw and Bih Jane Wu (Northampton: Edward Elgar Publishing, 2011), 131.

[51] Ministry of Economy, Trade and Industry, "White Paper on International Economy and Trade 2007: Japan's Trade Strategy on Improving Industrial Productivity and Accelerating Economic Growth," July 2007, accessed 26 April 2019, https://www.meti.go.jp/english/report/downloadfiles/2007WhitePaper/Overview0712.pdf.

[52] Liberalization was neither consistent nor complete throughout the 1990s, as the Israeli government continued to play an important role in attracting large foreign enterprises and subsidizing high-tech startups. See: Michael Shalev, "Have Globalization and Liberalization 'Normalized' Israel's Political Economy?" Israel Affairs 5, nos. 2–3 (1998): 121–55.

[53] Ibid., 128.

[54] Ibid., 131.

3.3.3 Diplomacy

Diplomatic relations began to warm between the late 1980s and early 2000s. Motivated by a realization that it needed to play a more active role in international politics, especially in areas of strategic importance such as the Middle East, Japan recalibrated its policy toward the region in general and Israel in particular. To exemplify this point, it joined the Middle East peace process in October 1991, denounced the Arab boycott on Israel (1994),[55] provided financial support to the newly established Palestinian Authority (PA)[56] as well as to other Arab countries involved in the peace process, and, from January 1996, contributed to the United Nations Peace-keeping Operations (PKO) in the Golan Heights.[57] The tectonic shifts in the international arena also prompted Israeli elites to seek improved relations in East and South Asia; shortly after the demise of the bipolar order, and during a single week in January 1992, Israel established full diplomatic relations with both India and China.

Beginning with the Israeli Cabinet's decision to approve Israeli President (1983–1993) Chaim Herzog's attendance at Emperor Hirohito's funeral (February 1989),[58] the number of audiences granted to government officials rose through the 1990s, including Prime Minister Rabin in 1994, after which six audiences were granted to ministers and ambassadors through 2004. In 2000, Ben-Ami Shillony was awarded the Order of the Sacred Treasure, Gold and Silber Star, in perhaps the clearest sign of warming royal relations between the countries. Likewise, government diplomacy thawed, and following the first visit of a cabinet minister to Israel in 1988, Japanese foreign ministers began to visit Israel on an

---

[55] The Arab boycott on Israel diminished somewhat in the 1990s, as several declarations made by Arab countries mitigated the policy. Japan followed suit, and during Prime Minister Yitzhak Rabin's visit in December 1994, it announced it would reconsider its policy on the matter. See: Shaoul, "Japan and Israel," 280–82.

[56] As of September 2018, Japan's assistance to the PA since 1993 amounted to 1.9 billion dollars. See: Ministry of Foreign Affairs of Japan, "Japan's Assistance to the Palestinians," September 2018, accessed 4 October 2019, https://www.mofa.go.jp/files/000 042388.pdf.

[57] Japan's Self-Defense Forces finished their mission in the Golan Heights in December 2012.

[58] Two cabinet ministers opposed the decision, citing Japan's role in WWII and specifically its cooperation with Nazi Germany. See: Hugh Orgel, "Herzog to Attend Hirohito's Funeral," *Jewish Telegraphic Agency*, 23 January 1983, 3.

annual basis.[59] Even more indicative of warming government ties, two prime ministers visited Israel during the period (Maruyama in 1995 and Koizumi in 2005). Relations between private industry and organizations also began to warm, albeit slowly; for instance, a large Israeli delegation visited Japan in early 1992 and met with government officials, economic organizations, and business leaders. As Shaoul has recounted, the climax of the visit was a seminar on Israel organized by the Keidanren, in which eighty Japanese executives participated.[60] Study abroad programs began and Japan-bound tourism doubled over the period, ushering in a new era of people-to-people exchange.[61]

4   The Diplomatic Turn

In the following section, we delve more deeply into the significant rapprochement underway between Japan and Israel during the second decade of the twenty-first century. Security and economic interests aligned for the first time since both countries gained their independence after the end of WWII. Along with systemic synergy between security and economic systems, strong political leadership in both countries looking to forge new alliances, diversify trade networks, and increase international diplomatic presence has brought Japan–Israel relations to a level is begining to resemble those of allied partners.

4.1   Hot Rising Sun Relations: 2012–2019

4.1.1   Security
Japan and Israel's overall security calculi have changed dramatically over the past decade. In addition to a severe energy crisis as a result of the 2011 triple disasters in northeastern Japan, the country has had to deal with a severe external security environment, including growing arms-spending and arms build-up in the region, nuclear proliferation

---

[59] For all diplomatic visits, see: Ministry of Foreign Affairs, Japan, Diplomatic Archives at www.mofa.go.jp/about/hq/record/service.html. Also see the online database "The World and Japan" at https://worldjpn.net. For a description, see: Matthew Brummer and Akihiko Tanaka, "The World and Japan: An introduction to a database."

[60] Shaoul, "Japan and Israel," 284.

[61] These data were drawn from: Japan Tourism Statistics, https://statistics.jnto.go.jp/en/.

concerns, and China's growingly assertive behavior in the region.[62] Relations with China have been particularly tenuous since 2010, as concerns about violent conflict over the Senkaku/Diaoyu Islands were raised for the first time in decades.[63] More recently, Japan has been exposed to a growing number of cyber-attacks directed at government institutions and vital infrastructure.[64] Further exacerbating this sense of insecurity was the election of Donald Trump (2016–), whose a-typical foreign and security policies, as well as unpredictable personal character, have generated anxiety among decision-makers in Tokyo about the credibility of America's defense commitment to their country.[65] It is in this context that the Japanese government has been pursuing a mix of external and internal balancing measures, including its outward-looking foreign policy of "proactive contribution to peace"[66] and the conceptual "Free and Open Indo-Pacific" strategy.[67] Other security-related initiatives comprise the reinterpretation of Article 9, so as to allow for collective self-defense,

[62] See, for example: Andrew L. Oros, "Japan's Security Future," in *The Routledge Handbook of Asian Security Studies*, ed. Sumit Ganguly, Andrew Scobell, and Joseph C. Liow (New York: Routledge, 2009), 39–50.

[63] The year 2015 marked a substantial improvement in relations between Japan and China. See: Akihiko Tanaka, *Japan in Asia: Post-Cold-War Diplomacy*, trans. Jean Connell Hoff (Tokyo: Japan Publishing Industry for Culture, 2017). For a review, see: Matthew Brummer, "Bridges over Troubled History: Japan's Foreign Policy in Asia," *International Studies Review 21*, no. 1 (2019): 172–74.

[64] National Institute of Information and Communications Technology, "NICTER Analysis Report 2017," *in NICT Report 2019* (Tokyo: NICT, 2019), 43–44.

[65] Smith, *Japan Rearmed*.

[66] The Proactive Contribution to Peace is the fundamental principle of Japan's first ever National Security Strategy, issued in December 2013. The principle "refers to Japan's commitment to contribute to ensuring international peace, stability and prosperity even more proactively and in a manner proportional to Japan's national power." See: Ministry of Defense, *Defense of Japan 2018* (Tokyo: Ministry of Defense, 2018), 217.

[67] This strategy was formulated in Japan and later promoted by US administrations (as well as by Australia, India, and Indonesia). At the core of Japan's version of the regional strategy are two principles: Respecting the rule of law, and the freedom of navigation and overflight in the seas. See: ibid., 55–57.

the relaxation of the "three principles on arms export," and, relatedly, the Specially Designated Secrets Act legislation in 2014.[68]

Israel is also dealing with a complex security environment, although it is much improved in terms of the nature and intensity of these issues compared with earlier periods. Importantly, the "classical" threat of conventional war with one or more of its neighbors has further diminished, and Israel now engages a range of state and non-state actors in the region, both publicly and privately. Nonetheless, its security environment continues to be rife with risks, most notably the threat of nuclear proliferation and the negative repercussions of the ongoing conflict with the Palestinians.[69] The bloody civil war in Syria also brought about the increased involvement of Israel's primary rival, Iran, whose nuclear aspirations have long undermined the former's sense of security. The Iranian factor, in addition to the ongoing Israeli-Palestinian conflict and the prospects of further violent clashes with Hamas in Gaza (the most recent of which was waged in the summer of 2014) and Hezbollah in Lebanon, kept Israeli defense planners busy. In order to address some of these challenges, Israel sought to obstruct actively the Iranian nuclear program and prevent "game-changing" weapon systems reaching the hands of what Israel perceived as Iranian proxies on its northern border, i.e., Syria and Hezbollah. Moreover, Israel has been bolstering its missile defenses, counterterrorism, and cyber-warfare capacities.[70]

As illustrated above, some of the security challenges facing both Japan and Israel are similar and some are different. In terms of shared security challenges, both countries share mostly a regional—not a global—strategic outlook. And in their respective regions, both now face three similar issues: A hostile neighbor pursuing nuclear weapon programs (North Korea and Iran, respectively), substantial missile threats (North Korea's repeated missile tests and Israel's recent wars with Hezbollah and Hamas, as well as a substantial missile threat from Iran, respectively), and,

---

[68] For a summary, see: Ministry of Foreign Affairs of Japan, "Japan's Legislation for Peace and Security: Seamless Responses for Peace and Security of Japan and the International Community," March 2016, accessed 4 April 2019, www.mofa.go.jp/files/000143 304.pdf.

[69] See: Dan Meridor and Ron Eldadi, *Israel's National Security Doctrine: The Committee Report on Formulation of the Security Concept (Meridor Committee), Ten Years Later* (Tel-Aviv: The Institute for National Security Studies, 2018), 17.

[70] Ibid., 23–29.

more recently, a growing number of sophisticated cyber-attacks against governments and vital infrastructure that originate within the region. There are also important differences between the security concerns facing both countries. Whereas Japan's regional security environment is at its most severe in the post-War period, as both North Korea (now demonstrably a nuclear power) and China pose intricate challenges to its national security, Israel's regional security has registered some important improvements, with old rivals (such as Saudi Arabia, Oman, and several of the Gulf countries) no longer perceived to be overtly hostile, and increased engagement with Cyprus and Greece (stemming in part from Israeli efforts to offset its souring relations with a once long-time friend, Turkey). The recent diplomatic engagement between the Israeli government and the oil-rich countries of the Gulf in particular bears important political and economic implications for the country's relationship with Japan, as it underscores the collapse of the Arab boycott.

Finally, the energy security outlook for both countries has changed considerably over the period. In Japan, the 3/11 triple disaster significantly changed its energy mix: Forced to shut down the country's nuclear power plants, it has now increased fossil fuel imports as a substitute for domestic nuclear power production. While several nuclear reactors have since been brought back online, Japan is still one of the world's leading importers of energy and the largest LNG importer.[71] In accordance with its new energy situation, Japan's Energy Plan (2015) has set a balanced energy supply as its 2030 policy pillar with roughly an equal share of coal, renewable energy, LNG, and nuclear power.[72] Israel's energy calculus has also changed considerably over the past few years, albeit for different reasons. Traditionally, it has relied on imported coal to generate electricity (about 70%). Since 2012, however, it has been importing fewer resources and producing more energy than ever before as a result of the 2009 discovery of large, domestic offshore natural gas deposits, which

---

[71] According to METI's Energy Plan 2015, Japan will continue to rely heavily on LNG for the foreseeable future (27% of the 2030 projected energy mix).

[72] Agency for Natural Resources and Energy, *Japan's Energy Plan 2015* (Tokyo: Ministry of Economy, Trade and Industry, 2015), https://www.enecho.meti.go.jp/en/category/brochures/pdf/energy_plan_2015.pdf.

currently provide about 60% of the nation's electricity needs and are esti-
mated to supply the current level of gas consumption for a century.[73]
Israel will soon begin to export its natural gas overseas, including to East
Asia, an enticing prospect for Japan.[74]

4.1.2   Economy

Along with the shared and divergent challenges in their security environments—both of which have enabled a favorable environment for
improved relations—Japan and Israel now share increasingly compatible
economic systems, from markets to institutions, to interests and capabilities. Despite recurrent economic recessions and a shrinking population,
Japan remains the world's third-largest and most complex economy, and
is currently ranked seventh in terms of global FDI outflows.[75] In addition
to large traditional industries such as automobiles and electronic goods,
manufacturing in Japan is currently centered on high-tech and precision
goods such as robotics and optical instruments. Since 2013, the economy
has experienced modest growth, generated by an economic revitalization
agenda led by Prime Minister Abe ("Abenomics"). In tandem with the
agenda's "Three Arrows"—monetary easing, fiscal stimulus, and structural reform—Japan is making progress toward ending deflation, although
the challenge of balancing its efforts to stimulate growth, alongside the
need to tackle its high public debt (now approximately 235% of GDP),
remains. Over the past few years, and in order to deal with the economic
challenges mentioned above, the Japanese government has sought to
open up the domestic economy to greater foreign competition, create
new export opportunities for Japanese companies, and, above all, enhance
the innovation of advanced technologies.[76]

[73] Tim Robinson and Geordie Jeakins, "Squaring the Triangle: Why Turkey
and the EastMed Project Need Each Other," *War on the Rocks*, 12 April
2019, https://warontherocks.com/2019/04/squaring-the-triangle-why-turkey-and-the-
eastmed-project-need-each-other/.

[74] Amiram Barkat, "Daewoo Hires Hoegh to Design Tamar Floating Gas Terminal,"
Globes, 4 December 2011, https://en.globes.co.il/en/article-1000703188.

[75] As of 2018, fifty-two of the Fortune 500 (the world's largest companies) were
Japanese. Accessed 21 April, 2019, http://fortune.com/global500/list/.

[76] Japan has been actively pursuing large-scale trade agreements, two of which came
into force earlier this year: The Comprehensive and Progressive Agreement for Trans-
Pacific Partnership (CPTPP), which reduces tariffs between eleven trading partners with
500 million people, and the Economic Partnership Agreement with the EU, which is the

Israel has a strong reputation for generating frontier technological solutions, and it is now an advanced free-market economy with strong indicators of innovation.[77] To further enhance its innovation ecosystem and connect it with the world's, Israel's Innovation Authority was established in 2016 and put in charge of formulating innovation policy goals and implementing all aspects of governmental support in technological innovation. Moreover, the nation's leading exports have become high-technology equipment, including aviation, communications, computer-aided design and manufacture, medical electronics, fiber optics, and, more recently, pharmaceuticals. To offset its substantial trade deficit—Israel imports crude oil, military equipment, rough diamonds, grains, and raw materials—it relies on significant foreign investment inflows as well as on tourism and other service exports. The global financial crisis of 2008–2009 prompted a short recession, but years of cautious fiscal policy and a resilient banking sector, as well as increasing participation in the labor market by social minorities, have enabled the economy to remain largely resilient to this debt shock. In September 2010, Israel became the thirty-third member of the OECD, in what further enhanced its international economic standing.

Throughout much of the post-war period, Israeli and Japanese economic interests were largely incompatible. Today, Israel offers a wealth of opportunities for collaboration in frontier science and technology, seen as critical for economic growth and national security. In particular, its recent reputation in Japan as a "start-up nation," rich with scientific know-how and technical expertise, harmonizes well with Japanese economic policies such as "Abenomics", which sees innovation as a key

world's biggest such deal to date, covering nearly a third of global GDP and 635 million inhabitants.

[77] According to the Global Innovation Index 2018, for example, Israel was ranked eleventh in the world in terms of innovation, two spots above Japan, whereas Japan ranked first in the following indicators: Gross domestic expenditure on R&D financed by business, patent families in two or more offices, and intellectual property receipts. See: World Intellectual Property Organization, "Global Innovation Index 2018: China Cracks Top 20. Top Rankings: Switzerland, Netherlands, Sweden, UK, Singapore, US," News release, 10 July 2018, https://www.wipo.int/pressroom/en/articles/2018/article_0005. html. For the full report, see: https://www.globalinnovationindex.org.

to generating growth, as well as with the more recent "Future Investment Strategy 2018" (announced in June 2018), which aims to draw on know-how and resources overseas.[78]

4.1.3   Royal Diplomacy

Royal diplomacy has recently been upgraded. After an interlude of sixteen years, in 2016, two Israeli citizens—Dr. Meron Medzini and architect Arie Kutz—received the Order of the Rising Sun, Gold Rays with Neck Ribbon for their contribution to promoting understanding between Japan and Israel. And, in 2018, Mr. Eli Cohen, the former Ambassador to Japan, received the Order of the Rising Sun.[79] Israel's PM Netanyahu was granted an audience with the Emperor in 2014, as was the Israeli Ambassador to Tokyo in both 2017 and 2018. Furthermore, the Israeli president met with Japan's FM Kono in December 2017, expressing his wish that the Emperor would visit Israel before abdicating in 2019. Kono then cautiously replied that he hoped a member of the Imperial Household would be able to visit the region in the near future.[80] Such a flurry of symbolic acts and practices exhibiting goodwill and shared understanding between Japan and Israel has been an entirely new development in their bilateral diplomatic relationship.

4.1.4   Government Diplomacy

Much of the recent positive trend in the bilateral relations is a result of government diplomacy, enhanced by both sides—most notably since 2014. The Israeli government Decision 2395 to improve economic relations and cooperation with Japan, approved by the Cabinet in January 2015, made a significant contribution in promoting the bilateral relationship. The decision, for example, allocated resources to bring hundreds of

---

[78] On how diplomatic alignment can foster innovation, see: Jon Schmid, Matthew Brummer, and Mark Z. Taylor, "Innovation and Alliances." *Review of Policy Research 34*, no. 5 (2017): 588–616. Also see: Matthew Brummer, "Innovation and Threats." *Defence and Peace Economics* 33, no.5 (2022): 563–584.

[79] The two Israelis were among 96 foreign recipients in total. The Order of the Rising Sun has been awarded for non-Japanese since 1981, and foreign women have been included since 2003.

[80] Israel Ministry of Foreign Affairs, "President Reuven Rivlin Meets with Japanese FM Tarō Kōno," News release, 25 December 2017, https://mfa.gov.il/MFA/PressRoom/2017/Pages/President-Rivlin-meets-with-Japanese-FM-Taro-Kono-25-December-2017.aspx.

young leaders from Japan for a tour in Israel, in order to develop ties with business, media, and scientific leaders, and to communicate Israel's image to Japanese audiences. There have also been reports about Netanyahu's personal chemistry with Prime Minister Abe, after the leaders met once in 2014, twice again in 2015, and then again in early May 2018. On the Japanese side, an increased number of visits to Israel by high-level officials, following the example of Abe, who visited the region for the first time after a decade of no such visits, as well as a growing number of MOUs and inter-governmental dialogues, testify to the GOJ's efforts.

In relative terms, enhanced cooperation between the governments has been most pronounced in the security sector. Israeli and Japanese diplomats now routinely hold national security dialogues in Tokyo and Jerusalem covering strategy, counterterrorism, and military technology. Additionally, a bilateral exchange initiative between defense establishments geared at knowledge and skill transfer, first adopted in December 2014, has contributed to building networks between personnel and solidifying relations between security apparatuses. And since 2014, the two countries have held a series of ministerial dialogues on cybersecurity, while in October 2018, they held their first politico-military dialogue, discussing a range of issues including regional situations and security affairs.[81] This upgrading of ties in the security realm is unprecedented in Japan–Israel relations.

In absolute terms, Israeli-Japanese economic relations have seen the most dramatic improvement. High-profile visits to Israel by officials from Japan's Ministry of Economy, Trade, and Industry resulted in a bilateral investment treaty, ratified in May 2016. The treaty's impact was immediate; for instance, since its enactment, foreign direct investment from Japan to Israel has increased exponentially. In May 2017, both governments issued a sweeping joint statement announcing a "Japan–Israel Innovation Partnership," which would extend cooperation in cybersecurity into joint trainings and workshops for officials, deepen the linkages between the countries' public and private sectors, and forge new bilateral research and development networks.[82] In addition, in 2018

---

[81] Ministry of Foreign Affairs of Japan, "First Joint Foreign Affairs and Security Consultation between Japan and Israel (Pol-Mil Dialog)," News release, 10 October 2018, https://www.mofa.go.jp/press/release/press4e_002186.html.

[82] Ministry of Economy, Trade and Industry, "Joint Statement: The Ministry of Economy, Trade and Industry of Japan and the Ministry of Economy and Industry of the

alone, JIIN conducted business networking for more than 1000 companies by organizing fifty events, including nine business missions and forty-one business seminars.[83]

4.1.5   Citizen Diplomacy

Citizen diplomacy is also currently its most pronounced and positive in the history of Japan–Israel relations. In addition to growing levels of trade and FDI, relations have seen an increase in humanitarian initiatives, as several Israeli organizations specializing in psychosocial care have launched projects in Japan in the aftermath of 3/11, as well as educational and research initiatives such as the JSPS-ISF Joint Academic Research Program (2016–), the Japan-Israeli Cooperative Scientific Research Program (2017), and the Japan–Israel R&D Cooperation Program (2018).

Trade figures have shown modest albeit steady growth year-on-year since 2014. In 2018, for example, the trade volume between both countries reached a record $3.5 billion, an increase of around 20% from 2017.[84] Israel's trade volume with Japan is modest when compared with China or India, and yet more relevant than aggregate volume of trade is its characteristics: Since 2009, trade between Japan and Israel has become increasingly diversified and complex, with a growing share of high-technology products, from medical equipment to chemicals, to advanced ICT and beyond.

Traditionally, Japanese-Israeli trade can be characterized as "cars for diamonds." Between 1966 and 2006, diamonds were the main export from Israel to Japan; similarly, beginning in 1978, Japan's main export to Israel was cars. Yet, in 2017, diamonds accounted for only 9.4% of Israeli exports to Japan, with high-tech products such as medical and measuring instruments accounting for about 30% of total outgoing trade. In the

---

State of Israel launch Japan-Israel Innovation Partnership," News release, 3 May 2017, https://www.meti.go.jp/press/2017/05/20170508004/20170508004-2.pdf.

[83] Ministry of Economy, Trade and Industry, "Japan-Israel Innovation Network 2.0," News release, 17 January 2019, https://www.meti.go.jp/english/press/2019/pdf/0117_001a.pdf.

[84] Japanese-Israeli trade volume first crossed the $2 billion US dollar threshold in 2006 and has since steadily grown towards $3 billion US dollars. See: Adi Pick, "Israel and Japan in Talk to Enter a Free Trade Agreement," *CTech by Calcalist*, 15 January 2019, https://www.calcalistech.com/ctech/articles/0,7340,L-3754321,00.html.

other direction and in the same year, machinery and electric equipment (such as photo lab equipment) accounted for 39% of Japanese exports to Israel, pushing cars back to second place (28%) for the first time in decades.[85]

In addition to changing trade characteristics, trends pertaining to FDI and cooperation in R&D testify to the strengthening of economic relations among countries. Between 2013 and 2017, investment flowing from Japan to Israel increased 120-fold, while the number of Japanese companies active in Israel almost tripled, from twenty-five to seventy-five.[86] FDI outflow from Japan to Israel doubled between 2014 and 2015 (to $45.7 million), including investments by Fujitsu, Mitsui, and Softbank.[87] In 2017, Japanese FDI reached a staggering $186 million, mostly due to investments by Softbank.[88] Several Japanese giants have purchased Israeli companies in recent years: in 2014, Japanese e-commerce company Rakuten Inc. acquired the Israeli messaging app Viber Inc. for $900 million; in 2016, Sony Corporation purchased Israeli chip manufacturing company Altair for $212 million; and in 2017, Japanese drug-maker Mitsubishi Tanabe Pharma Corporation acquired Israel-based pharmaceutical company NeuroDerm Ltd. for $1.1 billion. In the opposite direction, FDI from Israel to Japan increased, from $4 million in 2013 to $412 million in 2014.[89] In terms of R&D, leading Japanese technology companies, including Dentsu, Mitsui, Rakuten, Softbank, and Sony, invested and opened research facilities in Israel.[90] The diversification of trade

---

[85] See: Israel Export Institute, "Israel-Japan Trade Relations," *Israel-Japan Business Guide*, 10 August 2018, 14.

[86] Japan Israel Innovation Network, *Japanese Business Partners 2019*, 7 January 2019. https://www.jetro.go.jp/ext_images/israel/Japanese_Business_Partners_WEBver.pdf.

[87] The value of investment by Japanese firms in 2015 amounted to 4.7 times the amount in 2013, and twenty-six times the amount in 2012. See: Hidemitsu Kibe, "Japanese Companies Show Keen Interest in Israeli Startups," *Nikki Asian Review*, 6 December 2016, https://asia.nikkei.com/Business/Biotechnology/Japanese-companies-show-keen-interest-in-Israeli-startups; "Balance of Payments," Bank of Japan, accessed 4 October 2019, https://www.boj.or.jp/en/statistics/br/bop_06/index.htm.

[88] Yasmin Yablonko, "Following China and South Korea: Japan Puts Israel on the Agenda," *Globes*, 17 January 2019, https://www.globes.co.il/news/article.aspx?did=100 1269341.

[89] Data from Israel Central Bureau of Statistics website: https://www.cbs.gov.il/.

[90] Israel has been one of the world's leading spenders on research and development (R&D) as a percentage of GDP (4.25% in 2015). In order to encourage its private

between Japan and Israel, as well as increasing levels of FDI and R&D, represent a deeper trend toward higher economic compatibility between the two economies.

What social agents, aside from governments, have actively contributed to these positive trends? Among those agents committed to citizen diplomacy, we can cite long-standing organizations such as The Israel–Japan Friendship Association and Chamber of Commerce (established in 1956) and the Japan–Israel Friendship Association (JIFA, established in 1966), as well as emerging actors such as the Japan–Israel Innovation Network (JIIN, a business forum, established in May 2017 in order to strengthen business relations between both countries). The role of these organizations in promoting their relations has been crucial. Interestingly, whereas traditional Japanese organizations with a keen interest in Israel have tended to be religious (Christian groups such as Beit Shalom and the Makuya), today there is a growing interest in Israel across broader Japanese society, including but not limited to decision-makers, businesses, and individuals. Another aspect of citizen diplomacy that has registered an upward trend is tourism; specifically, the number of Israeli visitors to Japan has more than tripled over the past several years. Between 2000 and 2013, about 10,000 Israelis visited Japan annually, but by 2017, the number had risen to more than 32,000 visitors.[91]

5   Complex Synergy and International Relations

It is interesting to contemplate an entangled bank, clothed with many plants of many kinds, with birds singing on the bushes, with various insects flitting about, and with worms crawling through the damp earth, and to reflect that these elaborately constructed forms, so different from each

---

businesses to cooperate with companies overseas, the Israeli government launched four bilateral R&D funds and over forty R&D cooperation agreements with foreign governments, one of which was signed with Japan in 2014. See: Manuel Trajtenberg, "R&D Policy in Israel," in *Innovation Policy in the Knowledge-Based Economy*, ed. Maryann P. Feldman and Albert N. Link (Boston: Springer, 2012), 409–54.

[91] Tourists contribute much of this increase, as the number of visitors for business purposes has been fluctuating between 4000 and 6000 since the late 1990s.

other in so complex a manner, have been produced by laws acting around us.[92]

Throughout his seminal work *The Origin of Species*, Darwin gave credence to "the web of complex relationships" in nature, the "infinitely complex associations" among species, and the "marked interdependence" of organisms.[93] For Darwin, the entangled bank in the passage above was one of complex synergistic wonder. Centuries later, Stanford University biologist Peter Corning would pick up on this entangled metaphor in *The Synergism Hypothesis*, where, under the rubric Holistic Darwinism, he laid out a comprehensive bioeconomic theory of cooperation and complexity in the natural world. Corning argued that synergy has been a leading casual force of evolution, whereby biological systems come into functional alignment to produce cooperative interactions between diverse types that in turn yield otherwise unattainable combined effects. Thus, in this biological evolutionary principle, synergy is the genesis of Darwin's entangled bank of complex, interdependent life forms.[94]

Scholars of international relations will immediately recognize the metaphor of this entangled bank in their own theories of cooperation and conflict. Our walk through Japan–Israel relations since 1952 makes clear that diplomatic affairs progress over time as security and economic synergies progress. For nation-states to develop, nurture, tend to, upgrade and embed diplomatic relations, common ground must be found whereby both find benefit in such engagement. Importantly, this extends beyond power and security benefits to include economic, trade, and investment compatibility.

This speaks importantly to the foundations of neoliberal theory, perhaps most readily to "complex interdependence," where dependence means "a state of being determined or significantly affected by external

---

[92] Charles R. Darwin, *On the Origin of Species by Means of Natural Selection, or the Preservation of Favoured Races in the Struggle for Life* (Milford: Oxford University Press, 1859), 459.

[93] For a review, see: Peter Corning, *Nature's Magic: Synergy in Evolution and the Fate of Humankind* (New York: Cambridge University Press, 2003).

[94] See also: Peter Corning, *Holistic Darwinism: Synergy, Cybernetics, and the Bioeconomics of Evolution* (Chicago: University of Chicago Press, 2010).

forces," and interdependence means "mutual dependence,"[95] as well as to the folly of dividing international politics into "high" security and "low" economic affairs.[96] To be sure, "states are not motivated solely by national interest defined in terms of power."[97]

Indeed, the story of Japan–Israel relations suggests that it is the compatibility of security and economic interests that yields greater net-level gains than can be achieved without cooperation that best explains why relations have progressed in the manner they have done. And in order to understand the bilateral relationship we must look at both Japanese and Israeli interests across levels of diplomacy, including the "transmission belts" of royal and citizen affairs.[98] That is, it is the relative synergy, or lack thereof, between security and economic systems that best explains the evolution of Japan–Israel relations.

If we summarize the four periods across security synergy and economic synergy, we find compelling support for this reading of international relations as an entangled bank of shared futures. As our abbreviated case on the 1952 to the mid-1960s period shows, Japan and Israel shared relatively compatible security concerns at the outset of formal diplomatic relations, while in the economic domain there was little opportunity for cooperation. This "cool but diplomatically correct" period resulted in relatively robust, government-led diplomacy but lacked any substantial royal or citizen connection. In the following period, from the late-1960s to the late-1980s, security synergy dissipated while economic synergy remained low, resulting in "cold and at times openly hostile" relations. Royal, government, and citizen diplomacy were essentially non-existent. Yet, relations began to show signs of warmth in the late-1980s and into the 1990s, as both governments and industry began to identify synergistic compatibility amidst the globalization of trade and production. Security interests remained relatively incompatible, however, and the Palestine

---

[95] Robert O. Keohane and Joseph S. Nye, *Power and Interdependence: World Politics in Transition* (Boston: Little, Brown & Co., 1977), 8.

[96] Ibid.

[97] Marc A. Genest, *Conflict and Cooperation: Evolving Theories of International Relations* (Belmont: Thomson & Wadsworth, 2004), 133.

[98] According to Keohane and Nye, such organizations, including firms and NGOs, can have a considerable impact on both domestic and interstate relations. These actors, besides pursuing, "act as transmission belts, making government policies in various countries more sensitive to one another." See: Keohane and Nye, *Power and Interdependence*, 26.

issue endured as a bottleneck to building common understanding in the political-security sphere.

Finally, as our last case on the 2012 to present (2019) period demonstrates, synergy in both security and economic interests has resulted in significant rapprochement across all three levels of diplomacy. The "rising sun relations" of today's Japan–Israel relationship resemble that of allies, due to the upgrading of relations across royal, government, and citizen affairs. Nonetheless, even amidst the significant developments now underway, it would be premature to think of Japan–Israel relations as one of embedded mutual dependence. The countries are only just beginning to weave their national interests together across the tapestry of security and economic affairs, and to build the institutional and human networks upon which the shared futures of which Nye and Keohane speak are grounded. In this way, Japan–Israel relations are best understood "beyond power" yet "before interdependence."

In keeping with Darwinian and neo-liberal terms, we may conceive of this evolution as *complex synergy*, comprised of both security and economic synergies. For analytical purposes, these two interactions can be conceived of as dichotomous: Security and economic synergy can be conceived of as either "higher" or "lower." Fig. 1 describes this evolution in terms of synergy and Japan–Israel relations over the past seventy years.

Complex synergy so conceived yields three combinations of outcomes. The first is "weak," having the lowest possible positive effect on Japan–Israel bilateral relations. As seen in the upper-left quadrant of the typology, this is a period in which both security and economic synergies are relatively low. Here, synergy is "doubly incompatible," resulting in a "cold and at times openly hostile" relationship. The second "net level" of synergy yields a "moderate" outcome, seen in two different combinations. The first, in the top-right of the typology, is one in which security

		Security Synergy	
		Low	High
Economic Synergy	Low	Weak Complex Synergy Cold bilateral relations (1967 ~ late-1980s)	Moderate Complex Synergy Cool bilateral relations (1952 ~ mid-1960s)
	High	Moderate Complex Synergy Warm bilateral relations (1989 ~ 2011)	Strong Complex Synergy Hot bilateral relations (2012 ~ present)

Fig. 1 Complex synergy and Japan–Israel Post-War relations

compatibility is relatively strong but economic compatibility is relatively weak. Thus, a "mixed-incentive" exists for diplomatic actors, leading, in our case, to a "cool but diplomatically correct" relationship. The second combination that yields a "moderate" level of diplomacy, as depicted in the lower-left quadrant, is one in which security compatibility is relatively low but economic compatibility is relatively strong, thereby leading in our case to "warm but uncommitted" diplomacy. The third and final net level of synergy, as shown in the lower-right quadrant of the typology, is "doubly compatible," where both security and economic synergies come together to spur "hot" diplomatic relations.

What does synergy "look like"? In Fig. 2, we offer an illustration of how it describes Japan–Israel relations. The figure is compiled from the World Bank's Trade Complementary Index, which measures to what degree one state's export profile is in relative demand by a given partner's import profile, and it is thus a measure well-designed to capture synergy in economic systems.[99] From the 1960s through the mid-1980s, economic compatibility remained flat and relatively low, as did bilateral trade. This began to change in the late 1980s, as Japanese and Israeli import/export profiles slowly came into alignment. Since approximately 2014, synergy in economic systems has experienced a Cambrian explosion, as have diplomatic relations.

However, synergy exists beyond security and economic dimensions to include cultural, ideational, and political dimensions. Although it is beyond the scope of this study to explore these in depth, if we look briefly at the contemporary political environment in Japan and Israel, we see evidence that synergy does indeed appear to operate in yielding particular outcomes. The rise of Prime Minister Shinzo Abe and his administration's assertive foreign policy has ushered in an era in which Japan is no longer willing to remain on the sidelines of international affairs. Abe, elected with large majorities in 2012, 2014, and 2017, has fashioned a powerful political coalition that commands a supermajority in both houses of the Parliament—a rarity in Japanese politics that has expedited the prime minister's agenda. The country's current political alignment has allowed for the emergence of previously taboo debates concerning Japan's place in

---

[99] For data and computational formulas, see: "Trade Indicators," World Bank, accessed 24 October 2019, https://wits.worldbank.org/wits/wits/witshelp/Content/Utilities/e1.trade_indicators.htm.

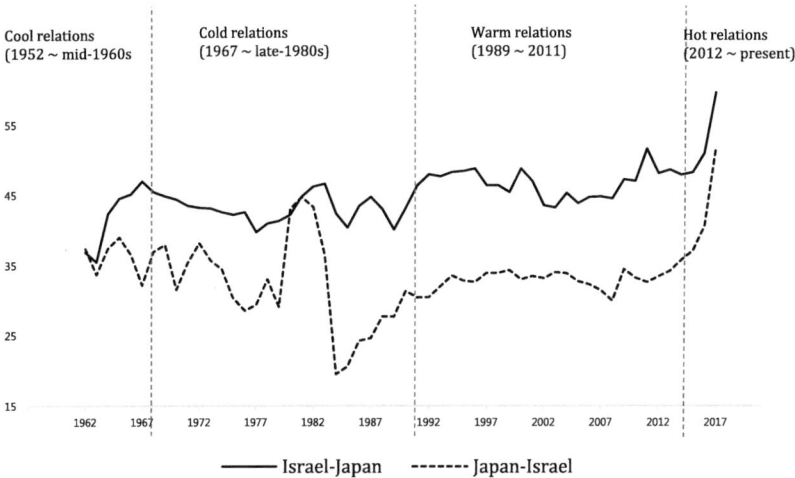

Fig. 2 Trade Complementary Index between Japan and Israel

the world,[100] and these in turn have led to proactively building strategic bridges with states once eschewed because of the country's preoccupation with natural resource scarcity and anti-military sentiments. Expanding strategic relations with Israel, a country at the frontier of both security and technology, is a natural result of this drive for a more independent and influential international presence.

At the same time, Israeli foreign-policy elites have long been preoccupied with the dual threats of *isolation* and *delegitimization* in the international arena, first as a result of the Arab boycott and later as a result of growing criticism from the liberal left in the Western hemisphere. Israel's government (led by Benjamin Netanyahu 2009 to 2021) has been at pains to address these concerns by diversifying its diplomatic engagement beyond Western Europe and the US toward Asia and elsewhere. Demonstrating this engagement while on a visit to Singapore in February 2017, Netanyahu declared that Israel was pivoting toward Asia in a "very clear and purposeful way."[101] It is in this context that he has found a

---

[100] Oren and Brummer, "Abe Shinzo's Japan."

[101] Herb Keinon, "Israel is Clearly Pivoting to Asia, Netanyahu Announces in Singapore," *Jerusalem Post*, 21 February 2017, https://www.jpost.com/Israel-News/Pol itics-And-Diplomacy/Israel-is-clearly-pivoting-to-Asia-Netanyahu-announces-in-Singapore-482131.

friend in Abe, whose security initiatives and foreign policy stance have meant that both leaders have much in common. In sum, political synergies are aligning in ways that have not existed previously in the Japan–Israel relationship.

6   Conclusion

Our survey of Japan–Israel relations from 1952 to 2019 offers a holistic account of bilateral affairs beyond the influence of "oil" and "Washington." While both are necessary for understanding the relationship, they are not sufficient: This paper's analysis of system and interest compatibilities, comprising security and economic factors, allows for introspection on the more general forces at work shaping the relationship across royal, government, and citizen affairs. The relationship is a storied one, complex in its nature, and always changing.

While our meta-analysis of Japanese and Israeli security and economic environments offers a valuable view of the evolution of the relationship, such an approach also leaves much to be covered. We have not explored, for instance, how synergy may operate within the cultural or ideational realms, and we have only briefly touched on how political synergy explains some aspects of the bilateral relationship. Similarly, we have not addressed certain compelling forces on the development of the relationship, including how the "history problem" of colonialism or the "social problem" of anti-Semitism have affected bilateral affairs. Future research must therefore square these approaches to understanding the relationship with the concept of complex synergy.

Synergy as a term has not been substantially developed in the study of international relations, which is surprising given not only its ubiquitous effect in nature but also its causal role in the evolutionary process of species. While our brief analysis of the Japan–Israel relationship demonstrates that synergy across security and economic systems and interests has clear applicability to the study of interstate affairs, this approach remains embryonic, both theoretically and methodologically. Similarly, the model of complex synergy presented in Fig. 1 is unidirectional in cause and effect, from changes in synergy to changes in diplomatic relations. Nonetheless, there may well be a mutual effect whereby, for example, better relations provide opportunities for increased synergy, and vice-versa, whereas worsening relations may in turn decrease synergistic compatibility. In other words, cooperative interactions of various kinds can produce otherwise unattainable combined effects—synergies—with functional advantages that may, in turn, become causes of better relations. While this "mutually determined system" conceptualization of diplomatic relations falls outside the scope of this paper, it nevertheless offers a compelling avenue for future research.

REFERENCES

Agency for Natural Resources and Energy. "FY 2017 Japan's Independent Development Ratio of Oil and Natural Gas." News release, Ministry of Economy, Trade and Industry, 27 July 2018.

Agency for Natural Resources and Energy. *Japan's Energy Plan 2015*. Tokyo: Ministry of Economy, Trade and Industry, 2015. https://www.enecho.meti.go.jp/en/category/brochures/pdf/energy_plan_2015.pdf.

Akiyama, Nobumasa. "Disarmament and the Non-Proliferation Policy of Japan." In *The Routledge Handbook of Japanese Foreign Policy*, edited by Mary M. McCarthy, 173–87. New York: Routledge, 2018.

Anderson, Nicholas D. "Anarchic Threats and Hegemonic Assurances: Japan's Security Production in the Postwar Era." *International Relations of the Asia-Pacific 17*, no. 1 (2016): 101–35.

Barkat, Amiram. "Daewoo Hires Hoegh to Design Tamar Floating Gas Terminal." *Globes*, 4 December 2011. https://en.globes.co.il/en/article-100 0703188.

Bialer, Uri. *Between East and West: Israel's Foreign Policy Orientation 1948–1956*. New York: Cambridge University Press, 1990.

Breznitz, Dan. *Innovation and the State: Political Choice and Strategies for Growth in Israel, Taiwan, and Ireland*. New Haven: Yale University Press, 2007.

Brummer, Matthew. "Bridges over Troubled History: Japan's Foreign Policy in Asia." *International Studies Review 21*, no. 1 (2019): 172–74.

Brummer, Matthew. "Innovation and Threats." *Defence and Peace Economics 33*, no. 5 (2022): 563–584.

Brummer, Matthew, and Eitan Oren. "Israel and Japan's Rising Sun Relations." *Foreign Affairs*, July 28, 2017. https://www.foreignaffairs.com/art icles/japan/2017-07-28/israel-and-japans-rising-sun-relations.

Brummer, Matthew, and Eitan Oren. "We Must Protect This Peace with Our Hands: Strategic Culture and Japan's Use of Force in International Disputes." *Journal of Advanced Military Studies* (2022): 88–111.

Cha, Victor D. "Abandonment, Entrapment, and Neoclassical Realism in Asia: The United States, Japan, and Korea." *International Studies Quarterly 44*, no. 2 (2000): 261–91.

Cohen, Avner. *Israel and the Bomb.* New York: Columbia University Press, 1998.

Cohen, Yaacov. "Japanese-Israeli Relations, the United States, and Oil." *Jewish Political Studies Review 17,* no. 1/2 (2005): 135–55.

Corning, Peter. *Holistic Darwinism: Synergy, Cybernetics, and the Bioeconomics of Evolution.* Chicago: University of Chicago Press, 2010.

Corning, Peter. *Nature's Magic: Synergy in Evolution and the Fate of Humankind.* New York: Cambridge University Press, 2003.

Darwin, Charles R. *On the Origin of Species by Means of Natural Selection, or the Preservation of Favoured Races in the Struggle for Life.* Milford: Oxford University Press, 1859.

de Boer, John. "Before Oil: Japan and the Question of Israel/Palestine, 1917–1956." *The Asia-Pacific Journal 3,* no. 3 (2005): 2159.

Desch, Michael C. *Power and Military Effectiveness: The Fallacy of Democratic Triumphalism.* Baltimore: John Hopkins University Press, 2008.

Fischer, Louise, ed. *Moshe Sharett: The Second Prime Minister, Selected Documents (1894–1965).* Jerusalem: Israel State Archives, 2009.

Genest, Marc A. *Conflict and Cooperation: Evolving Theories of International Relations.* Belmont: Thomson & Wadsworth, 2004.

Ginor, Isabella, and Gideon Remez. *Foxbats over Dimona: The Soviets' Nuclear Gamble in the Six-Day War.* New Haven: Yale University Press, 2008.

Halevi, Nadav, and Ruth Klinov-Malul. *The Economic Development of Israel.* New York: Praeger, 1968.

Hayashi, Fumio, and Edward C. Prescott. "The 1990s in Japan: A Lost Decade." *Review of Economic Dynamics 5,* no. 1 (2002): 206–35.

Heginbotham, Eric, and Richard J. Samuels. "Active Denial: Redesigning Japan's Response to China's Military Challenge." *International Security 42,* no. 4 (2018): 128–69.

Inbar, Efraim. "Israel's Strategic Environment in the 1990s." *Journal of Strategic Studies 25,* no. 1 (2002): 21–38.

Iokibe, Makoto, Caroline Rose, Junko Tomaru, and John Weste, eds. *Japanese Diplomacy in the 1950s: From Isolation to Integration.* New York: Routledge, 2008.

Israel Export Institute. "Israel-Japan Trade Relations." *Israel-Japan Business Guide,* 10 August 2018, 12–14.

Israel Ministry of Foreign Affairs. "President Reuven Rivlin Meets with Japanese FM Tarō Kōno." News release, 25 December 2017. https://mfa.gov.il/MFA/PressRoom/2017/Pages/President-Rivlin-meets-with-Japanese-FM-Taro-Kono-25-December-2017.aspx.

Japan Israel Innovation Network. *Japanese Business Partners 2019,* 7 January 2019.   https://www.jetro.go.jp/ext_images/israel/Japanese_Business_Partners_WEBver.pdf.

Kawai, Masahiro, and Shinji Takagi. "Why Was Japan Hit So Hard by the Global Financial Crisis?" In *The Impact of the Economic Crisis on East Asia: Policy Responses from Four Economies*, edited by Daigee Shaw and Bih Jane Wu, 131–48. Northampton: Edward Elgar Publishing, 2011.

Keinon, Herb. "Israel is Clearly Pivoting to Asia, Netanyahu Announces in Singapore." *Jerusalem Post*, 21 February 2017. https://www.jpost.com/Isr ael-News/Politics-And-Diplomacy/Israel-is-clearly-pivoting-to-Asia-Netany ahu-announces-in-Singapore-482131.

Keohane, Robert O., and Joseph S. Nye. *Power and Interdependence: World Politics in Transition*. Boston: Little, Brown & Co., 1977.

Kibe, Hidemitsu. "Japanese Companies Show Keen Interest in Israeli Startups." *Nikki Asian Review*, 6 December 2016. https://asia.nikkei.com/Business/ Biotechnology/Japanese-companies-show-keen-interest-in-Israeli-startups.

Kingston, Jeff. *Japan in Transformation, 1945–2010*. 2nd ed. New York: Routledge, 2014.

Krotz, Ulrich. *Flying Tiger: International Relations Theory and the Politics of Advanced Weapons*. New York: Oxford University Press, 2011.

Medzini, Meron. "Asian Voting Patterns on the Middle East in the UN General Assembly." In *Israel in the Third World*, edited by Michael Curtis and Susan A. Gitelson, 318–24. New Brunswick: Transaction Books, 1976.

Medzini, Meron. "From Alienation to Partnership: Israel–Japan Relation." *Contemporary Review of the Middle East 5*, no. 3 (2018): 232–40.

Medzini, Meron. *Golda Meir: A Political Biography*. Berlin: De Gruyter, 2017.

Medzini, Meron. "Reflections on Israel's Policy Toward Japan Since 1952." In *Japanese Studies in Israel as a Micro-cosmos of Japanese Studies in the World: Lectures Delivered at the Israel-Japan Symposium*, edited by Helena Grinschpun, Shalmit Bejarano, and Nissim Otmazgin. Jerusalem: Hebrew University of Jerusalem, 2012. http://japan-studies-org.stackstaging.com/ wp-content/uploads/2019/04/medzini-fulltext.pdf.

Meridor, Dan, and Ron Eldadi. *Israel's National Security Doctrine: The Committee Report on Formulation of the Security Concept (Meridor Committee), Ten Years Later*. Tel-Aviv: The Institute for National Security Studies, 2018.

Ministry of Defense. *Defense of Japan 2018*. Tokyo: Ministry of Defense, 2018.

Ministry of Economy, Trade and Industry. "Japan-Israel Innovation Network 2.0." News release, 17 January 2019. https://www.meti.go.jp/english/ press/2019/pdf/0117_001a.pdf.

Ministry of Economy, Trade and Industry. "Joint Statement: The Ministry of Economy, Trade and Industry of Japan and the Ministry of Economy and Industry of the State of Israel launch Japan-Israel Innovation Partnership." News release, 3 May 2017. https://www.meti.go.jp/press/2017/05/201 70508004/20170508004-2.pdf.

Ministry of Economy, Trade and Industry. "White Paper on International
Economy and Trade 2007: Japan's Trade Strategy on Improving Industrial
Productivity and Accelerating Economic Growth." July 2007. Accessed 26
April 2019. https://www.meti.go.jp/english/report/downloadfiles/2007Wh
itePaper/Overview0712.pdf.
Ministry of Foreign Affairs of Japan. "First Joint Foreign Affairs and Secu-
rity Consultation between Japan and Israel (Pol-Mil Dialog)." News release,
10 October 2018. https://www.mofa.go.jp/press/release/press4e_002186.
html.
Ministry of Foreign Affairs of Japan. "Japan's Assistance to the Palestinians."
September 2018. Accessed 4 October 2019. https://www.mofa.go.jp/files/
000042388.pdf.
Ministry of Foreign Affairs of Japan. "Japan's Legislation for Peace and Security:
Seamless Responses for Peace and Security of Japan and the International
Community." March 2016. Accessed 4 April, 2019. www.mofa.go.jp/files/
000143304.pdf.
Nakayama, Ichirō. *Industrialization of Japan.* Tokyo: Centre for East Asian
Cultural Studies, 1963.
National Institute of Information and Communications Technology. "NICTER
Analysis Report 2017." In *NICT Report 2019*, 43–44. Tokyo: NICT, 2019.
Oren, Eitan. "Japan's Evolving Threat Perception: Data from Diet Delib-
erations 1946–2017." *International Relations of the Asia-Pacific* 20, no.
3 (2020). https://academic.oup.com/irap/article-abstract/doi/10.1093/
irap/lcz016/5533104.
Oren, Eitan. *Japan's Threat Perception during the Cold War: A psychological
account.* New York: Routledge, 2023.
Oren, Eitan and Matthew Brummer. "How Japan Talks About Security Threats."
The Diplomat. August 14, 2020. https://thediplomat.com/2020/08/how-
japan-talks-about-security-threats.
Oren, Eitan, and Matthew Brummer. "Reexamining Threat Perceptions in Early
Cold War Japan." *Journal of Cold War Studies* 22, no. 4 (2020). https://doi.
org/10.1162/jcws_a_00948.
Oren, Eitan, and Matthew Brummer. "Threat Perception, Government Central-
ization, and Political Instrumentality in Abe Shinzo's Japan." *Australian
Journal of International Affairs* 74, no. 6 (2020). https://doi.org/10.1080/
10357718.2020.1782345.
Orgel, Hugh. "Herzog to Attend Hirohito's Funeral." *Jewish Telegraphic Agency*,
23 January 1983.
Oros, Andrew L. "Japan's Security Future." In *The Routledge Handbook of Asian
Security Studies*, edited by Sumit Ganguly, Andrew Scobell, and Joseph C.
Liow, 39–50. New York: Routledge, 2009.

Pick, Adi. "Israel and Japan in Talk to Enter a Free Trade Agreement." *CTech by Calcalist*, 15 January 2019. https://www.calcalistech.com/ctech/articles/0,7340,L-3754321,00.html.

Robinson, Tim, and Geordie Jeakins. "Squaring the Triangle: Why Turkey and the EastMed Project Need Each Other." *War on the Rocks*, 12 April 2019. https://warontherocks.com/2019/04/squaring-the-triangle-why-turkey-and-the-eastmed-project-need-each-other/.

Schmid, Jon, Matthew Brummer, and Mark Z. Taylor. "Innovation and Alliances." *Review of Policy Research 34*, no. 5 (2017): 588–616.

Senor, Dan, and Saul Singer. *Start-Up Nation: The Story of Israel's Economic Miracle.* New York: Hatchette Book Group, 2009.

Shalev, Michael. "Have Globalization and Liberalization 'Normalized' Israel's Political Economy?" *Israel Affairs 5*, no. 2–3 (1998): 121–55.

Shaoul, Raquel. "Japan and Israel: An Evaluation of Relationship-Building in the Context of Japan's Middle East Policy." *Israel Affairs 10*, no. 1–2 (2004): 273–97.

Smith, Sheila A. *Japan Rearmed: The Politics of Military Power.* Cambridge: Harvard University Press, 2019.

Steinhoff, Patricia G. "Portrait of a Terrorist: An Interview with Kozo Okamoto." *Asian Survey 16*, no. 9 (1976): 830–45.

Tanaka, Akihiko. *Japan in Asia: Post-Cold-War Diplomacy.* Translated by Jean Connell Hoff. Tokyo: Japan Publishing Industry for Culture, 2017.

Trajtenberg, Manuel. "R&D Policy in Israel." In *Innovation Policy in the Knowledge-Based Economy*, edited by Maryann P. Feldman and Albert N. Link, 409–54. Boston: Springer, 2012.

Varble, Derek. *The Suez Crisis.* New York: Rosen Publishing, 2008.

Wezeman, Pieter D., Aude Fleurant, Alexandra Kuimova, Nan Tian, and Siemon T. Wezeman. "Trends in International Arms Transfer, 2017." *SIPRI Fact Sheet*, March 2018.

World Intellectual Property Organization. "Global Innovation Index 2018: China Cracks Top 20. Top Rankings: Switzerland, Netherlands, Sweden, UK, Singapore, U.S." News release, 10 July 2018. https://www.wipo.int/pressroom/en/articles/2018/article_0005.html.

Yablonko, Yasmin. "Following China and South Korea: Japan Puts Israel on the Agenda." *Globes*, 17 January 2019. https://www.globes.co.il/news/article.aspx?did=1001269341.

Yarime, Masaru. "Integrated Solutions to Complex Problems: Transforming Japanese Science and Technology." In *Japan: The Precarious Future*, edited by Frank Baldwin and Anne Allison, 213–35. New York: New York University Press, 2015.

CHAPTER 8

Oil Market and Supply: From the Perspective of Japan's Energy Policy

Takeru Hosoi

1 INTRODUCTION

Oil is an essential resource in modern society. However, as Japan has no oil resources, it imports most of it from abroad and consequently has close economic relations with Middle Eastern countries, especially the Gulf countries, through its trade in oil. Japan and other Asian countries, such as China and India, which have been rapidly increasing their oil consumption in recent years, are important customers for Middle Eastern oil producers.[1]

In recent years, China and India's presence as oil export markets for Middle Eastern oil-producing countries has been increasing. Will Japan

[1] The oil industry in the GCC countries began in 1932 with the discovery of the first oil field in Bahrain, and exports began in 1934. As this was the first export destination of Bahraini oil to Yokohama, Japan, the historical relationship between Japan and the GCC countries through oil is also significant.

T. Hosoi (✉)
Kokugakuin University, Shibuya, Tokyo, Japan
e-mail: hosonaga@kokugakuin.ac.jp

© The Author(s), under exclusive license to Springer Nature Singapore Pte Ltd. 2023
S. Nakamura and S. Wright (eds.), *Japan and the Middle East*, Contemporary Gulf Studies, https://doi.org/10.1007/978-981-19-3459-9_8

continue to be as important a market as it has been in the past? Yoshihide Suga became the new Prime Minister in September 2020, and in his
first policy speech, he announced a goal of "virtually zero greenhouse gas
emissions by 2050". South Korea's President Moon Jae-in has announced
a similar policy, while Chinese President Xi Jinping also announced in his
September 2020 speech to the United Nations General Assembly that he
aimed to achieve zero greenhouse gas emissions by 2060. It is inevitable
that the consumption of fossil fuels in Asia's major consumer countries
will decline significantly in the future but will this fall in oil consumption
be a factor in changing the relationship between the oil-producing countries of the Middle East and Asian consumer countries such as Japan? As
described later, the basic policy of Japan's energy policy is 3E+S (Energy
Security, Environment, Economy and Safety). In this chapter, we try to
consider this question by reviewing the development of this policy and
the characteristics of the Japanese energy market.

First of all, we present an overview of the Japanese energy market, and
then we look at the current circumstances of oil in the energy market.
Oil played an important role in Japan's economic development in the
post-war period, known as "the Miracle". A stable supply of oil resources
is necessary for the growth of the Japanese economy, but as mentioned
above, the country has no oil resources and therefore relies mainly on
imports from the Middle East. As a result, its "energy security" perspective is extremely important compared to other countries, and the Middle
East is becoming more and more important as a target region. We also
summarise Japanese policy in terms of securing energy resources, especially oil, and examine the problems associated therewith, and finally, we
examine the characteristics of the Japanese oil industry from an industrial
perspective and demonstrate how its direction as the global oil industry is
undergoing major changes.

Through the above discussion, we summarise the oil market in Japan
and consider how to establish a relationship with the Middle East.

2   Macro Structure
of the Energy Market in Japan

In this section, we explain the macrostructure of energy supply and
demand in Japan, in comparison with other developed and Asian countries. We point out that the peak of energy consumption has already
passed in Japan and that energy-saving technologies are now being widely

used, before moving on to illustrate the importance of oil as an energy resource has been declining in Japan.

2.1 Trends in Energy Supply and Demand in Japan

The Economic White Paper (Annual Report on the Japanese Economy), published by the Economic Planning Agency in 1956, stated that "it was no longer the post-war period", thus heralding a period of rapid economic growth from the mid-1950s onwards,[2] which lasted until 1973 when the first oil shock occurred. During this period (1956–1973), Japan's real GDP growth rate averaged 9.1% per year, which was extremely high, peaking at 12.4% in 1968. Obviously, energy consumption also surges during periods of rapid economic growth. Figure 1 shows the change in energy consumption by industry in Japan from 1965. It is clear that the figure rose rapidly until 1973, when the first oil crisis occurred, actually doubling in five years, from 4.54 EJ in 1965 to 8.84 EJ in 1970. The oil crisis of the 1970s brought an end to Japan's rapid economic growth and put a brake on the growth in energy consumption. It was not until the Japanese asset price bubble (bubble economy) of the late 1980s that energy consumption showed a significant increase, and after bursting the bubble economy in the early 1990s, it remained at a high level until the mid-2000s. Japan's energy consumption peaked in 2005. Since 2007, around the time of the World Financial Crisis, energy use began to decline, and in recent years it has fallen to the level of the early 1990s.

2.2 A Comparison of Japan and Other Countries

This section illustrates the energy consumption composition ratio in Japan by sector. Figure 2 shows the energy consumption composition by the industrial sector since 1965. The following features can be noted from Fig. 2.

---

[2] See Miyazaki (1967) for a discussion on the Japanese economy during the period of rapid economic growth.

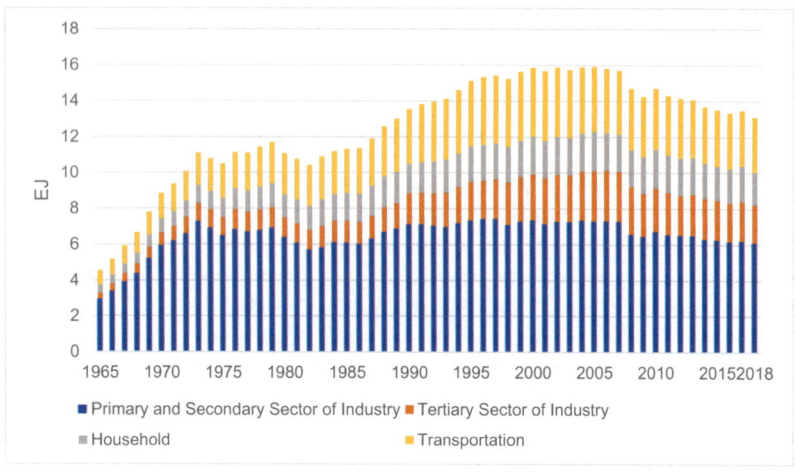

Fig. 1   Japan: Energy consumption by industry[3]

i. Manufacturing is the largest industry in terms of energy consumption in Japan; it used to account for over 60% during the rapid economic growth period, but it has fallen to less than 50% today.

ii. The percentage of energy consumption in the service industry is increasing significantly.

iii. The ratio for the transportation sector is also increasing.

We now explain how Japan's energy-saving technology has spread. The nation has a comparative advantage in manufacturing, and its post-war economy developed mainly through this industry.[4] In the past, heavy

---

[3] FY2019 Annual Report on Energy (Japan's Energy White Paper 2020).

[4] In terms of Japan's comparative advantage, the change in products subject to U.S.–Japan trade friction is a good example. From the 1950s to the early 1990s, there was a diplomatic row between Japan and the United States over trade. The basic structure of the dispute was that Japanese companies launched an offensive against the United States in terms of low prices, the United States posted a large trade deficit and U.S. companies sought a bailout from their government. Diplomatic negotiations were held between the U.S. and Japanese governments, and the solution was agreed after the Japanese side instructed its companies to impose voluntary export restrictions (voluntary export restrictions are prohibited under current WTO rules). These trade friction targets are similar to the development of Japanese industry: apparel in the 1950s, steel in the 1960s, colour

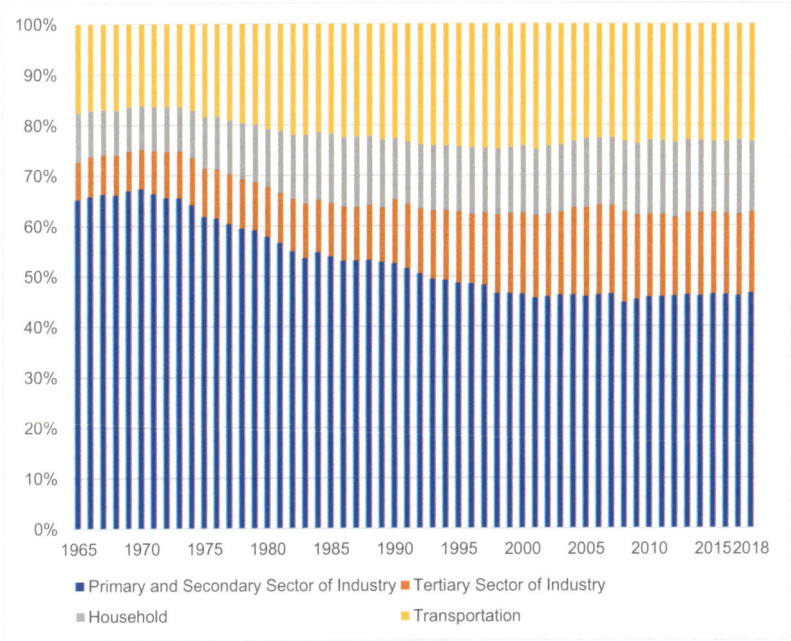

Fig. 2 Japan: Energy consumption ratio by industry[5]

industries, such as steel, were the main producers, and, consequently, consumers of energy. However, after the oil crisis of the 1970s, the machine and automobile industries came to the forefront in Japan, and today the materials and electronics industries predominate. Currently, the automobile industry is the most essential.

There are three important points to consider when discussing the spread of energy-saving technologies in Japan. The first is their rapid development during the oil crisis of the 1970s, when the prices of oil skyrocketed and had a significant impact on the economy.

TVs and automobiles in the 1970s and semiconductors in the 1980s. In particular, the oil crisis led to a surge in Japanese exports to the United States, and the automobile industry became a serious issue between the two nations. On trade frictions between Japan and the United States, see Cohen (1985), Holgerson (1998), Sato and Wachtel (1987) and others.

[5] FY2019 Annual Report on Energy (Japan's Energy White Paper 2020).

The second point is that along with these changes in industrial structure and technology, Japanese companies moved their production bases
abroad in droves as a result of trade friction between the country and
the United States, as well as the appreciation of the yen as a result of
the 1985 Plaza Accord. This was also a factor in limiting the growth of
energy consumption in the manufacturing sector.

Third, Japan is no exception to the phenomenon known as "Petty-
Clark's law",[6] whereby the services sector has increased remarkably in
accordance with economic growth.

However, unlike the manufacturing industry, the service industry does
not directly benefit from energy-saving technologies, so energy consumption has been increasing in line with the development of the service sector.
In the transportation sector, the spread of fuel-efficient technologies has
led to a decline in energy consumption itself, compared to the late 1990s
and early 2000s, when consumption was at its highest, but the proportion
in other sectors has been relatively high, particularly in the manufacturing
sector.

2.3   Trends in Japan's Energy Sources

Next, we look at the transition of energy sources in Japan's energy supply
(Fig. 3). After the end of World War II, most of Japan's primary energy
was supplied by domestic coal, since it was not possible to import oil
freely, due to foreign exchange restrictions running from 1945 to 1962.
However, oil imports were liberalised in 1962, and the ratio of oil as a
source of energy increased in the 1960s, partly due to rapid economic
growth and the government's policy of switching from coal to oil as an
energy source. The supply of oil as a primary energy source in Japan
peaked in 1995, but the highest share of oil in total was 75.5% in 1973.
Recently, the amount of oil supply has remained about the same as seen
in the late 1960s and early 1970s, and oil share of the total is now below
40%. While oil remains the largest primary energy source, it is not as
important as it once was, due to the diversification of energy sources.

When considering the transition of Japan's energy supply sources, the
two oil crises in the 1970s and the Great East Japan Earthquake in 2011
are significant turning points. During the oil crisis of the 1970s, the

---

[6] See Clark(1940).

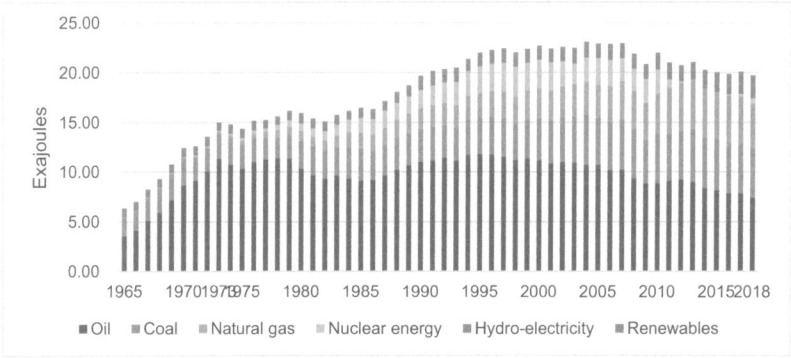

Fig. 3 Japan: Primary energy supply by fuel[7]

nation's over-reliance on oil, and its dependence on the Middle East, was strongly perceived as an energy problem.

Therefore, it tried to shift to other energy sources and to buy oil from outside the Middle East. As a result of this energy resource diversification, the share of natural gas and nuclear power increased,[8] while the share of nuclear power in the primary energy supply has remained at just over 10% since the 1990s.

The Great East Japan Earthquake in March 2011, and the resulting explosion at the Tokyo Electric Power Company's (TEPCO) Fukushima Daiichi Nuclear Power Plant, resulted in the shutting of all nuclear power plants in the country. As of 2020, some nuclear have been restarted, but only small amounts of power have been generated, and so, currently, nuclear power as a source of energy supply remains close to zero. As a result of the shutdown of nuclear power plants, the share of natural gas

---

[7] FY2019 Annual Report on Energy (Japan's Energy White Paper 2020).

[8] Japan first imported natural gas (LNG) came from the United States in November 1969. With regard to nuclear power, the first was generated in October 1963, and commercial operations began in 1966. From the 1970s, electric power companies such as Tokyo Electric Power Company and Kansai Electric Power Company increased the number of nuclear power plants in Japan.

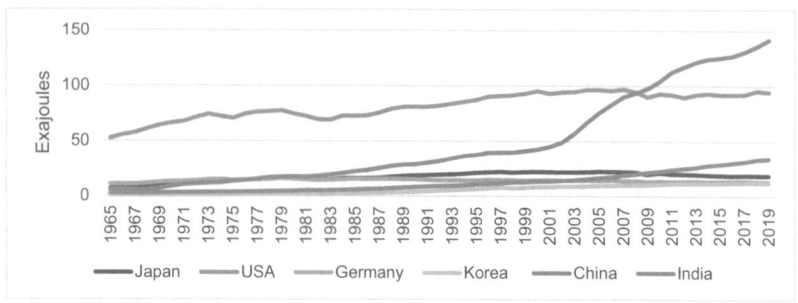

Fig. 4   Primary energy consumption[10]

and, to a lesser extent, coal, is increasing as an alternative source,[9] with natural gas recently accounting for about 20% of Japan's energy supply.

2.4   Comparison with Other Major Energy Consumers: Japan's High Dependence on Fossil Energy

We now compare Japan's energy situation with other countries. Figure 4 illustrates primary energy consumption in Japan, the United States, Germany, China, India and South Korea. In Japan and Germany, where people are highly concerned about energy issues and energy-saving technologies are widely spread, the peak primary energy consumption has already passed and is on a decreasing trend.

What is noteworthy here is the rapid increase in primary energy consumption in China and India, especially since the beginning of the twenty-first century. In particular, the increase in China's energy consumption since the beginning of the twenty-first century has been remarkable. China and India are the leading emerging economies, and they are also increasing their global presence in terms of energy consumption. Figure 5 shows these changes per person. In terms of per capita primary energy consumption, Japan, the United States and Germany are gradually declining. The emerging economies of China and India have

---

[9] As a result of shutting down nuclear power plants, plans to build new coal-fired power plants have been put forward, but there is opposition in many areas of the region, due to concerns of nearby residents about the negative impacts on the environment.

[10] BP Statistical Review of World Energy 2020.

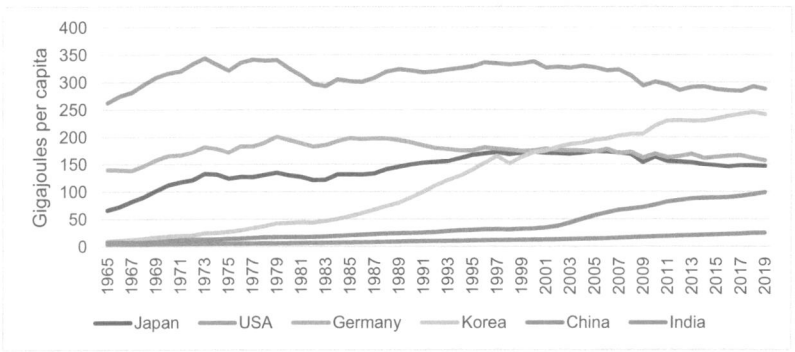

Fig. 5 Primary energy consumption per capita[11]

lower absolute per capita energy consumption, but the rate of increase since the 2000s has been substantial. Although this high growth in developed countries is not expected in the future, emerging economies are expected to continue to grow. It is a certainty that energy consumption will increase in emerging countries, and securing energy sources for economic growth will be a policy issue.

Table 1 shows the fossil energy dependence of major countries in 2019. Japan's dependence on fossil fuels was 87.5%, which is higher than that of the United States and Germany, making it one of the highest users among developed countries. Its dependence on oil in 2019 was 40.3%. France is highly dependent on nuclear power and has low dependence on fossil energy at 51.4%. Incidentally, Germany has a high share of renewable energy (about 16%). The emerging economies of China[12] and India are also highly dependent on fossil energy, as is Korea. In developed countries, dependence on oil and natural gas is high among fossil fuels, while emerging countries are more dependent on coal from a price perspective. Due to the perceived negative impact of coal on the environment, economic development will likely lead to a gradual shift to oil and natural gas.

Japan is also highly dependent on coal among developed countries. As will be explained in detail in the next section, oil and natural gas in Japan

[11] BP Statistical Review of World Energy 2020.

[12] China is notable for its relatively high percentage of hydropower (7.9%).

Table 1 Percentage of primary energy consumption by fossil energy (2019, %)[13]

	Japan	USA	Germany	France	China	India	Korea
Dependence on fossil energy	87.5	83.3	77.4	51.4	85.1	91	86.9
Oil	40.3	39.1	35.6	32.5	19.7	30.1	42.8
Coal	26.3	12	17.5	2.8	57.6	54.7	27.8
Natural gas	20.8	32.2	11.9	16.1	7.8	6.3	16.2

are mostly imported from the Middle East, and coal has been used from the perspective of diversifying energy sources and cost, as it is cheaper than oil and natural gas.[14] Furthermore, the nation has been developing efficient and environmentally friendly coal-fired power generation technologies, and in July 2020, the Ministry of Economy, Trade and Industry (METI) announced a policy to phase out inefficient units by 2030 and maintain highly efficient ones(*NIKKEI*, 3 July, 2020).

Since the collapse of the bubble economy in the late 1980s, Japan has been struggling with low long-term economic growth, and the country's population is declining and ageing. While Asia is expected to achieve rapid economic growth in the future, it cannot be expected in Japan. In addition, the nation's industrial structure is changing from traditional heavy industry to hi-technology or material industries, and energy-saving technology is spreading, so a significant increase in energy use itself is not expected in the future. Under these circumstances, Japan's dependence on fossil fuels the supply of almost all of which is dependent on foreign countries is a unique characteristic among developed countries.

3   The Structure of the Japanese Oil Market

This section summarises the supply and demand effect in the Japanese oil market, and it explains the deep relationship between Japan and Middle Eastern countries.

---

[13] BP Statistical Review of World Energy 2020.

[14] Most of the coal consumed in Japan is imported from Australia, Indonesia and Russia.

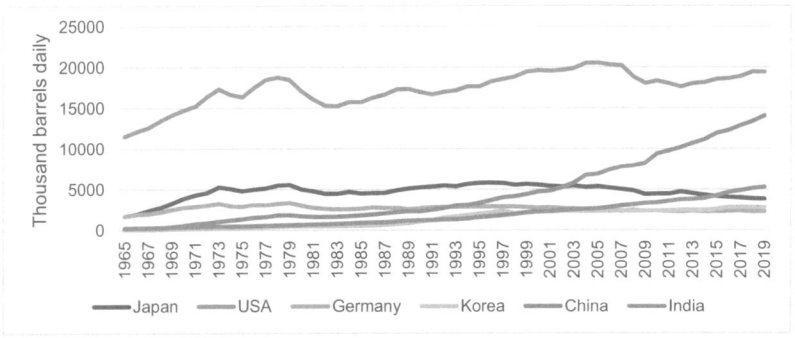

Fig. 6 Oil consumption of major countries[15]

3.1 Japan's Middle Eastern Oil Dependency

Figure 6 shows the transitions in oil consumption in major countries, including Japan. Japan's oil consumption expanded 2.2 times in just five years, from 1965 to 1970, a period of rapid economic growth. Thereafter, consumption levelled off in the 1970s as oil prices soared in the wake of the oil crisis. In the latter part of the 1980s, the Japanese economy turned around, due to the bubble economy. Still the development and spread of energy-saving technologies in response to the oil crisis did not lead to a significant increase in oil consumption. Japan's oil use peaked in 1996 at 5.08 million barrels per day and has been on a downward trend in recent years. In Japan and Germany and in the United States, where consumption is by far the largest, there is a downward trend in consumption. However, China and India have been rapidly increasing their oil utilisation since the 2000s.

Japan's dependence on oil for primary energy consumption is around 40%, and although the ratio of other energy sources such as natural gas is increasing, oil remains the most important. The country does not have any oil resources. To be more precise, Niigata[16] and Akita do produce oil, but only in quantities, and Japan is almost entirely dependent on

---

[15] BP Statistical Review of World Energy 2020.

[16] At the Niitsu oil field in Niigata City, a former oil facility has been turned into an industrial heritage museum, and in 2019, Saudi Aramco Japan donated 20 million yen to help develop it (*Nikkei Sangyo Shinbun*, 6JAN2020).

imports from other countries; for instance, its oil import dependency ratio exceeded 99% in 1964 and has remained so. Figure 7 shows the percentage of Japan's oil imports by country and its dependence on the Middle East, which rose until the first oil crisis in 1973, when it became over 90% dependent on the region. Based on the experience of the oil crisis of the 1970s, Japan decided that relying solely on the Middle East was dangerous from the perspective of ensuring energy stability, and so it worked to diversify its supply sources. As a result, it increased oil imports from China, Indonesia and other Asian countries, and by the 1980s, its dependence on the Middle East had diminished to around 60%.

Since then, however, China has switched to a policy of not exporting oil, due to its rising domestic demand. Indonesia has also drastically reduced its exports in recent years for the same reason. In terms of cost, Middle Eastern oil has a distinct advantage. As a result, dependence on the Middle East, including Saudi Arabia and the UAE, has increased again since the mid-1990s, and today its dependence on the Middle East stands at around 90%, which is an important factor when considering Japan's oil market.

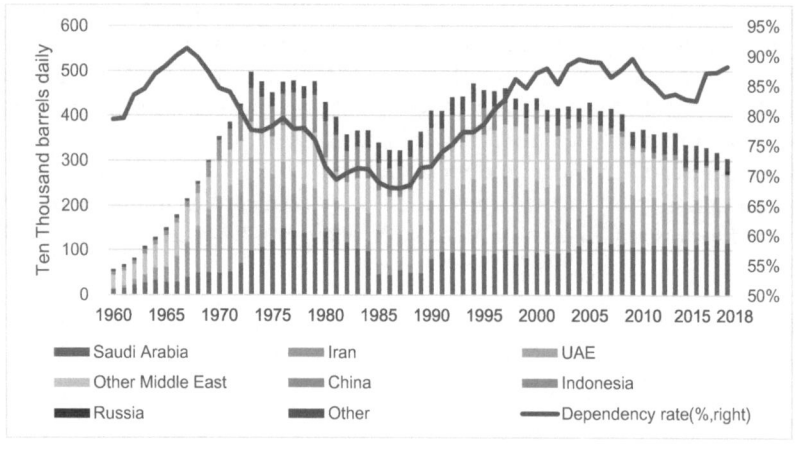

Fig. 7 Japan's crude oil imports and dependency rate on the Middle East[17]

[17] FY2019 Annual Report on Energy (Japan's Energy White Paper 2020).

3.2   Japan's Dependence on Middle Eastern LNG

I now explain from where major Asian countries import oil and LNG. Figure 8 is a graph of where Japan, China, South Korea and India imported oil from in 2019. One of this graph's features is Japan's remarkable dependence on the Middle East, which reached 88.9% in 2019, with Saudi Arabia and the UAE accounting for over 50% of this import share. South Korea is also relatively dependent on the Middle East, but at around 70%, which is less than Japan. Oil imports from the United States, Russia and Mexico have reduced South Korea's dependence on the Middle East. China's dependence on the Middle East for oil imports is 44.5%. While Saudi Arabia is the largest source of imports, it is noteworthy that imports from outside the Middle East, such as from Angola and Brazil, are high, thereby diversifying the sources of supply. India's dependence on the Middle East is 64%.

Figure 9 graphically indicates from where Japan, China, South Korea and India imported LNG in 2019. For LNG, except for India, all three countries are overall less dependent on the Middle East than on oil. Japan imports more than 50% of its LNG from Australia and Malaysia, with supplies from Qatar coming in third with an 11% share. South Korea's imports from Qatar and Oman account for 38% of the total, while India's imports from Qatar and the UAE account for 53%, making it more dependent on the Middle East for LNG imports than Japan and China. Unlike oil, LNG is not a commodity traded on the spot market, but rather on long-term contracts, and it is not possible to change suppliers easily.

3.3   Gulf Dependence on Japan's Market

I now explain the position of the Japanese market and its trade relationships with Gulf oil producers. Figure 10 shows Saudi Arabia's oil exports by region. Until the early 1980s, it exported much of its oil to Europe and North America. In the 1980s, when it played a role as a swing producer in OPEC to stabilise oil prices, exports fell sharply, and the Saudi economy fell into distress. In Europe, oil fields such as the North Sea developed in the 1970s, due to the high oil price, and exports from Saudi Arabia to Europe and the United States decreased up to the 1980s. From the 1990s onwards, economic development in Asia led to an increase in demand for oil, and the Saudi Arabian oil market replaced that of the Western countries. There was a remarkable increase in the volume of exports to

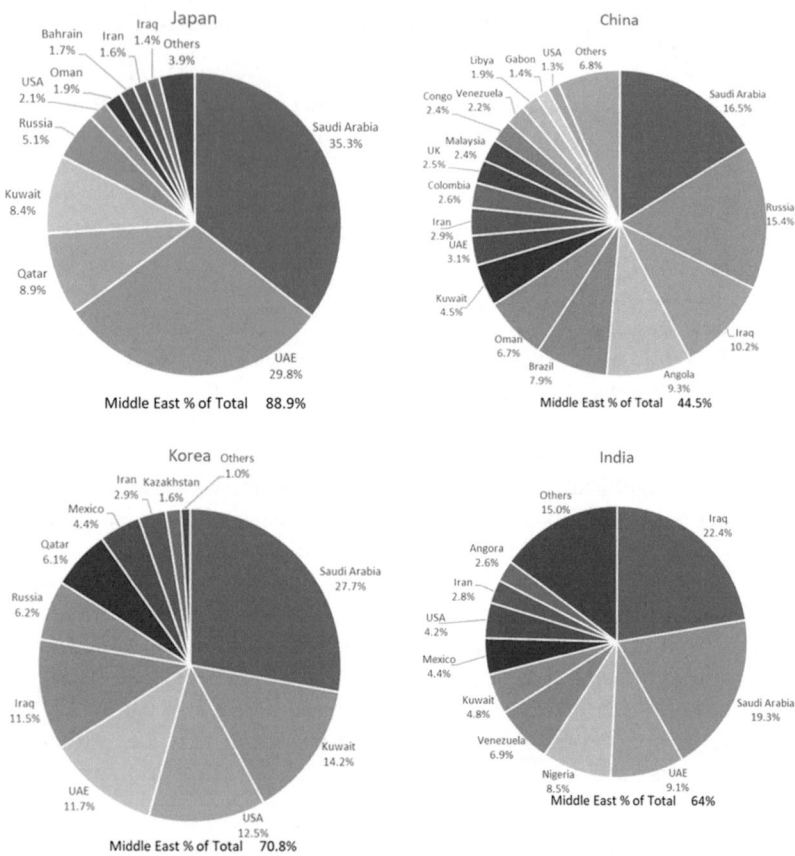

Fig. 8 Asian countries crude oil imports in 2019 ('000B/D)[18]

[18] MEES, 17 JAN 2020 (Korea) and 7 FEB 2020 (Japan, China and India).

Asia since the 2000s, when the economic development of China and India began in earnest. Saudi Arabia exported 70% of its oil exports to Asia in 2019, and with high economic growth assured for the future, the continent has become an important oil market for the Kingdom.

Figure 11 shows changes in the export values of Saudi Arabia, UAE and Qatar to Japan and China. These three countries' exports to Japan and China include some non-oil products, such as aluminium, but they

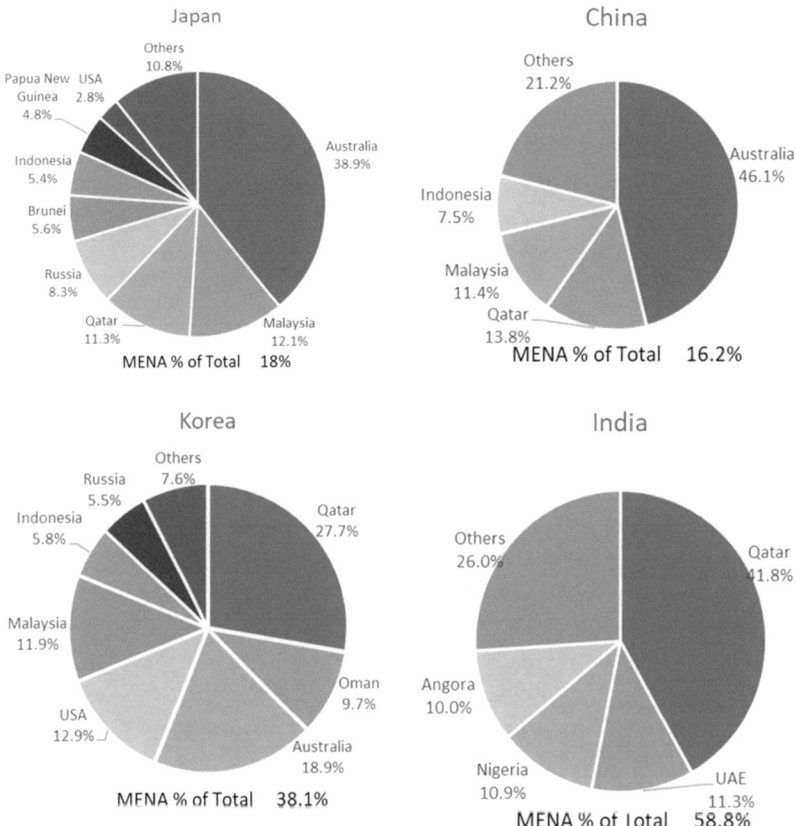

Fig. 9   Asian countries LNG imports in 2019 (Volume:MNT)[19]

[19] MEES, 17 JAN 2020 (Korea) and 14 FEB 2020 (Japan, China and India).

are not particularly large. Exports from these three countries are mostly oil, LNG and petroleum-related products. The fact that the trend in oil prices and the value of exports are almost identical shows that oil-related commodities make up the bulk of these exports. For Saudi Arabia, although the value of its exports to Japan fell during the period from the late 1980s to the 1990s, when the oil price was low, the value of

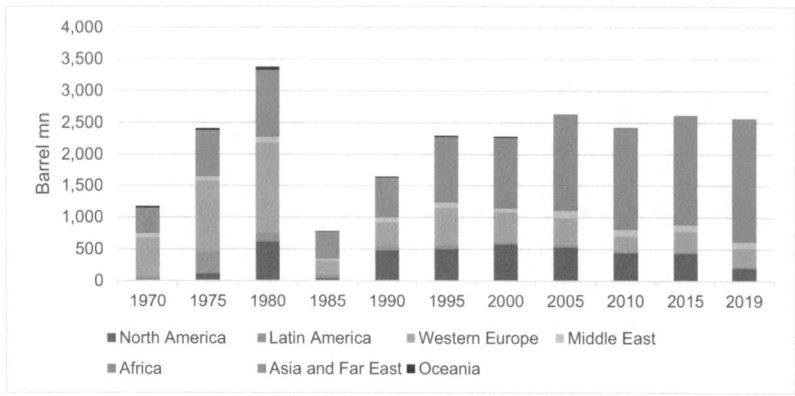

Fig. 10   Saudi Arabia's oil exports by region[20]

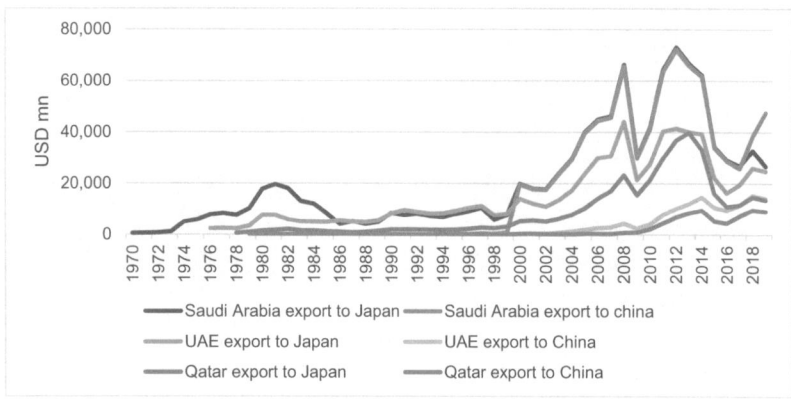

Fig. 11   Saudi Arabia, UAE, and Qatar export value to Japan[21]

exports has increased rapidly since the 2000s. At the same time, the value of exports to China has increased since the 2000s.[22]

[20] Ministry of Energy, Industry and Mineral Resources, Saudi Arabia.

[21] Source: IMF, DOT.

[22] It should be noted that China's trade statistics through 1999 may not be accurate especially the oil trade section.

Saudi Arabia established diplomatic relations with China in 1990,[23] and since Jiang Zemin became the first Chinese president to visit Saudi Arabia in 1999 and signed a number of oil-related agreements, Saudi Arabia has increased its oil exports to China, due to rising domestic demand. In monetary terms, since 2018, these exports have exceeded what the kingdom sends to Japan. The growth of the UAE and Qatar's exports to China has also been remarkable since the 2000s. Both countries are still exporting more to Japan than to China, but this will eventually be reversed as China's energy demand continues to rise.

3.4 Energy Interdependence and Its Fragility

Japan has traditionally been a trade surplus country, but since the 2010s, when nuclear power generation was shut down and fossil fuel imports increased, it has recorded trade deficits in some years. Looking at Japan's trade balance by region, the Middle East has traditionally recorded a trade deficit. Figure 12 shows Japan's trade balance with Saudi Arabia, UAE, Qatar and Kuwait indicating that the country's trade deficit with these four nations has increased since the 1970s when oil prices rose. The biggest export item from Japan to these four countries is automobiles, and when the oil-producing economies are in a boom period due to high crude oil prices, exports from Japan increase, but the impact of the oil price on the value of trade with the country is even greater than that.

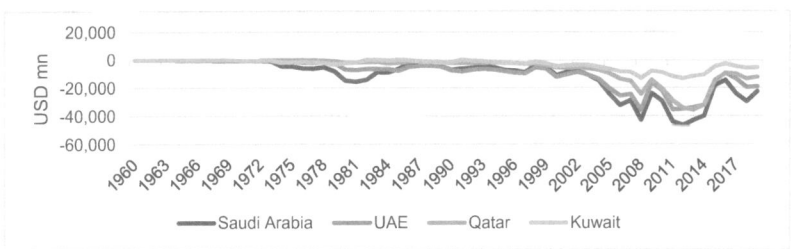

Fig. 12 Japan's trade balance with major Gulf countries[24]

---

[23] Saudi Arabia had diplomatic relations with the Republic of China (Taiwan) until 1990.

[24] Source: IMF, DOT.

To summarise Japan's oil market in a nutshell, its dependence on the Middle East is extremely high and more pronounced than other Asian countries, such as China and India. With regard to LNG, Japan is not as dependent on the Middle East as oil, but it does rely on Qatar for a significant amount of LNG. Likewise, the Asian market is an important position for the Middle Eastern oil-producing countries, as Asia is expected to grow in the future.

Moreover, transporting oil and LNG from the Middle East to East Asia requires passage through chokepoints such as the Strait of Hormuz and the Strait of Malacca, which makes transportation more unstable than in the case of exports to Europe. Needless to say, Japan must build a good relationship with Middle Eastern oil-producing countries in order to ensure the stability of its energy resources. In recent years, the Japanese government has taken actions to reduce the risk to its ships at chokepoints in the Middle East, including the deployment of the Japanese Self-Defense Forces (JSDF) for anti-piracy operations in the Gulf of Aden to protect Japanese-related vessels and the dispatching of a fleet to the Gulf of Oman for intelligence-gathering purposes.

To summarise Japan and Asia's oil market, Japan's oil consumption peaked in 1996 and has been on a decreasing trend in recent years. Its dependence on the Middle East, which declined in the 1980s, has risen to around 90% in recent years and is higher than that of any other major Asian country. For LNG, Japan's dependence on the Middle East is not as significant as it is for oil. As for relations between the oil-producing Middle Eastern and Asian countries, the Middle East's exports to Asia are dominated by oil and natural gas, with China's growth replacing that of Japan.

A stable and inexpensive energy supply is essential for economic development. As Japan has no oil and gas resources, building strategic relationships with resource-rich countries, especially the oil-producing countries of the Middle East, is a top priority in this regard. In addition, oil-producing countries cannot achieve their own economic development without a market through which to sell their oil, and so it requires building interdependent relationships. In the next section, we review Japan's policies for securing oil resources.

4   JAPAN'S ENERGY SECURITY VIA THE "3E+S" POLICY

This section first explains the trajectory of Japan's economic development and energy security and then considers the country's future direction. The meaning of energy security differs from country to country, depending on a variety of factors such as diplomacy, economic and geography. In recent years, factors such as global environmental issues and technologies that were not previously considered have also become more prevalent. While there are various definitions of energy security, this paper sees it as "the ability of a country to obtain (supply to the market) the energy resources it needs for its economy, national defence, and other activities, without excess or deficiency, at a reasonable price".[25] We would like to focus on the adequacy of the "quantity" and "price" of energy resources. The purpose of this section is to discuss what policies have been implemented to achieve this goal.

4.1   Energy Security: Japan's Pre-War Experiences

After World War I, there was a shift from coal to oil as a source of power for warships, and the nations of the Powers were eager to secure oil. Britain, for example, increased its procurement of oil from Persia and used it for military purposes. Countries without oil resources were at a military disadvantage, a typical example of which was Japan. Prior to World War II, Japan was dependent on imports from the United States for more than 80% of its domestic oil consumption. After the outbreak of the Second Sino-Japanese War in 1937, Japan fell into a confrontation with the United States, and when U.S. economic sanctions reduced oil exports, Japan tried to import oil from Indonesia, which was under Dutch colonial rule, but the embargo imposed by the United States made it impossible to secure the necessary amount of oil from abroad.

The Imperial Japanese Navy attempted to acquire oil fields in Brazil, Afghanistan and other countries through *Sogo Shosha* (a trading conglomerate, for example, Mitsui Cooperation), but again, all of these attempts failed due to American pressure. As a result, Japan was unable to obtain sufficient supplies to conduct its part in the war, including aircraft fuel. In August 1941, the United States, along with Britain, China and the

---

[25] On energy security, see Pascual and Elkind eds. (2010), Chester (2010), Goldthau ed. (2013), Douglas, Toman, and Walls eds. (1996), Wesley ed. (2007) and others.

Netherlands, imposed an oil embargo on Japan, and then, in December 1941, war broke out with the United States.

Japan's intentions were to end the war quickly, due to its shortages of resources, but it was defeated in 1945. Sakhalin Island had oil concessions in Japanese territory at the time, but this did not help secure oil resources during the war, due to conflicts with the Soviet Union. Japan was a bad example of a clash with a country to which it was exporting a key strategic commodity, oil, and thus the supply was disrupted. Following the post-First World War period, people become aware of the importance of energy security, which is directly linked to the nation's security.

As Winston Churchill stated, "Safety and certainty in oil lie in variety and variety alone" (Yergin 2006, p. 69). The basic idea of energy security is "diversification". Before World War II, Japan was dependent on the United States alone for its oil resources, and it foolishly tried to clash with it, which lead to the eventual suspension of its oil supply. Japan is now dependent on the Middle East for its oil resources. The implications of the lessons learned before the war have not diminished in their importance today.

4.2   Diversification as an Energy Security Option

When considering energy security, oil is given the highest priority. Vivoda (2009) attempted a detailed literature survey on energy security and oil and the diversification of its supply, while Stringer (2008) noted that there are two perspectives on "diversification", namely source and supplier. Source diversification refers to the realisation of an energy mix in which the energy sources used by a country consist of various commodities such as oil, coal, natural gas and nuclear power. Supplier diversification means diversifying the countries that supply oil, natural gas and other resources, and in the case of oil, it is important to diversify. Asian countries tend to be more dependent on the Middle East for oil, due to their geographic location, but as shown in Fig. 8, China is deliberately working to diversify its oil import sources as much as possible, including Africa and Latin America. Diversification of oil supplies in the context of energy security has been pointed out by many experts and incorporated into national policies in practice. In addition, there are suggestions that the perspective of an oil-importing industrialised country such as Japan is based on the four key factors: diversity of energy supply, diversity of oil imports, reduced dependence on Middle Eastern oil and low oil price volatility. Energy security should be based on four principles (Alhajji 2007, p. 29.)

4.3   Stable Supply as Japan's Energy Security: 1950s–1970s

We now turn to the main topic, Japan's energy security and its policies after World War II and up to the 1970s.[26] Energy security did not become a major concern in Japanese policy until the oil crisis and the problem of a "stable supply" of oil, at which point it was forced to change its policies. As mentioned above, Japan enjoyed a period of rapid economic growth from the late 1950s until the first oil crisis in 1973, and during this time, it did not encounter any major obstacles to its energy supply. While oil consumption increased in major Western countries as Anglo-American major producers supplied plentiful amounts of cheap oil to the market, Japan's main source of energy in the 1950s was domestically produced coal. It was unable to import oil freely, due to a lack of foreign currency, and the government restricted this practice in the 1950s.

These restrictions on oil imports were lifted in 1962, and from the 1960s onwards, the government's policies led to a shift from coal to oil as the main energy source. The reason for this shift is that imported oil was cheaper than domestic coal. The dependence on the Middle East as a supplier of oil also increased (Fig. 7). Japan had a resource and energy policy before the oil crisis, but it was not deemed particularly important.[27]

Japan's vulnerability in terms of its energy supply was exposed in the 1970s when oil prices rose sharply and the domestic economy was thrown into turmoil, due to the possibility of supply disruption from the Middle East. The oil crisis made Japan acutely aware of the need for energy security, and so in the 1970s, it placed the highest priority on a "stable supply". The term "energy security" used by the Japanese government means "stable supply".

The Yom Kippur War broke out in October 1973, and OPEC raised oil prices. In addition, OAPEC imposed an oil embargo on the United States, the Netherlands and other countries friendly to Israel. At that time,

---

[26] For an overview of Japan's energy policy, see Nihon Energy Keizai Kenkyusho (1986), Kikkawa (2011).

[27] Japan's development of foreign oil resources began in the late 1950s, when Arabian Oil successfully explored the Khafji oil field off the coast of neutral territory between Saudi Arabia and Kuwait in 1960, and production began in 1961.

Japan was not deeply involved in political or diplomatic issues with Israel and other Middle Eastern countries, but the United States and Japan had a military alliance, and they were both deemed friends by the Arab, which suggested an oil embargo. As a result, in December 1973, Deputy Prime Minister Miki Takeo visited eight Middle Eastern countries, including Saudi Arabia and Kuwait, to explain Japan's position on the shift to a pro-Arab policy. This visit enabled the Arab countries to understand Japan's position and to cease any supply restrictions.[28] The oil crisis led to the recognition of the importance of the Middle East to Japan in terms of energy security, and Japan's interest in the region thus increased.[29]

In the 1970s, when the oil crisis erupted, Japan provided Official Development Assistance (ODA) to Indonesia and other Southeast Asian countries and worked to diversify its import sources in order to reduce its dependence on Middle Eastern oil, which consequently declined. Efforts to diversify energy resources other than oil, such as natural gas, nuclear power and foreign coal, also began in the 1970s, and these efforts accelerated following the second oil crisis. The first oil crisis forced a change in Japan's energy policy. To summarise this shift simply, it was a move from a mere oil policy to a comprehensive energy policy, the main aim of which was to break away from dependence on oil.[30]

4.4   Awareness of Costs and the Environment: 1980s–1990s

When oil imports were liberalised in the 1960s, Japan tried to switch energy from coal to oil in order to reduce costs. Its energy policy in the 1970s focused on stable supplies of oil and coal, i.e. on "Energy Security". As the impact of the oil crisis eased in the 1980s, the Japanese government began to focus on the cost of energy. In 1983, the Ministry of International Trade and Industry (MITI) announced that balancing security and cost reduction would be the basis of energy policy (MITI 1983), thereby becoming aware of the economic perspective. From the mid-1980s onwards, oil prices remained at a low level and supply stabilised, allowing the world economy to return to a growth path. Japan entered

---

[28] Miki's visit to the Middle East has sometimes been described by the Japanese media as "Abura goi gaiko(seeking for oil diplomacy)".

[29] For more on Japan's diplomatic relations with the Middle East during this period, see Moese (1986) and others.

[30] For more details, see (Kikkawa, 2011) and others.

the bubble economy and enjoyed the era of "Japan as No. 1" (Vogel 1979).

Towards the end of the bubble economy, energy security once again became an issue as a result of the 1990 Gulf Crisis and the 1991 Gulf War. The Gulf War raised concerns about the uncertainty of oil supplies to Japan. At the same time, as an ally of the United States, Japan was required to be involved in Middle East diplomacy. The United States demanded that its allies, including Japan, should contribute to the war effort and participate in military operations, forcing Japan to make difficult decisions. Ultimately, Japan contributed $13 billion to the multinational force but did not participate in actual military and logistical support operations, citing constitutional provisions. The United States complained about the lack of Japanese action, and after the Gulf War, the Japanese government amended its laws to include the SDF in United Nations peacekeeping operations, in terms of mine clearance operations in the Arabian Gulf. Japan was keenly aware of the vulnerability of its energy security, due to the outbreak of war in the Middle East, on which it relied for most of its oil resources, but the fear did not continue, and the rest of the 1990s saw a period of increasing oil consumption and dependence on the Middle East, due to its favourable price.

In the late 1990s, another event led to Japan's choice to focus on costs. In 1958, the Arabian Oil Company was awarded the concession to the Khafji oil field, located in the neutral zone between Saudi Arabia and Kuwait, and it started producing in 1961. When this concession expired in 2000, Saudi Arabia and the Arabian Oil Company[31] negotiated to extend the concession. The former demanded the construction and operation of a railway for mine development, the expansion of Saudi oil imports and Japanese investment in Saudi Arabia. The Japanese government and Arabian Oil Company tried to meet Saudi demands, but it was clear that the railway construction would be unprofitable, so they urged Japanese companies to invest in Saudi Arabia, but none responded. The Japanese government did not actively support the concession negotiations

---

[31] Although Arabian Oil was founded by a private citizen, it was an extremely unusual business with Japanese interests in the Middle East, and although it was a publicly traded company, it was backed by the Japanese government. From 1976 onwards, it was headed by an alumnus of the MITI bureaucracy, making it a company with strong ties to the government. In my opinion, this is a good example of what can happen when a "descent president" with no sense of management takes the top job.

with Saudi Arabia, even to the extent of throwing in a budget, and the Japanese private sector was indifferent to the government's requests.[32] The concession with Kuwait expired in 2003.[33]

The 1990s was a period of heightened global awareness of environmental issues. Japan's energy policy was becoming more "environmentally" oriented in this period. The United Nations Framework Convention on Climate Change (UNFCCC) was convened at the Earth Summit in Rio de Janeiro, Brazil, in 1992. The UNFCCC's Conference of the Parties meets once a year, and the Kyoto Protocol was adopted at COP3 in 1997 to set targets for the reduction of greenhouse gases. In the 1990s, the world became increasingly concerned about environmental issues, particularly global warming. One of the causes of damaging greenhouse gas emissions is the use of fossil fuels, which led to the need to reduce the use of oil and coal. In Japan's energy policy in 1989, global environmental problems were recognised as an important issue (MITI 1989), following which the Cabinet approved a policy in 1990 to shift to non-fossil fuels in order to deal with environmental problems. During the 1990s, Japan's bubble economy burst, and the country entered a prolonged period of low growth until the present day. In addition to environmental concerns, this economic downturn led to a downward trend in energy demand itself. As Japan entered an era of low growth, there was no longer a need to adopt energy policies that prioritised economic growth as in the past. Additionally, in the 1990s, the nation's energy policy adopted an

---

[32] Japan has adopted policies to promote Japanese companies' investment in the Middle East in an effort to forge closer economic ties with Middle Eastern oil-producing countries. There is no denying the importance of this policy. However, Dubai is currently home to the largest number of Japanese companies in the Middle East, and this is not the result of the Japanese government's efforts to promote. The Japanese government is encouraging Japanese companies to invest into Saudi Arabia, Kuwait, Abu Dhabi and other countries in order to strengthen ties with oil-producing nations, but not in large numbers. Many companies have decided that "the market is not attractive enough to establish a subsidiary" or "it is sufficient to control it from Dubai", and if the local market is truly attractive, they will expand on their own without government support. I suggest that we should be clearer about where we stand on the balance between economic rationality and the national policy of energy objectives. If the national goal is to secure energy, the government should stop asking the private sector to pay for it.

[33] Japan's oil concessions in Saudi Arabia and Kuwait have expired, but the UAE's concession for the Zakum oil field was renewed in the 2010s. Naturally, there was some bargaining on the part of the UAE, but the "cost-effectiveness" of the project compared to Saudi Arabia, in addition to political decisions, was probably a significant factor in its appropriateness.

"environmental" perspective, in line with rising environmental awareness worldwide.

4.5 Formation of the 3E+S Policy

Reflecting the above-mentioned changes in circumstances, the Basic Act on Energy Policy, which came into effect in June 2002, stipulated the need to achieve the three E's, namely energy security, environment and economy, in parallel. In response to the enforcement of the Act, a Strategic Energy Plan was formulated in October 2003, which outlined three basic principles for implementing the policy: securing a stable energy supply, adapting to the environment and utilising market principles. The plan positions nuclear power as Japan's main source of power, with natural gas also set to play a major role, indicating an intention to reduce dependence on oil. The price of oil soared after 2004 and fell immediately after the collapse of Lehman Brothers, but it remained high until around 2015. In the face of these long-term high prices, the Japanese government refocused on energy security. In addition to the 3E's, the government's policy involved adding the goal of strengthening the security of resources. The plan was revised into the 2nd Strategic Energy Plan in March 2007 and the 3rd Strategic Energy Plan in June 2010, but the nuclear power plant accident in 2011 made it impossible to use nuclear power, and a change in policy became necessary.

In April 2014, the plan was revised into the 4th Strategic Energy Plan, covering the basic strategy of the 3E+S, alongside the addition of a safety perspective. The plan also referred to internationalisation and economic growth. In July 2018, the plan was revised into the 5th Strategic Energy Plan, with a basic approach of "more advanced 3E+S". The plan positioned fossil fuels, including oil, as the main energy source until such a time at which renewable energy was the main source, and it enumerated measures such as independent development of fossil fuels, promotion of resource diplomacy and improving the efficiency of thermal power generation technology.[34]

ODA is supposed to not be provided to developing countries that have reached a certain income level, and GCC countries with high per capita incomes are not eligible for it. In recent years, the perspective of energy

---

[34] The Ministry of Economy, Trade and Industry began discussions on the drafting of the 6th Strategic Energy Plan in October 2020.

security has also been added to ODA policy. To the GCC countries, in fact, limited aid has been provided since 1960s; it was only technical cooperation. In February 2015, the Japanese government revised its Development Cooperation Charter to provide ODA to regions strategically important to its security and economy, even if they were above a certain income level. As a result, Japan institutionalised its policy to provide ODA more flexibly to the GCC countries on which it depends for most of its energy resources. In addition, it has recently implemented a number of other measures with an eye on securing energy resources, such as oil stockpiling, which has been secured for around 200 days in accordance with IEA regulations and seeks to promote Japanese companies' investment in the GCC countries in response to requests.

4.6   Evaluations of Energy Security Performance

While the historical overview of Japan's energy policy shift is outlined above, let us now take a look at an evaluation of some studies, to see how it can be assessed. It can be said that these conclusions largely summarise the essentials of Japan's energy policy. Sovacool (2013) suggested that six perspectives should be considered in the analysis of energy security: availability, affordability, technology development and efficiency, environmental sustainability, regulation and governance. He points out that Japan is the best-performing country in terms of energy security, citing the importance of policy interventions as a factor in its success. Lesbirel (2013) also points out the effectiveness of policies in considering Japan's energy security. Using the insuring state concept, she argued that Japan had been balancing and diversifying the source of its imports, such as continuing to import oil from Iran even though Iran's position in the international community had deteriorated, and the U.S.–Japan alliance existed. Vivoda (2010) evaluated the reduction of fossil fuel demand in Japan through policy.

On the other hand, Vivoda (2009) noted that Japan has tried to reduce its dependence on the Middle East for oil imports through various measures, but it has not succeeded in doing so and remains vulnerable to disruptions in the region. The reason for this lack of progress in diversification is that Japan has limited incentives to diversify, including declining oil consumption and the existence of the U.S.–Japan alliance. Even from Japan's point of view, oil imports from the Middle East are overwhelmingly cost advantageous, while imports from other regions, such as Africa and Latin America, are not possible unless consumers accept a significant cost increase.

In this section, the transition of Japan's energy policy in the post-World War II period is described. After the oil crisis in the 1970s, the main theme was the stable supply of oil, following which, in the 1980s, Japan began to diversify its energy sources from a cost perspective. Environmental factors have been taken into account since the 1990s, and the basic policy of 3E+S has been the main pillar of policy since the 2000s. Since the nuclear disaster of 2011, the perspective of safety has also come into consideration. As the Japanese economy has entered an era of low growth, the "quantity" of energy is no longer a concern. This is an era in which the quality of energy is becoming more important in terms of how diverse energy resources can be combined to meet domestic energy needs.

Finally, a stable oil supply is a high priority. In extreme cases, no matter how much the Japanese government diversifies its dependence on the Middle East for oil imports, the overwhelming dominance of Middle Eastern oil in terms of cost makes it a rational decision to continue with this strategy, unless there is some kind of financial subsidy for companies and consumers. Of course, we cannot talk about energy security based on economic rationality alone, but oil is no longer the strategic commodity it once was, and it is appropriate to give priority to this point. Japan's economy has already entered a period of shrinkage, and it is unlikely that oil demand will increase significantly in the future. However, it is expected to increase in China, and it is not surprising that the Chinese government is eager to secure resources and diversify its import sources.

5   Japan's Oil Industry Lacks International Competitiveness

This section summarises the characteristics of the Japanese oil industry at the industry level and discusses the issues involved.

The following is a discussion by Takeo Kikkawa, a leading scholar in the history of the energy industry in Japan.

5.1   Two Weak Points

The world's major oil companies are divided into three categories: *Majors* (former known as seven sisters) such as ExxonMobil and BP, national oil companies in oil-producing countries such as Saudi Aramco and ADNOC and national-flag oil firms in the oil and natural gas importing countries, such as CNPC and Total. There are no national-flag oil firms in Japan. He then identifies the following two weaknesses of the Japanese oil industry and points out that they are inherent:

i. A split between upstream sectors (development and production) and downstream sectors (refining and distribution).
ii. A surplus of excessively undersized upstream companies (Kikkawa 2012a, p. 8).

We explain the "split between upstream sectors and downstream sectors". Before World War II, the *Majors* foreign oil companies were extremely active in Japan, and they adopted the production site refining system (importation of petroleum products). Japanese oil companies competed by adopting the consumption-land refining system, and after the war, they continued to focus on downstream operations while relying entirely on *Majors* produces for upstream operations. In the Petroleum Industry Law, enacted in 1962, the division between upstream and downstream was authorised in Japan.

The problem is that even after the 1970s, when the influence of the *Majors*-affiliated companies began to wane, the division between upstream and downstream was maintained in Japan in a fixed manner. As is well known, the upstream sector has higher profit margins in the oil industry. This focus on the downstream sector means that Japan's oil industry is structured in a way that makes it difficult to generate profits.

Next, there is the problem of "too little for too many". There are many Japanese oil companies that are small in size, and if all the upstream and downstream divisions of these firms were added together, they would be as large as Total and ENI, which are among the largest in the world. Japan's oil industry as a whole is not small, but there are so many companies in the industry that no one company is on the global level.

How did this condition arise? It was due to the strong influence of the Japanese government's modes of intervention. After the 1970s, securing the stability of the nation's oil resources became an important issue, but the structure of the division between upstream and downstream created during the high economic growth period of the 1960s did not change.

Since the 2000s, Japanese oil companies have been merging to expand their scale.

To put it simply, Japan's oil industry cannot have a global presence because it is concentrated in the downstream sector, which is less profitable, and its bargaining power in relation to oil-producing countries is weak. In the case of China's oil industry making efforts to ensure a stable supply of oil from abroad, the three major national oil companies, China National Petroleum Corporation (CNPC), China Petrochemical Corporation (Sinopec Group), and China National Offshore Oil Corporation (CNOOC) hold a dominant position in the industry. It has been active in acquiring concessions and production activities outside of the country with the backing of the Chinese government, which is strongly promoting its national credo, "One Belt, One Road". In the face of the overwhelming power of China's oil industry, Japan's oil industry is probably too powerless at present. In recent years, Exxon Mobil and Royal Dutch Shell have also withdrawn their capital from a Japanese market (in 2012 and 2019, respectively) that is shrinking, thereby indicating that it is no longer an attractive proposition for foreign capital.

5.2   The Roadmap for Japan's Oil Industry

As for the future of the Japanese oil industry, Kikkawa (2012b) noted that there is a necessity for a new approach to building refineries and petrochemical plants in oil-producing countries, i.e. "attacking upstream with downstream technology", rather than just the traditional approach of acquiring oil field concessions to ensure energy security. He cited Sumitomo Chemical's Petro Rabigh in Saudi Arabia and the Nghi Son Project in Vietnam, in which Kuwait Petroleum, Idemitsu Kosan and PetroVietnam are participating, as examples of the new approach, noting that such initiatives will not only contribute to strengthening the international competitiveness of Japan's petroleum and petrochemical industries and revitalising the local economy, but will also help ensure energy security. It is important to acknowledge the need to develop the upstream sector for Japan's energy security and to point out the need to provide the high value-added technologies that oil-producing countries demand, in order for Japan to win in the face of intensifying global competition.

Bearing in mind that the Middle East is a very important region in terms of Japan's energy security, I quote Kikkawa's argument at length:

We need to know exactly what the oil-producing countries of the Middle East expect from Japan and respond to those expectations in an appropriate way, which is essential to ensure Japan's energy security. For a long time, Japan has been an attractive market for Middle Eastern oil-producing countries. This situation is still the same today, but with the emergence of China and other powerful rivals (competitors in crude oil imports) these days, this is not enough to keep the Middle Eastern countries interested in Japan. What the oil-producing nations of the Middle East expect of Japan, and what Japan has that China does not, is, to put it simply, technology. In this sense, attacking the upstream market with downstream technology is particularly important in Japan's relations with Middle Eastern countries. (Kikkawa 2012b, p. 299)

The main points are as follows: how can the Japanese oil industry, which has a weak upstream sector, participate in the development of the upstream sector in the Middle East? In order to do so, the first step is to build cooperative relationships with Middle Eastern countries in the downstream sector. This is a very important suggestion, as there is no way that Japan can win by competing head-on with China's overwhelming financial power. Thus by providing the technology and human resource development needed by the oil-producing countries, Japan should take measures to make inroads into the upstream sectors.

The above discussion of Kikkawa's argument makes it clear that Japan's oil industry is not internationally competitive, so Japan needs to be aware of this situation and seriously consider how it should build its relationship with the Middle East.

6   Concluding Remarks: Trends in the Japanese Economy and Oil Market

This paper has assessed the current conditions in Japan's energy and oil markets, summarised its energy security and policies, which depend on the Middle East for oil resources, and summarised the characteristics of the nation's energy industry.

In the first section, it was established that the peak of energy and oil consumption in Japan has passed, and growth in this regard is not expected in the future. Also, its dependence on fossil fuels is one of the highest in the developed countries. In the second section, Japan's dependence on and deep ties with Middle Eastern oil-producing countries for oil supply. In Sect. 4, we reviewed Japan's energy security history, which led to the current "3E+S" policy employed by the government. In Sect. 5, it was illustrated that Japan's oil industry is not internationally competitive.

Finally, I would like to consider the outlook for the Japanese economy and its relation to the oil market.

As many scholars have pointed out, energy security in the twentieth and twenty-first centuries has different implications. While the twentieth century was the age of oil, the twenty-first century has become the age of electricity, and today's energy security has come to mean diversifying sources of electricity supply while ensuring energy sustainability and climate change mitigation (Tanaka 2013, p. 244).

The use of fossil fuels as a source of power generation in developed countries will decline in the future in terms of environmental concerns. The two main roles of oil, other than as a source of power generation, are as a fuel, such as gasoline, and as a feedstock for industrial products. Of these two, industrial product materials will continue to grow in significance, because there is currently no other alternative.

Among the fuel applications, there are insufficient alternative technologies for aircraft and marine fuels, and oil will therefore continue to be the main source of power for some time in the twenty-first century. The problem is motor fuels. As shown in Fig. 2, the percentage of energy consumption in the transportation sector is increasing in Japan. The share of the transportation sector is relatively large, due to a significant decline in the manufacturing sector, but how should this be viewed in the context of the automotive industry's growing need to deal with the environment?

CASE, which is an innovation with which the automotive industry needs to deal, is an acronym for Connected, Autonomous/Automated, Shared and Electric. Of these, electricity is directly related to oil demand. Electric vehicles (EVs), which use motors as a power source to replace internal combustion engines in cars, are reaching the level of commercialisation. In addition, hydrogen fuel cell vehicles are also being developed as a carbon-free technology. The environmental policies of various countries have also been announced; for example, the UK will ban the sale of petrol cars by 2035, and France by 2040.[35] In China, Asia's largest auto market, incentives for environmentally friendly vehicles, including

---

[35] One of the most important parts of an EV is the battery, which currently depends on China for its supply. If EVs are to be more widely used in Western countries than they are now, they will need to overcome this dependence on China for components.

EVs, are also being offered to boost the spread of EVs. Then, in January 2021, Japan's Prime Minister Suga expressed in the Parliament that the country would achieve 100% electric vehicle sales by 2035.[36]

Currently, EVs prices are high and governments may be subsidising their spread, but Japan is lagging behind other countries in this regard, due to the fact that Toyota and the rest of the Japanese automotive industry are not very active in developing EVs. Hybrid technology is used primarily in Japan, the main reason for which is that its automotive industrial policy has not led to the explosive growth of EVs, albeit this is due to the industry's ineptitude in EV technology.

EVs are relatively easy for non-traditional automotive companies to enter the market. China's BYD, for example, was originally a battery manufacturer. For Japanese manufacturers who have produced vehicles based on thoroughly "integrating" with their own suppliers, there are many aspects of the EV manufacturing philosophy that are incompatible with theirs. For this reason, Japanese automotive companies are reluctant to introduce a strategy to promote EVs as an environmental measure, and if the Japanese government tries to promote EV policies without offering preferential treatment to Japanese automotive companies, it is likely that the nation's companies will not be able to compete.[37] Similarly, Thailand, which has become one of Asia's largest production bases for Japanese automakers, has not yet adopted policies to promote EVs actively.

This is because of the huge impact they will have on the domestic industry. Thus, Japan is likely to continue to produce vehicles with mainly internal combustion engines for a relatively long time compared to other developed countries. In this regard, the absolute amount of fuel demand will decrease with the development of fuel-saving technologies, but the use of fuel for automobiles will not dissipate so easily.

However, since the automotive industry has a huge impact on the domestic economy, the global movement to expand the penetration of EVs as a way to boost the economy after the COVID-19 recession may

---

This could potentially cause a diplomatic dispute, as in the case of the conflict between Huawei and the Western nations over 5G technology.

[36] It will be allowed to produce hybrid vehicles.

[37] For example, Toyota has not released an EVs in any market in the world at the end of 2020. However, this does not mean that Toyota does not have the technology for EVs, but rather that its world-leading hybrid technology would enable it to develop electric vehicles easily.

accelerate. There is a significant "green recovery" movement in Europe, and it is possible that this could expand to other countries. Depending on this trend, it could have a significant impact on global oil demand. In addition, the flourishing of ESG investments in the capital markets will force companies to deal with environmental issues and lead to a move away from the use of oil. This capital market pressure is also an important perspective.

The most important aspect of the future of Japan's oil market is the Japanese economy's shrinkage. The declining birthrate and ageing population, said to be one of the fastest growing in the world, are affecting every aspect of the Japanese economy. Estimates of the nation's population, released in 2018 by the National Institute of Population and Social Security Research, a research organisation on Japan's demographic issues, predict that the population will decline from 127.09 million in 2015 to 88.08 million by 2065, according to a medium estimate. It is estimated that the population will decline by 30% in the next 50 years. Developed countries are similarly entering a period of population decline, with the UK estimated to shrink by 18%, France by 14% and Germany by 7% over the same period,[38] but Japan's 30% decline is by far the largest. A significant decline in population would mean market downsizing and, of course, a lower demand for oil.

From the Middle East oil-producing countries' point of view, this shrinkage of the domestic market and the inevitable development of energy-saving technologies means that Japan's importance in the Asian market will decline. When this happens, how will Japan be able to maintain its presence in the Middle East? Based on the good relations between the two factions, it is necessary to create a mechanism for mutual coexistence and co-prosperity through Japan's unique efforts to meet the Middle East's needs in a wide range of fields, including technological development and human resource development. We will not be able to eliminate oil consumption throughout the twenty-first century, even though technology improves. In spite of any change in the attitude of the Middle East, Japan, which has no oil resources, needs to continue to maintain good relations with the Middle East. Japan needs to establish that unique cooperative relationship. This will also encourage Japanese enterprises to expand their business in the Middle East.

---

[38] Incidentally, the United States is forecast to grow in population, by about 30% over the same period.

REFERENCES

Alhajji, A.F. 2007. What is energy security? Definitions and concepts. *MEES* 50 (45): 27–30.

Chester, Lynne. 2010. Conceptualising energy security and making explicit its polysemic nature. *Energy Policy* 38 (2): 887–895.

Clark, Colin. 1940. *The Conditions of Economic Progress*. Macmillan.

Cohen, Stephen D. 1985. *Uneasy Partnership: Competition and Conflict in U.S.–Japanese Trade Relations*. Ballinger Publishing.

Douglas R. Bohi., Micheael A. Toman, and Margaret A. Walls (eds.). 1996. *The Economics of Energy Security*. Kluwer Academic Publishers.

Goldthau, Andreas (ed.). 2013. *The Handbook of Global Energy Policy*. Wiley-Blackwell.

Holgerson, Karen M. 1998. *The Japan–U.S. Trade Friction Dilemma*. Ashgate.

Kikkawa, Takeo. 2011. *Tsushou Sangyo Seisakushi 10 Shigen Energy Seisaku 1980–2000* [The History of International Trade and Industry policies Vol.10. Resource and Energy Policy 1980–2000], Keizaisangyo Tyousakai (in Japanese).

Kikkawa, Takeo. 2012a. International Competitiveness of Japan's Petroleum Industry: A view from Business History. *The Kyoto Economic Review* 81 (1): 4–13.

Kikkawa, Takeo. 2012b. *Nihon sekiyu sangyo no kyosoryoku kochiku* [Building the Competitiveness of the Japanese Oil Industry], Nagoya Daigaku Shuppankai (in Japanese).

Lesbirel, S. Hayden. 2013. The insuring state: Japanese oil import security and the Middle East. *Asian Journal of Political Science* 21 (1): 41–61.

MITI. 1983. *Choki energy zyukuno mitoshito energy seisakuno soutenken [Long-term energy supply and demand outlook and comprehensive review of energy policy]*. Tsusanshoukouhou [Official bulletin MITI], 24AUG1983.

MITI. 1989. *2010 nenno energy shouhiryou genyukansan 4.44okukiloritoru – Sougou energy tyousakai tyukanhoukokukai souron-[Energy consumption in 2010: 444 million kiloliters of oil equivalent – Interim report on Comprehensive Energy Research Committee]*. Tsusanshoukouhou [Official Bulletin MITI].

Miyazaki, Yoshikazu. 1967. Rapid economic growth in post-war Japan. *The Development Economics* 5 (2): 329–350.

Moese, Ronald A. (ed.). 1986. *Japan and the Middle East in Alliance Politics*. University Press of America.

Nihon Energy Keizai Kenkyusho (ed.). 1986. *Sengo Energy Sangyoshi[Post-war History of Energy Industries]*. Toyo Keizai (in Japanese).

Pascual, Carlos, and Jonathan Elkind (eds.). 2010. *Energy Security: Economics, Politics, Strategies, and Implications*. Brookings Institution Press.

Sato, Ryuzo, and Paul Wachtel. 1987. *Trade Friction and Economic Policy: Problems and Prospects for JAPAN and the United States*. Cambridge University Press.

Sovacool, Benjamin K. 2013. An international assessment of energy security performance. *Ecological Economics* 88: 148–158.

Stringer, Kevin D. 2008. Energy security: Applying a portfolio approach. *Baltic Security & Defence Review* 10: 121–142.

Tanaka, Nobuo. 2013. Big Bang in Japan's energy policy. *Energy Strategy Reviews* 1 (4): 243–246.

Wesley, Michael (ed.). 2007. *Energy Security in Asia*. Routledge.

Yergin, Daniel. 2006. Ensuring energy security. *Foreign Affairs* 85 (2): 69–82.

Vivoda, Vlado. 2009. Diversification of oil import sources and energy security: A key strategy or an elusive objective? *Energy Policy* 37 (11): 4615–4623.

Vivoda, Vlado. 2010. Evaluating energy security in the Asia-Pacific region: A novel methodological approach. *Energy Policy* 38 (9): 5258–5263.

Vogel, Ezra F. 1979. *Japan as Number One: Lessons for America*. Harvard University Press.

CHAPTER 9

The LNG Sector in Japan's Relations with the Middle East

Steven Wright

1 THE EVOLUTION OF JAPAN'S ENERGY INTERESTS

When considering the drivers behind the emergence of Japanese political and economic interests in the Middle Eastern region and its relationship to the Liquefied Natural Gas (LNG sector), it is important to consider this based on two interrelated areas: first, how the Middle Eastern region progressively evolved to be viewed within the context of Japanese foreign policy calculations. This requires reflection on the foreign policy doctrines and strategic pillars that have existed within Japan's foreign policy in the

This chapter was made possible by a National Priorities Research Program Standard (NPRP-S) 12th Cycle grant no. NPRP12S-0210–190, 067 from the Qatar National Research Fund (a member of Qatar Foundation). The findings herein reflect the work, and are solely the responsibility, of the author.

S. Wright (✉)
Hamad Bin Khalifa University, Ar-Rayyan, Qatar
e-mail: stwright@hbku.edu.qa

post-Second World War era. Secondly, how the energy sector impacted on Japan's economic engagement with the Middle Eastern region, and how this proved to be a driver behind the progressive adoption of LNG.

In several respects, the history, and dynamics behind the growth of the LNG sector in Japan are interrelated with the question of Japan's progressive energy transition toward more efficient and cleaner energy sources. It is proven to be a significant driver of engagement with the key countries in the Middle East, and Qatar in particular, and has proven to be a means by which multifaceted interdependence can be furthered based on trade, technology transfer, and energy security calculations.

It is therefore necessary to reflect on how these have both evolved, the contexts that are shaped them within Japan, and finally how they have impacted on contemporary relations between Japan and the Middle East with specific regard to LNG exporting countries. By doing this, it is possible to provide a basis to identify that LNG has proven to be an enabler of complex multifaceted interdependence in Japan's bilateral relationships.

In terms of the background of Japan's energy transition phases, it is important to recall that, from 1945 to 1952, Japan was under US occupation and the reforms that were initiated form the basis of the rapid modernization and economic development that Japan experienced up until the 1980s. Japan's pacifist constitution of 1947 was a product of the US goals for democratization and demilitarization, however, with the victory of the Chinese Communist Party in 1949, and the Korean War commencing in 1950, the emergent Cold War calculations prompted the United States to see a rearmed Japan as best placed to further United States interests. Any moves toward rearmament were viewed by the Japanese government as conflicting with Article 9 of the Japanese Constitution which committed Japan to pacifism.[1] It is significant here that, within this context, foundations of Japan's postwar foreign policy began to take shape within what can be described as a tripartite prism which Japanese leaders gravitated to depending on the outlook.[2] Even prior to the Second World War, Japan had been sensitive to its need for foreign resources to further its economic development. Indeed, Japan's

---

[1] David Arase, "New directions in Japanese security policy," *Contemporary Security Policy* 15, no. 2 (1994): 44–45.

[2] Bert Edström, *Japan's evolving foreign policy doctrine: from Yoshida to Miyazawa* (New York, N.Y.: St. Martin's Press, 1999), 173–78.

interests in 1931 in Manchuria were underlined by the drive to secure natural resources, yet in the post-Second World War era, it's a rapid postwar reconstruction saw its energy consumption rise rapidly which understandably informed calculations on how to safeguard economic development.

By 1951, the United States and Japan negotiated a treaty for the ending of the US occupation, and it was within this context that the 1952 Security Treaty Between the United States and Japan was signed. This treaty is significant in that it permitted the continued presence of US military forces within Japan, but also located Japan under the US security umbrella. Under the Japanese Prime Minister Yoshida Shigeru, the Yoshida Doctrine was adopted whereby Japan placed a priority on reconstructing its domestic economy while relying on its overall economic, political, and security linkages from the United States to safeguard Japan's national interests.

Japan's foreign policy came to be aligned with that of the United States and allowed Japan to reach a postwar consensus that the government's focus should be on economic development. This led to Japan adopting a strategy (*seikei bunri*), where entailed a separation of economic from political objectives within Japan's foreign policy, as it afforded Japan the ability to prioritize its economic development and modernization, thereby benefiting from the security provided by the United States.[3]

To appreciate the way Japan's economic development unfolded, by 1951, Japan's industrial production had recovered to prewar levels, and this was driven by what can be understood as a developmental state approach whereby the government focused on industrial output and internal capacity development. This was further driven by the demand for manufactured goods and supplies due to the Korean War given the need for goods to be provided given the logistical problems in supplying the war effort from the United States mainland. Indeed, the outbreak of the Korean War proved to be a significant driver in Japan's balance of trade at that time which spurred overall economic development and energy demand.[4]

---

[3] William Nester and Kweku Ampiah, "Japan's oil diplomacy: Tatemae and honne," *Third World Quarterly* 11, no. 1 (1989): 72–73.

[4] Ryutaro Takahashi, "Trade Policies of the New Japan," *Foreign Affairs* 30 (1951): 295.

During the US occupation, Japan's energy needs were heavily dependent on its domestic coal reserves which constituted more than 90% of Japan's total primary energy requirements. This catered to the main consumers of energy which were the iron and steel industry along with the electric power sector. Between 1950 to 1960, Japan pursued a "coal first—oil second" energy policy, that this was to change by the late 1950s. This was representative of the coal sector being essentially a government enterprise. Samuels notes that "Coal was the primary industrial fuel and feedstock for the first half-century of Japan's industrial transformation.

Long before the industrial revolution started, however, the coal mines had attracted state intervention. In fact, coal was the first business of the Japanese state."[5] By 1950, Japan's energy mix was heavily dependent on coal which amounted to 83.2% of total energy needs. This was followed by Hydro electricity production at 10.4%, and crude oil that 6.1%. While coal dominated the energy mix at this time, it was to decline as Japan's rapid economic development resulted in an energy revolution which saw crude oil increase as part of the energy mix. By 1960, coal amounted to 54.1% of total primary energy requirements, and had fallen to 24% by 1970 and 18% by 1973. Conversely, crude oil amounted to 38.1% of total primary energy requirements by 1960 and had increased further to 71.8% by 1970 and 77.8% by 1973.[6] Underlying this transition was a shift in Japan's energy policy toward an oil-focused economy which was driven by the cost of imported foreign crude oil being cheaper than domestically sourced coal. Furthermore, although Japan's coal sector was a major employer, it was also unionized and strike action, especially in 1952 and 1960, proved to be disruptive and further encouraged the government to focus on oil imports.

This was also followed by the lifting of oil price controls which further enabled Japan to deepen its trade with the United States and import energy at a cheaper cost than what was being domestically produced. It is this supply dynamic which made Japan's transition toward an oil-focused economy and a decline of its coal sector an inevitability. What is important here, is that it is this energy revolution and transition toward

[5] Richard J. Samuels, *The Business of the Japanese State* (Cornell University Press, 1987), 68.

[6] Satoru Kobori, "Japan's energy policy during the 1950s: reasons for the rapid switch from coal to oil" (Asia–Pacific Economic and Business History Conference, San Francisco Bay Area, 2009).

an oil-focused economy set the context for a subsequent substantive engagement with the Middle Eastern region based on national economic interests.

Japan's demand for oil expanded in line with its economic growth and as early as 1957, the Japan Arabian Oil Company had entered into agreements with Saudi Arabia and Kuwait for offshore drilling rights. This proved to be the onset of a progressive pursuit of any security through bypassing Anglo-American international oil companies. It was by the mid-1960s that Japan had emerged as the third-largest consumer of oil after the United States and the USSR. An increasing proportion of Japan's oil was progressively sourced from the Middle Eastern region to the extent that by 1962, Japan was the second largest consumer of Middle Eastern oil after the United Kingdom, and by 1973 Japan was the largest consumer of Middle Eastern oil.[7] It is worth noting that by 2021, although China had overtaken Japan as the largest consumer of Middle Eastern oil, Japan remained heavily integrated with the Middle Eastern market as it constituted 92% of total crude oil imports in 2020–21.[8]

As early as 1967, Japan had recognized in its *Economic and Social Development Plan (1967–71)*, that, "in order to modernize the industrial structure and to strengthen the international competitiveness of enterprises, it is necessary to secure a stable supply of cheap energy which is the basic material for all industry and for the people's livelihood. The essence of the energy policy in Japan is to pursue the possibility of the energy supply meeting these two requirements: stability and low cost."[9] This was also recognized in the subsequent *New Economic and Social Development Plan (1970–75)* which highlighted the vulnerability based on the global distribution of energy being dominated by key enterprises. This underlined a drive for energy security through the stability of the Middle Eastern region and having direct access to supply markets.

---

[7] Nester and Ampiah, "Japan's oil diplomacy: Tatemae and honne," 75–76.

[8] Petroleum Association of Japan, "Crude Oil Import by Countries and by Source," (Tokyo, Japan, 2021). https://www.paj.gr.jp/english/statis/.

[9] R. P. Sinha, "Japan and the Oil Crisis," *The World Today* 30, no. 8 (August 1974): 30.

2   THE EMERGENCE OF THE LNG SECTOR IN JAPAN

Japan's gas sector originated in Osaka in 1871, with the unveiling of Japan's first gas-powered lamp, which illuminated the Imperial Mint in Osaka. Coal was used to generate the gas. This occurred during Japan's Meiji Restoration, which was a fundamental period change of Japanese society. As a result, the use of gas lights as an alternative to kerosene lamps began to spread across other Japanese towns. Three years later, 85 street lights were installed in the vicinity of Japan's Diet. The individual who pioneered the introduction of gas streetlamps was the industrialist Eiichi Shibusawa, who is often referred to as the father of Japanese capitalism. Shibusawa played a central role in Japan's economic transformation, and one of his many accolades is that he advocated the adoption of gas lamps as a safer alternative to the traditional oil lamps which posed a risk to Japan's wooden buildings.

Shibusawa became the head of the city of Tokyo's Gas Board in 1879 and subsequently the first chairman of the Tokyo Gas when it was established in 1885. Subsequently, Shibusawa established the Tokyo Gas Railway Company to further a network of gas-powered trains across the city. He was important in the development of electricity across Japan, founding one of the country's earliest electric railway companies. Shibusawa had a remarkable impact on the establishment of several hundred companies and projects, and his contribution toward Japan's development cesium was recognized on the ¥10,000 note which is introduced in 2024.

Following victory in the Sino-Japanese War of 1897 and the Russo-Japanese War of 1904, Japan emerged as a significant industrial and military power. Rapid economic development came with increased demands for gas for home cooking and was broadly enabled by low prices which was a product of government regulation and price-fixing during this period. Moreover, following Japan's invasion of Manchuria in 1931, its abundant coal supplies gave Japan an ample supply from which to produce gas which maintained low prices and encouraged demand to grow. During the interwar years, infrastructure for gas processing, storage, and distribution through pipelines, saw severe damage due to the bombing raids Japan experienced and as a result it was not until the 1950s that a recovery began to emerge in the gas sector, but as the sector was based on coal–gas, the sector suffered from a lack of reliable access to coal, which gave way to crude oil as has been highlighted in the above text. Nevertheless, it is important to recognize here that gas had shown demand since the Meiji period, and the main challenge facing the sector was access to reliable supply.

By 1970, Japan relied on oil for more than 70% of its main energy requirements, and oil accounted for 60% of the fuel used in electricity production. While it was not until after 1973 that the LNG market saw its most significant growth, its emergence within Japan can be traced back to 1967 when the first agreement was made for importing LNG. While Shibusawa played a critical role in the establishment of a gas market, it was a future Tokyo Gas Chairman, Hiroshi Anzai, who can be credited with being the father of the LNG industry in Japan.[10] Anzai's impact was that he recognized the potential application of obtaining gas from alternative sources than the traditional coal–gas method that had dominated Japan's gas sector since the Meiji period. His first initiative was to derive gas from oil as this, was a significantly less expensive option than obtaining it from coal which also suffered from supply challenges. His initiative was to see Tokyo Gas move into oil gas production in 1953. His longer-term objective however was to recognize that natural gas was a more cost-effective and sustainable option for Tokyo Gas, but the challenges want transportation to Japan as the only technical solution for the issue at the time was pipeline-based supply.

It was, however, by 1958 that Anzai established a collaboration with the Chairman of British Gas Council, Sir Henry Jones, that technical cooperation on LNG shipping and reapplication took place. With his conviction that LNG had a commercial future that could be transformative in Japan's energy sector, engaged in collaboration with Tokyo Electric Power to establish the Negishi LNG in Yokohama. Anzai's visionary efforts in this regard would subsequently prove to be the onset of a return to a progressive increase in the gas market, which was first pioneered by Shibusawa during the Meiji restoration.

As previously stated, Japan's energy consumption increased dramatically in the 1960s as a consequence of population growth and spectacular postwar reconstruction. However, urban air pollution and other forms of pollution had developed into social issues in Japan, and the country faced an urgent need to transition away from conventional coal and oil-based

---

[10] S. Stapczynski (Stephen Stapczynski), "Japan imported its 1st shipment of liquefied natural gas 50 years ago today. Now the nation is the world's largest buyer of the fuel (and pioneered the industry). Hiroshi Anzai is the little known maverick who played a key role in Japan becoming an LNG juggernaut," Twitter, 4 November 2019.

materials and toward environmentally friendly and reliable energy sources that did not jeopardize future economic efficiency. Tokyo Gas concluded that Liquefied Natural Gas (LNG) was the best option for addressing such societal issues, since it was expected to be both environmentally and economically sustainable.[11]

With this goal in mind, Japan inked its first contract for LNG imports in March 1967, when Phillips Petroleum and Marathon Oil signed a deal with Tokyo Electric Power and Tokyo Gas for the supply of 1 million tonnes of LNG per year. This was to be obtained in the United States, since Alaska's Kenai gas field was founded in 1959. The deal allowed Tokyo Electric to use 75% of the gas to fuel a 700-MW power plant. For the remaining, Tokyo Gas was to reform the remaining gas into town gas for distribution to its consumers.

The LNG was transported by two ships, the *Polar Alaska* and the *Arctic Tokyo*. *Polar Alaska* was launched in August 1969, followed by sistership *Arctic Tokyo* in December of the same year. Each steam turbine ship was equipped with six cargo tanks, an ice-resistant hull, and was able to travel at a maximum speed of 17 knots to make the 3,234 nautical mile trip. Marathon Oil managed both ships, with the Polar Alaska departing from the Nikiski facility on the Kenai Peninsula in southern Alaska on October 26, 1969. It arrived in Japan on 4 November and discharged its LNG on 11 November. The ship docked at Yokohama's Negishi terminal. This cargo marked the first LNG export from the United States and the first LNG import into Japan and Asia. Arctic Tokyo, the second ship, made her maiden cargo discharge in Negishi on March 11, 1970.[12]

By 2004, oil's proportion of primary energy had fallen to 52% and its part of electricity production had fallen to 8%. Nuclear and LNG were the major winners in this shift.[13] Nuclear and gas together contribute for about 13% of primary energy and 35% and 27%, respectively. Rapid expansion began in 1972, with the commencement of exports to Japan by a new liquefaction facility in Lumut, Brunei. By 1977, this plant was

---

[11] Tokyo Gas, *LNG 50th For the Next 50 Years: Integrated Report*, Tokyo Gas, (Tokyo: Tokyo Gas, 2019), 3.

[12] Mike Corkhill et al., "LNG shipping at 50, SIGTTO at 35 and GIIGNL at 43. A commemorative SIGTTO/GIIGNL publication 2014," (2014): 25.

[13] Michael D Tusiani and Gordon Shearer, *LNG: a nontechnical guide* (PennWell Books, 2007), 55.

providing Japanese customers with over 7 MMt/y (9.8 Bcm/y) of gas.[14] Abu Dhabi and Indonesia joined the list of Japanese LNG suppliers the next year. Malaysia followed in 1983 and Australia in 1989. Japan got its first LNG shipment from Qatar in 1997, followed by Oman in 2000.

3   THE OIL 1973 CRISIS: IMPACT ON JAPAN'S FOREIGN POLICY AND THE LNG SECTOR

While concerns about Japan's economic development's access to a dependable and cost-effective energy source have persisted for a lengthy period, in the run-up to the 1970s, Japan experienced a range of contextual challenges which began to raise questions about its reliance on the United States as a guarantor for its national and economic security and the role of oil in its energy mix. It should not be forgotten that in 1972, US President Richard Nixon's strategic engagement with China was a pivotal moment in the context of Cold War politics and had implications on Japan's own engagement with China and with Taiwan.

Indeed, prior to this tumultuous event, Zbigniew Brzezinski had notably characterized Japan in 1972 as a "Fragile Blossom" owing largely to vulnerabilities within its economy, which further compounded its own perceptions of regional and global insecurity. Such unexpected upheaval was also added to through the broader recognition of the widening Sino-Soviet tensions, along with the context of US stagnation in Vietnam, and the unexpected onset of negotiations between North and South Koreans. All this fed into a broad context in which Japanese policymakers would have viewed as a period of upheaval and uncertainty. It was, therefore, with the onset of the Arab oil embargo in October 1973, that the understanding of the nexus between energy insecurity and the inability to rely on the United States to secure Japanese interests under a Pax Americana, crystallized into what was to mark the onset of a new era in how Japan engaged with the Middle Eastern region.

The 1973 Arab oil embargo was undoubtedly a turning point in how Japan was to engage with the Middle East. Japan's dependency on imports for its energy needs left it vulnerable to both supply security and prices. The oil shock resulted in Japan facing its first trade deficit since 1964 and prompted a public panic with surging prices driven by

---

[14] Tusiani and Shearer, *LNG: a nontechnical guide*, 55.

an inflation rate which exceeded 20% and the economy retracted for the first time during the postwar era. Indeed, this was a time now known as experiencing a "price frenzy" (*kyōran bukka*), which had an impact on common consumables whose manufacturing included a petroleum derivative.[15] Daniel Yergin aptly noted that for Japan, "the confidence that had been built up with strong economic growth was suddenly shattered all of the old fears about vulnerability rushed... The fears aroused by the embargo ignited a series of commodity panics that we called the violent "rice riots" that had shaken Japanese governments in the late 19th and early twentieth centuries. Taxicab drivers staged angry demonstrations, and housewives rushed out to buy and hold laundry detergent and toilet paper."[16]

Stemming from the social anxiety brought on by the oil crisis, the broader ramifications over the 1973 oil crisis was that it prompted the Ministry of International Trade and Industry (MITI) to reconceptualize how Japan can achieve energy security. It is worth recalling that in terms of Japan's energy security (*enerugi anzen-hoshō*), "oil accounted for 74.9% of Japanese primary energy supply in fiscal 1972... of which 99.7% was imported, and only the remaining 0.3% produced domestically. Of this imported oil, 80% came from the Middle East - 43% from Arab oil-exporting countries and 37% from Iran alone."[17] When this domestic context is considered along with the above-mentioned international forces, a more proactive foreign policy toward the Middle Eastern region, based on national strategic interests, became a necessity for the Japanese government in foreign policy terms.

In terms of Japan's own energy security, the oil crisis bird MITI to envisage a new energy mix for Japan whereby imports of crude oil were diversified, nuclear energy was to be developed along with alternative energy sources such as LNG and renewables. More broadly than this, Daniel Yergin reminds us that it also prompted a strategic shift in Japan's industrial base from heavy fuel industries toward low energy intensive electronics and semiconductors. Indeed, he makes the point that Japan's

---

[15] B. Bryan Barber, *Japan's Relations with Muslim Asia* (Cham, Switzerland: Palgrave Macmillan, 2020), 43.

[16] Daniel Yergin, *The prize: the epic quest for oil, money, and power* (New York: Simon & Schuster, 1992), 616.

[17] Saburo Okita, "Natural resource dependency and Japanese foreign policy," *Foreign Affairs* 52, no. 4 (1974): 714.

energy insecurity and vulnerability to global oil geopolitics and geoeconomics which prompted an economic and industrial revolution.[18] It was also, however, a pivotal moment for the progressive growth and rapid expansion of the LNG sector in Japan's energy mix. Indeed, it gave impetus and drive behind the initial establishment of the sector by Hiroshi Anzai, and it was to grow and expand in nature as both a cleaner and more cost-effective alternative to crude oil, but also later as a transitional fuel to a carbon-neutral future involving renewables and the hydrogen sector.

During this time, the overarching structure of Japan's international relations remains shaped by the Yoshida doctrine and an alignment with US foreign policy, but the pursuit of national economic interests proved to be the key driver behind Japan reformulating its Middle Eastern policy thereby requiring a balancing against its relationship with the United States. Stockwin reminds us of the conventional wisdom on Japan's relations with the Middle East and the 1973 oil crisis:

> Japanese policy towards the Middle East has predominantly been affected by two considerations: US policies and the need for oil. When the first oil crisis halted Japanese economic growth in 1973-4, Japan promptly substituted broadly pro-Arab for pro-Israel policies in order to secure continued sources of oil. It is probably true to say that up to that time Japan was dependent on the US for much of its Middle Eastern expertise, and tended to follow the US line. But economic imperatives forced a change of policy.[19]

While the oil crisis certainly led to a more pro-Arab stance in Japanese foreign policy and overt policy shifts, most notably in Japan's relations with Israel, it is not necessarily accurate to view this as a purely binary shift. Indeed, Jun'ichirō Shiratori has convincingly shown how Japan's involvement in the formation of the International Energy Agency (IEA) in the aftermath of the 1973 oil embargo as evidence of how Japan cooperated with the United States and other Western powers, to counterbalance the potency of OAPEC's influence over supply and price.[20] This

[18] Yergin, *The prize: the epic quest for oil, money, and power.*

[19] J. A. A. Stockwin, *Governing Japan: divided politics in a resurgent economy* (Malden, Massachusetts: Blackwell Publishing, 2008), 261.

[20] Jun'ichirō Shiratori, *"Keizai taikoku" Nihon no gaikō: enerugī shigen gaikō no keisei,1967–1974-nen* (Tōkyō-to Chūō-ku: Chikura Shobō, 2015).

is important as it challenges the conventional wisdom that Japan shifted to a pro-Arab position in spite of its relations with the United States, and a more accurate reading of Japan's conduct at this time saw it adopt a foreign policy strategy to maximize its national interest. Such calculations dealing with the supply security and pricing of crude oil, allowed LNG to be seen as a credible alternative and gave impetus behind its progressive adoption.

This allows us to view the 1973 oil crisis as an *initial departure* by Japan toward a more sophisticated diplomacy, which balances strategic interests from tactical initiatives to maximize the national interest. This contrasts what has been the conventional wisdom that Japan prioritized its national economic interests over its relations with the United States. Nevertheless, the tangible impact of this shift toward greater foreign policy engagement with the Middle Eastern region has allowed for a deepening of the relationship across the region and for it to evolve in a complex manner. While Japan interpreted safeguarding its national economic interests as an overarching objective to pursue despite to balance this in a sophisticated manner with its entrenched bilateral relationship with the United States, it can be argued here that this was to set the course of Japan's future complex relationship with the Middle Eastern region which is the subject of this book. Based on this, it is therefore appropriate to provide some reflections on the characteristics of Japan's foreign policy before moving toward an overall conceptualization which will reflect the case studies on Japan's bilateral relations in addition to thematic studies that are the subject matter of this volume.

It can be argued here that 1973 proved to be an important juncture in Japan's foreign policy as it was faced with the reality that there was an inherent incompatibility between the pursuit and advancement of national economic growth and economic security, against its bilateral support for the US position. It is also worth noting that the oil crisis proved to be a shock to Japan's self-perception as a pacifist and friendly nation to others as the Organization for Arab Petroleum Exporting Countries (OAPEC) did not initially classify Japan as a friendly country.

Japan's ability to rely on the United States to safeguard its interests came into question as US Secretary of State Henry Kissinger could not provide guarantees that the United States would safeguard Japan's oil supplies. It is on this basis that Prime Minister Kakuei Tanaka outlines Japan's new strategy for "resource diplomacy" (*shigen gaikō*) was initiated, yet as highlighted in the above text, it should not be viewed as a binary strategy at the expense of Japan's strategic relations with the United States, but rather the contemporary onset of Japan exercising a sophisticated statecraft to further Japan's strategic national economic interests, of which LNG was increasingly recognized as a credible alternative.

Nevertheless, it is also clear that it marked the onset of Japanese diplomacy that was able to advance interests it's the Middle Eastern region which facilitated the growth of its engagement regionwide. This necessarily has seen it evolve in a complex and multifaceted manner. Nevertheless, it is also clear that the relationship can also be described as one of interdependence where both Japan and energy exporting Middle Eastern states arguably have a mutually dependent relationship. In the case of the LNG sector, this was particularly the case about Qatar, but also the United Arab Emirates who was the first supplier of LNG to Japan. It is therefore appropriate to move on to a discussion of how the LNG sector grew in the Gulf region and the nature of Japan's engagement both as a consumer of LNG, but also as a stakeholder in the LNG sector's development. This will be shown to given the under-line increased interdependence between Japan and the LNG supplying countries concerned.

4   Growth and Expansion of Japan's Trade in LNG with the Gulf Region

By 2021, Japan was importing LNG from three countries within the Middle Eastern region: Qatar, the United Arab Emirates, and Oman. While the United Arab Emirates was the first country in the Middle East from which Japan was to import LNG, it is Qatar which it dominates the volume of supply to Japan followed by Oman. LNG is a critical thematic issue in understanding the evolution of Japan's energy interests in the Gulf region with the three supplying countries in question. It is also an important thematic issue which factors into calculations on crude oil consumption and overall energy security. With the first shipment of LNG to Japan taking place in 1977, for more than four decades LNG has been a factor in shaping the Japan's engagement with specific countries in the region.

The UAE was the first to recognize the need to put an end to the wasteful flaring of associated gas linked with the country's growing oil output during the 1960s. By 1972, the Abu Dhabi National Oil Company (ADNOC) signed a 20-year sales and purchase agreement (SPA) with

Tokyo Electric Power Company (TEPCO) for the supply of 2 million tonnes per year (mta) of LNG and 800,000 tonnes per annum (tpa) of LPG. Abu Dhabi Gas Liquefaction Company (ADGAS) was formed the following year to own and manage the Das Island LNG facility. Das Island is a small piece of land (2.5 km), 160 km northwest of Abu Dhabi, and it is home to the Middle East's first LNG facility. ADNOC, Mitsui, BP, and Total are the joint venture company's shareholders. Following this agreement, on April 29, 1977, the UAE exported the first LNG from the Gulf, on the tanker *Hilli* which left Das Island with the country's first LNG cargo headed for Japan. On May 14, 1977, *Hilli* successfully unloaded the cargo at the Sodegaura import terminal in Tokyo Bay. The LNG project showed that gas flaring could be offset, but more broadly it was the onset of a future relationship between the Gulf region and Japan through LNG.[21]

In 1989, gas discoveries led to the establishment of the Oman LNG plant in the city of Qalhat, which is situated a little over 20 km north of Sur in northeastern Oman's Ash Sharqiyah Region. Qalhat was a vital stop on the larger Indian Ocean commerce network, as well as the ancient Kingdom of Ormus's second city. In 1994, Sultan Qaboos created the Oman Liquefied Natural Gas (Oman LNG) by royal decree. The first two-train project, which began exporting gas in 2000, had a capacity of 7.4 million tons per year (10 billion cubic meters per year), but has not run at full capacity owing to supply challenges. This heralded Oman's entry into the LNG sector and the 12th exporting country globally. In November 2005, a third liquefaction train with a capacity of 3.7 MMt/y (5 Bcm/y), known as Qalhat LNG, was commissioned, and dispatched its first cargo in December 2005. Qalhat LNG subsequently merged with Oman LNG in 2013.

Oman LNG's ownership comprises institutional and governmental shareholders. While the government of the Sultanate of Oman is the dominant shareholder at 51%, followed by shale gas at 30%, and hotel at 5.54%, it is noteworthy that several Japanese companies are shareholders. These are Mitsubishi Corporation (2.77%), Mitsui & Co. (2.77%), and Itochu Corporation (0.92%). While the majority of Oman's LNG is exported to the Korea Gas Corporation, both Osaka Gas and Itochu Corporation are contracted for a combined total of 1.4 million tons per

---

[21] Corkhill et al., "LNG shipping at 50, SIGTTO at 35 and GIIGNL at 43. A commemorative SIGTTO/GIIGNL publication 2014," 81.

year. Since this, the LNG sector is important for Japanese companies not only as consumers, but also as shareholders in the LNG sector in Oman. The creation of stakeholders in Oman's LNG sector coupled with supply agreements demonstrates a strategic engagement which can be accounted for under the multifaceted complex interdependence conceptualization offered within this volume.

Although the UAE and Oman have been important suppliers to Japan, it is Qatar which has dominated the supply of LNG both to Japan but also on a global level as it is the world's leading LNG supplier. A noteworthy feature of Qatar's natural gas industry is that it was deliberately developed with a long-term perspective in mind. Qatar's North Field, discovered in 1971, is the world's biggest unassociated gas field, with an estimated reserve of 900 trillion cubic feet (TCF). Despite its discovery, the energy market was dominated by crude oil demand rather than natural gas demand. Indeed, demand for natural gas was very low, and as a result, oil companies usually flared a significant amount of natural gas. Nonetheless, a strategic decision to exploit the gas reserves was taken in 1984. This resulted in the creation of Qatargas, which was predicated on the choice to utilize the resource both for local consumption and export. The field's development began in 1987, and the first crop was harvested in 1991. Within Qatar, it was recognized that this was a strategic advantage, and the task would be to develop and find markets for natural gas, allowing Qatar to profit from its natural resource.

A noteworthy feature of Qatar's natural gas industry is that it was deliberately developed with a long-term perspective in mind. Qatar's North Field, discovered in 1971, is the world's biggest unassociated gas field, with an estimated reserve of 900 trillion cubic feet (TCF). Despite its discovery, the energy market was dominated by crude oil demand rather than natural gas demand. Indeed, demand for natural gas was very low, and as a result, oil companies usually flared a significant amount of natural gas. Nonetheless, a strategic decision to exploit the gas reserves was taken in 1984.[22] This resulted in the creation of Qatargas, which was predicated on the choice to utilize the resource both for local consumption and export. The field's development began in 1987 and its first export of LNG took place in 1996 to Japan.

---

[22] Steven Wright, "Advancement of environmental sustainability through LNG: The case of Qatar–China relations," in *Green Finance, Sustainable Development and the Belt and Road Initiative* (Routledge, 2020).

Qatar's determination to capitalize on its natural gas industry resulted in the establishment of a gas hub in Ras Laffan, enabling Qatar to export its gas. This cost approximately US$2 billion, which Qatar had to finance via foreign funding. The strategy's long-term objective was for Qatar to become a significant worldwide supplier of natural gas. To accomplish this, three pillars of Qatar's natural gas industry were identified: first, the adoption of a fully integrated gas sector. This necessitated developing a new way of providing LNG, one that included production, gas liquefaction, transportation, and ultimately a receiving terminal and re-gasification. In this respect, Qatar's natural gas business was a fully integrated enterprise that enabled market access and the acceptance of natural gas as a source of energy. Qatar's LNG strategy's second pillar was cost optimization. The strategy here was to use the company's involvement in all sectors to reduce the cost of producing and transporting LNG to the customer. The last pillar was built on reliability as establishing a brand that is synonymous with dependability, price competitiveness, and delivery quality, Qatar was able to use this to secure long-term energy supply deals with key customers.

Japan's engagement with Qatar's energy sector is intertwined with its overall development and has been central to the expansion of ties between Qatar and Japan and the realization of an interdependent relationship. After the establishment of Qatargas in 1984, it is noteworthy that the first sale and purchase agreement for LNG 1992 was signed with Chubu Electric for the delivery of 4 million tons per annum of LNG. This established Qatar as a leading supplier of LNG to Japan and was the onset of a strategic relationship.[23] After the first shipment of LNG from Qatar to Japan departed in 1996 and was delivered in January 1997, a variety of opportunities existed for Japanese companies to become engaged in the energy sector. In comparison to the case of the Sultanate of Oman where shareholders of Oman LNG were established, the approach undertaken in Qatar was for shareholders to be granted a stake in the development and future profits from gas trains developed. Prior to the merger between Qatargas and Rasgas in 2018, the following data can be observed in Table 1, which underlines that although most

---

[23] Satoru Nakamura, "Challenges for Qatar and Japan to Build Multilayered Relations," *Gulf Monographic Series*, no. 2 (2016).

stakeholders in Qatar's energy sector were American international energy companies, Japanese trading companies were notable stakeholders.[24]

Although Japan and Korea are the largest consuming countries of Qatar's LNG, this is not necessarily translated into them being the dominant shareholders in Qatar's LNG sector. It is important here to note that there was a move toward merging Qatar's two LNG companies, Rasgas and Qatargas in 2016 and this was realized in 2018. The main motive behind this was cost saving measures and an increasingly competitive operating environment which was a product of the transformative effects of the shale industry within the United States. While ExxonMobil, Shell, and Total are the main international energy companies operating within Qatar, the role of a variety of Japanese trading companies has nevertheless been important particularly as they also play a role as being a long-term customer. This is an issue which can differentiate the role of Japanese companies to other companies which are the dominant shareholders. The central importance of Japanese companies relates to their significant role as consumers of LNG as Japan, along with Korea, constitute the largest export markets for Qatar's product. What can be argued observed here is that while being a shareholder in the energy sector is an important means of facilitating interdependence, what is arguably more important is the role that the country plays as a destination market for the export of LNG. In this regard Japan has played a unique role in Qatar's economic development given it is the largest trading partner of Qatar, and this trading relationship has allowed for a broadening and deepening of relations to take place on several levels. Indeed, it was after the 2011 Tōhoku earthquake and tsunami, that Japan's suspension of all nuclear reactors in the country led to LNG being seen as the solution for Japan's domestic electricity needs. It was this event which led to a further deepening of Japan's trade with Qatar as a significant proportion of that excess LNG was sourced from Qatar.

It is also worth noting here that in line with the conceptual framework presented in this volume for multifaceted interdependence, a similar pattern has been observed whereby Japanese trading companies have participated in corporate social responsibility activities. A notable contribution was made by Marubeni through a US$6 million endowment made to Qatar University for the promotion of Japan–Qatar relations on April

---

[24] Maha Khalid Al Subaey, "An Analysis of the bilateral relations between Qatar and Japan: Case studies on Energy, Culture and Diplomacy" (2017).

Table 1   Qatar LNG Shareholders and Customers[25]

Operator	Trains	mn t/y	Start-up	Expiration	Shareholders	Key long-term customers
Qatargas 1	T1–3	9.9	1997	2021	Up until March 2021: QE (65%) ExxonMobil (10%) Total (10%) Marubeni (7.5%) Mitsui (7.5%)	Japanese utilities
Qatargas 2	T4	7.8	2009	2034	QE (70%) ExxonMobil (30%)	ExxonMobil (UK)
Qatargas 2	T5	7.8	2009	2034	QE (65%) ExxonMobil (18.3%) Total (16.7%)	CNOOC (China), Total (various destinations)
Qatargas 3	T6	7.8	2010	2035	QE (68.5%) ConocoPhillips (30%) Mitsui (1.5%)	Centrica (UK), CNOOC (China), Chubu/Kansai (Japan)*
Qatargas 4	T7	7.8	2011	2036	QE (70%) Shell (30%)	Shell, PetroChina (China), Marubeni (Japan)
Rasgas 1	T1&2	6.6	1999	2024	QE (63%) ExxonMobil (25%) KORAS (5.0%) Itochu (4.0%) LNG Japan (3.0%)	Kogas (Korea)
Rasgas 2	T3	4.7	2004	2029	QE (70%) ExxonMobil (30%)	Petronet (India), Edison (Italy)
Rasgas 2	T4	4.7	2007	2030	QE (65%) ExxonMobil (30%) CPC (5.0%)	CPC (Taiwan), EDF, Eni (Belgium)
Rasgas 2	T5	4.7	2007	2031	QE (65%) ExxonMobil (30%) CPC (5.0%)	
Rasgas 3	T6	7.8	2009	2034	QE (70%) ExxonMobil (30%)	Kogas (Korea), Petronet (India)
Rasgas 3	T7	7.8	2010	2035	QE (70%) ExxonMobil (30%)	
Total: 14 trains, 77.4 mt/y						

25 Jamie Ingram, "Qatar Petroleum Moves to Take Full Ownership of LNG Facilities." MEES, 2 April, 2021.

29, 2012. This yielded a range of Japanese cultural activities at the University of Japan, in addition to the development of the first encyclopedia in Arabic on Japan which was distributed to all schools within the country. Moreover, it also led to the establishment of two endowed Professorships at Qatar University with the respective faculty teaching on the social sciences and history of Japan, respectively. This was also coupled with the recruitment of a lecturer in Japanese language which students could take as an elective course. Indeed, it is the role of Japanese Corporations in corporate social responsibility which has had a discernible impact on fostering greater understanding and relations between the two countries.

It is because of the scale of the investment and trade that is taking place that has allowed such large-scale corporate social responsibility activities to take place within Qatar which has further the relationship. In essence it is evidence of a cycle of engagement which leads to a deepening of the relationship and achievement of multifaceted complex interdependence and the bilateral relations between the two countries concerned.

5   Geopolitics and LNG: Key East Asian Market Dynamics

The broader backdrop of energy supply and demand dynamics is illuminating, since significant developments have happened that enable us to see the global energy market as entering a new age. Two trends are observable: the shifting nature of demand, and emerging cooperation between buyers of LNG. This shift in the global environment was most visibly shown in 2018 when the United States reclaimed its position as the world's biggest oil producer. For the better part of the past century, the United States was the world's biggest producer of oil, a position it retained until 1974, when it was surpassed by the Soviet Union during the Cold War's height. The Soviet Union was eventually surpassed by Saudi Arabia in 1976—from that point on, it was the Saudis who would control the oil market for the next four decades. The way in which the United States surpassed Saudi Arabia in the global energy markets requires a wider examination of geopolitical shift in the global energy markets and the implications for United States involvement with the Middle East and supply to global markets.[26]

While the changing fortunes of the United States have undoubtedly had a global impact, a broader pattern that can be observed is a shift in the global center of gravity for energy demand, which is primarily characterized by demand shifting from OECD to non-OECD countries, with a particular emphasis on China and India.[27] Since the 1990s, this change in demand has been driven by the increasing economic affluence of billions of people in emerging nations. Given China's and India's size and population, they have been the primary drivers of world energy consumption. China has been the primary driver of demand for natural gas over the past decade, and this trend is expected to continue. However, on a geopolitical level, it is critical to realize that south and northern East Asia account for the lion's share of global natural gas consumption. China, Japan, South Korea, and India together account for more than sixty percent of world consumption.[28] These nations constitute the Big-4 in terms of LNG consumption. As a result, these markets will inevitably be critical for Qatar and other major LNG suppliers in terms of present and future market demand.[29]

Related to this is the move toward a cooperation between LNG buyers to secure more flexible supply contracts and pricing. The nature of this Corporation stems from the changes in the global energy market and can be observed to be operating on two levels: the first is a cooperation between Japanese LNG buyers, and the second is international where Corporation also takes place with key consuming countries. It is noteworthy here that in 2014, Tokyo Electric Power Group (TEPCO) and the Chubu Electric Power Group, established a joint venture alliance, JERA, which was geared toward collaboration in the entire supply chain from upstream fuel investment and fuel procurement. With respect to LNG, this amounted to a collaboration between consuming companies

---

[26] Steven Wright, "Energy Geopolitics in 2019," *Aljazeera Centre for Studies* 24 (2019).

[27] Steven Wright, "Shifting markets of liquid gas: emerging producers and alternative geostrategies," *Al Jazeera Centre for Studies* 12 (2018).

[28] Steven Wright, "Qatar's LNG: Impact of the changing east-asian market," *Middle East Policy* 24, no. 1 (2017).

[29] Wright, "Shifting markets of liquid gas: emerging producers and alternative geostrategies."

on procurement so the most effective pricing and contract terms could be achieved. In its current form, JERA, is the world's largest purchaser of LNG, and can be viewed as a devolution of Japan this historical move toward achieving energy security. What is particularly interesting about the move toward a collaborative procurement market is that the logic of a buyer's alliance amounts to an inverse relationship that can be observed in the oil market through the Organization of Petroleum Exporting Countries (OPEC).

In March 2017, JERA, China National Offshore Oil Corp (CNOOC), and Korea Gas Corp (KOGAS) signed an agreement to share information and collaborate on cooperative LNG purchase. The three firms together acquire a third of worldwide LNG output, giving them a powerful hand in challenging tight contract conditions that have strained purchasers' budgets. Prior to 2014, high LNG prices forced Asian importers to come up with new strategies to limit losses, resulting in the initial discussions regarding combined purchases involving India, Japan, South Korea, China, and Taiwan. Numerous joint LNG purchases have been made since then, but while initial cooperation agreements were made between countries, it is the move toward actual buyers collaborating that is the most significant change. This move started a new form of cooperation to exert pressure on exporters such as Qatar, who has traditionally preferred to lock customers into long-term fixed supply contracts that require purchasers to accept set monthly quantities regardless of demand, with no right to resell excess supplies to other end users. While the 2017 agreement was an important development, by 2022 there was little evidence that it had yielded a tangible cooperation in terms of procurement of LNG.

In terms of how this related to Japan's complex interdependence with LNG supplying countries in the Gulf region, the efforts toward increased collaboration in terms of the procurement of LNG should be interpreted as a reflection of economically driven market dynamics and energy security calculations, but not one which runs counter to interdependence. As highlighted above, an inverse relationship exists in the oil market where a cartel of sellers maximizes the revenue from their export commodity, but given the nature of the LNG sector and how consumer demand is dominated by key markets, the opposite relationship exists. This does not necessarily mean that it is a trend running counter to complex interdependence, but rather a reflection of states pursuing their national interests and also energy companies maximizing their respective revenue.

6   OPPORTUNITIES AND CHALLENGES

While global energy prices have been low since 2014 but began a resurgence in the post-Covid recovery era in 2021, one of the major distinctions in this cycle is the emergence of a new era due to the extraction of oil and gas reserves in shale and tight formations. This has enabled the United States to become more energy secure and to position itself as an oil and gas exporter, but it is the commercial viability of shale producers that acts as a depressant on global oil prices: the higher the price, the more commercially viable it is for producers to exploit shale, and thus increased oil production results in price depression. While it is true that national oil firms have lower production costs and are thus more competitive on pricing, their economies remain reliant on oil and gas income. As a result, the new energy environment helps to keep prices low for the foreseeable future, which has obvious consequences for the Arab Gulf area, further encouraging an eastward direction. Additionally, as the US's perspective and interests evolve, the nexus of oil and geopolitics is defining a new age for the Gulf.

The outbreak of the COVID-19 pandemic in 2020 led to a substantial decrease in crude oil prices, which had a ripple effect on the economic capacities of the GCC countries. These have subsequently recovered, but the economy remains highly reliant on OPEC supply cutbacks. Given their greater barrier to entry, it's worth noting that historically, declining fossil fuel prices have delayed the adoption of more energy-efficient products and renewable energy sources. Most energy-importing nations, on the other hand, have set a strategic objective of attaining a carbon–neutral collective economy by approximately 2050. While carbon neutrality aims to balance CO_2 emissions by actively mitigating their effect via measures to remove greenhouse gases, it also stresses the need for renewable energy, possibly decreasing future oil and gas use. The European Union (2050); Japan (2050); China (2060); South Korea (2050); and the United States (2050) have all made significant pledges (2050). LNG may gain from the shift away from oil and coal, since LNG is a cleaner fossil fuel than oil, but the question is how the next 30 years' carbon-Neutral targets will affect its longer-term usage.[30]

---

[30] Steven Wright, "COVID-19 and the global energy market: implications for international and domestic policies in the Arab Gulf states," *Global Discourse: An interdisciplinary journal of current affairs* 10, no. 4 (2020).

While LNG is more cost-effective than renewables in this instance, the long-term trend indicates a continuous rise for cost-effective renewables. As the world's first cargo of blue ammonia arrived in Japan on September 27, 2020 from Saudi Arabia, a further challenge facing the LNG sector is the progressive growth of the hydrogen sector in the longer term. While LNG can be turned into blue ammonia thereby becoming a cleaner fuel source than its current form, the key issue will be how this can be done economically to make it more competitive. Nevertheless, the move toward a hydrogen-based economy and the recognition that blue ammonia from LNG may be a viable fuel source and the future, also opens opportunities for research and development and technological innovation in making that option a more cost-effective solution. Given Japan's research and development sector, there is a good opportunity for it to become increasingly engaged in blue ammonia technologies and to work with partners within the region toward the emergence of a new energy sector.

7 Concluding Observations

The wider view on Japan's energy ties with the Middle East is that they have been critical to Japan's national economic growth, given the country's energy deficit. Additionally, it is evident that Japan illustrates how energy changes have been critical to overall national growth. Coal was the first fuel source to be phased out, followed by oil and coal gas, and then nuclear, LNG, and renewable energy.[31] Each of these changes shaped Japan's engagement with certain nations in the area, inevitably resulting in substantial bilateral commerce between countries. Indeed, significant observations can be made about Japan's commerce with the Middle Eastern region's major oil-producing nations and how this has facilitated the development of interaction and intricate interdependence among the countries involved.

In the case of LNG, it has been a critical commodity that has influenced Japan's ties with three major nations in the Gulf area, most notably with Qatar, which is the world's biggest supplier of LNG. In many ways, LNG adoption has been accelerated by Japan's own internal energy transitions and energy security policy. These have unavoidably been affected by global contextual variables, but the critical point here is that the issue

---

[31] Wright, "Energy Geopolitics in 2019."

of Japan's energy security is dynamic and ever-changing. What we can deduct from this is that, at the time of writing, the shift to a carbon–neutral future and the development of green technology are likely to be the defining variables determining how LNG fits into Japan's energy mix. LNG, as a more environmentally friendly alternative to crude oil, has the potential to profit from the energy revolution and assist Japan in its goal of reaching carbon neutrality by 2050.

It is conceivable that as a carbon–neutral future heralds the rise in the use of renewable technology and a mix of blue and green fuel sources, natural gas processed into blue ammonia is a key area that Qatar's trade with Japan will see progress growth into as part of a diversification from LNG. The strength of natural gas is that it can be turned into LNG or blue ammonia, so there is long term potential for Japan's engagement with Qatar in terms of bilateral energy trade. Despite this, history has shown how significant energy transitions have been, so it is reasonable to conclude that Japan's trade with Qatar will necessarily evolve given how changes to Japan's energy mix to incorporate cleaner sources of energy (blue ammonia in particular) will alter the character of future bilateral trade.

References

Arase, David. "New Directions in Japanese Security Policy." *Contemporary Security Policy* 15, no. 2 (1994): 44–64.

Barber, B. Bryan. *Japan's Relations with Muslim Asia*. Cham, Switzerland: Palgrave Macmillan, 2020.

Corkhill, Mike, Syd Harris, Andrew Clifton, Bill Wayne, and Jean-Yves Robin. "LNG Shipping at 50, Sigtto at 35 and Giignl at 43. A Commemorative Sigtto/Giignl Publication 2014." (2014).

Edström, Bert. *Japan's Evolving Foreign Policy Doctrine: From Yoshida to Miyazawa*. New York, N.Y.: St. Martin's Press, 1999.

Ingram, Jamie. "Qatar Petroleum Moves to Take Full Ownership of LNG Facilities." MEES, 2 April, 2021.

Kobori, Satoru. "Japan's Energy Policy During the 1950s: Reasons for the Rapid Switch from Coal to Oil." Asia-Pacific Economic and Business History Conference, San Francisco Bay Area, 2009.

Nakamura, Satoru. "Challenges for Qatar and Japan to Build Multilayered Relations." *Gulf Monographic Series*, no. 2 (2016).

Nester, William, and Kweku Ampiah. "Japan's Oil Diplomacy: Tatemae and Honne." *Third World Quarterly* 11, no. 1 (1989): 72–88.

Okita, Saburo. "Natural Resource Dependency and Japanese Foreign Policy." *Foreign Affairs* 52, no. 4 (1974): 714–24.

Petroleum Association of Japan. "Crude Oil Import by Countries and by Source." Tokyo, Japan, 2021. https://www.paj.gr.jp/english/statis/.

Samuels, Richard J. *The Business of the Japanese State*. Cornell University Press, 1987.

Shiratori, Jun'ichirō. "Keizai Taikoku" Nihon No Gaikō: Enerugī Shigen Gaikō No Keisei, 1967–1974-Nen. Tōkyō-to Chūō-ku: Chikura Shobō, 2015.

Sinha, R. P. "Japan and the Oil Crisis." *The World Today* 30, no. 8 (August 1974).

SStapczynski. "Japan Imported Its 1st Shipment of Liquefied Natural Gas 50 Years Ago Today. Now the Nation Is the World's Largest Buyer of the Fuel (and Pioneered the Industry). Hiroshi Anzai Is the Little Known Maverick Who Played a Key Role in Japan Becoming an LNG Juggernaut." Twitter, 4 November 2019.

Stockwin, J. A. A. *Governing Japan: Divided Politics in a Resurgent Economy*. Malden, Massachusetts: Blackwell Publishing, 2008.

Takahashi, Ryutaro. "Trade Policies of the New Japan." *Foreign Affairs* 30 (1951): 289.

Tokyo Gas. *LNG 50th for the Next 50 Years: Integrated Report*. Tokyo Gas, (Tokyo: Tokyo Gas, 2019).

Tusiani, Michael D, and Gordon Shearer. *LNG: A Nontechnical Guide*. PennWell Books, 2007.

Wright, Steven. "Advancement of Environmental Sustainability through Lng: The Case of Qatar–China Relations." In *Green Finance, Sustainable Development and the Belt and Road Initiative*, 159–76: Routledge, 2020a.

Wright, Steven. "Covid-19 and the Global Energy Market: Implications for International and Domestic Policies in the Arab Gulf States." *Global Discourse: An interdisciplinary journal of current affairs* 10, no. 4 (2020b): 475–80.

Wright, Steven. "Energy Geopolitics in 2019." *Aljazeera Centre for Studies* 24 (2019).

Wright, Steven. "Qatar's LNG: Impact of the Changing East-Asian Market." *Middle East Policy* 24, no. 1 (2017): 154–65.

Wright, Steven. "Shifting Markets of Liquid Gas: Emerging Producers and Alternative Geostrategies." *Al Jazeera Centre for Studies* 12 (2018).

Yergin, Daniel. *The Prize: The Epic Quest for Oil, Money, and Power*. New York: Simon & Schuster, 1992.

CHAPTER 10

Investment and Trade Promotion Policies: Gulf and Japan's Non-energy Sector Interdependence

Jun Saito

1 INTRODUCTION

As energy resource suppliers for Japan, the GCC countries have been important economic partners and outstanding benefactors of the Japanese economy and its prosperity since World War II. With the aim of the steady supply of energy, Japan steadily reduced its dependence on oil and natural gas and moved towards nuclear power for many years, thus diversifying its energy source and relying less on the GCC countries. However, after the Great East Japan Earthquake in 2011, Japanese energy policy changed

---

This chapter is based on Saito and Janardhan (2020) and has been significantly revised by Saito.

J. Saito (✉)
Institute Developing Economies (IDE-JETRO), Chiba, Japan
e-mail: Jun_Saito@ide.go.jp

© The Author(s), under exclusive license to Springer Nature
Singapore Pte Ltd. 2023
S. Nakamura and S. Wright (eds.), *Japan and the Middle East*,
Contemporary Gulf Studies, https://doi.org/10.1007/978-981-19-3459-9_10

remarkably and is now reverting back once again to fossil fuel energy and its previous dependence on these oil-producing nations.

Longstanding economic relationships through energy-related trade have also laid solid foundations for economic interchanges in the non-oil economies of the GCC countries and Japan. In 1997, for instance, Japan called for "Comprehensive Partnership toward the Twenty-First Century," based on political, economic and new areas of cooperation, following which Saudi Arabia and Japan witnessed the signing of "Japan-Saudi Arabia Cooperation Agenda" in 1998.[1] The economic exchange between the two countries grew considerably thereafter. In 2016, then Vice Crown Prince Mohammed bin Salman Al Saud agreed with the Japanese government on a detailed programme of cooperation in relation to its "Saudi Arabia vision 2030."

In a similar way, with respect to the United Arab Emirates, Prime Minister Abe visited the UAE in 2013 and announced a "Joint Statement on the Strengthening of the Comprehensive Partnership between Japan and the United Arab Emirates towards Stability and Prosperity," in order to strengthen the bilateral relationship in the fields of education, science, technology, healthcare, infrastructure, agriculture and so on.[2]

Japan and oil-producing countries in the Middle East have been important economic and trading partners in the energy field for many years. Changes in Japan's energy policy, instability in the Middle East and the economic diversification of Middle Eastern countries have promoted a transformation of economic relations through trade in natural resources. Japanese corporate expansion and investment in the Middle East have gradually increased, and Middle Eastern companies, especially those from the GCC countries, have also expanded their overseas markets in recent years.

How has the close economic relationship between the GCC countries and Japan changed? Have the investment promotion policies adopted by them strengthened the economic relationship between the two regions?

---

[1] Ministry of Foreign Affairs of Japan "Joint Press Release: On the Occasion of Crown Prince Abdullah's Visit to Japan," October 23, 1998. https://www.mofa.go.jp/region/middle_e/saudi/visit9810.html (Accessed November 9, 2020).

[2] Ministry of Foreign Affairs of Japan "Prime Minister Shinzo Abe's visit to the Middle East," May 4, 2013. https://www.mofa.go.jp/region/page6e_000028.html (Accessed November 9, 2020).

What are the challenges facing governments and the private sector in the GCC countries and Japan to further strengthening economic relations? This chapter will clarify—via a range of aggregated statistical data— economic interactions between the GCC countries and Japan that are deemed necessary to solve these questions. First, we summarize trade and investment promotion policies between the GCC countries and Japan, following which we analyse changes in economic relations in trade, foreign direct investment, bank lending and business expansion. Finally, we evaluate changes in "interdependence" between the two trading blocs.

In this chapter, therefore, Sect. 2 presents the findings of previous research on trade, direct investment, firm entry and changes in trade policies. Sect. 3 summarizes the investment promotion policies of the GCC countries and Japan, and Sect. 4 analyses changes in economic relations with reference to trade and foreign direct investment (FDI) statistics, and to trends in overseas affiliations. Finally, the last section concludes on the interdependence of the GCC countries and Japan.

2   Impact of Trade and Foreign Direct Investment on Economic Development in Developing Countries

What effects do trade, direct investment, entry of firms and changes in trade policies have on the economies and economic dealings between the GCC countries and Japan? In this section, we summarise the findings of previous research in this field.

2.1   Trade and Economic Development

If the GCC countries export natural resources such as oil and natural gas to trading partners, how does this practice affect the economic development of the GCC countries themselves? Is it a rational policy choice to expand the domestic production of non-petroleum products and switch major exports from oil and natural gas-related products to non-petroleum products? Herein, we discuss the relationship between trade and economic development, and between the export of natural resources and the development of the domestic industry.

There are two conflicting theories, namely staple theory and Dutch disease, on the impact of the comparative advantage brought about by the presence of resources on economic growth. According to the staple theory, proffered by Innis (1956) and Watkins (1963), an export industry based on natural resources leads the economy, and the ripple effect from that industry to other industries promotes economic growth. In the early stages of economic development, exports of abundant natural resources promote the development of industries other than export industries through spillover effects such as backward linkage, forward linkage and increased final demand accompanying increased income (Kimura 2000). When one "major primary product (staple)" is at a stage of exhaustion, through this ripple effect (and if it is possible to produce products dependent on other natural resources), economic growth will continue (Hayami 1995).

Dutch disease, contrary to staple theory, argues that rich natural resources can be a barrier to economic growth. The sharp increase in exports of natural resources will bring about an appreciation of the effective exchange rate through an increase in the balance of payments surplus, thereby reducing the international competitiveness of non-resource traded goods and leading to stagnation and unemployment in the sector. In general, the mining sector, which includes oil and natural gas, has a high capital-labour ratio and a weak ability to absorb employment. Thus, the expansion of the natural resources sector cannot compensate for the decline in employment brought about by non-natural resource trade sectors, such as agriculture and manufacturing, contracting (Hayami 1995).

While the development of these theoretical aspects has been discussed for many years in terms of the relationship between trade in natural resources and economic growth, there is no firm consensus or empirical analysis at either the macroeconomic or the sector level. Although the correlation between trade liberalization and economic growth has been pointed out in many papers, using macro-level data, its causality is still controversial (Kimura 2000). Also, it has been argued that maintaining restrictions on trade and exclusionary trade policies impede long-term economic growth (Rodríguez and Rodrik 2000; Fukui 2008).

2.2   Trading Policies

Negotiations on the conclusion of international agreements on trade liberalization have been conducted by international bodies such as General Agreement on Tariffs and Trade (GATT) and World Trade

Organization (WTO), but international trade liberalization negotiations surrounding GCC countries have slowly progressed. Though since 2000s, the GCC countries have been actively negotiating for the conclusion of the Free Trade Agreement (FTA) between them and Japan, and within the MENA (Middle East and North Africa) region.

Although the FTA aims to allow many goods to be freely traded among the countries that signed this agreement, it does not guarantee the removal of trade barriers for countries that have not signed up, and so for this reason, it can sometimes be an obstacle to multilateral free trade (Fukui 2008). For developing countries, the benefit of participating in an FTA is to promote the import of cheap goods from the region (Viner and Oslington 2014) and to improve the productivity of participating countries through the transfer of technology and the expansion of capital (Balassa 1961). On the other hand, there is also a disadvantage that high-productivity products in the FTA region will be replaced with low-productivity goods (Fukui 2008).

Furthermore, with regard to the effect of improving productivity in the region, it is important for developing countries to select a developed partner country to enter into the FTA, because if they can later source capital and technology from this developed partner, they can enhance their productivity. On the other hand, when developing countries mutually conclude FTAs, there are few tradeable goods, low production technology and a small number of production factors, so it is difficult to expect trade expansion through the formation of FTAs.

2.3 FDI and Economic Development

For many developing countries, how to raise a large amount of money to foster domestic industry is an important issue for economic development. As developing countries generally have low savings rates and lack of domestic funding, financing from overseas countries, especially in the form of foreign direct investment, contributes significantly to industrial development (Meier and Rauch 2005). Meier and Rauch (2005) point out the advantages and disadvantages of countries that accept FDI and attract foreign companies. In the first instance, it benefits workers in the host country through real-term wage rises. Second, foreign investment benefits consumers, as product prices decrease as a result of improved productivity. Third, the increase in tax revenue is a financial benefit to the host government. Finally, foreign investment brings many benefits, such as the acquisition of overseas "knowledge" through the realization of the external economy. On the other hand, it can come at a cost to the recipient country, such as excessive concessions made to domestic and foreign investors, negative impacts on domestic savings due to declining profits in domestic industries, deterioration in trade terms and balance of payments adjustments.

To the best of the author's knowledge, there is not enough prior research on how a rentier state regime such as that of the GCC countries affects the attraction of foreign direct investment, and whether transitioning to a de-rentier or late-rentier state will promote foreign direct investment. However, as pointed out by Daude and Stein (2007), countries with better governance systems and higher "Government Effectiveness" and "Regulatory Quality" (from World Bank's Worldwide Governance Indicators) are able to attract more foreign direct investment.

These scores tend to be higher in typical rentier states such as the UAE, Qatar and Saudi Arabia than other Middle Eastern countries. The ratio of natural resource rents to GDP, also calculated from the World Bank's World Development Indicators, has been on a downward trend in the GCC countries since the 2000s, suggesting that de-rentierization of the GCC countries is in progress in the short term. These findings suggest that rentier states, such as the GCC countries, are more likely to attract a lot of foreign direct investment because they have better governance systems compared to other Middle Eastern countries. On the other hand, the GCC countries could introduce further FDI if they can maintain and upgrade their good legal systems in promoting economic development through de-rentalization income.

2.4   Investment Promotion

In addition, the asymmetry of economic and institutional conditions between the GCC countries and Japan needs to be taken into account when concluding new investment agreements between the two blocs to promote investment. Promoting FDI between developed and developing countries can create institutional problems. Foreign direct investment drivers are often companies in the developed country, and policy rule changes are often imposed on developing countries only when investment rules are imposed bilaterally and internationally. Due to the asymmetry involved in these policy changes, developing countries have a strong desire to attract direct investment while at the same time hoping to avoid being squeezed out of policy, if possible (Kimura 2000). Thus, even if concluding new investment promotion rules that are "fair" to both sides would institutionally facilitate FDI between the GCC countries and Japan, it would not necessarily lead to symmetrical expansion of companies from both sides into the other country.

Moreover, as Kimura points out, if a bilateral investment protection agreement is already in effect, it will be difficult to develop it into a multilateral investment agreement that may be beneficial in the long run if the multilateral investment agreement does not provide any advantages over existing bilateral agreements. If Japan is to promote investment in the GCC countries, it may be more expedient to promote bilateral investment promotion first, rather than concluding an investment agreement with the GCC countries, which is a regional framework.

3 Institutional Framework of Trade and Investment Promotion in the GCC Countries

The GCC countries' governments have recognized the importance of foreign trade and foreign investment in promoting domestic economic development, and they have developed institutional frameworks for trade expansion and investment promotion from the early stages of economic development.

3.1 Free Trade Agreements (or FTAs) for the GCC Countries

The GCC Supreme Council adopted the Common Economic Agreement in 1981 to develop unified laws and regulations in various areas, including the economy and trade, in accordance with the Cooperation Council Charter. After the GCC Unified Economic Agreement, which was signed and ratified in 1981, the Free Trade Area (FTA) Agreement among the GCC countries entered into force in March 1983, while the GCC Customs Union, which was established in January 2003, reached its declaration with the GCC Common Market on January 1, 2008 (Alshakhanbeh 2012). Greater Arab Free Trade Area (GAFTA)[3] was declared within the Social and Economic Council of the Arab League

---

[3] In the Arab League, it is called the Pan Arab Free Trade Area (PAFTA) instead of GAFTA.

as an executive programme to activate the Trade Facilitation and Development Agreement that had been in force since January 1, 1998 (Table 1). The GAFTA includes in its membership 17 Arab countries.

Negotiations for the conclusion of an FTA between developed countries, including Japan, and the GCC countries have been in progress in recent years. Table 1 outlines free trade agreements that currently exist with the GCC countries and shows that the FTA between the GCC countries and Japan is currently under negotiation.

Negotiations on the FTA between the GCC countries and Japan agreed to start negotiations in March 2006 covering the goods and services sector, and the entry into negotiations was announced in April in a joint statement by the Prime Minister and Crown Prince of Saudi Arabia. Negotiations were subsequently launched in September 2006, and by March 2009, two formal meetings and four interim meetings were held between the GCC countries and Japan. However, in July 2009, the negotiations were postponed at the request of the GCC side, and Japan is currently working on the resumption of the negotiations.

As pointed out in the previous section, the GCC countries such as Saudi Arabia have maintained a cautious stance on establishing an FTA with developed countries. Since the late 2000s, the United States and European countries have begun negotiations to conclude a bilateral free trade agreement with the GCC countries. In 2004, although the United States and Bahrain had been negotiating their free trade agreement, the Saudi foreign minister criticized that bilateral trade agreements between individual GCC members and developed countries would harm the efforts of the Arabian Gulf nations as a whole to integrate their economies. However, despite Saudi Arabia's criticism, Bahrain held its first meeting in 2006 via the Bahrain-US Free Trade Agreement Executive Committee, with an eventual agreement coming together in August 2008.

When Prince Sultan of Saudi Arabia visited Japan in April 2006, he met with Prime Minister Koizumi and issued a joint statement that included notification of the resumption of negotiations on a bilateral investment agreement and formal negotiations on a free trade agreement.

With regard to the UAE, in August 2006, Nakagawa, Minister of Agriculture, Forestry and Fisheries, met with Prince Muhammad of Abu Dhabi and discussed bilateral relations in line with strengthening economic cooperation between the GCC countries and Japan, which then led to the start of FTA negotiations.

Table 1 Free Trade Agreements (FTA) issued or being negotiated by the GCC countries

FTA name	Member countries	Type	Effective date
PAFTA/GAFTA	Iraq, Kuwait, Bahrain, Qatar, UAE, Oman, Saudi Arabia, Lebanon, Syria, Jordan, Egypt, Libya, Tunisia, Yemen, Sudan, Morocco, Palestine, Algeria	FTA	1988/1
GCC	Saudi Arabia, UAE, Kuwait, Bahrain, Oman, Qatar	Customs Union*1	2003/1
UAE-Morocco FTA	UAE, Morocco	FTA	2003/7
US-Bahrain FTA	Bahrain, US	FTA	2008/8
US-Oman FTA	Oman, US	FTA	2009/1
GCC-Singapore FTA	GCC, Singapore	FTA	2013/9
EFTA-GCC FTA	EFTA*2, GCC	FTA	2014/7
TPS-OIC*3	OIC 56 countries/area	preferential trade agreement	2014/1(signing)
GCC-New Zealand FTA	GCC, New Zealand	FTA	2009/10(provisional signing)
GCC-Japan FTA	GCC, Japan	FTA	under negotiation(interrupted)
GCC-China FTA	GCC, China	FTA	under negotiation
GCC Turkey FTA	GCC, Turkey	FTA	under negotiation
GCC-Pakistan FTA	GCC, Pakistan	FTA	under negotiation
GCC-India FTA	GCC, India	FTA	under negotiation
Thailand-Bahrain FTA	Thailand, Bahrain	FTA	under negotiation(interrupted)
GCC-Australia FTA	GCC, Australia	FTA	under negotiation(interrupted)
GCC-Korea FTA	GCC, Korea	FTA	under negotiation(interrupted)
GCC-Malaysia FTA	GCC, Malaysia	FTA	conceptual phase

Source JETRO (2019)
*1 GATT/WTO defines FTAs (elimination of tariffs and quantitative restrictions between members) and customs unions (FTAs plus common tariffs with non-members) as "regional trade agreements." In this table, the term "FTA" includes the Customs Union
*2 European Free Trade Association
*3 Trade Preferential System of the Organization of Islamic Cooperation

3.2   Investment Promotion Policies

Essentially, an investment promotion policy is divided across two dimensions that relate to national and international matters (UNCTAD, 2015). For national policy, enterprise development is an important approach to investment promotion and sustainability in any given country. The number of GCC-listed companies has increased over the last ten years.

To regulate and promote investment, investment promotion agencies (IPAs) can be effective in advocating inward FDI. Among the GCC countries, Oman has been a pioneer in this regard, establishing its own IPA in 1996 (Table 2). Both the public and private sectors in Saudi Arabia have sought to introduce foreign capital and facilitate the establishment of joint ventures. In 1998, the Ministry of Industry and Electric Power of Saudi Arabia was responsible for governing foreign investment law, and the Foreign Investment Department played a central role in attracting foreign investment. Besides, the International Relations Department also backed up joint venture promotion with foreign countries (JETRO 1998). In the Ministry of Foreign Affairs, the Bilateral Economic Department and International Economic Department deal with bilateral and international issues related to the economy, with a particularly strong interest in investment promotion activities. The Ministry of Commerce is in a position to promote "Saudisation" for existing joint ventures in the domestic distribution industry, but it also focuses on promoting the export of domestic Saudi products. In the private sector, the Chamber of Commerce plays a central role in promoting investment. The current SAGIA (Saudi Arabian General Investment Authority, established in 2000) is an investment promotion agency that originated from the Industrial Studies and Development Center (established in 1967) and the Saudi Consulting House (established in 1979).

3.3   Bilateral Investment Treaties

In terms of international investment promotion policies, The GCC countries and Japan have made progress since the latter half of the 2000s, but compared to the advanced economies and Southeast Asian countries, the development of the mutual legal and institutional investment environment has been delayed. The implementation of the current bilateral international investment policies between the GCC countries and Japan, specifically Kuwait, Saudi Arabia and Oman, began in 2014 (Table 3).

Table 2 Investment Promotion Agency in the GCC countries

The GCC country	Investment Promotion Agency	Establish date
Abu Dhabi	Abu Dhabi Investment Office (ADIO)	2018
Dubai	Dubai Investment Development Agency (Dubai FDI)	2014
Saudi Arabia	Saudi Arabian General Investment Authority	2000
Qatar	Qatar Investment Promotion Department (IPD)	2019
Kuwait	Kuwait Direct Investment Promotion Authority (KDIPA)	2013
Oman	Public Authority for Investment Promotion and Export Development (Ithraa)	1996
Bahrain	Bahrain Economic Development Board (EDB)	2000

Source Compiled by the author from each organization's website

Table 3 Investment Protection Agreement (IPA) between Japan and MENA countries

MENA countries	Signed date	Effective date
Egypt	1977/1/28	1978/1/14
Turkey	1992/2/12	1993/3/12
Kuwait	2012/3/22	2014/1/24
Iraq	2012/6/7	2014/2/25
Saudi Arabia	2013/4/30	2017/4/7
Oman	2015/6/19	2017/7/21
Iran	2016/2/5	2017/4/26
Israel	2017/2/1	2017/10/5
UAE	2018/4/30	2020/8/26
Jordan	2018/11/27	2020/8/1
Morocco	2020/1/13	tentative

Source METI (2020), METI website

Among the GCC countries, Kuwait signed an IPA[4] with Japan for the first time in March 2012, but in order to improve transparency, with Japan in March 2012, setting up a legal framework to improve the transparency, legal stability and predictability of the investment environment in both countries and to protect bilateral investment and investor rights. Specifically, (1) non-discrimination treatment on and after the establishment of an investment property, (2) fair treatment and adequate protection for the

[4] Agreement between Canada and the State of Kuwait for the Promotion and Protection of Investments.

Table 4   Progress of Japan's Economic Partnership Agreement (EPA)

	Countries
Effective	ASEAN (2008), Mexico (2005), Chile (2007), Switzerland (2009), India (2011), Peru (2012), Australia (2015), Mongolia (2016), TPP11 (2018), EU (2019)
Signed	TPP (2016), UK (2020)
Under negotiation	Korea (interrupted), Japan–China-Korea FTA, RCEP*, GCC (postponed), Turkey, Canada, Columbia

Source METI (2020), METI website
*RCEP stands for Regional Comprehensive Economic Partnership. The East Asian countries have so far formed economic partnership agreements with ASEAN, but this concept is designed to develop them into a broad-based EPA that includes major neighbouring countries such as Japan

investment property, (3) the prohibition of requirements that may inhibit investment, (4) the prohibition of expropriation without justification and (5) a dispute settlement procedure between the receiving country and the partner country investor.

3.4   Economic Partnership Agreements (EPAs)

EPAs are more comprehensive agreements than investment protection agreements and FTAs. In general, EPAs are intended to strengthen economic relations over a wide range of areas, including the elimination or reduction of tariffs, deregulation or removal of regulations in the services sector, improvement of the investment climate and mutual development of the business environment. Japan currently has no EPAs with the Gulf States (Table 4).

4   GCC-JAPAN ECONOMIC RELATIONS

This section observes changes in economic relations, using trade, FDI and bank lending statistics and by looking at trends in the GCC and Japanese overseas companies.

4.1   GCC Trade Partners

The GCC countries have been important trading partners for Japan over many years (Ehteshami 2013). For instance, according to JETRO (1975),

Japan was listed after the United States, Australia, the United Kingdom and France as the UAE's main trading partner in 1972/1973. The export value of the UAE to Japan was 149.8 billion yen, and the import amount was 43.9 billion yen, while UAE exports have been excessive since the beginning of trade transactions between the two countries. The total import value of Qatar in 1972 was about 600 million QAR, and the top importers of Qatari goods were the United Kingdom (27%), Japan (11%) and the United States (10%), with Japan cited as another important trading partner.

Figures 1 and 2 illustrate trade relations between the two blocs from 1980s to 2010s. Trade in natural resources from the GCC countries, and in machinery and textiles from Japan, have promoted industrial development in the GCC countries. The trade volume increased from 1980s to 2010s, and GCC-Japan trade relations have been changing since the turn of the century. Whereas the GCC countries depended on trade with Japan and other developed countries throughout the 1980s, they have diversified their trading partners since the early 2000s, and so contributions made by both sides are far fewer in the 2000s than they were in the 1980s.

One of the characteristics of trade relations between the GCC countries and Japan is that the GCC countries are more dependent on trade with Japan than their neighbours. According to the IMF's Direction of Trade Statistics (DOT), a similar trend can be seen in trade relations between Japan and MENAP (MENA, Afghanistan and Pakistan). The share of exports to Japan in total exports of MENAP countries has declined from 16.5% in 1980 to 8.1% in 2017. Compared to the ratio of the GCC countries' exports to Japan over the same period (from 21.6% in 1980 to 10.2% in 2017), the GCC countries are more dependent on Japan for export than other MENAP countries. Similarly, the dependence of the GCC countries on Japan for imports is also high among MENAP countries.

From 1990 to 2017, trade between the GCC countries and Japan was dependent on oil and natural gas, and increasingly dependent on mineral fuels. The amount of trade, excluding oil and natural gas, between the two blocs expanded from 2.8 billion dollars in 1990 to 4.2 billion dollars in 2017, but the proportion of non-petroleum to total trade value decreased from 11.3% to 6.2% during the same period (Table 5). In particular, Saudi Arabia and Oman's trade with Japan was highly dependent on oil and natural gas, and compared with other GCC countries, UAE had exported

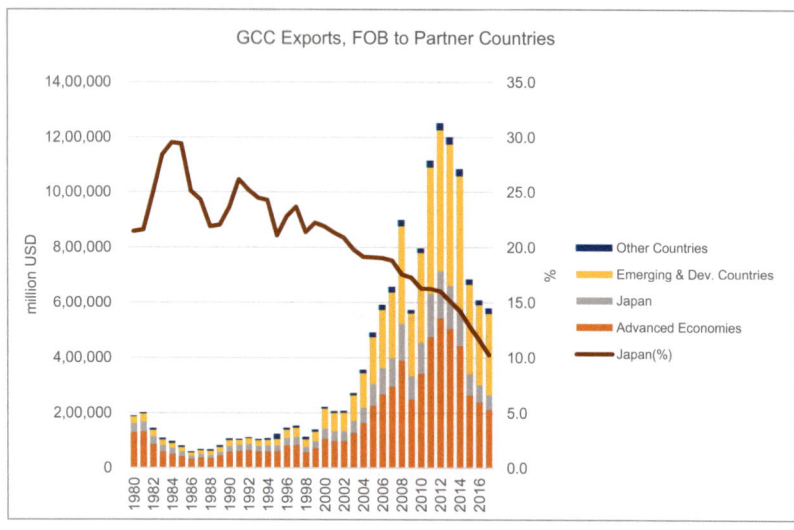

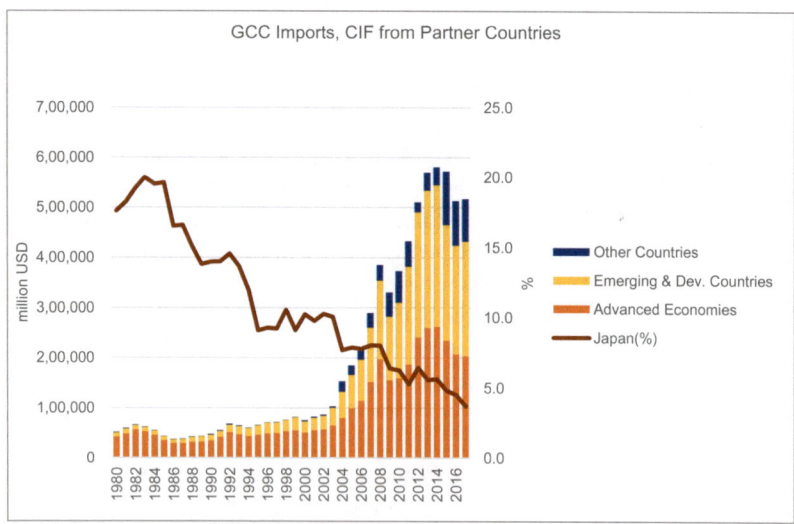

Fig. 1   GCC trade partners and Japanese contribution (*Source* IMF, Direction of Trade)

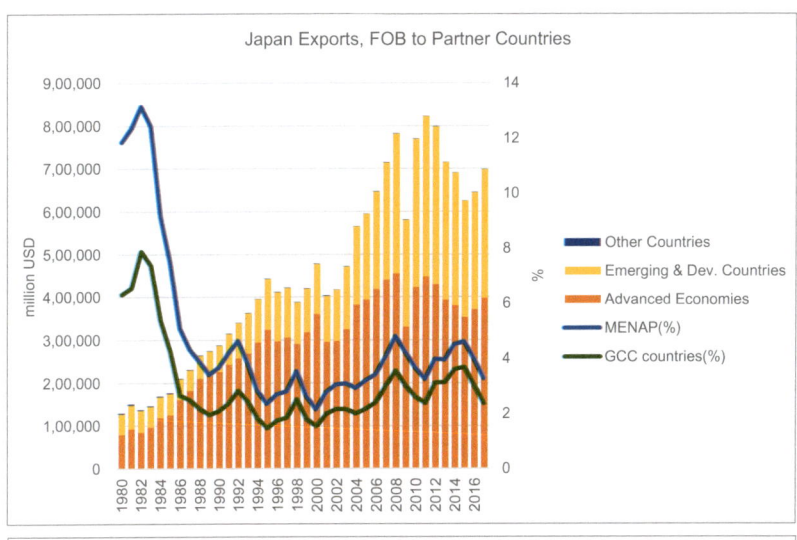

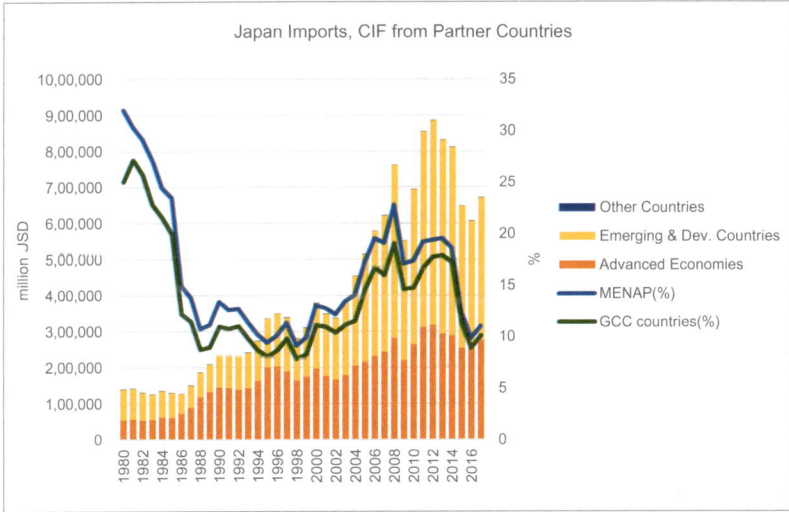

Fig. 2 Japanese trade partners and the GCC countries contribution (*Source* IMF, Direction of Trade Statistics [DOT])

more non-oil products to the country.[5] In economic affairs between Japan and the UAE, non-oil trade is now becoming more important.[6] In 2017, for instance, it totalled USD 14.3 billion, and the compound average growth rate (CAGR) from 1990 to 2017 was 1.3%. Major non-oil imports goods from UAE to Japan were iron or non-alloy steel, liquefied propane gas and aluminum in 2017. Saudi Arabian non-oil export goods to Japan were methyl alcohol, aluminum and liquefied propane gas.

The slowdown in international oil prices since late 2014 has had a major impact on trade between the GCC countries and Japan, in particular the amount of exports from the GCC countries to Japan. For example, while Saudi Arabia's total crude oil exports increased from 396 million tonnes in 2014 to 404 million tonnes in 2015, the value of exports halved from SAR 1.04 trillion ($277.7 billion) to SAR 573.5 billion ($152.9 billion), according to the General Authority of Statistics. The impact of falling oil prices has therefore been significant.

Since 2014, trade between the two regions has been sluggish in terms of both imports and exports, the main reason for which is due to the slump in oil prices, but it is also attributable to the cooling of the domestic economy in Saudi Arabia and other GCC countries and declining exports of construction machinery and raw materials following the postponement or cancellation of large projects.

4.2   Foreign Direct Investment

In contrast to trade relations, GCC-Japan FDI has expanded in recent years. Although investment from Japan, or west Asia more generally, comprises a small amount of total FDI in the GCC countries, bilateral FDI has expanded, particularly with Saudi Arabia and the UAE (Fig. 3). The FDI databases of JETRO and UNCTAD used in this graph are not well developed, making it difficult to get an accurate picture of FDI trends

---

[5] The economic relationship between Japan and the UAE became fully fledged in 1967 when Abu Dhabi Oil Co. Ltd. of Japan signed an oil concession agreement with the Abu Dhabi emirate. Since the formation of the UAE in 1971, Japan has been one of the largest export destinations for crude oil from the UAE.

[6] *Gulf News*, April 30, 2018.

Table 5 Japanese Oil and Non-oil imports (CIF) from the GCC countries

	1990		2000		2010		2017	
	Oil trade (*1) Million USD	Non-oil trade Million USD	Oil trade Million USD	Non-oil trade Million USD	Oil trade Million USD	Non-oil trade Million USD	Oil trade Million USD	Non-oil trade Million USD
Bahrain	307	75	141	94	561	92	322	54
Kuwait	1549	233	4544	451	9310	954	5346	528
Oman	1896	7	2024	13	4491	29	1768	95
Qatar	2082	31	5549	316	19,186	2505	10,198	721
Saudi Arabia	8727	1495	11,793	2416	33,848	2030	26,230	1349
UAE	7875	1013	13,419	1425	26,746	2518	19,187	1431
Total	22,436	2854	37,469	4715	94,142	8129	63,492	4207
	%	%	%	%	%	%	%	%
Bahrain	80.4	19.6	59.98	40.02	85.89	14.11	85.67	14.33
Kuwait	86.92	13.08	90.98	9.02	90.7	9.3	91.01	8.99
Oman	99.61	0.39	99.36	0.64	99.35	0.65	94.89	5.11
Qatar	98.53	1.47	94.61	5.39	88.45	11.55	93.4	6.6
Saudi Arabia	85.38	14.62	83	17	94.34	5.66	95.11	4.89
UAE	88.61	11.39	90.4	9.6	91.39	8.61	93.06	6.94
Total	88.72	11.28	88.82	11.18	92.05	7.95	93.79	6.21

Source Ministry of Finance, Trade Statistics of Japan
*1 Crude oils (2,709,009), Petroleum oils and oils from bituminous minerals, not crude (2710) and liquefied, natural gas (271,111) in Harmonised System Codes (HS Code 2017)

between the GCC countries and Japan and other Middle Eastern countries. Only a few countries in the UAE, Saudi Arabia, Oman, Kuwait and Iran are listed as Middle Eastern countries in either database, and detailed data for other Middle Eastern countries is not available. According to JETRO data, in 1996, FDI outstanding from Japan to Middle East countries was $960 million, of which $480 million was in Saudi Arabia and $310 million was in the UAE. In 2018, Japan invested $5.22 billion in Saudi Arabia and $2.15 billion in the UAE in FDI, with the share of Japanese investment in the Middle East as a percentage of total foreign direct investment in the region increasing slightly from 0.37% to 0.54%.

With regard to the economic relationship between Saudi Arabia and Japan, Japanese companies' investments in Saudi Arabia have lagged

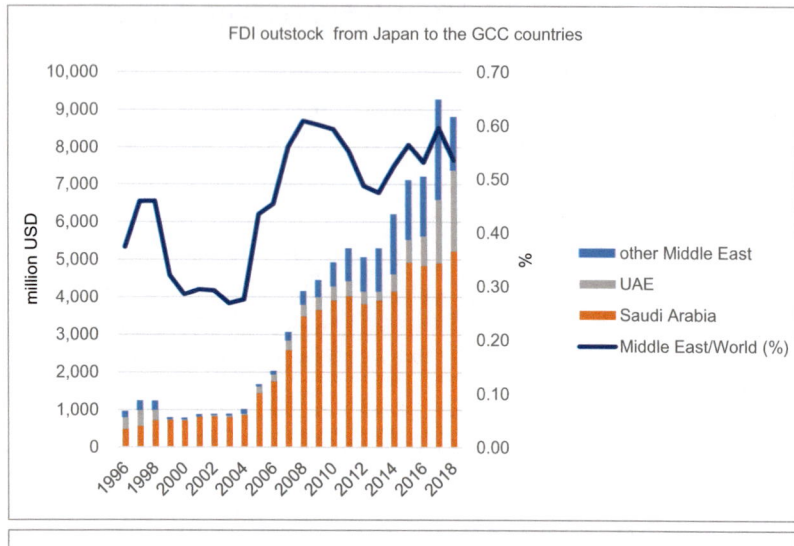

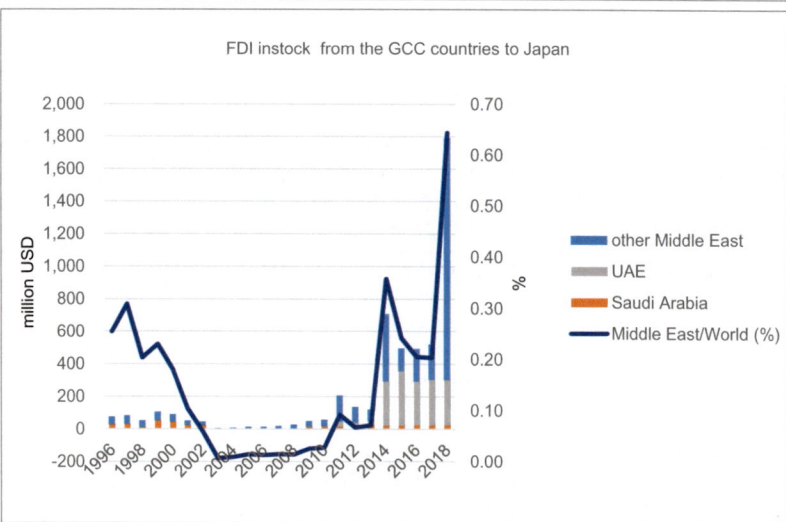

Fig. 3 Foreign direct investment between the GCC countries and Japan. (*Source* JETRO)

behind in trade terms for some time. For example, of the 2117 manu-facturing licences issued by the Ministry of Industry and Electricity in Saudi Arabia by the end of 1980, 464 were related to a joint venture with a foreign partner, but only seven involved Japanese investment. In 1980, manufacturing permits for foreign business partners were: neigh-bouring Arab countries, such as Lebanon (61), Palestine (31) and Jordan (25), alongside the United States (48), the United Kingdom (28), etc. In the United States and Europe, many permits were issued, with very few going to Japanese projects (JETRO 1983).

Oil mining concessions of the Arabian Oil Company Ltd. in Saudi Arabia, which expired in February 2000, contributed to the resurgence of the Japanese government and Japanese companies' Saudi investment at that time. The Japanese government has traditionally assisted the private sector in Saudi Arabia, and in May 1999, it presented a $600 billion investment promotion policy for Gulf countries, including Saudi Arabia, over a 10-year period and supported the extension of this concession. However, as a result of the lapse of this concession, some Japanese compa-nies were also expected to postpone or stop investing in the non-oil sector.

However, in the late 2000s, the foreign direct investment environ-ment changed in Saudi Arabia. During this period, FDI from Japan to Saudi Arabia surged, mainly due to the involvement of Japanese compa-nies in the mega infrastructure construction projects promoted in the kingdom. In August 2005, Sumitomo Chemical Co. Ltd. announced plans to invest $8.5 billion in the world's largest integrated petrochemical plant, which was planned on the Red Sea coast in a joint venture with the state-owned oil company, Saudi Aramco. Saudi Petrochemicals Develop-ment Co. Ltd. (SHARQ), which was funded by 60 companies, including Mitsubishi Chemical, Mitsubishi Corporation and Japan Bank for Inter-national Cooperation, started producing ethylene in a joint venture with a local company in 1987 and subsequently expanded production capacity in the 2000s. The latter half of the 2000s was a period when foreign direct investment from Japan also rapidly expanded in the UAE. Nippon Sheet Glass Company Ltd., for example, announced in its medium-term management plan for the 2006 to 2010 fiscal years that it would invest 24 billion yen in Abu Dhabi to establish a production base for flat glass for the Gulf countries.

Foreign direct investment by foreign companies is also expected to further boost foreign direct investment by foreign companies as a measure to diversify domestic industries and promote employment, as mentioned in the Saudi "Vision 2030" announced in April 2016; however, inward FDI in 2016 was 7453 million USD, down 8.5% from the previous year. FDI from Japan to Saudi Arabia in 2016 was also down 34% from the previous year, totalling 289 million USD (JETRO, net, flow). However, the numbers of Japanese investments in Saudi Arabia have been steadily increasing. In 2016, Ebara Corporation established a joint venture in Dammam as a new manufacturing, sales and service base in the kingdom, while the Unicharm Corporation built a new plant in Riyadh in the same year, in order to expand diaper production. In addition, the "Softbank Vision Fund," established by SoftBank Corporation in October 2016, was expected to be active in the financial investment sector in Saudi Arabia, and the Bank of Tokyo-Mitsubishi UFJ was the first Japanese bank to obtain branch establishment approval from the Saudi General Investment Authority (SAGIA) in 2017 and opened the Riyadh branch in October 2018.

4.3   Japanese Banks' Claims on the GCC Countries

In analysing private fund transfers between the GCC countries and Japan, besides foreign direct investment, it is not possible to ignore financial transactions such as loans by commercial banks and other financial institutions, or portfolio investments in securities and bonds. This section clarifies the trend of cross-border funding flows across the bloc in recent years through the analysis of international financial transactions between the International Settlement Bank (BIS) and the GCC countries (the international sector assets and liabilities transactions of banks). As seen in this section, trade transactions in the real sector have expanded, direct investment by Japanese has extended and at the same time capital movements have also increased. In particular, Japanese banks' willingness to issue credit has provided financial support for economic development and business activities in the GCC countries. Figure 4 shows from which GCC countries GCC countries have accepted bank loans and the extent to which Japanese banks have contributed.

After the second oil shock that started with the Iranian Revolution in 1979, and as oil prices fell rapidly and oil money flowing into the GCC countries decreased, governments in these nations struggled to maintain their expansive fiscal policies and suffered significant deficits. Japanese banks were the major suppliers of GCC bank loans in the late 1980s and

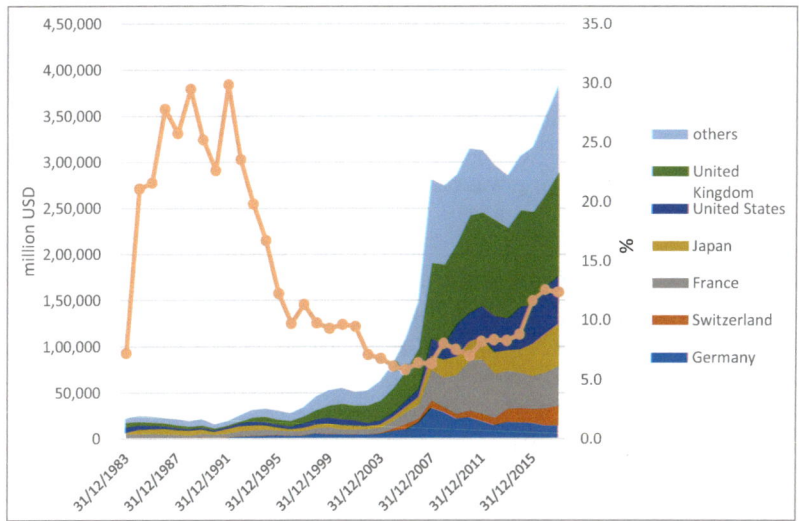

Fig. 4   Credit balances for the GCC countries, by nation (*Source* BIS, consolidated positions on counterparties resident in the GCC countries)

early 1990s. For example, of the $17.5 billion lent to the GCC countries at the end of 1991, Japanese banks provided $5.2 billion of credit, accounting for 30% of the total (Fig. 4).

The development of the private sector, aligned with attracting foreign companies, became a priority for the GCC economies as rising energy demands in emerging market countries raised international oil prices in the 2000s. The GCC governments promoted the establishment of systems aimed at expanding the private sector, such as the privatization of state-owned enterprises, investment law and competition law. As a result, the demand for funds from domestic and foreign companies also increased, and credit from foreign financial institutions expanded to the GCC countries. The average value of credit to the GCC countries was $38.7 billion in 1996–2000, but it rapidly swelled to $64.3 billion in the next five years (2001–2005) and $235.2 billion in 2006–2010.

According to BIS data, banks in the United States and Europe have extended their credit to the GCC countries since the 2000s, and Japanese banks also have their credit from $3.8 billion in 1996–2000 to $4.4

billion in 2001–2005, and $16.8 billion in 2006–2010 (five-year averages). Sumitomo Chemical Company Ltd., for instance, signed a $2.5 billion loan from the Japan Bank for International Cooperation in the petrochemical field in March 2006. In December 2006, Sumitomo Mitsui Banking Corporation co-financed $4265 million to build 16 LNG carriers in Qatar. This co-financing was attended by 24 financial institutions inside and outside of Japan.

As described above, Japanese financial institutions' credit to the GCC countries expanded in the 2000s, but the growth rate was not necessarily high compared to their counterparts in Western countries and emerging countries. The credit ratio of Japanese financial institutions, which accounted for 10–30% of GCC credit from the late 1980s to the early 1990s, dropped to less than 10% in the early 2000s.

4.4   Japanese Companies in the GCC Countries

The expansion of Japanese companies into the Middle East is not necessarily a recent phenomenon. Major Japanese trading companies, in particular, have been planning to expand into the Middle East since before and after World War II. In June 1933, Sumitomo Corporation established an office in Tehran, and in September 1933, it reorganized its operations to become a Japan-Persian Trading Company, and thus began to do business in the Middle East in earnest. The company opened representative offices in Alexandria in October 1933, Cairo, Istanbul and Tehran in 1954, and Baghdad in 1955.

Sumitomo Corporation's entry into the GCC countries began after oil exports began, with the opening of representative offices in Kuwait in August 1959, Abu Dhabi in November 1969, and Dubai in December 1970. Marubeni's business in the Middle East began in August 1955 with the signing of an import contract for Iraqi barley; it opened a dispatch office in Tehran in 1953 and in Beirut in 1955, and participated in and invested in the establishment of Arabian Oil in November 1957. Our business in the GCC countries began when we received a joint order with Japan Radio for radio station-related communications equipment.

Mitsui began in April 1954 with a barter agreement with the Anglo-Iranian Oil Company to import crude oil and export steel. In September 1971, Mitsui signed a basic contract with the Emirate of Abu Dhabi for the development of LNG from Das Island. Sumitomo Corporation's Middle East business also began in 1954 with the opening of a representative office in Cairo, and in the GCC countries it opened representative offices in Kuwait in November 1966 and Abu Dhabi in March 1968.

Thus, major Japanese trading companies started their business in the Middle East with trade and oil development projects with Iran, Iraq and Egypt. However, a series of political turmoil and conflicts in this region and the development of oil in the Gulf Arab countries have shifted the focus of their business to the GCC countries.[7]

Next, we turn to trends in Japanese companies with GCC affiliations. Figure 5 outlines when Japanese companies established their foreign offices, using data from Ministry of Foreign Affairs of Japan, Annual Report of Statistics on Japanese Nationals Overseas. From this data, we can observe that the Middle East, and in particular the GCC countries, are not primary markets for Japanese enterprises. However, the UAE is an attractive market as an overseas operation for Japanese companies, while other data from *Toyokeizai* shows the expansion of overseas subsidiaries in the UAE and Saudi Arabia throughout the 2000s.

As of 1998, there were 31 joint ventures between Saudi Arabia and Japan with a total of 5.7 billion Saudi riyals invested (total investment including Saudi capital was 11.6 billion Saudi riyals). At that time, joint ventures with foreign capital in Saudi Arabia were dominated by Saudi Basic Industry Corporation (SABIC), while non-SABIC projects were somewhat limited. Of the number of projects, 26 were non-industrial joint ventures established by a trading company, a heavy electric manufacturer, a plant engineering company, etc., with local partners, in order to operate in Saudi Arabia (JETRO 1998).

4.5 The GCC Companies in Japan

Compared to the number of Japanese companies operating in the GCC countries, the number of the GCC companies currently operating in

---

[7] The closure and relocation of representative offices and branches due to political changes and conflicts in the region was also observed in the case of major Japanese banks. For example, the Bank of Tokyo was the first Japanese bank in the Middle East to open a branch in Alexandria in 1955 to handle loans primarily related to the export of Egyptian cotton to Japan. The Bank of Tokyo opened representative offices in Beirut in July 1956 and Cairo in July 1962, but closed them in March 1987 and February 1967, respectively, due to the civil war and increased government censorship.

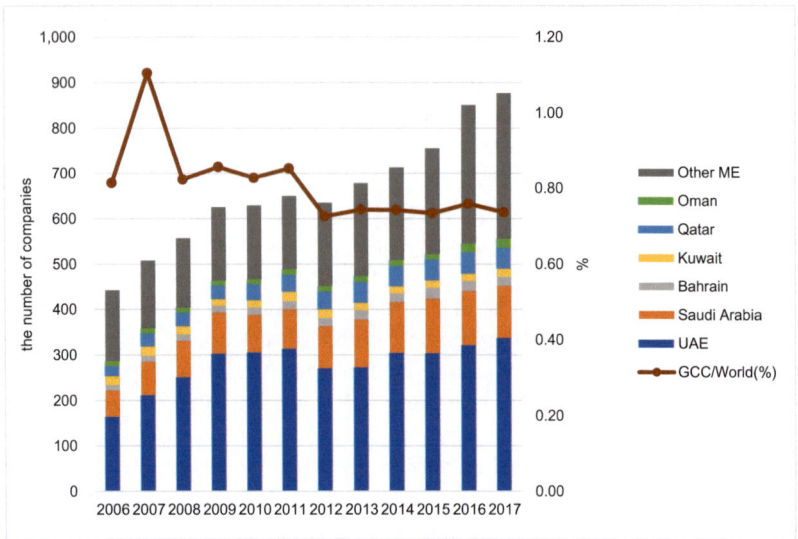

Fig. 5 Japanese companies in MENA (*Source* Ministry of Foreign Affairs of Japan, Annual Report of Statistics on Japanese Nationals Overseas

Japan is very small. The Japanese Ministry of Economy, Trade and Industry (METI) publishes the "Survey of Trends in Business Activities of Foreign Affiliates" every year and reported just 29 Middle Eastern companies operating in the country in 2016. These included 12 businesses in the wholesale sector, 6 in services provision, 6 in manufacturing, three in information and communications and two in transport. In general, the main function of the Japanese offices is for sales and marketing to the domestic market, which is true across the whole sample and not just for Middle Eastern companies. METI also cites the large number of consumers with high income levels and the large market size for products and services as key advantages of doing business in Japan. On the other hand, it points to the high cost of doing business in Japan, especially with regard to labor and taxes, and the difficulty in finding skilled human resources as obstacles to the Japanese market. Language is also a barrier. The reasons for the reluctance of companies from the GCC countries and other Middle Eastern countries to expand into Japan are not clear, but based on the results of the METI survey, the Japanese market, which is generally attractive to foreign companies as a consumer market, does not match the needs of the GCC companies which are mainly engaged in oil-related businesses and exporting Japanese products back home. In other words, a preferential tax system and the development of human resources are required to promote Middle Eastern investment in Japan.

According to Toyo Keizai (2017), in 2017, there was a list of 45 Middle Eastern companies operating in Japan, including 23 from the UAE, 17 from Israel, 2 from Egypt, 2 from Kuwait and 1 from Saudi Arabia. The list includes a number of subsidiaries from the UAE, of which Cosmo Energy Holdings[8] is the parent company, and a number of oil-related companies from Saudi Arabia, including SABIC Japan, in which SABIC has a stake.

5   Conclusion: Interdependence of the GCC Countries and Japan

This chapter attempts to analyse the recent changes in economic relations between the GCC countries and Japan in terms of trade, foreign direct investment, financial transactions and corporate expansion. The GCC countries have gained abundant oil revenues by exporting their rich natural resources to developed countries, such as Japan, and developing countries, and have used these funds to purchase imported goods and to develop their domestic economies. On the other hand, it is only in the last decade that various arrangements have been established between the GCC countries and Japan to promote trade and foreign direct investment. Among rentier states that depend on natural resources for a large portion of their national revenues, the GCC countries' governments have been engaged in improving governance and various regulations. The building of a system to strengthen economic relations, including trade and direct investment between the two blocs, has been expected to further increase the interdependence of the economies between the two blocs.

The analysis of economic relations between the two blocs from the 1980s to the 2010s shows that the interdependence between the GCC countries and Japan in terms of trade has been declining due to the economic development of the GCC countries and the diversification of their trading partners. This trend should not necessarily be seen as a

---

[8] Cosmo Energy Holdings' largest shareholder is Infinity Alliance Limited, a special purpose company (SPC) established in 2007 by IPIC, which was converted into Mubadala Investment Company in 2017.

pessimistic one, but rather as a consequence of the significant growth in economic activity in the GCC countries and the quantitative and qualitative expansion of their consumer markets over the past 40 years. On the other hand, direct investment and financial transactions between the GCC countries and Japan are on the rise, and the interdependence is expected to continue to strengthen through further extensions of the Investment Protection Agreement and the Economic Partnership Agreement.

However, the interdependence of the two blocs, mainly with respect to the FDI side and the enterprise expansion, is currently asymmetric: The importance of Japan to the GCC countries far outweighs the importance of the GCC countries to Japan. Attracting FDI from the GCC countries to Japan and facilitating the entry of the GCC companies into the Japanese markets would contribute to making the interdependence between the two blocs more symmetrical. Thus, the GCC governments will need to further support the development of domestic companies and further develop their legal systems to expand overseas economic transactions. The Japanese government needs to improve measures to reduce various business costs, such as taxation and labour costs, and to mobilize domestic human resources in order to promote the entry of foreign companies, including those from the GCC countries, into Japan markets.

The impact of Covid-19, which is set to become a global pandemic from the end of 2019, is having a significant impact on the economies of the GCC countries and Japan, as well as on economic relations between the two blocs. Many global and national institutions have also predicted that the future economic stagnation caused by Covid-19 will not end in the short term. However, the Investment Protection Agreement between Japan and the UAE, which came into force at the same time, in August 2020, and the "Abraham Agreement" between the UAE, Bahrain and Israel, signed in September 2020, have the potential to significantly change the economic structure and business environment in the GCC countries. I hope that international exogenous shocks such as Covid-19 will be taken as an opportunity to expand and sublimate the interdependence between the two blocks, both quantitatively and qualitatively.

References

Alshakhanbeh, N. 2012. GCC Integration with International Trade Mechanisms. In *The GCC in the Global Economy*, ed. R. Youngs, 121–140. Gerlach Press.

Balassa, B. 1961. *The Theory of Economic Integration*. Richaed D: Irwin.
Daude, C., and E. Stein. 2007. The Quality of Institutions and Foreign Direct Investment. *Economics and Politics* 19 (3): 317–344.
Ehteshami, A. 2013. Asianization of the Persian Gulf. In *Dynamics of Change in the Persian Gulf – Political Economy, War and Revolution*, 89–105. Routledge.
Fukui, S. 2008. Economic Development and Trade. in *Economic Development Theory*, ed. M. Takahashi and S. Fukui, 145–160. Tokyo: Keisou Shobou. (in Japanese).
Hayami, Y. 1995. *Development Economics*. Tokyo: Sobun Sha. (in Japanese).
Innis, H.A. 1956. *Essays in Canadian Economic History*. Toronto: Canada, University of Toronto Press.
JETRO. 1975. *Economic Development and Foreign Investment Relations in the UAE and Qatar* (in Japanese).
JETRO. 1983. *Case Study of a Foreign Company in Saudi Arabia* (in Japanese).
JETRO. 1998. *Investment Climate Survey Report: Saudi Arabia* (in Japanese).
JETRO. 2019. *List of FTAs with Japan* (in Japanese).
Kimura, F. 2000. *Introduction to International Economics*. Tokyo: Nippon Hyoron Sha (in Japanese).
Meier, G. M., and J. E. Rauch eds. 2005. *Leading Issues in Economic Development*, 8th ed. Oxford University Press.
METI. 2018. *The 2017 (51st) Survey of Trends in Business Activities of Foreign Affiliates* (in Japanese).
METI. 2020. *White Paper on International Economy and Trade* (in Japanese).
Rodríguez, F., and D. Rodrik. 2000. Trade Policy and Economic Growth: A Skeptic's Guide to the Cross-National Evidence. *NBER Macroeconomics Annual* 15 (1): 261–325.
Saito, J , and N. Janardhan. 2020. Gulf-Japan Ties, Beyond the Energy Sectors. in *The Arab Gulf's Pivot to Asia. From Transactional to Strategic Partnerships*, ed. N. Janardhan, 49–64, Gerlach Press.
Toyo Keizai. 2017. *Foreign Companies Overview 2017*. Toyo Keizai.
UNCTAD. 2015. *Investment Policy Framework for Sustainable Development* http://investmentpolicyhub.unctad.org/ipfsd.
Viner, J., and P. Oslington. 2014. *The Customs Union Issue*. Oxford University Press.
Watkins, M.H. 1963. A Staple Theory of Economic Growth. *The Canadian Journal of Economics and Political Science / Revue Canadienne D'economique Et De Science Politique* 29 (2): 141–158.

CHAPTER 11

Origin of Japan's Relations with Middle Eastern Countries by Practical Internationalism

Satoru Nakamura

1 LACK OF STRATEGY VERSUS PRACTICAL INTERNATIONALISM

The National Security Strategy of Japan stated in 2013, "Stability in the Middle East is an issue that is inseparably linked to the stable supply of energy, and therefore Japan's very survival and prosperity.[1]" In fact, since the very First Oil Crisis in the 1970s, the primary crisis for Japan's energy security was not a matter of the supply quantity of imported energy, but rather of soaring its price (Shiratori 2015, 191–192). Japan's oil consumption has declined since then through energy saving efforts. Furthermore, after the oil crisis, due to the success in diplomatic efforts

---

[1] Cabinet Secretariat. National Security Strategy. December 17, 2013. 27. https://www.cas.go.jp/jp/siryou/131217anzenhoshou.html.

S. Nakamura (✉)
Kobe University, Kobe, Japan
e-mail: satnaka@kobe-u.ac.jp

Contemporary Gulf Studies, https://doi.org/10.1007/978-981-19-3459-9_11

and structural change in energy consumption, even fear of an energy price rise was regarded as of secondary importance in the 1990s in Japan. However, in the twenty-first century, due to the return of soaring energy prices and the long-term forecast of an increase in world energy demand in developing countries, the Japanese government again seriously set the goal of strengthening bilateral relations with Middle Eastern countries and increasing self-developed energy sources.[2]

After the Gulf Crisis in 1990, Japan's policy priorities in the Middle East have shifted. Maintaining stable bilateral relations with Middle Eastern countries is on the baseline, as before, but security concerns about how to contribute to conflict prevention came to be at the forefront. Thus, Japan dispatched a marine sweeping mission to the Gulf and enhanced support to Palestine after the Gulf War in 1991,[3] followed by fuel supply activities of the Japanese Maritime Self-Defense Force (JMSDF) for coalition force in the Indian Ocean after the September 11th incident, anti-piracy activities in the Gulf of Aden and the Coast of Somalia, peacebuilding in Afghanistan, and humanitarian and reconstruction assistance in Iraq.

Abe administration announced "proactive contribution to peace" in 2013, which intended to construct security interdependence with the countries in the world, including the U.S., to counter potential threats for Japan. New threat pointed by Abe administration was China. "China has been rapidly advancing its military capabilities in a wide range of areas through its continued increase in its military budget without sufficient transparency. In addition, China took actions that can be regarded as attempts to change the status quo by coercion based on their own assertions, which are incompatible with the existing order of international law, in the maritime and aerial domains, including the East China Sea and the South China Sea."[4]

However, after the withdrawal of Japan Ground Self-Defense Force (JGSDF) from South Sudan in 2017, the Japanese Self-Defense Forces (JSDF) revalidated their dispatch to ongoing conflict areas Japan's Middle East policy is not well explained in official publications, including the

---

[2] Cabinet Secretariat. *op. cit.* 34.

[3] Kohei Hashimoto (1995). *Senryaku Enjo: Chuto Wahei Sien to ODA no Shourai.* Tokyo: PHP Kenkyujo.

[4] Cabinet Secretariat. *op. cit.* 12.

Diplomatic Blue Book. The Middle East section in it explains the course of major incidents and conflicts that occurred in the Middle East, and part of Japanese government reactions, but there is a gap in understanding its policy, strategy, direction, and methods. Japan's diplomacy is a perplexing research theme, since the evaluation of Japan's diplomacy can be split into different academic interpretations. Japan's foreign policy cannot be understood instantly by reading government statements and publications in Japan, especially in the case of Middle East policy.

Hisahiko Okazaki (1930–2014), founder of strategic thinking in Japan, who was former Japanese ambassador in Saudi Arabia (1984–88), wrote, "[The best strategy towards] developing countries by major powers is forming no alliance because it enables analysing sudden and unpredictable crisis situations and allows space for flexible response to it" (Okazaki 1983, 139). This statement coincides with Japan's Middle East diplomacy, which seems operated by rationality based on the principle of analysing sudden and unpredictable crisis situations and making flexible responses to it.

This chapter will reveal Japan's foreign policy direction, bilateral relations, political economy policies, and efforts towards peace and security in the Middle East. In truth, the direction of Japan's diplomacy after the Cold War was marked by its "practical internationalism." Japan's "practical internationalism" is a complex concept composed of neo-classical realism (or realism oriented for defence and economic prosperity) and multilateralism, and it is constrained by Article 9 in Japanese constitution. It is oriented to democracy, human rights, free trade, and anti-nuclear proliferation, but is far from ideological obstinacy and has been applied flexibly with soft approach. The "mutual interests with other nations" is recognised widely as Japan's right direction, though new nationalists criticise it as "losing national interest" and pacifists regard it as "national interests" and "dangerous."

Japan's practical internationalism has strengthened relations with Middle Eastern countries by adapting to the regional complexity of the Middle East, in which the West intervenes. Japan has no political ambition to struggle for hegemony in the Middle East, and pursued maintaining balance and trilateral mutual interests among the Middle East, the West and Asia. Japan produced highly active performance in peacebuilding activities with self-control in accordance with Japan's norm of not resorting to military powers, but Japan cannot provide superpower solutions to Middle East conflicts. Hereafter, this chapter mainly deals with Japan's Middle East policy up to the 1980s.

2   "REACTIVE STATE" CONTROVERSY AND METHODOLOGY FOR "THE MIDDLE EAST-JAPAN RELATIONSHIP"

2.1   Evaluations of Japan's Diplomacy by Middle East Critics

It is extremely difficult to research and evaluate Japan's diplomacy, since evaluations of it vary by different political stands of critics. Views outside Japan can be summarised as split in support and against it. Observers in Japan's neighbours, China and Korea, are split into pro-Japan and anti-Japan. Pro-Japan experts on Japan are numerous in China and Korea, while issues of historical awareness and "comfort women" issues in the imperial Japan era drag on until today. Chinese military and communists maintained a world view formed in the pre-Second World War era of hostility to Japan. Others however, such as Lee Teng-hui (1923–2020) in Taiwan, Mahatir bin Muhammad (1925–) in Malaysia, and Lee Kuan Yew (1923–2015) in Singapore are well known for evaluating Japan's development and foreign aid with high regards.

Edwin O. Reischauer (1910–1990), who was the authority on Japanology and the U.S. ambassador in Japan (1961–66), praised the manner in which democracy blossomed in Japan after the Second World War (Reischauer 1988, 38). Among the U.S. experts on Japanese affairs, M.J. Green, former director for Asian affairs of the National Security Council (NSC) and special assistant to the president (2001–2005), known as "Japan-handler," called Japan's diplomacy "reluctant realism (Green 2001)." K.E. Calder (1948–), current director at Edwin O. Reischauer Center regarded Japan as a "reactive state" that never changes policy without foreign pressure (Calder 1988). These sceptics underestimate Japan's leadership as enjoying prosperity by mercantilism and as a free-rider on international security. Similar assessments include "realism from behind" (Rix 1993, 65) and "circumscribed balancer" (Twomey 2000, 195).

Views of Japan in Middle Eastern countries, based on writings by their ambassadors in Japan, tend to be supportive of Japan by often pointing to Japan's values as similar and familiar to theirs but in culturally distinct ways. Hisham Mohamed Mostafa Badr, former Egyptian ambassador in Tokyo (2003–2007), writes, "Japanese sword and Egyptian Sphinx are both symbols representing that strength is sustained by reason" (Badr 2008, 38). Eli Cohen, former Israeli ambassador in Tokyo (2004–2007), writes, "Bushido (Japanese chivalry) is a philosophy identical with Jewish one in that both ennoble self spiritually" (Cohen 2006, 14). Muhammad Bashir Ali al-Kurdi, former Saudi ambassador in Tokyo (1998–2004), writes, "Decisions are not made by top down, but in the opposite in Japan. This is well read in early Muslims who brought message of Allah too far and wide" (Kurdi 2015, 50). Middle Eastern countries are imagined as regions with disputes and conflicts, but to a surprise, their views are in concert with familiarity and a high evaluation of Japan. This is a contrast with splits in views on Japan in Asia and the U.S.

2.2 The Competition of Five Perspectives in Interpreting Japan's Foreign Policy Direction

In Japan, the evaluation of Japan's diplomacy is an issue of contention given the various forces at play. Previous studies identified four competing perspectives over Japan's diplomatic direction (as mentioned later); this chapter revises them as five perspectives: (1) mercantilism, (2) pacifism, internationalism are divided into (3) middle-power perspective and (4) normal nation[5] perspective, and (5) new nationalism. This classification clarifies the middle-power perspective, which has not been recognised clearly, but can be identified as de fact Japan's foreign policy. The middle-power perspective and the normal nation perspective have been prime driver of Japan's Middle East policy after the Gulf Crisis in 1990.

Politicians, bureaucrats, intellectuals, activists, media, and citizens of the five perspectives utter, behave, organise groups, and distinguish each other in accordance with specific patterned code of each perspective.

---

[5] Internationalists want to see Japan as a "normal nation" which means it utilises its military forces in the pursuit of its national goals when the need arises. It would therefore allow for a militaristic character. Despite this, it needs to be recognised that there are no "normal nations" in the world. Countries vary in their size, power, goals, and behaviours. A "normal nation" is a saying by Japanese internationalist policy advocators to appeal to Japanese mass because Japanese people prefer to behave same as others (along with something normal). Japanese power projection, goal, and behaviour pattern have been unique up to today. No other state is the same as Japan yet. Take any examples; military behavior of Japanese JSDF is still very different from other major powers or small states.

Each perspective permits some degree of difference and sway, but the five perspectives go parallel with each other in political issues. No specific nationwide membership or certification is formed by these five perspectives, but they can be distinguished from each other by listening and reading specific term usage. They are in essence, the identifiable world-view perspectives, which feed into foreign policy debate, construction, and implementation.

Thus, it is quite hard to grasp Japan's diplomacy in a comprehensive manner by reading and listening to only one opinion because they merely interpret and explain it in the pattern of their affiliated perspective. This adds to the ambiguity that exists on the nature of Japan's foreign policy and makes it a more intriguing case to examine. Major Japanese newspapers and monthly journals can be classified within one of the five perspectives.[6] Thus, one can understand the view of a perspective by reading a paper or monthly journal, but it only represents a view of a given perspective and does not help to grasp Japan's diplomacy comprehensively. Japan's Middle East policy is implemented in this context and it adds to its inherent ambiguity. The five perspectives are further explained below.

After the culmination of the Gulf Crisis in 1990/91, the five perceptions for Japan's diplomatic directions, politically weigh more than official decision-making process. During the Cold War era, Japan's diplomatic direction was static, and bureaucrats dealt with them. However, after the Gulf Crisis, five perceptions began true struggle to redirect its diplomatic direction. After 1990s, the Cabinet Office began to lead political changes, and governmental coalition parties checked and backed them. In 2000, Koizumi administration realised the perception of normal nation to dispatch the JSDF to Indian Ocean and the Iraq.

---

[6] Yomiuri newspaper is founded on "normal nation perspective," Asahi newspaper and Mainichi newspaper on combination of pacifism and the middle-power perspective, Sankei newspaper on new nationalism, Nikkei newspaper on middle-power perspective. Opinion trends of monthly journals are hard to clearly divided, but loosely saying, *Zeneii* is pacifism as it is communism, *Sekai* is leftists of pacifism and middle-power perspective, *Chuoukouron* is of internationalism of the middle-power perspective and the normal nation perspective, and *Seiron* is of the normal nation perspective and new nationalism. *Bungeishunjuu* and *Voice* are mixed.

2.3   The Controversy Over "Reactive State Theory"

The "reactive state theory" claims that Japan's diplomacy is pressured by the U.S. and Europe and that Japan's diplomatic autonomy and independence are constrained by it. Controversy over autonomous diplomacy has been a hot issue among five perspectives on Japan's foreign policy. In this section, after reviewing the academic controversy over "reactive state theory" and its critic, Japan's practical internationalism will be examined.

Miyashita and Sato (2001) examined cases of Japanese regional diplomacy in Southeast Asia, China, Russia, and the Middle East and cases of thematic issues of political economy, including the Asian Financial Crisis and international organisations. They pointed out that Calder (1988) is the most elaborated work among "reactive state theory." In fact, Calder (1988) offers a literature review of six publications. Calder reviewed Japan's international political economy, and Japan changed its policy only by foreign pressure. It says that even during periods without foreign pressure, Japan is not willing to take international leadership (Calder 1988, 521).

Miyashita and Sato (2001) undertook a far-reaching study on this. In their volume, some are in favour of reactive state theory, but others counter-argue it. Miyashita proposed a methodology for a suitable case selection that points out that cases of Japanese diplomacy in which Japan did not face any pressure are not an adequate case study selection. Moreover, cases of Japanese diplomacy in which Japan's national interests are not of great value were deemed to not be an adequate case selection either. Thus, he pointed out that adequate case selection is the one in which Japan has large national interests which clash with those of foreign countries, and they lead to pressure on Japan to change its policy. Two cases of China's Tiananmen square uprising and foreign aid to Russia after the Cold War are such cases in which Japan gave in to Western pressures (Miyashita 2001, 38-41).

Cases of Japan's Indochina diplomacy indicate that during the period Japan faced no friction with the U.S., and Japan pursued independent diplomacy. But one can notice more implications with this conclusion. Japan did not simply ask major powers to accept or refuse Japan's policy. Rather, Japan has attempted to change major powers' diplomatic preference. Japan investigated the reasons of the U.S. to oppose Japan's diplomacy towards Indochina, and succeeded in changing the U.S. diplomatic stance to Indochina. Here, it can be pointed out that Japan has a third diplomatic option besides winning and losing to foreign pressure. Japan can change diplomatic stance of the Western countries for a third option, which will satisfy Japan's foreign policy orientation and interests. Such choice finds a balance among the West, developing countries, and Japan in the long term.

Hook pointed out Japan's "quiet diplomacy" and "Aikido state" (Hook et al. 2001). Japan's "quiet diplomacy" can be examined further by focussing on Japan's diplomatic dialogue, conciliation, and coordination of interests among nations. Japanese government is not proud to show off opposing other governments as its strength, but prefers finding common interests through diplomatic steps. Examples of Japan's quiet diplomacy can be seen in cases supporting the establishment of a regional framework and the invitation of major powers to it in the Asia–Pacific region.

Japan played a significant role in the establishment of the Asia–Pacific Economic Cooperation (APEC) and its reforms to coordinate the interests of the U.S. and Pacific countries. After the end of the Cold War, Prime Minister Hashimoto invited Russia for entry to the APEC to get it involved in Asian politics. He seized the chance that Russia was isolated by the U.S. and established a good relationship with Russian President Eltisin. He expected that Russia would realise a solution to the territorial dispute over the Kurlic Islands (Iokibe and Miyagi 2013, 81–82). His diplomatic skills were soft and inclusive. Prime Minister Abe created the inter-regional concept of Indo-Pacific in 2007 (Nakamura 2018, 1). Japan's initiative is quiet, but it has pulled the U.S. into this inter-regional framework, invited India to the East Asian security issue, and exerted Australia to be a part of the "Quad" partnership of the U.S., India, Japan, and Australia in Open Indo-Pacific. Japan's trace of such initiatives is hardly recognised by experts in international relations studies within and outside Japan. It is a "quiet diplomacy."

Japan's Middle East policy has also been a case for examination of "reactive state theory." Pacifists are critical to the Japanese government, as they accuse Japan of having lost independent diplomacy. Kuroda examined two case studies of Japan's diplomacy during the First Oil Crisis and the Gulf Crisis (1990–1991) and pointed out that Japan did not relent to U.S. pressures (Kuroda 2001). Kuroda's evaluation of Japan's diplomacy was precise. At the First Oil Crisis, U.S. Secretary of State Henry Kissinger visited Japan and requested that it break relations with the Arab. However, the Tanaka cabinet (July 1972–December 1974) did not comply with it (Nakasone 2012, 240–1). During the Gulf Crisis, the U.S. requested Japan to dispatch JSDF, but Japan did not until the ceasefire of the ground battle at the Gulf War in 1991.

Kuroda elaborated on finding concepts to portray Japan's diplomacy in the Middle East. Kuroda adopted the concepts of "fuzzy," "unbinary diplomacy," and "Rashomonesque"[7] to Japan's diplomacy. They indicate Japan's attempts to maintain good relations with all directions to the U.S., the Arab, and Israel and did not replete to foreign pressure or take up total autonomy. Kuroda's analysis is precise in light of the latest study based on diplomatic documents by Shiratori (2015). Kuroda points out that Japan was consenting to all parties involved in the First Oil Crisis but maintained its principle and did not comply fully with any of one country's request. Japan expressed condemnation of Israel and requested that it withdraw from the occupied territory and was admitted as friendly to the Arabs. Japan enhanced its relationship with Palestine. However, Japan did not break off diplomatic relations with Israel. Shiratori pointed out that Japanese diplomats recognised that they did not change Japan's Middle East policy, but simply clarified its neutral policy and principle. Japan did not oppose the U.S., and joined in the process to establish International Energy Agency (IEA) (Shiratori 2015, 365–373).

Kuroda pointed out that Japan's "unbinary diplomacy" was exerted during the Gulf Crisis. As a result, Japan did not dispatch JSDF for the ground battles in the Gulf War not to violate its constitution prohibiting participation in wars, but it should be pointed out that internationalists, composed of politicians of the middle-power perspective and the normal nation perspective tried to comply with the U.S. request by legislating "Act on Cooperation with United Nations Peacekeeping Operations and Other Operations," which was approved in 1992 to dispatch JSDF for United Nations Peace Keeping Operations (UNPKOs).

Kuroda ascribed the cause of Japan's "unbinary diplomacy" to the structure of the Japanese language and culture, which makes the standpoint of the speaker unclear and blurs binary code in recognition. He is an expert in cultural study, and his analysis is absolutely insightful but lacks two tasks. His analysis of the cause of "unbinary diplomacy" succeeds in explaining Japan's Middle East diplomacy but fails in

---

[7] The Rashomon effect is a term related to the notorious unreliability of eyewitnesses. It describes a situation in which an event is given contradictory interpretations or descriptions by the individuals involved. https://en.wikipedia.org/wiki/Rashomon_effect.

providing detailed case studies of Japan's diplomacy. Japan's Middle East policy can be described with a combination of political science concepts. Japan's autonomy can be pointed out as relative autonomy instead of absolute one and Japan's foreign policy tools to maintain it are probably unique though it may be quiet.

2.4   Methodology

"Reactive state theory" was not applied suitably in the case of Japan's Middle East policy, as revealed by Kuroda. Japan's "quiet diplomacy" displayed subtle dimensions and diplomacy, although they are not militaristic. This section discusses three methodologies for overcoming the "reactive state theory" of Japan's foreign policy in the Middle East.

The first method is to focus on analysing Japan's Middle East diplomacy in its own context in relations with Middle East. In other words, Japan's Middle East policy maintains relative autonomy in Japan's regional diplomacy and bilateral relations with Middle Eastern countries nevertheless the U.S. pressure. Japan's political method of how to realise relative autonomy may be quiet and unique. It is also a product of Japan's domestic politics. Hereafter, Japan's domestic policy formation is discussed as an interaction of the five perspectives over foreign policy orientation. Practical internationalism will be the key of this discussion.

The second method is citation of primary sources including governmental reports, memoirs of diplomats and politicians, journalistic records, and the latest academic results. It is sometimes hard for scholars and students to confirm Japanese laws and reports. Memoirs uncover the true perception of foreign decision makers behind official standpoint. Japanese politicians and administrators' sayings and words are frequently different from what laws legislate. Politicians aim to appeal to the mass, while parliament politics has its own dynamic.

Among former prime ministers, Yasuhiro Nakasone (1918–2019. prime minister 1982–86), Toshiki Kaihu (1931–. prime minister 1989–1991), Ryutaro Hashimoto (1937–2006. prime minister 1996–1998) were interviewed by scholars, and the records are published. Among diplomats are Ryohei Murata, former ambassador in the U.S. (1989–1992), former ambassador in Iraq, Kunio Katakura (1990–1991), etc. Among the memoirs of JSDF commanders, Shun Ochiai contributed a web essay.

The study of Japan's diplomacy during the First Oil Crisis by Junichiro Shiratori utilised diplomatic documents from the Ministry of Foreign Affairs (MOFA). He Liqun studied Prime Minister Nakasone's resource diplomacy (He 2011), and Murakami Tomoaki studied Kishi administrations' engagement in Lebanon Crisis, and examination to dispatch JSDF to UNPKO (Murakami 2003).

The third method is evaluation by concepts from political studies experts. Realist scholars, Matake Kamiya and Tsuyoshi Kawaski will be discussed since they debate what type of realism Japan's foreign policy has adopted.

3 The Internationalists' Perspective on Japan's Middle East Policy

This section debates the emergence of a split in Japan's diplomatic direction that formed five major perspectives prior to the Gulf War. They are mercantilists, pacifists, internationalists (middle-power perception and normal nation perception), and new nationalists.

One has to consider the bias inherent in the above-mentioned sources and studies, which reflect the five perspectives in Japan's foreign policy. This section discusses (1) what internationalists are and (2) the origin of Japan's engagement in the Middle East by internationalists.

The rise and fall of the five perspectives represent domestic debates and power struggles over the nature of the world order, political economy policy, relations with the U.S., diplomacy towards developing countries, and Japan's role in the globalising world. The history of the interaction among the five perspectives is complex. However, the outline is as follows: the pacifists and mercantilists declined after the end of the Cold War, and after the Gulf Crisis internationalists led Japan's foreign policy. New nationalists never positioned themselves in the mainstream in Japan's foreign policy, but they are disrupting Asian diplomacy.

3.1 Internationalism in Japan's Diplomacy

Internationalism presupposes that cooperation among sovereign states would realise prosperity and peace in the world. It can be a diplomatic policy or a diplomatic process of a state. Internationalism was formed in nineteenth century through development in international law, cooperation beyond borders among individuals and organisations, and the establishment of international organisations in Interwar period. Internationalism was conceived as liberal internationalism, socialist internationalism, cultural internationalism, realist internationalism, etc. Early liberal internationalists in the nineteenth century deemed that interdependence would prevent wars. The opposite of internationalism is nationalism, isolationism, unilateralism, and hegemonism. E.H. Carr is well known, as he criticised internationalism as utopianism (Bablik 2013). Internationalism is a dynamic process of decline and circulation (Morgan 2010).

In Japan, internationalism is usually articulated as "international collaborationism (Kokusai Kyoutyou Shugi)" instead of simple "internationalism (Kokusai Shugi)." This Japan's version of internationalism (hereafter "internationalism") is not associated with "specific type of" internationalism, such as liberal, socialism, and realism, and is shared with citizens and governments, not only academic circles. However, "Internationalism in Japan" emerged in 1980s as goal of Japan's diplomacy. Scholars such as Mochizuki, Pile, Samuels, and Hirata all agree that internationalism emerged as diplomatic goal in Japan in 1980s, though they apply different names (Hirata 2009, 50).

The Gulf Crisis placed internationalism as a mainstream diplomatic course in Japan in 1990. Internationalism is classified into a middle-power perspective and a normal nation perspective. Normal nation perspective is well known, as its name was given by Ichiro Ozawa in his 1993 book *Blueprint for a New Japan*. Famous advocator of the middle-power perspective is Professor Yoshihide Someya at Keio University. Besides him, advocates of various new views do not label themselves with middle-power theory, but they can be classified as variance of middle-power theory. After 2017, the Japanese government is low profile with a "pro-active security policy," which was once the star policy of the Abe administration. The Japanese government follows the middle-power perspective line after the withdrawal of JGSDF unit from United Nations Mission in Sudan (UNMIS) in 2017.

Advocators of the normal nation perspective and those of the middle-power perspective share views on Japan's global role, alliance with the U.S., and non-military use of JSDF. Supporters of normal nation theory are more uncompromising with China and Korea, overseas dispatch of JSDF, and military solutions, while those for middle-power perspective prefer minimum role of military, such as dispatch of JSDF to overseas for only non-military purpose, no amendment of constitution, check on U.S. wars, non-military solution for armed conflicts and terrorism, world disarmament, and reconciliation with China and Korea. After the Gulf Crisis in 1990, diplomacy and international security policy by the Japanese government were gripped by internationalists of the normal nation perspective and middle-power perspective. Distribution of parliamentary seats in Japan makes it unlikely a constitutional amendment will be adopted. The practical difference between the two, the middle-power perspective and the normal nation perspective has become somewhat blurred in recent years (Table 1).

Pacifists maintain anti-war, anti-military, anti-U.S., anti-JSDF, anti-nuclear, and anti-imperial sovereignty. They prefer solidarity, especially with the Third World and the former Eastern bloc. Condemnation to the Second World War has been at the centre of the pacifist world view. Previous studies have pointed out that Pacifists peaked in the 1960s and then declined and ran off the political mainstream in Japan after the 1970s (Hirata 2009, 51). However, pacifists should be regarded as having been influential in public opinion and in the diplomatic decision-making process in Japan thereafter. To a surprise, Tomiichi Murayama (1924–), Socialist Party, took the office of Prime Minister in June 1994 in coalition with LDP, and in the next month, as well known, he overturned the platform of Socialist Party and affirmed both of the JSDF and alliance

Table 1   Characteristics of five perspectives for Japan's foreign policy

Foreign policy perspective	Defence	Diplomacy
Mercantilism	Minimum for self-defence	Pro-U.S
Pacifism	No army, no war	Anti-U.S
Middle-power perspective	• Dispatch of JSDF at minimum • Reinforcement of JSDF • Defensive	• Pro-U.S • Enhancing relations with Asia and Europe • Global role
Normal nation perspective	• Active Dispatch of JSDF • Reinforcement of JSDF • Defensive—Limited offensive measures if necessary	• Pro-U.S • Enhancing relations with Asia and Europe • Global role • Equal with Korea and China, but insensitive to them
New nationalism	• Reinforcement of JSDF • World view of Pre Second World War	• Nationalistic identity is priority • No practical agenda

Source This author

with U.S. constitutional. It revealed that the socialist platform on Japan's diplomacy "neutrality without arms" was an impractical platform. Then, the socialist party's pacifist stand lost authority among its supporters.

However, after the decline of the Socialist Party, pacifism has maintained a powerful influence on Japan's diplomacy. The Socialist Party exerted its influence over Japan's security policy as a minor coalition partner for the LDP, which formed the Hashimoto coalition cabinet. After the Socialist Party left the coalition with the LDP, it lost supporters rapidly and downfall to a tiny party with a huge loss of parliamentary seats. However, they disguised, pretending to be supporters of the middle-power perspective. In place of the Socialist Party, the Komeito Party, a minor party, formed a coalition with LDP and became its stable partner. In February 1992, it cooperated with the LDP to legislate the budget for the coalition force in Saudi Arabia to liberate Kuwait. It cooperated with the Koizumi administration to dispatch the JMSDF to the Indian Ocean in 2002. Supporters of the Komeito Party believe that they placed brakes on LDP diplomacy, not to expand into military activities (Miyazaki 2018, 268, 271). Komeito's official diplomatic platform is classified as a middle-power perspective.

The "fortress" of pacifists is Article 9 of the Japanese constitution, which renounces wars for Japan's option. It remains as it is unless constitutional amendment is legislated in parliament, which will not happen in foreseeable future. Constitutional amendment is legislated with two-third votes both in Upper House and Lower House in Japanese parliament, which is extremely difficult for any political party or coalition in Japan. Therefore, pacifists can rely on Article 9 of the Japanese constitution to prohibit military action of the JSDF.

Mercantilists aim at a trade state with economic prosperity. It is known as Yoshida[8] doctrine, which formed a keynote of Japanese diplomacy after the Second World War with plights of light-armed army, pro-U.S. diplomacy, and economic prosperity. They tried to reopen relations with Asian countries by paying post-war compensation, which was the origin of Japan's overseas development assistance (ODA). It was a severe blow for Japan that Prime Minister Tanaka met anti-Japan demonstrations in Thailand and Indonesia in 1974.

---

[8] Shigeru Yoshida (1878–1967: prime minister, May 1946–May 1947, October 1948–December 1954).

3.2 Emergence of Internationalists after 1970's

Japan's foreign policy began transforming from mercantilism to the middle-power perspective at diplomatic and economic crisis. 1970s was the transitional phase. The Fukuda administration (December 1976–December 1978) declared three principles of foreign policy called "Fukuda doctrine" to Southeast Asia in 1977 to appease critics to Japan's mercantilism. They are (1) rejection of militarism, (2) building confidence, trust, and mutual understanding with the South East, and (3) equal partnership with South Asia.

Ohira administration (1978–80) advocated "comprehensive security" after the First Oil Crisis. It was a strategy to achieve energy security and food security through the utility of all policy tools, including strategic distribution of ODA and excluding military. Prime Minster Zenkou Suzuki (1911–2004, Prime minister July 1980–November 1982) described the Japan–U.S. relationship as alliance for the first time as premier, but refused the U.S. request for military cooperation, and made the U.S. give up such request (Wakatsuki 2017). Then the U.S. and Japan found a balance between their stance at the Nakasone administration. Prime Minister Nakasone aimed at departing from Yoshida doctrine and shifting to internationalism to strengthen relations with Asia, as well as the U.S. and Europe.

Internationalists have been fully awake to Japan's rise in economic power and tried to find out Japan's appropriate international role and burden sharing since 1980s. While they regard security cooperation with the U.S. as a stable pillar of Japan's diplomatic and international security, they aim to deepen relations with Europe and Asia. At the break of the Gulf Crisis in 1990, they were determined to depart from mercantilism or the Yoshida doctrine.

Politicians who can be classified as holders of middle-power perspective are prime ministers Yasuhiro Nakasone, Toshiki Kaihu, and Kichi Miyazawa (1919–2007, prime minister November 1991–December 1992), Yukio Hatoyama (1947–, prime minister September 2009–June 2010), etc., and the prime ministers of the "normal nation perspective" are Ryotaro Hashimoto, Junichiro Koizumi (1942–, prime minister April 2001–October 2005) and Shinzo Abe (1954–2022, prime minister September 2006–September 2007, December 2012–September 2020).

Nobusuke Kishi (1896–1987, prime minister February 1957–June 1960) was a politician of "normal nation" internationalist even though he did not dispatch JSDF to UNPKO at a request from UN secretary General in 1950s, in consideration not to provoke political oppositions prior to renewal of Japan–U.S. security treaty in 1960 (Murakami 2003) (Table 2).

Internationalists currently agree with the reinforcement of the JSDF to deter military threats posed by North Korea and China currently. They officially apologised for the invasion of Japan at Fifteen Years' War,[9] but they believe it ended Western colonialism in their heart. They pursue friendly relations with China and Korea, but some of the holders of normal nation perspective are insensitive to angering China and Korea by praying at Yasukuni Shrine.[10] They insist to be equal with China and Korea. They in fact want to collect votes from new nationalist organisations in elections by praying at Yasukuni Shrine. Internationalists institutionalised the legal and political framework for the JSDF to participate in international peace activities by legislating UNPKO law in 1992. They dispatched JMSDF to the Indian Ocean and legislature of Peace and Security Law in 2015. They expanded the definition in interpretation of right of collective self-defence and non-military activity of JSDF, while amendment of constitution is hard to realise.

A "normal nation" advocator, former Prime Minister Shinzo Abe, publicised his proposal to amend article nine of the Japanese constitution in 2018. He proposed leaving Clause 1 and Clause 2[11] of Article 9

---

[9] Pacific War is the name for the battles in the Pacific front that began in 1941 and ended in 1945. Japan began its war in 1931 in Manchuria, expanded the front to China's mainland and ended all battles in 1945. Thus, the Fifteen Years' War represents comprehensive fronts, including the Chinese front.

[10] This is a Shinto shrine that commemorates those who died in service of Japan since nineteenth century, and was revealed by a news report in 1978 that it had started to enshrine war criminals of the Second World War (Akazawa 2015).

[11] Article 9. 1 Aspiring sincerely to an international peace based on justice and order, the Japanese people forever renounce war as a sovereign right of the nation and the threat or use of force as means of settling international disputes.

2 To accomplish the aim of the preceding paragraph, land, sea, and air forces, as well as other war potential, will never be maintained. The right of belligerency of the state will not be recognised. "The Constitution of Japan," http://www.japaneselawtranslation. go.jp/law/detail_main?id=174.

Table 2 Political trend of major prime ministers

Name	Terms of office	Political trend
Shigeru Yoshida (1878–1967)	May 1946–May 1947, October 1948–December 1954	Mercantilist perspective
Nobusuke Kishi (1896–1987)	February 1957–July 1960	Normal state perspective
Hayato Ikeda	July 1960–November 1964	Mercantilist perspective
Eisaku Sato	November 1964–July 1972	Mercantilist perspective
Kakuei Tanaka	July 1972–December 1974	Middle-power perspective
Takeo Fukuda	December 1976–December 1978	Transition from mercantilism to the middle-power perspective
Masayoshi Ohira (1910–80)	December 1978–June 1980	Transition from mercantilism to the middle-power perspective
Zenkou Suzuki (1911–2004)	July 1980–November 1982	Transition from mercantilism to the middle-power perspective
Yasuhiro Nakasone (1918–2019)	November 1982–November 1986	Middle-power perspective
Toshiki Kaihu (1931–)	August 1989–November 1991	Middle-power perspective
Kichi Miyazawa (1919–2007)	November 1991–December 1992	Middle-power perspective
Tomiichi Murayama (1924–)	June 1994–January 1996	Transition from pacifist to middle-power perspective
Ryutaro Hashimoto (1937–2006)	January 1996–July 1998	Normal state perspective, coalition with Pacifists
Keizo Obuchi (1937–2000)	July 1998–April 2000	Normal state perspective
Junichiro Koizumi (1942–)	April 2001–October 2005	Normal state perspective
Yukio Hatoyama (1947–)	September 2009–June 2010	Middle-power perspective
Shinzo Abe (1954–2022)	September 2006–September 2007, December 2012–September 2020	Normal state perspective

Source Author

in the constitution and adding Clause 3 to admit JSDF.[12] His proposal is

---

[12] Yuuki Murohashi. Abe Seiken ga Mezasu Kenpou Kaisei wo Tettei Kaisetsu. 'Kaiken 4Koumoku' tte Nanda. *Business Insider*. January 8, 2018. https://www.businessinsider.jp/post-159342.

controversial, but it can be pointed out that his proposal is not aiming at the militarisation of Japan, since article one and article two are untouched. Internationalists criticise Japan's pacifists as unilateral pacifists and mercantilists as seekers of unilateral prosperity. On the contrary, pacifists do not distinguish the middle-power perspective from the normal nation perspective and are wary of all internationalists as militarists. Internationalists are "practical" in that they set democracy and capitalism as principles. However, they are not bound by any specific ideology or dogma, including liberalism, and are flexible to make situational adoptions. They can respect values and thoughts in other counties. They seek equal partnerships with China and Korea instead of concessions.

Toshiki Kaihu, prime minister at the onset of the Gulf Crisis in 1990–91, was a middle-power supporter and was attacked by both pacifists and normal nation advocators. Prime Minister Miyazawa was affiliated with a political perspective within the LDP called Kouchikai, of tradition from former Prime Minister Yoshida, but he elaborated to legislate UNPKO law and dispatch of PKO to UN peace activities in Cambodia, UNCTAD. Thus he can be classified to a middle-power perspective. Two policemen were killed during their mission in Cambodia in 1992, but Premier Miyazawa had a sense of responsibility and valour to order the Japanese mission to stay there to complete the mission.

The perception of the middle power may be regarded as similar to that of the normal nation. The difference is that the politicians of the middle-power perspective do not pray at Yasukuni Shrine and do not provoke China and Korea for this cause. They exert their efforts on disarmament and soft-power. Kochikai, a major inner group within LDP led by Miyazawa, was split in 2000 after he resigned as premier. The Democratic Party (1998–2016) was formed through unprincipled unity by the former Democratic Party, Socialist Party, Conservative Party, etc., and produced three prime ministers from September 2009 to December 2012. The Diplomacy of the Democratic Party was a variation of the middle-power perception, but lacked diplomatic skill and worsened relations with the U.S. and China. They could not work on bilateral relations with Middle Eastern countries, and left it to diplomats' hand. However, they ceased extension of fuel supply activities for the coalition force in the Indian Ocean and chose to commit deeper to peacebuilding in Afghanistan after 2010. The Democratic Party badly lost in the general election in December 2012, and extinguished in 2016 after it joined the Ishin Party (Innovation Party).

New nationalists are neo-conservatives that emerged after 1990s among politicians.[13] This perspective is a mix of parties and individuals. Their concern is mainly on domestic issues. They legitimised Japan's invasion of Asia in the Second World War and are emotionally against China and Korea. They are against internationalists and the pacifists. They are in favour of reinforcing the JSDF and expanding rule of engagement (ROE) for JSDF to counter China and North Korea.[14] Although they still advocate only militaristic defence, but did not advocate any militaristic offences, pacifists cannot distinguish internationalists from new nationalists and regard both simply as militarists. New nationalists criticise both the middle-power perspective and the normal nation perspective as "weak diplomacy" to Asia. For example, they criticised premier Koizumi for not praying at the Yasukuni Shrine on August 15, the memorial day for the end of Japan's fighting in the Second World War. They do not think about diplomacy beyond Asia and have no practical diplomatic proposals (Hirata 2009, 76).

The highest political positions held by new nationalists were Governor of Tokyo by Shintaro Ishihara (1932–, Governor 1999–2012), and former defence minister Tomomi Inaba (August 2016–July 2017), at Abe administration (Fuse and Miura 2018, 32). Defence minister Inaba resigned in July 2017, and they did not produce any other ministers yet.

The risk of new nationalism for the future of Japan is two points. The first is that some holders of normal nation perspective are rumoured to hide new nationalist perspective in their heart. The former prime ministers Kishi and Abe were interpreted to be sympathetic to that perspective. But they are practical in their diplomatic behaviour, and promote harmony in the pro-U.S. and pro-Asia diplomacy. The second risk is real problem; parliament members of internationalists rely on groups of new internationalists, such as the Association of Bereaved Family (of the soldiers in the Second World War; Izokukai) and the Japan Conference (Nihonkaigi), to gather votes in elections.[15] Internationalists expect good relations with China and Korea, but pray at Yasukuni Shrine with the intention of

---

[13] This chapter distinguishes the new nationalists who hold official positions from the traditional nationalists who are radical outsiders. See (Yasuda 2018) on genealogy of nationalists' claims, terrorism, resurrection, groups, and on-line nationalism.

[14] An example; Shintaro Ishihara. Toushutouron. *Jisedai no Tou*. Tadashi Nakamura. dated December 4, 2013. http://tadashiism.jp/26731204-ishihara.php.

[15] Masahiro Yamazaki (2016). *Nihon kaigi: senzen kaiki he*. Tokyo: Shueisha. 19–20.

performing in line with new nationalist claims to gather their votes, which worsens relations with China and Korea.

The course of the power struggle by the five perspectives is as follows: during the Cold War, the mercantilists were mainstream, and the opposition was pacifists. However, they survived together the period the political structure called the "1955 regime," which framed a patterned hostile relationship and the strange coexistence of the government party LDP and the opposition party, the Socialist Party. Japan's diplomacy began shifting towards internationalism in 1970s. Nakasone's premiership stabilised Japan's internationalism as main diplomatic direction in the 1980s, with a pro-U.S. base line, towards the assumption of defence responsibility, strengthening Asian diplomacy, and carrying out of global role.

Internationalists' attempts are often mistaken as new nationalist. An example was Japan's proposal of the Asian Monetary Fund to relieve Asian countries in the Asian financial crisis, in which the Clinton administration doubted Japan's hegemonic initiative, although Japan had no ambition to monopolise Asia to kick out the U.S. During the Abe administration (September 2006–September 2007, December 2012–September 2020), the longest premiership in Japan ever for more than eight years did not achieve constitutional amendment. In other words, the fortress of pacifists, Article 9 of Japan's constitution, has been unchanged. Although Abe administration modified the definition of collective security and legislated the Peace and Security Law in 2015, Clause 2, Article 9 of the Japanese constitution, "The right of belligerency of the state will not be recognised" is unchanged.

The Socialist Party until the 1990s, and Komeito Party after the 2000s, as minor coalition partner parties, deterred LDP from militarism. The Democratic Party was of a middle-power perspective, but it extinguished. After the 2000s, new nationalists emerged and disrupted Japan's Asian diplomacy but had no hand in the diplomatic decision-making process and no vision worth considering on Japan's Middle East policy.

Therefore, mercantilists and new nationalists did not play a significant role in Japan's Middle East policy. Hereafter, this chapter discusses mainly internationalists, to examine the development of the Japan's Middle East Policy.

3.3   Japan's Middle East Policy by Internationalists

Pacifists in Japan are against colonialism, Orientalism, the Israeli occupation of Palestine, and U.S. military operations in the Middle East. They opposed battels of coalition forces to liberate Kuwait in 1991, the Afghanistan War in 2001, and the Iraqi War in 2003. Pacifists are among musicians, artists, religious figures, journalists, teachers, students, housewives, and university professors (Blanco 2005). They are critical of the lack of Japanese government in terms of autonomous and independent foreign policy, solidarity, and civil politics. Most of the Middle East studies researchers are probably pacifists in Japan. Demonstrations and protest movements took place against the Gulf War and Iraq War by novelists, religious figures, war victims, intellectuals, ordinary citizens, etc. (Blanco 2005).

Internationalists unfold more active diplomacy in the Middle East than mercantilists. One early Japanese internationalist was probably Premier Nobusuke Kishi (February 1957–July 1960), who supported Japanese enterprises in starting business in the Middle East since the MOFA analysed that the Middle East would be potential market. Kishi cabinet made cabinet approval that the Japanese government would cooperate with necessary measures for the Arabian Oil Co. Ltd. to obtain oil concessions in Saudi Arabia (Hasegawa 2015, 369–70).

In 1958, the Kishi cabinet was against the U.S. for dispatching forces to the Lebanon Crisis, and tried to mediate the United Arab Republic (UAR) and the U.S. at the United Nations, and proposed reinforcement of United Nations Interim Force In Lebanon (UNIFIL) to the UN Security Council. The proposal was rejected by the USSR, but UNIFIL was reinforced, and Lebanon resumed stability. Prime Minister Kishi considered dispatching the JSDF to UNPKO for the first time in Japan. But he did not because the renewal of the Japan–U.S. security treaty was scheduled after a short period, and he was afraid to provoke anger of public opinion against his security policy (Murakami 2003, 148, 149, 152–155). It is well known that he could barely renew the Japan–U.S. security treaty in June 1960 in waves of demonstration on streets.

Premier Tanaka began a tour to France, the UK, West Germany, and the USSR from September 1973, and during his stay in Moscow, the Fourth Middle East War (October War or Yom Kippur War) broke out. He was later accused of corruption in the "Lockheed Bribery Scandal," and he received severe criticism of his money politics. He did not visit the Middle East personally but dispatched three special envoys after the break of the First Oil Crisis. Takeo Miki, the vice prime minister (August 1972–July 1974), was dispatched to eight countries, including Egypt, Libya, Saudi Arabia, and Iraq, from December 1973 to January 1974. Former Foreign Minister Zentaro Kosaka (minister in 1960) was dispatched to another eight countries, including Morocco, Algeria, Libya, and Jordan. Then the minister of Trade and Industry, Yasuhiro Nakasone, was dispatched to Iraq and Iran. These three special envoys explained Japan's stand on the Israel–Arab conflict and promised a large sum of economic cooperation (Shindo 1986, 209). Japan was recognised as a friendly country by the Arabs, and took a firm step forward to deepen relations with Middle Eastern countries hereafter.

Yasuhiro Nakasone professed himself as an innovative-conservative, neo-liberal, and neo-conservative, but his foreign policy was most precisely described in the summer of 1987 at the study meeting of the LDP, saying that he would shift "Japan from nationalism to internationalism" (Nakasone 1986). Nakasone cabinet (November 1982–November 1987) challenged to shift Japan's foreign policy to internationalism in earnest. In January 1983, premier Nakasone declared the "final settlement of the post-war politics," meaning departure from Yoshida doctrine in his first general policy speech. He aimed to shift Japan from a country of "peace and economy" to a country of "politics and culture" (Nakasone 2012, 321). He expected the world centre would shift to the Pacific and advocated for the Pacific Cultural Regional Initiative once (Nakasone 2012, 275). However, no Japanese commentator described him as an internationalist. Those academics who applied the concept of internationalism to the foreign policy of Japan, from the premier Nakasone to Koizumi, were all based in universities outside Japan.

Mr. Nakasone displayed concern that Japan's diplomacy was one-sided with only the U.S. and aimed at deeper relations with Asia. He was one of the early pro-Arab politicians in Japan. He joined in a tour to Arab countries in 1957 and met with Nasser in Egypt. This tour resulted in the establishment of the Japan Arab Association in 1958.[16] He was the Minister of Economy, Trade, and Industry (METI) at the First Oil Crisis and added a clause to support Palestine Cause to the historic statement by Chief Cabinet Susumu Nikaido (1972–1974) in November 1973 to

---

[16] Takeyo Nakatani, who initiated the tour, endeavoured to establish the Japan-Arab society. He was the chairman of the society (1969–1990).

clarify the stand of the Japanese government on the Israel-Arab conflict (Nakasone 2012, 242–243). Nakasone stated in his memoir that he noticed that the Arabs would sell oil to Japan if Japan issue statements to support Arab side (Nakasone 2012, 242). Kissinger, the U.S. Secretary of State, visited Japan in November 1973 and talked with prime minister Tanaka, foreign minister Ohira, etc. Official records confirm that Kissinger opposed Japan's neutral stand over the Arab-Israel conflict but accepted that Japan would remain at the same stand as the EC (Shiratori 2015, 206–7). Then he met with Nakasone. He threatened him that if Japan collapsed the world oil order created by international oil majors, it would be involved in trouble. Nakasone answered that Japan had to purchase oil. Japan would not violate international law and have no intention of causing friction (Nakasone 2012, 240–1).[17]

Prime Minister Nakasone visited Pakistan after the USSR invasion of Afghanistan (Yasutomo 1986, 190). He visited Iraq in November 1990 while the Gulf Crisis and met Iraqi president Saddam Hussein al-Tikriti in Baghdad. Nakasone told him that the U.S. was ready to attack the Iraq army after a short term and requested that Iraq implement all UN Security Council resolutions, peaceful solutions to the Gulf crisis, and the liberation of all alien hostages. Saddam freed 74 Japanese hostages on November 8, 1990, and they returned to Japan with Nakasone. Thereafter, Nakasone visited the U.S. Embassy in Tokyo and requested to give Iraq the option to withdraw from Kuwait with peace (Nakasone 2012, 519–527).

After the First Oil Crisis, the MOFA was reformed to enhance Japan's Middle East diplomacy. Diplomat experts in the Arabic language, Persian language, and Turkish language were aimed to increase to 100, 20,

---

[17] Mr. Nakasone told in an interview for memoir that he understood years later what "the trouble" is. Kissinger visited Japan again and told him, "It was a mistake to have struck Tanaka" (Nakasone 2012, 237), which meant that the U.S. trapped Premier Tanaka into the Lockheed bribery scandal and forced him to resign the premiership, since his resource diplomacy around the world was seen as disrupting the world oil order ruled by international oil majors. However, a recent study argued that Kissinger used the Lockheed bribery scandal to achieve the downfall Tanaka, since Tanaka disrupted his diplomacy towards the USSR, China, and the Arab which ran against Kissinger's world strategy. No clear evidence was found that oil Majors had hand in Lockheed scandal. But in fact, Nakasone was allegedly bribed by Lockheed, and he was trying to hide it (Haruna 2020, 275, 364–379, 389–397, 426–430, 449, 562).

and 20 each in the ministry, which was achieved in 1979. The Middle East section in the MOFA was expanded to double, the Middle East 1st Section and the Middle East 2nd Section (Murata 2008a, 240–244). Embassies of Japan were opened and established in all Middle Eastern countries where they were not. Japanese embassies established good communication with all Japanese residents in Middle Eastern countries. METI set up the Japan Cooperation Center for the Middle East (JCCME) in 1973.

The Nakasone cabinet was an early version of the middle-power perspective. Minister of foreign affairs at Nakasone cabinet was Shintaro Abe (April 1924–May 1992), the father of later Prime Minister Shinzo Abe. He visited Iran and Iraq in 1983 to challenge mediating Iran–Iraq War. The U.S. navy began an escort mission in the Gulf during the Iraq–Iran war. Prime Minister Nakasone then examined the possibility of dispatching a marine sweeping mission to the Gulf as the U.S. requested Western countries, including Japan, to dispatch marine sweeping ships. He gave up the consideration due to opposition within the cabinet and by the Socialist Party (Kato 2012, 33–38). The Nakasone administration was probably an embryo for internationalism consolidated in the next decade. Thus, the next drastic change in Japan's Middle East policy occurred after the Gulf crisis.

4   Conception of Japan's Internationalism

From the constructivist view, Japanese security policy is derived by values and identity diffused in Japan after the Second World War, and domestic politics and institutions produced by them (Berger 1996). However, Japan's security policy, foreign policy, and Middle East policy have drastically shifted after the Gulf Crisis.

"Circumscribed balancer" or "circumscribed realism" regards Japan as defensive realism but also as mercantilism and uncooperative to its ally, the U.S. (Twomey 2000). Internationalists in Japan, especially advocates of normal nations, expect the Japanese government and public opinion to comprehend the urgency to expand Japan's defence capability and expansion of the operation of the JSDF.

Professor Matake Kamiya, one of Japan's exemplary scholars in security studies, asserted that the country's security policy behaviour after the Fifteen Years' War was based on a different type of realism than that prevailing in the West. The "realists" in Japan have comprehended the limited effect of the use of weapons and consider non-militaristic tools, such as economic interdependence, the sharing of common values and the provision of foreign aid and international organisations, to deter wars. Kamiya framed Japanese realists as sharing the perspective of liberalists in the Western definition and even deems it fitting to call them "realistic liberals" (Kamiya 2012, 66–81). It is true that Japan does not have any ambitions for new territory and expansion.[18] The Japanese view of the balance of power is based on defensive realism, which conforms with liberal order.

Kawasaki analysed Yoshida doctrine and considered it a neo-classical realism. Neo-classical realism is defensive, and prefers equipping minimum arms. Neo-classical realism aims at security and economic prosperity together. Kawasaki pointed out that the Yoshida doctrine refined the types of threats for small-scale wars and prepared for it. It implements arms policy to avoid the trap of security dilemmas in Northeast Asia (Kawasaki 2015, 110–135). Japan continues realism for defensive goals after the end of the Cold War.

Kawasaki's analysis limits its scope to only Yoshida doctrine, but neo-classical realism is probably the foundational behaviour of Japan throughout the post-Second World War period up to today. Three behaviour patterns of the Japanese government—mercantilism, middle-power perspective, and normal nation perspective—are variations within neo-classical realism thinking and behaviour. All three share features of

---

[18] Japanese stance on territorial disputes on the Kurile islands, Takeshima Islands, the Senkaku Islands is not expansionism. Japanese government proposes Korea and China to bring two each cases of Takeshima Islands and the Senkaku Islands to International Court of Justice (ICJ). Japanese government is confident that it will win both cases. Details of Japan's claim: Ministry of Foreign Affairs of Japan. "Japanese Territory," https://www.mofa.go.jp/territory/index.html. April 4, 2014. Japanese government does not propose to bring the case of Kurile Islands to ICJ. It was domestic politics of Japan that impeded a decision to respond to rare chance that Russian president was willing to reach agreement with Japan in around 1999–2000. Maximum Russian offer was agreement over two islands of the Kurile Islands, but hardliner in Japan insists on return of four islands from Russia, and impede negotiation over return of only two islands. Then, the Russian side change their mind and lost very rare opportunity for good. The nationalisation of Senkaku Islands was done in 2010 by misreading of the then Democratic Party administration with poor diplomatic skill as it had sought improvement of good relations with China. "Senkaku, Zettai ni Kokuyuuka wo, Ishihara shi tono Kaidan de Kimeta Noda Shi." Asahi. September 12, 2017.

neo-classical realism, such as defensiveness, preference for equipping with minimum arms and aims at security and economic prosperity together.

Kawasaki also analysed Japan's initiative to establish the ASEAN Regional Forum (ARF) after the Cold War. Conception for its establishment was founded on diplomatic thinking by diplomats and scholars around them. They aimed to strengthen the confidence-building function and sense of security among Japan, China, and the U.S. to avoid security dilemma in Asia. For that purpose, they judged multilateral organisations to be more efficient than repeating bilateral negotiations. They conceived that the ARF would be a mechanism to exchange information to create a sense of security among trilateral countries (Kawasaki 2015, 95–109).

This is a case of Japan's foreign policy, which aims at inclusive and multilateral regional order, and prosperity with defensive security founded on realism oriented towards balance among major powers through confidence building.

In sum, the principles of Japan's internationalism are summarised from the above review as follows.

   i. Free trade and interdependence with nations at maximum.

   ii. Multilateral diplomacy, if efficient.

   iii. Lack of clear political ambitions for hegemony, colonialism, imperialism, and expansion of territory, although Japanese maintain vague hope to be "No. 1" in various competitions.

   iv. Strengthening relations with Asia, with regard to relations with the U.S., is the baseline.

   v. Responsibility of global role except military engagement for war.

   vi. Promotion of democracy and human rights with non-intervention in other nations.

   vii. Practical application of internationalism. These principles contradict each other. But the Japanese government or specific leaders do not set priority among them as dogma, but they make foreign policy decisions on context. They struggled within five perspectives of Japanese diplomacy, and the struggle took place within governmental leaders of mercantilists and internationalists.

Thus, Japan's Middle East policy after the Nakasone administration will be discussed in the next chapter.

REFERENCES

Akazawa, Shiro. 2015. *Senbotusha to Yasukuni Jinja*. Tokyo: Yoshikawakobunkan.

Badr, Hisham. 2008. *Sphinx to Nihontou*. Tokyo: Tachibana Publishing, Inc.

Berger, T.U. 1996. "Norms, Identity, and National Security in Germany and Japan." In P.J. Katzenstein (ed.). *The Culture of National Security: Norms and identity in World Politics*. New York: Columbia University Press. 317–356.

Blanco, Sebastian. 2005. *Faces of Protest: Two Global Movements against the Gulf Wars, a View from Japan*. Master thesis. Honolulu: University of Hawai'i.

Calder, Kent E. 1988. "Japanese Foreign Economic Policy Formation: Explaining the Reactive State." *World Politics* 40, no. 4: 517–41.

Cohen, Eli. 2006. *Taishi ga Kaita Nihonjin to Yudayajin*. Translated by Aoki Isaku. Tokyo: Chukei Shuppan.

Fuse, Yujin and Miura Hideyuki. 2018. *Nippou Inpei*. Tokyo: Shueisha.

Green, Michael J. 2001. *Japan's Reluctant Realism : Foreign Policy Challenges in an Era of Uncertain Power*. NY: Palgrave.

Haruna, Mikio. 2020. *Lokkido Giwaku: Kakuei wo Houmuri Kyoaku wo Nogasu*. Tokyo: Kadokawa.

Hasegawa, Hayato. 2015. *Kishi Naikaku no Naisei, Gaikou Rosen no Rekishiteki Saikentou: Fukushi Kokka, Keizai Gaikou toiu Shiten Kara*. Ph.D. dissertation. Tokyo: Hitotsubashi University.

Hashimoto, Kohei. 1995. *Senryaku Enjo: Chuto Wahei Sien to ODA no Shourai*. Tokyo: PHP Kenkyujo.

He, Liqun. 2011. "Daiichiji Sekiyu Kiki Zengo no Nakasone Yasuhiro: "Shigen Gaikou" wo Megutte." *Kokusai Koukyou Seisaku* 15, no. 2: 83–99.

Hirata, Keiko. 2009. Nihon no Anzenhoshou Seisaku to Kokunai Giron. In Hara Kimie (ed.). *Zaigai Nihonjin Kenkyusha ga Mita Nihon Gaikou*. Tokyo: Fujiwara-Shoten.

Hook, Glenn D. et al. 2001. *Japan's International Relations : Politics, Economics and Security*. London: Routledge.

Iokibe, Shin, and Miyagi Taizo (eds.). 2013. *Hashimoto Ryutaro: Diplomatic Memoire*. Tokyo: Iwanami Shoten.

Kamiya, Matake. 2012. "Nihonteki Genjitsushugisha no Nationalizumu Kan." *Kokusaianzenhoshou* 39, no. 4: 66–81.

Kato, Hiroaki. 2012. "Nationalism and Jieitai: 1987, 91 nen no Soukaitei Haken Mondai wo Chuushinni." *Kokusaiseiji* 170, 30–45.

Kawasaki, Tsuyoshi. 2015. *Shakaikagaku toshiteno Nihon Gaikou Kenkyuu*. Kyoto: Minerva.

Kurdi, Muhammad Bashir Ali al-. 2015. *Sauji Arabia Taishi ga Mita Nihon*. Tokoyo: Japan Saudi Arabia Society.

Kuroda, Yasumasa. 2001. Japan's Middle East Policy: Fuzzy Nonbinary Process Model. In Miyashita and Sato (eds.). 101–118.

Miyashita, Akitoshi. 2001. Consensus or Compliance? Gaiatsu, Interests, and Japan's Foreign Policy Aid. In Miyashita and Sato (eds.). 37–61.

Miyashita, Akitoshi, and Sato Yoichiri. 2001. *Japanese Foreign Policy in Asia and the Pacific: Domestic Interests, American Pressure, and Regional Integration.* New York: Palgrave.

Miyazaki, Youko. 2018. '*Tero tono Tatakai*' *to Nihon: Renritsuseiken no Taigaiseisaku heno Eikyou.* Nagoya: Nagoya University Press.

Morgan, Patrick. 2010. Liberalism. Alan Collins (ed.). *Contemporary Security Studies.* 2nd ed. New York: Oxford University Press.

Murakami, Tomoaki. 2003. "Kishi Naikaku to Kokuren Gaikou: PKO gentaiken toshite no Lebanon Kiki." *Kokusaikyouryoku Ronshu* 11, no. 1: 141–165.

Murata, Ryohei. 2008a. *Murata Ryohei Kaiso Roku: Sokoku no Saisei wo Jisedai ni Takushite. Jou.* Kyoto. Minerva Bookstore.

Nakamura, Satoru. 2018. "The Role of Japan and Potential Cooperation with the GCC for the Stability and Prosperity of the Indian Ocean Rim Region (IORR)." *Bulletin of Graduate School of Intercultural Studies, Kobe University* (December 2018), 21–58.

Nakasone, Yasuhiro. 1986. "Shinjidai wo Kizuku Jimintou no Shimei—1986 nen Taisei no Sutaato." *Gekkan Jiyuminshu* 403, 38–51.

Nakasone, Yasuhiro. 2012. *Nakasone Yasuhiro ga Kataru Sengo Nihon Gaikou.* Tokyo: Shinchosha.

Okazaki, Hisahiko. 1983. *Senryaku teki Shikou toha Nanika.* Tokyo: Chuokoron-shinshoa, Inc.

Reischauer, Edwin O. 1988. *The Meaning of Internationalization.* Tokyo: Tuttle English House.

Shindo, Eiichi. 1986. *Heiwa Senryaku no Kouzu.* Tokyo: Nippon Hyoron sha.

Shiratori, Junichiro. 2015. *Keizai Taikoku Nihon no Gaikou: Enerugii Shigengaikou no Keisei 1967–1974.* Tokyo: Chikura Shobou.

Twomey, Christpher P. 2000. "Japan, A Circumscribed Balancer: Building on Defensive Realism to Make Predictions about East Asian Security." *Security Studies* 9, No.4: 167–205.

Wakatsuki, Hidekazu. 2017. *Reisen no Shuuen to Nihon Gaikou: Suzuki, Nakasone, Takeshita no Gaikou* 1980–1989. Tokyo: Chikura publishing Co.

Yamazaki, Masahiro. 2016. *Nihon Kaigi: Senzen Kaiki he.* Tokyo: Shueisha.

Yasuda, Kouichi. 2018. '*Uyoku*' *no Sengoshi.* Tokyo: Koudansha.

Yasutomo, Dennis T. 1986. *The Manner of Giving: Strategic Aid and Japanese Foreign Policy.* Lexington, Mass.: Lexington Books.

CHAPTER 12

Nonmilitary Contribution by Japan in the Gulf Crisis 1990–1991: Funding, Intelligence Gathering, Releasing Hostages, and Minesweeping

Satoru Nakamura

Japan's internationalists began to play a central role in leading Japan's foreign policy formation after the Gulf Crisis of 1990–1991. Nevertheless, Japan's foreign policy was not carried out solely by their views and actions. Although Antonio Inoki's release of hostages in Iraq is not well known in the world, his pacifist-tone conducts pushed the Iraqi government to free foreign hostages.

This chapter will deal with aspects of Japan's engagement in the Gulf Crisis, including funding to the coalition force, appreciation by the Arabs to Japan, relief of hostages in Iraq, intelligence gatherings in Iran, and

S. Nakamura (✉)
Graduate School of Intercultural Studies, Kobe University, Kobe, Japan
e-mail: satnaka@kobe-u.ac.jp

© The Author(s), under exclusive license to Springer Nature
Singapore Pte Ltd. 2023
S. Nakamura and S. Wright (eds.), *Japan and the Middle East*,
Contemporary Gulf Studies, https://doi.org/10.1007/978-981-19-3459-9_12

325

minesweeping activities in the Gulf. These Japan's activities were kept unknown to the world, and they seem to be a part of the *quiet diplomacy*. During the Gulf Crisis and the following Gulf War, Japan was known to have been criticised as a "slow response" and "invisible diplomacy" and humiliated by being forced to "check book diplomacy". These were based on images of Japan as mercantilists or free riders. Japan's failure was to have been represented in newspaper advertisements by the Kuwaiti government to express their gratitude for the liberation of Kuwait. Japanese bitterly remember that the Japanese flag was not printed in this advertisement, which they thought that a huge amount of funding was not an adequate method for international contribution.

However, data collection by the Tokyo Shinbun Newspaper revealed that the Kuwaiti government and citizens deeply appreciated Japanese support for them during the Gulf Crisis.[1] It was clarified that the Kuwaiti advertisement for appreciation in U.S. newspapers was drafted by the U.S. government, and the Kuwaiti government was negligent in checking its contents in advance of the publication (details are later in this chapter). The U.S. government officials and the commander of the U.S. Middle East Force also appreciated Japan's efforts during the Gulf Crisis. The sequence of the diffusion of the above-mentioned false claim about Kuwaiti lack of appreciation of Japan indicates that high-ranking officials in the Japanese government and intellectual adherents to them knew the truth but have repeated the fake story that Kuwait did not appreciate Japan's efforts during the Gulf Crisis to Japanese citizens to make them support their claim that Japan has to dispatch the Japanese Self-Defense Forces (JSDF) abroad.

Japan did not relent to U.S. pressure in that Japan did not dispatch the JSDF to the Gulf Crisis. However, instead, Japan offered huge funding to the coalition force. Does this funding mean that Japan gave in to foreign pressure? In reality, the Japanese government established the Gulf Peace Fund (GPF) with the Arabian Gulf Cooperation Council (GCC) and managed the funds together with the GCC to mitigate U.S. pressure. Japan's funds were distributed to the U.S., and countries in Europe, the Middle East, Africa, and Asia through GPF. In short, previous studies over Japan's funding to the coalition force have examined the delay of the decision-making process for up to one week due to coordination within

---

[1] Wangan Sensou deno 'Kuueto 'Kansha Koukoku' kara no Nihon Hazushi' no Trauma ha 'Jieitai Haken no Koujtsu'. *Tokyo Shinbun.* September 10, 2015. p. 8.

the Japanese government, which resulted in the U.S. media criticising Japan severely. But Japan's funding was to maintain officials' budgetary responsibility to Japanese citizens, and the payment was done more swiftly than those of the U.S. Congress and Saudi Arabia.

The Japanese government never planned to participate in the ground campaign to liberate Kuwait, and up to today, Japan's JSDF has not participated in any military conflicts in the contemporary era. Japan contributed to bringing intelligence over Iran's intention towards the Gulf War in 1991, which assisted the coalition force to concentrate in the battle in Kuwaiti front. Only Japan had an intimate diplomatic channel with Iran along with the Western countries, and could talk with the Iranian government over their militaristic intention, which relieved the coalition force of unexpected risk in the ground campaign. Japanese Maritime Self-Defense Force (JMSDF) played a unique role in cleaning all the marine mines set by Iraq in the Gulf, where Western countries could not operate.

All these unknown stories will reveal Japan's different perspective to the Gulf Crisis which goes beyond the "reactive state" debate. Japan's actions contributed to the resumption of peace and security in the Gulf. Japan's actions were appreciated by the U.S., Europe, and the Middle East for its unique roles. Japan did not take military action, but Japan provided indispensable resources for funding, intelligence gathering, relief of hostages, and minesweeping.

1 THE U.S. DOMESTIC RESPONSE TO THE GULF CRISIS

Immediately after the Iraqi invasion of Kuwait, the U.S. option was not certain. The main military scenario of the U.S. in the Gulf was planned during the Cold War. The U.S.S.R would invade Iran through Caucasus. In July 1990, the previous month of the real Iraqi invasion, the commander of the newly established U.S. Central Command, Herbert Norman Schwarzkopf Jr. (1989–1991), had just created a new scenario with his strong leadership that Iraq would invade Kuwait (Schwarzkof 1992, 285–289). However, after the invasion on August 2, 1990, he and the Chairman of the Joint Chiefs of Staff, Colin L. Powell, thought to wait and observe the ongoing occupation of Kuwait by Iraq, and prepare for the defence of Saudi Arabia and the Gulf states. They did not conclude that Kuwait was worth fighting for by the U.S. army, but they expected that the U.S. army would fight with the Iraqi army if it invaded Saudi

Arabia. On August 4, at the national security council meeting presided by the U.S. President George H.W. Bush, who agreed to push back Iraqi troops in Kuwait, and then began considering military options to fight the Iraqi troops occupying Kuwait (Schwarzkof 1992, 298–302). On August 6, Iraq President Hussein threatened the world that it would attack Saudi Arabia if Iraq oil pipe line were closed. On August 7, the first U.S. fighter jets and the Airborne Division left the U.S. for Saudi Arabia.

The tone in media in the U.S. was clear-cut since the first day of Iraq's invasion of Kuwait, blaming it as "naked invasion", "challenge to world law", and "Hitler". The approval rate for President Bush raised remarkably high (Gomi 1992, 42). But the tone of the argument in the media was ad hoc. In November, 1990, anti-war sentiment appeared in the major press in the U.S. The U.S. media began to express concern of a repetition of morass and trauma of the Vietnam War (Gomi 1992, 44). In fact, after the coalition force started the military campaign against Iraq, demonstrators marched in Washington, D.C., and San Francisco on January 27, 1991.[2] On January 12, 1991, both the Upper House and Lower House in the U.S. Congress passed a resolution to approve military action against Iraq. This was due to the Democrats controlling both Houses of the 101st U.S. Congress (January 1989–January 1991), and the votes to favour it won by a narrow margin of only five votes in the Upper House (52–47).

President Bush, Secretary of the Defence Richard B. Cheney (1989–1993), and congressman of importance John McCain (1936–2018) worded their understanding of Japan's constitutional constraint that it could not participate in ground battels (Kunimasa 1999, 98). However, Senator McCain pointed out that Japanese nationals could engage in humanitarian assistance and the rescue of refugees, and that Japan had an important role as the world's largest creditor (Kunimasa 1999, 98–99). His view was similar to that of Premier Kaihu.

[2] War in the Gulf: Antiwar Rallies; Day of Protests Is the Biggest Yet. *New York Times.* January 27, 1991.

2   THE TRUTH ABOUT FUNDING: GULF PEACE FUND (GPF)

The Japanese government made three decisions to fund the coalition force during the Gulf Crisis. The first was on August 30, 1990 (1 billion U.S. dollars for coalition). The second was September 14, 1990 (1 billion U.S. dollars for the coalition and 2 billion U.S. dollars for the Middle Eastern countries; that is, 3 billion U.S. dollars in total). The third was on January 24, 1991 (9 billion U.S. dollars for coalition). This payment was legislated in Japan's parliament in March 1991 as a supplementary budget in 1990. This fund was not paid directly to the U.S., but donated to the GPF managed together by Japan and the GCC, although the largest amount was distributed to the U.S.

This payment was not examined by Japanese scholars. Record of proceeding for the Committee of Closing Account at the Upper House of the Japanese parliament, 129th national assembly dated February 28, 1994, approved the report "Regarding the Funding to the Gulf Peace Fund" submitted by the Ministry of Foreign Affairs (MOFA), Japan. According to this report, the Japanese government disbursed four times to the Fund. The distribution of the fund began in September 1990 and sustained the U.S. force dispatched in Saudi Arabia. The funding was approved by the Japanese Parliament on March 6, which caused no trouble for the U.S. account procedure, although the ground battle ended around 20 days ago on February 27, 1991 (Kuriyama 1997, 30).

Premier Kaihu stated in his memoir that the funding at the Gulf Crisis was set to disburse to the GPF. The motivation of this measure was to manage the intended use of the fund. Japan conditioned the recipients of the fund not to spend on arms and munitions (Kaihu 2005, 285). Premier Kaihu recollected President Bush appreciating him for Japan's funding (Kaihu 2005, 286). Not only the U.S., but the U.K. and France also requested that Japan disburse the funds for them (Kaihu 2005, 287).

The disbursement of Japan's funding was implemented through the GPF, which was established based on letters exchanged by the Japanese government and the Council of the GCC on September 21, 1990. Japan's funds were disbursed to 16 countries through the GPF. Its total amount was around $11.4 billion U.S. dollars.[3] Administrative committee for

---

[3] Sangiin. *Dai Hyaku Nijuu Kyuu Kai Kokkai Sangiin Kessan Iinkai Giroku Dai Ichi Gou.* Dated February 28, 1994. p. 36.

GPF was formed on September 21, 1990 as a body responsible for the management of the Fund. The administrative committee was composed of Japan's ambassador in Saudi Arabia (Takashi Onda from August 1990, and Hiroshi Ota from April 1992) and the Secretary General of the GCC, Abdullah Y. Bishar (1981–1993). GCC was established in 1981, and the Gulf Crisis was the first major blow to it. The committee held 15 meetings. The Japanese government disbursed funds four times from the GPF. The first disbursement occurred on September 21, 1990 (around 0.9 billion U.S. dollars). The second was on December 24, 1990 (around one billion U.S. dollars). The third was on March 12, 1991 (around 9 billion U.S. dollars). The fourth was on July 9, 1991 (around half a billion U.S. dollars).[4]

The exchanged documents on the first disbursement and the second disbursement provided purposes of the fund exclusively for (i) financial cooperation and (ii) material cooperation related to the procurement, transportation, and installation of materials and equipment.

The administrative committee stated that financial cooperation was spent on expenditures to rent aircrafts, ships, and other transportation. The material cooperation was spent on the procurement, transportation, and installation of (1) equipment for the protection of heat, (2) equipment related to water, (3) equipment related to vehicles and other transport machines, (4) accommodation and its attachment, (5) construction equipment and communication equipment, (6) office equipment, (7) food provision, medicines, and medical equipment, and (8) equipment for marine resource and environment.[5] The third disbursement and the fourth disbursement had almost similar conditions.

The first and second disbursements were distributed to the US (8.5 billion yen[6]), UK (6.2 billion yen), Egypt (3.2 billion yen), Syria (1.7 billion yen), followed by Pakistan, Kuwait, Morocco, Bangladesh, Senegal, Philippine, and Poland. The third and fourth disbursements were distributed to the U.S. (1.1 trillion yen), the UK (39 billion yen),

---

[4] Sangiin. *Ibid.* p. 37.

[5] Sangiin. *Ibid.* p. 37.

[6] 1 U.S. dollar was around 138 Yen in September 1990. Bank of Japan. Shuyou Jikeiretsu Toukei Deeta Hyou. Updated on May 1, 2021. https://www.stat-search.boj.or.jp/ssi/mtshtml/fm08_m_1.html.

Saudi Arabia (19 billion yen), Egypt (14.7 billion yen), followed by Syria, France, Pakistan, Senegal, Bangladesh, Morocco, Kuwait, and Niger.[7] It was appropriate for the U.S. to be afforded the largest sum of the funding. Kuwait was given 999 million yen at the first and second disbursements, and 626 million yen at the third and fourth disbursement.[8] The amount disbursed directly to Kuwait was not a large sum for Kuwait's financial power, but the total amount of funding through the GPF was enormous, which mitigated the financial burden on the Kuwait government.

3 THE U.S. AUDIT AND THE EVALUATION OF JAPAN'S FUNDING

Five days after the Iraq invasion of Kuwait, the Bush administration swiftly began dispatching the U.S. troops to Saudi Arabia before Congress approved a large-scale budget allocation for it. During the first dispatch for defence of Saudi Arabia and following preparation to liberate Kuwait, Congress's reaction was slow. In December 1990, the House of Senate held a public hearing and discussed the appropriateness of economic sanctions on Iraq and the use of force against Iraq. Three days ahead of the dead end of the ultimatum against Iraq, on January 12, 1991, the two Houses voted for a resolution to approve Operation Desert Storm to liberate Kuwait (Bennett 1994, 53–54).

The Secretary of Defense took measures to reallocate 2.1 billion U.S. dollars within the budget of the Department of Defense (DOD) by the use of Revised Statute 3732 during August and September 1990. The U.S. Congress only approved it prior to April 1991. Therefore, the DOD probably attached importance to Japan's funding to run the U.S. forces in early its dispatch to Saudi Arabia and the Gulf. At the beginning of 1991, the DOD again relocated its budget and took measures to borrow a quarterly budget in advance using Revised Statute 3732.

At the visit of Nicholas F. Brady (1930–), the Secretary of Treasury of the U.S. (September 1988–January 1993), President Bush stated in advance to Premier Kaihu that they would not be able to fight without funds (Kaihu 2005, 291). Karl D. Jackson, Special Assistant

---

[7] Sangiin. *Ibid.* p. 37.
[8] Sangiin. *Ibid.* p. 37.

to the President for National Security Affairs (1989–?), was assigned a task to elucidate the financial condition of the U.S. forces to Japanese government. He visited Japan numerous times and repeatedly stated that the U.S. government would not request dispatch of the JSDF but funding, since the U.S. Armed Forces held huge quantities of arms and ammunitions untested yet but lacked the fund (Kaihu 2005, 291).

Schwarzkopf, the commander of the U.S. Central Command, who commanded Operation Desert Shield and Operation Desert Storm, wrote in his memoir, "Had it not been for the Japanese, Desert Shield would have gone broke in August (Schwarzkof 1992, 365)", thus expressing frank gratitude to Japan. The U.S. Armed Forces needed funds for various uses at every step they were deployed in Saudi Arabia, but the U.S. Congress did not allocate a sufficient budget. The DOD took measures to relocate its budget within it, as mentioned above. Saudi Arabian funding for the coalition force was delayed for disbursement due to administrative inefficiency (Schwarzkof 1992, 363–365). At this circumstance, he wrote, "the Japanese Embassy in Riyadh quietly transferred tens of millions of dollars into Central Command's accounts (Schwarzkof 1992, 365)". His memoir described the transfer of Japan's funding as began in August 1990, but it was probably a slight lapse in his memory since the GPF was opened in September 1990. In any case, the commander of the U.S. Central Command highly appreciated Japan's swift transfer of its funds (Kato 2012, 40).

On April 10, 1991, the U.S. Congress legislated the Operation Desert Shield/Storm Supplemental Appropriation Act. It established the Persian Gulf Regional Defense Cooperation Fund to receive funding from other countries, including Japan, and approved 42.6 billion U.S. dollars for the expenditure of the DOD. It also approved 15 billion U.S. dollars for the Reserve Fund to provide a stopgap fund in case of delinquency of payment from abroad (Provide Comfort P.L.102–55, $320 million).[9]

The Report of the General Accounting Office (GAO), dated September 1991, outlined the expenditure at the Gulf War. It states that DOD reported in May 1991 that the total expenditure at the Gulf

---

[9] CQ Researcher. Calculating the Cost of the Gulf War. March 15, 1991. https://library.cqpress.com/cqresearcher/document.php?id=cqresrre1991031500 (Accessed on June 1, 2020); GAO Report to the Chairman, Committee on Armed Services, House of Representatives. Operation Desert Shield/Storm Costs and Funding Requirements. September 1991. GAO/NSISD-91-304. https://www.gao.gov/assets/220/215041.pdf. p. 3.

War was 47.5 billion U.S. dollars, but the auditing by the Office of Management and Budget pointed out that the prospective expenditure was excessive since it had included early orders for transportation, fuel, administration, ammunition, and equipment replacement, which turned out to be cancelled after the end of the ground battle.

It pointed out that the pledged funding from abroad reached 48.3 billion U.S. dollars; thus, 800 million U.S. dollars would be a balance remaining in the account. It is estimated that 15 billion U.S. dollars for the Reserve Fund were not needed for expenditure. It also asserted that they could not conclude a reliable figure for the total amount of expenditure during the Gulf War due to a defect in the DOD financial mechanism.[10]

In February 1990, the spokesman at the White House said that they did not find any problems with the constraints on the use of Japan's funding for nonmilitary purposes (Kunimasa 1999, 277). In summary, in Japan, from August 1990 to March 1991, debates about the decision-making process for Japan's funding seemed like reconciliation to pressure by the U.S. Japan's cooperation by providing funding for the Gulf Crisis was considered inferior in Japan. However, in consideration of the U.S. process of expenditure and budgetary decision-making from 1990 to 1991, Japan's funding was not slow but faster than others, including the U.S. Congress, and fast enough for budgetary procedures in the U.S.

Japan's decision-making took one week to consider the prospect expenditure of the U.S. Armed Force in Saudi Arabia, since the prospect and its grounds told by the U.S. officers were uncertain, and they were accused of delay and slowness.

It was naturally impossible for any U.S. officer to estimate the exact amount of expenditure at Operation Desert Storm in advance. However, Japanese decision makers accepted. It was natural that exact war cost could not be estimated in advance; however, the budgetary account system of the DOD was incomplete then, and the total amount of the expenditure was not clarified up to today, although it is estimated by certain experts that all funding from other countries had a surplus to it. Japan's funding at the time is worth restoring its reputation to some degree.

---

[10] GAO Report, pp. 5–7.

Former Japan's Ambassador Murata wrote in his memoir that the bashing of Japan by the U.S. media was based on economic envy to Japan. The bashing by the U.S. media of Japan in 1990 created pressure on the Japanese government, but the governments in the U.S., Germany, Kuwait, and Saudi Arabia appreciated Japan's funding then. In April 1991, President Bush met with Premier Kaihu and ended all of the U.S. Japan disputes over the Gulf Crisis (Murata 2008, 118–121).

The Upper House of the Japanese Parliament recorded foreign evaluations. President Bush again expressed his gratitude to Japan for its cooperation on July 11, 1991. The U.S. Secretary of Defense, Les Aspin (1993–1994), evaluated Japan's funding positively in his report to the U.S. Congress regarding the defence burden of allies. Kuwait Chief, Jabir al-Sabaha expressed his gratitude for Japan's support of Kuwait and international cooperation in his letter to premier Kaihu. GCC countries, the UK, and other countries conveyed their appreciation to Japan.[11]

Japan provided a large amount of funding to the U.S., but the GPF was the direct manager to distribute the fund, which legitimised the authority of the GCC and its member countries. GPF fund was distributed to countries in Europe, Asia, the Middle East and Africa, too, which meant it turned to be a multilateral scheme. The use of the expenditure was authorised by procedural and nominal approval of Saudi Arabia, then the nation of the Secretary General of the GCC. It was Japan's representation of respect for the sovereignty of the GCC countries. Japanese government was seen to have succumbed to the pressure of the U.S., but the highest authorities in countries comprehended the significance of Japan's funding, and established a GPF to protect the honour that Japan did not fund arms and ammunition.

4   GRATITUDE OF SAUDI ARABIA AND KUWAIT

Japan's funding contributed to countries besides the U.S. Pledges from countries towards the U.S.. costs from the beginning of the Gulf deployment from August 1990 through March 31, 1991 was $48.3 billion U.S.

---

[11] Sangiin. *Ibid.* pp. 37–38.

dollars in total. Saudi Arabia, and the government of Kuwait pledged $16 billion each, followed by Japan with $10.7 billion.[12]

Japanese government officials evaluated the state of the global economy at the time and decided that making a significant financial contribution to the Gulf Crisis would have the greatest impact. The U.S. fell into recession after eight years, and Germany had a financial burden after reunification (Kunimasa 1999, 270–271). Kuwait suffered Iraq occupation, and Saudi Arabia shouldered huge burden. Thus, Japan's funding for the coalition force also contributed to supporting the finance of world economics and other fund raisers, including Germany, the UAE, and Korea.

This section will deal with Japan's episodes with Saudi Arabia and Kuwait, two victims of the Iraq invasion, and the largest fund providers. These are the stories behind them.

4.1   Saudi Arabia's Appreciation and Diplomacy Towards Japan

Saudi Arabia expected Japan's funding immediately after the Iraqi occupation of Kuwait. Then the NHK (Japan Broadcasting Corporation)'s branch manager in the Washington D.C., Ryuichi Tejima recorded meetings of then Japan's ambassador in the U.S., Ryohei Murata and Saudi ambassador, Bandar bin Sultan Al Saud. Tejima writes that the Japanese government was excluded from the company of participating countries in the coalition force, and was subjected to a glacial look. By contrast, all diplomats wanted to see and talk with Ambassador Bandar, as he was close to President Bush, and was best informed about the inside conditions of the Gulf Crisis, since his nation was the party concerned and hosting the coalition forces.

Ambassador Bandar invited Ambassador Murata, who had sought an appointment with him for lunch one day in August 1990. They talked for more than two hours by themselves. Ambassador Bandar disclosed his analysis. The Kuwait Crisis would inevitably result in a large-scale military campaign (Tejima 1996, 52). The military campaign started in mid-January 1991. The analysis was grounded on his knowledge of weather

---

[12] CQ Researcher. Calculating the Cost of the Gulf War. March 15, 1991–Volume 1. https://library.cqpress.com/cqresearcher/document.php?id=cqresrre1991031500.

forecasts of storms, ongoing arms preparation, Ramadan month sched-
ules, waxing, waning of the moon, and tide in the Gulf (Tejima 1996, 53).
This was the most accurate forecast information for Ambassador Murata
(Tejima 1996, 54).

Why did Ambassador Bandar treat Japan with high regards? The U.S.
requested that Saudi Arabia fund the war, and he predicted that it would
be a serious financial burden for Saudi Arabia. Thus he regarded Japan as
having economic power to provide funding. Ambassador Bandar intended
to make Japan confront the bold reality that the ground battle would
break out, and drop any faint hopes (Tejima 1996, 70). The intelligence that Ambassador Bandar provided was one of the most accurate
estimations for the Japanese government.[13]

Japan provided the largest funding for coalition forces, after Kuwait
and Saudi Arabia. Saudi Arabia was more grateful for the fund than for
additional armed forces at that time, since the country had suffered a long
period of oil glut in 1980s. Japan's funding was limited in scale, but it was
directed towards having some impact on stability in the Middle East.

4.2   Kuwaiti Advertisement for Appreciation in Newspapers

Japanese citizens believed that Kuwait did not appreciate Japan's cooperation during the Gulf Crisis since it was not dispatched of forces but
only funding. The basis was that the Kuwait government did not list the
Japanese flag in the newspaper advertisements publicised in the U.S. after
the liberation of Kuwait, as it expressed its appreciation for nations that
supported Kuwait during the Iraqi occupation of Kuwait. For example,
Premier Abe stated in November 2013, "After the Gulf War, it was
shocking that Kuwaiti advertisements did not list Japan" and "unilateral
pacifism would not protect peace in Japan.[14]"

---

[13] Premier Kaihu did not mention this intelligence source in his memoir. He remembered that Ryuzo Sejima (1911–2007), former staff of the General Staff Office in Imperial
Army, advised him the on the likely start of the military campaign for the Gulf War. Kaihu
also wrote that Henry Kissinger visited Japan in summer 1990 and told him his forecast
that the U.S. would engage in a short-term military campaign against Iraq (Kaihu 2005,
315–316).

[14] Kawaru Nihon no Mamori (Chuu): Shuudanteki Jieiken ni Michi Jieitai Katsudou
Ryouoiki Hiroku. *Nikkei*. November 20, 2013.

However, on September 10, 2015, the Tokyo Shinbun Newspaper published an article about the truth of the Kuwait advertisement. Kuwaiti diplomat residing in Tokyo disclosed that the list of countries in the advertisement was not made by Kuwait government. Then, the Kuwaiti ambassador in the U.S., al-Sabaha[15] asked the U.S. DOD to provide him with a list of participatory nations of coalition forces. It did not include Japan. He ordered the newspaper advertisement, and the list was used for it.

Takashi Onda, Japan's ambassador at that time in Saudi Arabia, where the Kuwaiti government was in exile, received direct words of gratitude from the Kuwaiti chief and undersecretary of the Kuwaiti MOFA in February 1991. An anonymous former undersecretary of Japan's MOFA told Tokyo Shinbun Newspaper that some staff at Japan's Embassy in the U.S. used the Kuwaiti advertisement for political purpose without doubt. They had been blasted by the U.S. Congress members, and insisted funding was not sufficient as they had claimed. The director general at the bureau of the Middle East and Asia at MOFA, Japan, Mitsuru Watanabe, indicated the probability that the advocators of the normal nation perspective used the story of Kuwaiti advertisements to prove their claim against pacifists that Japan should dispatch JSDF abroad.

Japan's ambassador to Kuwait, Tsuyoshi Kurokawa, then asked the Kuwaiti MOFA immediately after the publication of the advertisement. They answered that the Kuwaiti Embassy in the U.S. did not check the list well before publicising it. It was not done by the direction of the home government. Kuwaiti memorial stamp sheet issued after the Gulf War listed Japan's flag, and the Kuwaiti War museum exhibits a special panel to show the amount of Japan's funding of "13 billion U.S. dollars".

One can conclude that the Kuwaiti advertisement incident was politically used by Japanese politicians and intellectuals who were holders of the normal nation perspective, although the Japanese government collected sufficient proof to confirm that the Kuwaiti government appreciated Japan for the funding. The politicians who insisted on the Kuwaiti omission of appreciation for Japan in Japan's parliament were listed in the Tokyo Shinbun Newspaper. They were foreign minister Michio Watanabe (1991–1993), premiers Keizo Obuchi (July 1998–April 2000), Junishiro Koizumi, Taro Aso (September 2008–September 2009), Shinzo Abe,

---

[15] Tokyo Shinbun newspaper did not exactly list the full name. Kuwaiti ambassador in the U.S. was Saud al-Sabaha at the time.

and defence minister Shigeru Ishiba (September 2007–August 2008). They are politicians of a normal nation perspective. It is a good political option for Japan to participate in international security cooperation by dispatching the JSDF, but they should not put false blame on Japan's reputation and Kuwaiti's sincere appreciation of Japan during the Gulf Crisis.

5   Relief of Hostages Through Peace Festival Held in Baghdad

Hostages in Kuwait during Iraq's occupation were officially treated as "guests" by the Iraqi government. The last thousand were released in December 1990. Despite their presence, the coalition declared war on Iraq on January 17, 1991. How were captives who had been imprisoned in Kuwait and transported to Iraq suddenly released?

The incident involving a Japanese wrestler hosting a peace festival in Baghdad was not well publicised. On December 1 and 2, 1990, 43 Japanese prisoner women were permitted to visit Baghdad to see art performances by musicians from the U.S states, Europe, and Asia, as well as sports activities conducted during the peace festival, with their husbands captured in Iraq. Following its conclusion, Hussein ordered the Iraqi National Assembly to debate and decide on the release of captives. Given this, it is an episode in Japanese diplomacy and engagement which deserves greater attention and scrutiny.

Antonio Inoki (1943–2022. Parliament member 1989–1995, 2013–2019), whose actual name is Kanji Inoki, has been a professional wrestler since 1964. In June 1976, he fought Muhammad Ali, a Muslim, in a bout in Las Vegas with the match being declared a draw. In December 1976, he faced Akram Pahalwan, Pakistan's wrestling star, and won. Two bouts established him as a world-renowned wrestler, particularly in the Muslim World. From 1972 until 1989, he served as president of the Shin Japan Professional Wrestling Company. In June 1989, he founded the Sports Peace Party, campaigned for and won a seat in Japan's Upper House of Parliament. He stated his belief that athletics might help bring peace to the globe. Sports Peace Party was a political party that operated independently of major political parties. Despite his notoriety, he played an important role in aiding Japanese foreign policy. As former secretary general of the Sports Peace Party, Hisashi Shinma, who was also a financial manager of Shin Japan Professional Wrestling Company, revealed Inoki was notorious for his financial mismanagement and had ran for parliament after his business went bankrupt and possessed a number of character flaws (Shinma 2002, 96, 133–140, 176, 179). Masaru Sato, a writer and former diplomat, recounts Inoki's diplomacy in Russia and praised his ability to create a deep network inside the Russian government for the Ministry of Foreign Affairs of Japan (Sato 2014). But he does not mention to Inoki's initiative in Iraq. Both Shinwa and Sato's descriptions fell short of conveying the whole story of Inoki's peculiarity, and this section seeks to explain it.

On August 14, 1990, around two weeks after the Iraqi invasion, foreign residents in Iraq were prohibited to leave Iraq thereafter, and foreign residents in Kuwait were ordered to move into Iraq. This included Japanese residents. On the other hand, the Japanese Embassy in Kuwait received 15 American citizens and embassy staff and provided them with protection in the Embassy of Japan, which was safer than the U.S. Embassy. It seemed that since the U.S. Embassy in the world was frequently targeted at foreign attacks, its staff tried to diffuse their location of stay to other embassies.

The U.S. government appreciated the Japanese government's protection of the U.S. citizens (Katakura 2005, 67–68). On August 18, 1990, Iraq declared using hostages (called *guests* by the Iraqi government) as a human shield, but the U.S. government did not have an information source to confirm where they were stationed (Schwarzkof 1992, 326). Japanese network provided it to the U.S. government. Japanese hostages stationed separately in various facilities in Iraq were allowed to write letters and receive materials, including food. Thus, Japan's ambassador in Iraq, Kunio Katakura,[16] formed loose network that brought such information to the Japanese Embassy (Katakura 2005, 96–122).

Jesse L. Jackson, a Baptist minister, and political activist in the U.S., visited Kuwait and Iraq on an individual basis and advocated that the UN and the Arab League do more to solve the Gulf Crisis. He also requested the release of foreign hostages. On August 28, 1990, the Iraqi government announced freeing women, children, and sick and aged men hostages. Approximately 700 people from various nations were allowed

---

[16] Premier Kaihu calls him *a considerable Samurai* (Kaihu 2005, 288).

to go home.[17] Around 70 Japanese were freed and allowed to exit Iraq to go back home.[18]

After the Iraq invasion, Mr. Inoki states in his memoir that he began thinking about Iraq's situation through his own investigation. He met with an Iraqi ambassador in Tokyo. He then visited Peking and met separately with the Chinese vice prime minister and Iraqi ambassador in China. He was convinced that Iraq did not want a military solution to the Gulf Crisis. He wrote that he was determined to engage in peace for the Iraqi people and the release of foreign hostages. Inoki visited Iraq three times in September, October, and December 1990 (Inoki 1990, 27–35).

His visit was the first among Japanese diplomats, politicians, and parliament member. He has become a famous wrestler in Iraq due to his match with Muhammad Ali. During his first visit to Baghdad, he met with Udai, the son of Hussein, Chief of Sports Committee in Iraq (1984–2003), and proposed holding an international peace festival in Baghdad. Udai immediately agreed to it. Back in Tokyo, he received approval from Hussein, the Iraqi president, on October 9, via the Iraqi Embassy in Tokyo. At his second visit to Baghdad (October 24–29, 1990), the date of the peace festival was decided as December 2 and 3, 1990. Sports players, musicians, and artists from Japan, the U.S., and Europe agreed to participate in it.

The Japanese government expressed its stance during the Gulf Crisis that it should not deal with criminals in hostage cases, since it had made concessions to hijackers in the past, which became the focus of international criticism. The Japanese government regarded this principle "no deal with criminals in hostage cases" as international cooperation during the Gulf Crisis (Katakura 2005, 76). Premier Kaihu took a firm stance towards the Japanese in Iraq: "Do not be fooled by sweet talk (by Iraqis). That's for the nation (Japan). One should speak to Iraq 'Withdraw your troops (from Kuwait)' with a resolute attitude (Kaihu 2005, 321: parenthesis are supplemented by this author)". It is not certain if the Japanese

---

[17] Freed Hostages Relieved, Angry After Ordeal. Liz Sly, Chicago Tribune. September 3, 1990. The U.S. Embassy in Kuwait was made electricity and water stopped their supply after August 25, 1990. The food was not supplied, and it confronted with dangerous situation. In Iraq, men and women were separated, and then men were forcibly sent to infrastructure facilities to stay there as hostages.

[18] Confrontation in the Gulf; As 700 Hostages Fly to Freedom, There Is Relief but Little Rejoicing. *New York Times*. Elaine Sciolino, September 3, 1990 (Katakura 2005, 75).

government felt a sense of inferiority to the U.S., which made it refrain from dispatching Japanese diplomats and politicians to Iraq, and taking principle "no deal with criminals in hostage cases".

A Japanese businessman, Ryuzou Ikeda, held as a hostage at the Gulf Crisis recollects a testimony by a veteran businessman resided in Baghdad who supported Japanese government activities. He gave logistical supports for Japanese government to dispatch politicians to Baghdad to meet president Hussein and liberate Japanese hostages. Nakasone was the first among them. Then Inoki visited Baghdad without any arrangements with Japanese government, and liberated all hostages, which disrupted all secret arrangements by the Japanese government. The MOFA planned to give such politicians "rewards" of fame to liberate hostages, but they got angry and ceased to visit there. Takako Doi, then the leader of the Socialist Party, was among them (Ikeda 2017, 187–190).

Women played an important role in resolving the hostage crisis in Iraq. The wives who were freed from the Iraqi government on August 28, 1990, reformed the *Association of Ayame (iris)*, a Japanese women's association in Iraq. Its members came back to Japan, and began new activities as victims of hostage cases in Iraq at home. These members were the wives of Japanese hostages. They began new activities to rescue their husbands. They sent a letter to Iraq president Hussein. They met with premier Kaihu and former premier Nakasone to entreat them. A parliament member Toshiko Yamaguchi agreed with them to visit Iraq on behalf of the *Association of Ayame* but was stopped by MOFA. Japanese hostages, their family, and Japanese residents who were not allowed to leave Iraq thought that the Japanese government lost the flexibility to negotiate with the Iraqi government due to diplomacy subordination to the U.S., and considered the possibility that the hostages would not be freed.

Dozens of wives in the Association of *Ayame* visited Inoki's office at Upper House of the Parliament on October 11, 1990. Inoki proposed them to visit Iraq together and take their husbands back. All of them answered that they wanted to visit there, and see their husbands even once again, although they might not get them freed, and shed tears.

In late October 1990, Iraq released hostages of some hostile nations. On October 22, Iraq released French hostages, followed by Bulgaria, Italy, Switzerland. The Western media called it the *bargain sale of hostages*. Former UK Prime Minister Edward Heath (1970–1974), who visited Baghdad for talks with the Iraqi president, was credited with securing the release of the hostages on October 23. But it was not clear when British hostages would be released exactly.[19] Probably it was because the UK premier, Margaret Thatcher was a hard liner against Iraq. Former West German Chancellor Willy Brandt visited to meet President Hussein in Baghdad, and returned with 174 Westerners on November 8.[20] The last hostages that remained captured were those from the U.S., the UK, and Japan.

Former premier Nakasone announced his visit to Iraq on October 26, and arrived in Baghdad by JAL special plane on November 5. He saw President Hussein, and 74 Japanese hostages were released and returned home with him (Katakura 2005, 110). Nakasome and Inoki did not consult with each other. Japanese government commented that Nakasone's action had nothing to do with them, but they provided a special government flight for him. Of course, the Japanese government and Nakasone worked together. However, it is not clear if Inoki received tacit supports from the Japanese government in Tokyo. At least, it is certain that, Ambassador Katakura welcomed Inoki in Baghdad, and handed him a list of sick and aged Japanese hostages at his first visit. Neverthless, after the end of the Gulf War, Ambassador Katakura remains silent on his support for Inoki in his publication. This can be because it would be a scandal if Japanese government had cooperation with Inoki who was later revealed to have had relations with some right-wing groups.

The legendary boxer Muhammad Ali arrived in Iraq, met with President Hussein on November 28, and succeeded in releasing 15 U.S. hostages.[21] Shinma writes that Inoki asked Muhammad Ali to convey his request of meeting to Saddam Hussein (Shinma 2002, 144). Turkish President Turgut Ozal (1927–1993. President 1989–1993) provided Turkish aeroplane for Inoki and his accompanies of 46 family member of hostages. They arrived in Baghdad on December 1.

---

[19] Heath Gains Accord on the Release of Some British Hostages. *Christian Science Monitor*. October 23, 1990. https://www.csmonitor.com>oe.

[20] Brandt Arrives in Frankfurt with 174 U.S., Other Foreign Hostages With AM-Gulf Rdp. *AP*. November 10, 1990. https://apnews.com/article/f8b42c368967189a95 6a952a9cf1402d.

[21] How Muhammad Ali secured the release of 15 U.S. hostages in Iraq. New York Post. Maureen Callahan. November 29, 2015. https://nypost.com/2015/11/29/the-tale-of-muhammad-alis-goodwill-trip-to-iraq-that-freed-us-hostages/.

The next day, a welcome ceremony was held at the Conference Palace in Baghdad, and the speaker of Iraq National Assembly Saadi Mehdi Saleh (1990–1996) made opening address. The peace festival[22] began with a rock concert (Inoki 1990, 187). Hostages were brought to see their families of the *Ayame Association* prior to the beginning of the peace festival, and stayed together to its end. At the first day of the peace festival, soccer matches were played et al.-Shaab stadium with 35,000 of audience. At the National Theatre, with an overflowed audience, musicians from Japan, the U.S., and France performed concerts. On the next day, December 3, the Karate tournament was held from the morning, and the finale was a wrestling match from six o'clock in the evening. Inoki could not fight, owing to an injury in his feet.

At eight o'clock on that day, Inoki saw Udai, the chairman of the sports committee in Iraq, and reported the success of the festival. Mr. Nozaki, branch manager of Itochu Co. Ltd. in Iraq, a veteran among the Japanese there, almost preached to Udai (Kadota 2015, 273–274). Then Udai told Inoki to write a request to President Hussein, which he did. On the following day, at 11 in the morning, their return flight to Japan was reserved, but hostages were not released yet. Thus, wives did not take their flight, thinking they would not go home until hostages were released. Mr. Nozaki persuaded Inoki not to leave Iraq since the high official at Ministry of Information had some signs of concession, and Inoki did not neither. On December 5, in the evening, Udai appeared to see wives, and told them 36 hostages would be released. At eight-thirty in the evening, hostages were transferred to the office of the Olympic committee, and saw their wives again. All those who were present shook

---

22 This author could confirm only the following sports players and artists who performed at peace festival in Baghdad.

A basketball team composed of professional and amateur players in the U.S.
  Professional wrestlers: Bad New Allen, Shinya Hashimoto, Riki Tyoushuu, Masa Saitou.
  Musicians: Jonny Ookura and Please, Panic in the Zoo, 25 musicians from Suwa Daiko, Kawauchike Kikusuimaru, Christine who was a U.S. country musician.
  Artist: Three craftsmen to make Japanese kite Rendako.

hands with Udai (Kadota 2015, 275–278). Udai stated words of apology. He said Iraq took the hostages to avoid war.[23]

Inoki and Mr. Nozaki then negotiated for the rest of the 78 Japanese hostages and other Japanese residents staying in Iraq. Hussein proposed holding an Iraq Revolutionary Council meeting to discuss the release of hostages, which began in the morning on December 7. Inoki and 10 more Japanese participated it in the front seats to listen. The debates were heated over the treatment of hostages from the UK and the U.S., but the votes approved the release of all foreign hostages as probably ordered by Hussein. Inoki was invited to the stage, and greeted, saying, "I welcome this decision. I would work hard for peaceful solutions to the Gulf Crisis". He received a large applaud.[24] On December 7, all foreign hostages, including the Japanese, began their return back home. Were the final foreign captives freed as a result of Inoki's efforts? This remains uncertain. Iraq had declared at the end of November 1990 that it would free all captives gradually during the Christmas and subsequent three months.

The letter of President Hussein addressed to the speaker of the National Assembly Saleh was reported in a Japanese newspaper, and the reasons for releasing hostages were mentioned as below. "Pleas of brothers, decision of the Democratic Party,[25] invitation by the European Parliament to Iraq, those positive changes will have significant influence over public opinion in the West to deter evil attempts by war provokers".[26] *Pleas of brothers* was one of the three reasons behind Hussein's decision, and Inoki was a Muslim who converted to Islam during his first visit to Iraq in September 1990. His conversion ceremony was treated splendidly in Karbala as that of a king (Inoki 1990, 88).

The discarded bill of Japan's international cooperation law to legislate the dispatch of JSDF abroad on November 8 was probably tail wind for Inoki. Iraq was afraid of the participation of Japanese soldiers in the coalition forces. The Arabs remember Japan's history as having won the Japan–Russian War and Japan's military campaign in the Pacific War (Kadota 2015, 218). The discarded bill heightened Inoki's persuasiveness

---

[23] Tokubetsuki haken wo kentou. *Asahi News.* December 6, 1990. Evening. p. 1.

[24] Iraku Hitojichi Kaihou no Shingi, Inoki Giin ra Mimamoru. *Asahi Newspaper.* December 8, 1990.

[25] The U.S. Congress majority then at both Houses.

[26] Hitojichi Zeninn Kaihou wo Yousei no Husein Shokan (Youshi). *Asahi Newspaper.* December 7, 1990.

as Japan's parliament member to devote himself to a peaceful solution to the Gulf Crisis. Iraq ended the reinforcement of occupying its troop in Kuwait in November 1990, with which, in case of a ground battle break, Iraq would not be defeated, and hostages turned to be a card for deterrence of war to promote changes in the Western countries towards peaceful solutions.

The resignation of Margaret Thatcher from the UK premiership (1979–1991) on November 29, and Nakasone's visit in November, were also probably a chance to make Hussein conceive that hardliners were losing ground in the West. Nakasone told Hussein that he would persuade the U.S. President Bush, and on November 30, he proposed a plan to negotiate with Iraq. President Bush would meet Tariq al-Aziz, Iraq foreign minister (1983–1991), and could dispatch Secretary of State James Baker (1989–1992) to meet the Iraq president, Hussein.

However, Hussein knew that President Bush was a hawk and had no intention of conceding to him (Salinger 1991, 207). Hussein expected that the Democratic Party would stop the U.S. president. The peace festival was held at this time of heightened expectation of a peaceful solution. Its success made Iraqi politicians expect that appeals at Baghdad for peace would reach the world. Inoki was not a high-ranking governmental officer, and could not meet Hussein in face, but provided Iraq excuse (peace festival) to liberate hostages. Thus Inoki's initiative and success was probably indispensable as checkmate for hostage release. All hostages went home by Christmas in 1990. But the war between Iraq and the coalition forces was not prevented and broke out on January 17, 1991.

According to Shinma, Inoki appealed to Iraqis by claiming to have a large sponsor for a private business through which he might import Iraqi oil to Japan (Shinma 2002, 147). It's difficult to verify the truth of this presentation, which is devoid of specifics yet may be accurate. Another tale revealed by Inoki's former secretary was that Inoki agreed to deliver 100 old trucks to a Russian General in exchange for a concession in Russia, but did not fulfil the pledge and was thrown out of the Kremlin (Sato 1993).

At the very least, one can attest to his fascinating character. During his visits in Baghdad, Inoki exchanged pleasantries with Iraqis on the streets. He was unaffiliated with existing political parties and acted as a pacifist. He was unconcerned about being taken prisoner by Iraq and voiced his admiration for Iraqi, Islamic, and Iraqi political leaders as potential discussion partners. He said that his objective was to ensure the Iraqi people's

peace. His admirers enabled his many encounters with high-ranking officials, including meeting with Udai, sending letters to President Hussein,
and delivering addresses to the Iraq Revolutionary Council. He oversaw
the international peace festival in Iraq when the country was sanctioned
and offered heartfelt encouragement to the captives' families. He got
support from Japanese private sector employees in Iraq and their families,
journalists, his worldwide network, athletes, artists, singers, Iraqi politicians, authorities, and friendship organisations, as well as the Turkish
government and business sector. He was also a member of parliament,
yet his behaviour resembled that of a citizen diplomat at the time.

Despite this notoriety and impact on Japan's engagement with Iraq,
Inoki was charged with tax evasion, violation of the Political Funds
Control Act, and close relations with right-wing organisations, among
other charges. He resigned as party head in June 1993 and by 1994, the
Sports Peace Party splintered. Inoki had another triumph in April 1995,
when he organised the Pyongyang Peace Festival. All of the party's candi-
dates, including Inoki, lost in the July 1995 Upper House election. In
1998, the party was declared illegal as a political party and was eventually
disbanded in 2006.

6   Intelligence Gathering
to Confirm Iran's Intention

Japan's cooperation with intelligence gathering during the Gulf War was
revealed by journalist Ryuichi Tejima (1996), but it was not known in
the world. Japan offered precise intelligence over Iran's intentions during
the Gulf War, which stabilised relations between Iran and the coalition
forces. It helped the coalition forces concentrate on the military campaign
to liberate Kuwait.

The Embassy of Japan received surprising intelligence that, on January
16, 1991, more than 40 first-class fighter jets affiliated with the Iraq air
force entered Iran and landed in airports. They were Mig 29, Mig 23,
Mig 21, Suhoi 21, Mirage 2000F-1, etc. The timing was one day before
the break of the air combat phase. The Embassy confirmed the fact that
by January 20—more than 100 Iraqi aircraft entered Iran.

This incident was not reported in the media at the beginning, and
the Embassy did not know the intentions of both the Iraqi government
and the Iranian government if they had a secret deal to cooperate with
any military operations against the coalition forces fighting in Kuwait and

the Gulf against the Iraqi forces. Japanese government then found that the U.S. government did not obtain any information about this mysterious flight of Iraq air crafts. It was known then that the vice chairman of the Iraqi Revolutionary Council had visited Teheran on January 8, 1990. Iranian aircrafts scrambled around the entering Iraqi aircrafts but did not shoot them down, and they landed on some airports in Iran, which added another mysterious impression.

The White House requested more information about them from the Japanese government. What is their intention and next operation? If those Iraq first-class fighter jets made a surprise attack on the coalition forces from the Iranian direction while it was busy attacking Iraq troops in Kuwait front, the coalition forces would face severe damage.

The Japanese ambassador in Tehran enquired from a good number of government officials in Iran, who replied, guaranteeing that the Iranian government had no plan to attack the coalition force with the Iraqi aircrafts. On January 26, the Iran News Agency reported the entrance and stationing of the Iraqi air fighters to Iran, but the U.S. Secretary of the State, James Baker, told the U.S. media that they had evidence that the Iraqi fighters would maintain neutrality and would not attack the coalition forces. He did not disclose the intelligence source, but Tejima guessed it was the Japanese Embassy in Tehran (Tejima 1996, 193–225).

The Iraqi regime's real motivation for sending planes to Iran remains unclear. Saudi Arabia and Iran eased their hostility and restored diplomatic relations after Iraq's invasion of Kuwait. Japan has maintained cordial ties with Iran, and the Japanese Ministry of Foreign Affairs has nurtured diplomats who are 'Persian language experts.' Japanese diplomats were able to gather information and analyse the result of the mystery Iraqi fighters' movement, which aided coalition forces commanders, whereas the US lacked diplomatic connections with Iran and therefore could not conduct intelligence operations there. Japan's intelligence services aided the Iranian regime in communicating its objectives to the U.S. through Japan. Nevertheless, while critics of Japan during the Gulf Conflict benefited from diplomatic secrecy to hide this incident, senior US government officials and commanders recognised Japan's critical contribution in information collection throughout the war.

7   MINESWEEPING IN THE GULF

Premier Kaihu dispatched the JMSDF to the Gulf for a minesweeping mission after the end of the ground battle during the Gulf War. It was interpreted constitutional. The premier thought the JSDF should go since private companies were working to pump out oil flown in the sea with oil recovery vessels (Kaihu 2005, 328). He made diplomatic decision to delay elucidation of the dispatch to Southeast countries after the departure of the mission, since departure had to be hurried up due to the weather in the Arabia (Kaihu 2005, 344).

Japanese Premier Kaihu at the time of the Gulf War had the experience of propelling legislation for the establishment of Japan Overseas Cooperation Volunteers in 1965. He thought that Japan had to take Africa into consideration, not only Asia. It was thus a quirk of fate that he was deeply involved in the Gulf Crisis during his premiership. He explained to members of the Japanese parliament at a budgetary committee meeting that since the establishment of the Overseas Cooperation Volunteers until the start of the Gulf War in 1990, 50 of the volunteers had passed away from various causes, even though it did not comprise a military force. He insisted that Japan did not support the solution of international conflicts through the use of arms, but it had "sweated and bled" for international causes.

On April 12, 1991, after the end of ground and air campaign to liberate Kuwait from Iraq, Premier Kaihu decided to dispatch a marine-sweep mission to the Gulf. On April 24, the Japanese cabinet meeting approved the mission in accordance with article 99 of the Self-Defense Forces Act. Its six ships, with 511 crew members, comprised the largest minesweeping mission among the coalition forces. They arrived in the UAE on May 27 and started their mission on June 5 with the other coalition forces from eight nations: Britain, the U.S., France, Belgium, Italy, Holland, Germany, and Saudi Arabia.

At the time, the minesweeping technique and equipment of JMSDF were skilled enough to conduct a mission at sea close to Japan, but they had not caught up with the latest information about new types of marine mines invented by the Iraqi navy (Kazushige, 2014). However, the US, Dutch, and German navies provided precious information on the location of mines and how to handle the latest and most dangerous model. This was Japan's first experience conducting a mission with coalition forces.

The U.S. troop was the only one that could function in a "common infrastructure" to operate logistics, intelligence gathering, and the management of task forces for the coalition.

However, in June, all European forces withdrew from the mission, owing to their interpretation of the UN security resolution. Moreover, the U.S. could not enter the sea area that Iran claimed as its territory. Thus, JMSDF had to sweep approximately 400 mines, remaining in the most dangerous sea zone alone. As a result, they cleared the largest number of mines in the Gulf during the mission, which was completed on September 11. The JMSDF commander was pleased to find that a local shop started to sell T-shirts painted with the Japanese national flag as a sign of the people welcoming their mission (Yoshida 2011, 5–20; Ochiai 2001). As lessons were learned during this mission, the JMSDF improved its technology to clear marine mines. Its capability is currently of the highest standard in the world.

Shuzo Kimura suggested that Japan began to aim at "diplomacy to attract attention to its performance (Kimura 2009, 31–32)", but the reality was that the JSDF did not make use of their experience in the Gulf War for international public diplomacy. Shun Ochiai, the JMSDF mission commander for minesweeping in the Gulf, noted that he instructed the crew by saying, "Pride is something to be put inside your heart (Ochiai 2001)". British security experts have highly evaluated minesweeping by the JMSDF (Orita 2013, 145).

8   Conclusion

It would be a simplistic debate to evaluate Japan's Middle East foreign policy with only a "reactive state" perception. Japan made unique contribution to the solution of the Gulf Crisis, but many stories were confidential and not translated to the World which enhanced the impression of Japan's quiet diplomacy.

This chapter crossed the barriers made by a split into five factions of Japan's foreign policy perspective, and collected sources for the unknown aspects of Japan's foreign policy. Kuwait advertisements are still widely conceived by the Japanese as the Kuwait government's intentional omission of appreciation of Japan. Japan's diplomacy was quiet due to Japan's weak ability to make Japan understood in the world. Intelligence gatherings in Iran, Inoki's initiative for peace festival, the release of foreign hostages, and the outcome of minesweeping are probably not well known.

Japan's funding at the Gulf Crisis was bashed by the U.S. media, but its funding to the coalition forces was disbursed fastest among nations, including the U.S. Congress; it was quick enough for the U.S. budgetary process, and was evaluated as indispensable by a U.S. commander and the White House. Funding was disbursed to countries in the West, the Middle East, Africa, and Asia, and contributed to the legitimacy of the GCC and the budget of Saudi Arabia. It may be added that Japan learned the lesson that dispatching JSDF is cheaper than disbursing funds during international crises.

Japan made the most of its diplomatic relations and channel with Iran, and succeeded in collecting intelligence over mysterious cutting-edge Iraqi aircrafts. Only Japan could clean marine mines in the Gulf in difficult political environments after the Gulf War. Japan did not have to beget tensions in the Gulf, which meant that it had contributed to maintaining stability in the Gulf. Japan did not participate in military operations during the Gulf Crisis and the Gulf War, and the JSDF expanded its operations to the maximum in the minesweeping at the time within Japan's constitutional interpretation.

Foreign hostages were released by governments through the actions of the governments and citizens of the world. Antonio Inoki contributed to the release of the last hostages by holding an international peace festival in Baghdad. As a result, the Japanese government and Inoki seemed to divide their roles and cooperated in the release of hostages, but Inoki's efforts were disturbed by it. He did not receive supports from established political parties in Japan. Inoki had dialogues with Iraqi government officials and citizens about the peace of Iraq partly due to his pacifist-oriented stance to understand the cultures and political position of Iraq.

References

Bennett, Andrew, Joseph Lepgold, and Danny Unger. 1994. Burden-Sharing in the Persian Gulf War. *International Organization* 48 (1): 39–75.

Gomi, Toshiki. 1992. American Public Opinion during the Persian Gulf Conflict and Its Image of Japan. *Journal of American and Canadian Studies* 8: 33–52.

Ikeda, Ryuzou, 2017. *Daitouryou no Kyakujin: Ningenn no Tate to Sarete.* Tokyo: Shinchousha.

Inoki, Antonio. 1990. *Tatta Hitori no Tousou.* Tokyo: Shuueisha.

Inoki, Antonio. 2014. *Toukon Gaikou: Naze Ta no Seijika ga Sakeru Kuniguni ni Tobikomunoka?* Tokyo: President Inc.

Kadota, Takamasa. 2015. *Nihon, Haruka Nari: Erutuururu no Kiseki to Houjin Kyushutsu no Meisou.* Tokyo: PHP Kenkyuujo.

Kaihu, Toshiki. 2005. *Kaihu Toshiki Oraru Hisutorii.* Part 2. National Graduate Institute for Policy Studies (GRIPS).

Katakura, Kunio. 2005. *Arabisuto Gaikoukan no Chuuto Kaisouroku: Wangan Kiki kara Iraku Sensou made.* Tokyo: Akashi.

Kato, Hiroaki. 2012. Nationalism and Jieitai: 1987, 91 nen no Soukaitei Haken Mondai wo Chuushinni. *Kokusaiseiji* 170, 30–45.

Kazushige, Humiya. 2014. Jitsuryoku Sekai Ichi ni Kaeri Zaita Kaijou Jieitai. *Gunji Kenkyuu* 49 (1): 106–117.

Kimura, Shuzo. 2009. Nihon no Chuto Seisaku. In *Nihon Gaikou to Koku-saikakei,* ed. Kanazawa Kyougyou, vol. 13, no. 38. Daigaku Kokusaigaku Kenkyuujo.

Kunimasa, Takeshige. 1999. *Wangan Sensou to Iu Tenkai Ten: Douten Suru Nihon Seiji.* Tokyo: Iwanami Shoten Publisher.

Kuriyama, Shoichi. 1997. *Nichibei Doumei: Hyouryuu kara no Dakkyaku.* Tokyo: Nikkei Inc.

Murata, Ryohei. 2008. *Murata Ryohei Kaiso Roku: Sokoku no Saisei wo Jisedai ni Takushite Ge.* Kyoto: Minerva Bookstore.

Ochiai, Taosa. 2001. *Operation Gulf Dawn (Wangan no Yoake Sakusen). Self-Defence Force.* Ministry of Defence. https://www.mod.go.jp/msdf/mf/001.pdf.

Orita, Masaki. 2013. *Wangan Sensou, Hutenma Kichi, Iraku Sensou.* Hattori Ryuji and Shiratori Jun'nichiro eds. Tokyo: Iwanami Shoten Publisher.

Salinger, Pierre. 1991. *Wangan Sensou: Kakusareta Shinjitsu,* trans. Tamio Akiyama. Tokyo: Kyodotsushinsha (Salinger, Pierre. 1991. Guerre du Golfe. le dossier secret. O. Orban).

Sato, Kumiko. 1993. *Giin Hisho Sutemi no Kokuhaku: Nagata Cho no Abunai Joshiki.* Tokyo: Kodansha.

Sato, Masaru. 2014. Antonio Inoki Gaiko nit suite. In (Inoki 2014), 188–191.

Schwarzkof, H. Norman. 1992. *It Doesn't Take a Hero.* NY. Inda Grey Bantam Books.

Shinma, Hisashi. 2002. *Antonio Inoki no Hukumaden.* Tokyo: Tokumashobou.

Tejima, Ryuich. 1996. *1991 Nen Nihon no Haiboku.* Tokyo: Shinchosha.

Yoshida, Masaki. 2011. Kaijo Jieitai niyoru Kokusaikatsudou no Jissen to Kyokun: Perushawan ni okeru Soukai Katsudou to Indoyou ni okeru Hokyu Katsudou wo Chushin ni. *Kokusaianzenhoshou* 38 (4): 5–20.

CHAPTER 13

Empirical and Conceptual Conclusions on Japan's Interdependence with the Middle East

Satoru Nakamura and Steven Wright

1 ESTABLISHMENT OF COMPLEX INTERDEPENDENCE

Japan's relations with nations in the Middle East, such as Egypt, Iran, and Turkey, have a long history and date back to the nineteenth century. The first formal diplomatic relations were established via an exchange of imperial envoys with the Ottoman Empire, followed by the recognition of Egyptian independence in 1922 and the establishment of Japan's embassy in Tehran.

S. Nakamura (✉)
Graduate School of Intercultural Studies, Kobe University, Kobe, Japan
e-mail: satnaka@kobe-u.ac.jp

S. Wright
College of Humanities and Social Sciences, Hamad Bin Khalifa University, Ar-Rayyan, Qatar
e-mail: stwright@hbku.edu.qa

353
S. Nakamura and S. Wright (eds.), *Japan and the Middle East*, Contemporary Gulf Studies, https://doi.org/10.1007/978-981-19-3459-9_13

Japan reestablished diplomatic relations with Middle Eastern nations after WWII, seeing Egypt and Turkey as vital crossroads for trade. Japan was able to acquire an oil concession in Saudi Arabia and Kuwait, and was also able to become involved in the energy sector in the United Arab Emirates prior to its independence. Nonetheless, it was only after the first oil shock in 1973 that Japan recognised the critical need of ongoing engagement with Middle Eastern countries in the face of persistent regional tensions. While the relationship was to gradually grow and interdependence deepened further, we can also observe that after the 2000s, Japan's engagement and interdependence with Israel grew significantly, which echoed the trend that has been observed across the region.

Japan's involvement with the Middle East in the 1970s increased interdependence on a range of issues beyond energy commerce with Gulf nations. The relationships grew via a variety of government agencies, the business sector, as well through royal linkages. After the 1970s, the Japanese government established embassies in all Middle Eastern nations, and a Representative office in Palestine. It is worth noting that the private sector periodically served as an informal conduit for official diplomacy: for example, the Abu Dhabi government regarded the Abu Dhabi Oil Company (ADOC) as Japan's representation until the creation of the Japanese Embassy. This is an important observation in that while conventional assessments would normally focus on political relations, the role of the business sector in addition to that of royal linkages have served to reinforce and enable the relationship to grow.

Although this book was unable to cover all of Japan's international non-governmental organisations' operations in the Middle East, Japanese volunteers to disaster areas such as during earthquakes in Turkey have proven to be important. While such examples vary by context and country, they nevertheless represent an example of how linkages deepen at a social base which serves to strengthen the overall interdependence. Civil society organisations have also added to this, and the Japanese Institute of Anatolian Archaeology is a good example where the imperial family took initiatives to strengthen linkages in partnership with the government sector and society.

Multinational corporations have also been shown in this volume to have been important in promoting transnational connections, largely through their activities in increasing cultural activities. They supported seminars, publications, events, and friendship associations played an important role in fostering cultural awareness. Multinational corporations also created non-profit organisations (NPOs) with the purpose of transferring technology, such as the Japan Cooperation Center for Petroleum (JCCP) and the Saudi Electronics and Home Appliances Institute (SEHAI). All these forms of linkages constitute layers in what is a multifaceted relationship and serve the broader purpose of deepening the relationship towards greater interdependence between Japan and countries within the Middle East.

Japan has virtually no oil and gas reserves, but was able to accumulate a 180-day supply of oil and created a comprehensive and balanced energy strategy known as 3E+S (Energy, Security, Environment, and Safety). It allowed Japan to overcome a great deal of sensitivity to price fluctuations. The reforms enacted towards energy saving were done in a largely successful manner as it was able to withstand the 1990s price increase in crude oil. Japan has progressively increased its reliance on Middle Eastern oil imports, and Japanese companies have been involved in the development of the oil and Liquefied Natural Gas (LNG) energy sector, particularly in the UAE and Qatar.

Although China has since surpassed Japan as the Middle East's biggest energy importer, Japan's has remained an important market for Middle Eastern supply countries. Following the 2010s, Japan suffered from high LNG prices but was insulated from fluctuations due to long-term contracts. Japan now faces the challenge of the next energy-era and costs related to a shift to renewable energy. While Japan's reliance on Middle Eastern energy sources is not expected to significantly decline, the changing energy mix will naturally have an impact over the coming decades as progress is made towards a carbon–neutral future which will lessen the volume of its conventional trade in this area. Opportunities exist however in cleaner energy. It can be expected that this will constitute an increasingly important area of Japan's trade with the Middle East as part of the energy transition.

2   THE FORMATION OF BILATERAL INTERDEPENDENCE

Certain political, economic, and regional security issues have been shown to influence the nature and extent of Japan's connection with the Middle East. A nation that is engaged in an armed conflict, whether civil war or inter-state warfare, has had a bearing on Japan's diplomatic relationship. Concerns over stability have been shown to be a dampening effect on political and economic relations. From an economic perspective, the key observation here is that Japan's commercial entities have broadly shown a reluctance to engage in commercial contracts without stable security and diplomatic relations existing as this impacts on legal enforcement of contracts.

In the context of international economic sanctions, there is a broad unwillingness by Japanese companies to engage in trade and this has an impact on other contacts with Japan which counteracts the trend towards interdependence. As the Japanese government selects which developing countries get Official Development Assistance (ODA) based on a variety of factors, including income level, economic structure, diplomatic access, and national and human security conditions, it is the issue of security which has proven to be the greatest obstacle for the deepening of the bilateral relations and growth of multifaceted relations towards interdependence.

The level of Japan's bilateral interdependence with Middle Eastern countries may be deduced from the findings of this book's case studies, as well as from the thematic issues that have been discussed. What is important here is that there are nuances and differential reasons for each country's respective relations with Japan, have underlined the importance of not essentialising the relationship. For example, Turkey and Egypt are viewed as strategic partners by Japan. They have a historical civilisational heritage, and are recognised for their geopolitical and geostrategic location. The Japanese government sees them as playing critical roles in the Middle East's stabilisation and future development.

In contrast, Saudi Arabia, the United Arab Emirates, and Qatar, also have a central role in Japan's strategic calculations towards the region, but in these cases it is by virtue of their roles as major energy producers, but also for the critical role they play in the Gulf region's stability and beyond. They have been shown to have a special role in Japan's national interest for energy security and the freedom of navigation within the Persian Gulf.

Additionally, nations such as Iran and Israel who are embroiled in difficult-to-resolve regional and international wars have experienced setbacks in their ties with Japan. Japan has maintained diplomatic and large-scale energy transactions with Iran, despite it being isolated in economic terms by US sanctions. Japan constantly pressed for the restoration of open and stable ties with Iran, but wars and natural catastrophes hampered the endeavour. Also, Iran's nuclear issue served to undermine Iran's interdependence with Japan, despite the fact that Japan retained a diplomatic channel to convey its good intent towards Iran. Nevertheless, the broader conclusions are that in spite of these variances, there is an identifiable broader pattern towards multifaceted interdependence between Japan and the respective Middle Eastern countries.

It is worth noting that nations such as Palestine, Yemen, and Afghanistan have maintained diplomatic ties with Japan even though they have suffered through continuous wars, instability, and economic stagnation. Their ties with Japan, on the other hand, are largely reliant on Japanese foreign aid assistance. Their commerce with Japan may expand if incentives are established via conflict reduction, infrastructure development, and marketing of distinctive competitive goods and services, among other things. Thus, Japan's ODA establishes objectives to assist these countries in achieving self-reliance in the Country Assistance Policy document,[1] and is a further aspect that has proven to be important in furthering bilateral relations.

3   FIVE TYPES OF JAPAN–MIDDLE EAST INTERDEPENDENCE

We have observed that the official conclusion of partnerships between the Japanese government and Middle Eastern states is a sign of their close relationship, but it does not precisely explain the type and depth of their interdependence.

Official partnerships concluded by the Japanese government and Middle Eastern states diplomatically have a variety of forms: simple partnership; strategic partnership; comprehensive partnership; educational partnership; and innovative partnership (see Tables 1–5). Although these types of partnerships are explicitly referred to by Japan's Ministry of Foreign Affairs' (MOFA), each kind of collaboration is not structured, except for educational and innovation collaborations.

Since multifaceted complex interdependence is taking place between Japan and the Middle East and characterises their relationship, for the purposes of this study, it is instructive to provide a typology on the specific bilateral relationships that have emerged. Japan's engagement with the

---

[1] MOFA. Kunibetsu kaihatsu kyoryoku houshin (kyu kunibetsu kyoryoku houshin). jigyou tenkai keikaku. September 11, 2020. https://www.mofa.go.jp/mofaj/gaiko/oda/seisaku/kuni_enjyo_kakkoku.html; MOFA. Kunibetsu deta shuu 2016 nendo ban. https://www.mofa.go.jp/mofaj/gaiko/oda/shiryo/kuni.html.

Table 1 Interdependence type A: Objects of promotion of self-reliance

Country (income level)	Main ODA type	Opening of the embassy of Japan	Official partnership with Japan	MOU on defence exchange
Afghanistan (LDC)	Grants	1934 (55)	None	None
Palestine (LMIC)	Grants	General mission (1998)	None	None
Yemen (LDC)	Grants	(1990) (closed since February 2015)	None	None
Libya (UMIC)	None	1973 (closed since 2014)	None	None

Source This author based on MOFA webpages on countries in the Middle East, Africa and International Cooperation Data. Classification of economic level is as of 2018–2019 as follows: least developed countries (LDCs; with less than $1025 GNI per Capita), low-income countries (LICs), lower middle-income countries (LMICs; with more than $1026 less than $3955 GNI per Capita), upper middle-income countries (UMICs; with more than $3956 less than $12,235 GNI per Capita)[2]

Table 2 Interdependence type B: Expectation of stabilisation partners

Country (income level)	Main ODA type	Opening of the embassy of Japan	Official partnership with Japan	MOU on defence exchange
Algeria (UMIC)	Loans	1964	None	None
Iran (UMIC)	Loans	1929 (55)	None	None
Iraq (UMIC)	Loans	1939 (60)	Comprehensive (2009)	None
Lebanon (UMIC)	Loans	1954 (1959a)	None	None
Syria (LMIC)	Loans	1954 (1962a) (closed since March 2012)	None	None

Source This author obtained this information from MOFA webpages on countries in the Middle East, Africa, and International Cooperation Data. a: A delegation was upgraded its status to an embassy

Middle East in general is best conceptualised as non-militaristic equal-partner relationship, and one which is characterised by a multifaceted complex independence, that can be classified into five types based on the bilateral relationship concerned:

Table 3 Interdependence type C: Strategic cooperation partners

Country (income level)	Main ODA type	Opening of the Embassy of Japan	Official partnership with Japan	MOU on defence exchange
Egypt (LMIC)	Yen Loans Triangular cooperation	1936 (54)	Partnership (2007) Deauville partnership (2011) Education partnership (2016)	None
Jordan (LMIC)	Yen Loans Triangular cooperation	1974	Partnership (2004) Strategic partnership (2013)	2016.10 signed
Morocco (LMIC)	Yen Loans Triangular cooperation	1961	Partnership (2005)	None
Tunisia (LMIC)	Yen Loans	1969	Deauville partnership (2011)	None
Turkey (UMIC)	Yen Loans (semi-Graduates) Triangular cooperation	1925	Strategic partnership(2013)	2012.7 Expressed intention

Source This author based on MOFA webpages on countries in the Middle East, Africa, and International Cooperation Data

(A) Promotion of self-reliance (Palestine, Afghanistan, Yemen, etc.).
(B) Stabilisation efforts (e.g., Iran).
(C) Strategic cooperation (Turkey, Egypt etc.).
(D) Energy security (Saudi Arabia, UAE, Qatar, etc.).
(E) Emerging Cooperation (Israel).

Japan's interdependence with these nations is influenced by their stability and security, income level, energy transactions, strategic importance, and ODA type. It is clear however that the ODA distribution constitutes a significant determiner of the level of interdependence that Japan will have with a given Middle Eastern country as this serves to direct diplomatic engagement which has a broader effect on the bilateral relationship.

ODA is the system that allows Japan's Ministry of Foreign Affairs to utilise a significant budget, and it has profound impact on both developing and developed countries. Japan's ODA spending is divided into three categories: grants-in-aid, Yen Loans, and technical support. Japan's ODA began with technical aid in 1954 but is known to have developed

Table 4   Interdependence type D: Energy security cooperators

Country (income level)	Main ODA type	Opening of the embassy of Japan	Official partnership with Japan	MOU on defence exchange
Bahrain (ODA Graduates)	Technical cooperation	1983	Comprehensive partnership (2013)	Signed April 2012
Kuwait (ODA Graduates)	Technical cooperation	1963	Comprehensive partnership (2013)	None
Oman (ODA Graduates)	Technical cooperation	1980	Comprehensive partnership (2014)	Signed March 2019
Qatar (ODA Graduates)	Technical cooperation	1972 (1974) [a]	Comprehensive partnership (2013)	Signed February 2015
Saudi Arabia (ODA Graduates)	Technical cooperation	1960	Strategic partnership (2006) Comprehensive partnership (2013)	Signed September 2016
United Arab Emirates (ODA Graduates)	Technical cooperation	1974	Comprehensive partnership (2013) Comprehensive and strategic partnership (2018)	Signed May 2018

Source This author based on MOFA webpages on countries in the Middle East, Africa, and International Cooperation Data
[a] At first, the Embassy of Japan in Kuwait administered jointly Embassy of Japan in Qatar after 1972, which was independently established in Doha in 1974

Table 5   Interdependence type E: Emerging partner

Country (income level)	ODA	Opening of the Embassy of Japan	Partnership with Japan	MOU on defence exchange
Israel (ODA Graduates)	None	1952 (63)	Innovation partnership (2017)	None

Source This author based on MOFA webpages on countries in the Middle East and Africa and International Cooperation Data

Table 6 Technical cooperation (total of dispatch, receipt, and dispatch of investigation team during 1954–2018)

Table 5–1. (A) Objects of support for self-reliance

Country	Afghanistan (LDC)	Palestine (LMIC)	Yemen (LDC)	Libya (UMIC)
Total number	7772	9822	2766	156

Table 5–2. (B) Expectation of stabilisation

Country	Algeria (UMIC)	Iran (UMIC)	Iraq (UMIC)	Lebanon (UMIC)	Syria (LMIC)
Total number	1682	7352	11,749	515	5187

Table 5–3. (C) Strategic cooperation partners

Country	Egypt (LMIC)	Jordan (LMIC)	Tunisia (LMIC)	Morocco (LMIC)	Turkey (UMIC)
Total number	3987	6533	4462	5616	9377

Table 5–4. (D) Energy Security Partners

Country	Kuwait (Graduate)	Oman (Graduate)	Qatar (Graduate)	Saudi Arabia (Graduate)	UAE (Graduate)
Total number	241	2113	186	4076	590

Table 5–5. (E) Emerging partners

Country	Israel (Graduate)
Total number	62

Source The author, based on the following reference. JICA. Gijutsu kyoryoku (Bunya bunrui betsu. Nendo betsu ninzuu jisseki). https://www.jica.go.jp/activities/achievement/index.html

2 MOFA. *Kokusai kyouryoku hakusho 2019.* p. 13. https://www.mofa.go.jp/mofaj/gaiko/oda/press/shiryo/page1w_000019.html. Classification of income level is applied to the Middle Eastern countries based on theirs in 2018–2019.

with an emphasis on Yen loan supply and infrastructure development as economic growth approaches. Japan's ODA has expanded its contribution to poverty reduction initiatives in the medical, educational, and water sectors since the 1980s. Japan's ODA strategy was revised in the 2010s to emphasise economic growth via the promotion of high-quality infrastructure building and the promotion of Japan's unique technology.

In 1992, Japan issued its first ODA Charter and boosted ODA spending in conflict-affected and post-conflict nations, including Palestine and Cambodia (Hashimoto 1995). Security-related development aid, including as peacebuilding after conflict and human security, were included to the ODA Charter's revised menu in 2003. The 2015 Development Cooperation Charter renamed ODA "cooperation" to show respect for the indigenous ownership of the aid recipient and to encourage private sector and non-governmental groups to engage in ODA as partners. Additionally, the Charter underlines Japan's commitment to human security as a pillar of its development aid.

Prior to the first oil shock, Japan's ODA to the Middle East was significantly reduced. It is well known that during the first oil shock, the Japanese government sent special envoys to Arab nations and Iran. During 1973 and 1975, however, the first oil shock slowed Japan's total ODA budget growth. Japan then changed the geographical allocation of ODA funds, which had previously been focused on East Asia. Japan reallocated its ODA funds to the Middle East, Africa, and South America.

According to Japan's ODA white papers, the primary objective of Japan's ODA in the Middle East is to promote security and stability. Based on the calculation of data recorded in ODA budget, Japan's ODA budget distributed for bilateral assistance channels to the Middle East from 1954 to 2016 totalled 637 billion yen. During the same period, East Asia received 46.3% of total ODA funding, Oceania received 1.2%, South Asia received 17.8%, Central Asia and Caucasus received 1.5%, Central and South America received 7.6%, the Middle East and North Africa received 12.4%, Sub-Sahara Africa received 12.6%, and Europe received 0.6%.[3]

In 2016, Pakistan ranked top in terms of ODA distributed by Japan to Middle East, North Africa, and Pakistan (MENAP) nations, followed by Egypt, Iraq, Turkey, Afghanistan, Jordan, Tunisia, Morocco, Syria, Yemen, and Iran (see Table 7). Japan's ODA assistance to the Arabian

---

[3] MOFA. Wagakuni nikokukan ODA gaiyou 2016. pp. 4, 55, 106, 138, 171, 277, 319, 494.

Gulf nations has been very restricted, owing to the fact that they are high-income countries receiving solely technical assistance. Thus, it would be incorrect to believe that Japan prioritises ODA to resource-rich nations. Japan's cumulative ODA disbursement to MENAP in 2016 included an 11.4% allocation to Least Developed Countries (LDCs), a 59.5% allocation to Lower Middle-Income Countries (LMICs), a 28.5% allocation to Upper Middle-Income Countries (UMICs), and a 0.1% allocation to graduates. In other words, by 2016, just 0.1% of Japan's ODA budget was given to the Arabian Gulf nations.

4   Classifying Japan–Middle East Interdependence

This section explains each of Japan–Middle East interdependence type: (A) Promotion of Self-reliance; (B) Stabilisation Efforts; (C) Strategic Cooperation; (D) Energy Security; (E) Emerging Cooperation (Fig. 1).

(A) Promotion of Self-Reliance

Japan's ODA plan sets ODA goals for Afghanistan, Palestine, and Yemen as promotion of their self-reliance under the Country Assistance Policy. Libya has received no ODA from Japan until its admission of involvement in the Pan-Am terrorist incident and civil conflict after the Middle Eastern regionwide uprisings in 2010/11. Libya is currently considered a nation that should strive for self-reliance. Japan's ODA to these countries has been significant, since Japan is committed to conflict resolution and Middle East stability. After 1991, the Japanese government increased ODA to Palestine, and in the 1990s, to Yemen. Japan's ODA towards Afghanistan's peacebuilding efforts since 2001 totalled 6.9 billion US dollars in 2021.[4] It is worth noting here that Japan's formal connection with countries of this kind is mostly based on ODA distribution, and Japan has not concluded into a formal partnership or a defence Memorandum of Understanding (MOU) with them.

(B) Stabilisation Efforts

---

[4] Nippon.com. Nihon no Afghanisutan Enjo: 20 Nen de 7500 Okuen Kibo. September 1, 2021. https://www.nippon.com/ja/japan-data/h01105/.

Table 7 Japan's ODA to countries in the MENAP (1954–2016) (100 million Yen)

Interdependence type/Main ODA type	Country	Grants	Non-grant (Yen Loans)	Technical coopera-tion	Total amount (Grants, Loans, Technical cooperation)
(A) Object of support for self-reliance/Grants	Afghanistan (LDC)	5225.57	7.2	601.26	5834.03
	Palestine (LMIC)[5]	960.98	0	143.03	1104.01
	Yemen (LDC)	734.72	608.49	104.75	1447.96
	Libya (UMIC)	6.48	0	3.71	10.19
(B) Expectation to stabilisation /Non-grant (Yen Loan)	Algeria[6](UMIC)	13.9	148.5	79.98	242.38
	Iran (UMIC)	71.67	810.28	295.76	1177.71
	Iraq (UMIC)	1897.80	6891.74	204.44	8993.98
	Lebanon (UMIC)	62.87	130.22	17.4	210.49
	Pakistan (LMIC)	2728.43	9922.83	582.91	13234.17
	Syria (LMIC)	373.31	1563.05	307.15	2243.51
(C) Strategic cooperation partner /Triangular cooperation (recipient of non-Grant, Yen Loans)	Egypt (LMIC)	1568.14	7613.73	814.07	9995.94
	Jordan (LMIC)	863.98	2826.59	360.59	4051.16
	Morocco (LMIC)	370.8	3116.09	389.74	3876.63
	Turkey (UMIC, Graduate)	43.4	6971.80	486.4	7501.6
	Tunisia (LMIC)	60.84	3045.01	273.45	3379.3
(D) Energy security partner/ Technological Cooperation	Kuwait (Graduate)	0	0	9.48	9.48
	Oman (Graduate)	0	0	141.32	141.32
	Qatar (Graduate)	0	0	11.01	11.01

(continued)

[5] Per capita income was 3380 US dollars in Palestine (World Bank), which is the level of LMICs. World Bank. West Bank and Gaza. https://data.worldbank.org/country/PS (reference on November 13, 2020). More than 100 countries recognise Palestine as sovereign state.

[6] Income level of Algeria fell from high income in 1980s.

Table 7 (continued)

Interdependence type/Main ODA type	Country	Grants	Non-grant (Yen Loans)	Technical coopera-tion	Total amount (Grants, Loans, Technical cooperation)
	Saudi Arabia (Graduate)	0	0	204.89	204.89
	United Arab Emirates (Graduate)	0	0	37.35	37.35
(E) Emerging partner/None-ODA	Israel (Graduate)	0	0	0.45	0.45

Source The author, based on the following references: Gaimusho. Seihu Kaihatsu Enjo (ODA) Kunibetsu Deta Shu 2016. April 3, 2017. https://www.mofa.go.jp/mofaj/gaiko/oda/press/shiryo/page1w_000019.html

Countries with expectations of stabilisation include Algeria, Iraq, Iran, Syria, and Lebanon. Their potentiality for economic growth is high, but their security has not been stable in the long term. Although Algeria, Iraq, and Iran are large energy resource reservoirs, Iraq, and Iran have suffered from hard economic sanctions since the 1980s. The Algerian economy suffered low energy prices in the 1980s, falling into a severe civil war after 1992. Japan maintained diplomatic channels with Syria, a socialist country, and disbursed ODA to it even during the Cold War era, but the Japanese embassy had to close in 2012 due to the intensifying civil war. Thus, Syria, after 2012, can be classified as a type A partner.

Japan's ODA disbursement to Type B countries has been mainly through the Yen Loan. Japan's Yen Loan offers a concessional interest rate (nominal rate), which is far lower than the market standard. Repayment is scheduled in the long term. Japan's philosophy of providing loans as ODA is an effective option to stimulate incentives for economic development to UMICs and LMICs. Grants-in-aid will spoil these countries, and high interests will impede their sustainable growth.

Japan provided Iran with a good amount of ODA loans, technical assistance, and disaster cooperation, but this support ranked 11th largest among the MENAP countries in amount as discussed above. Japan did

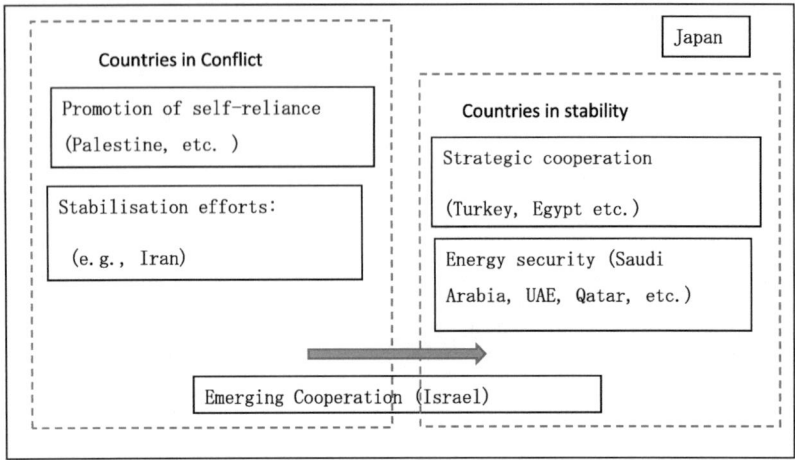

Fig. 1 Types of bilateral interdependence between the Middle East and Japan (*Source* This author)

not conclude an official partnership or defence MOU with any type B countries, except for a comprehensive partnership concluded with Iraq in 2009. This allocation represents Japan's intension to support Iraq's reconstruction, although Iraq's diplomatic and regional leadership cannot be expected yet.

(C) Strategic Cooperation

Countries of which can be understood as strategic cooperation partnership type are Egypt, Jordan, Tunisia, Turkey, and Morocco. Their security is stable. They are receivers of Japan's ODA loans, and in this sense, they are not different from type B partners. In fact, they assume the role of cooperating with the disbursement of Japan's ODA to other countries in the Middle East, Africa, and Asia. This is called "triangle aid". Japan makes use of "south-to-south aid" as a mechanism to distribute Japan's ODA. Thus, these countries are classified as "strategic cooperation partners" of Japan's relations with the Middle East. The governments of these countries have high skills and can play active roles. Notably, type C countries are located in strategic geo-political areas of the Middle East.

The Japanese government explains that Japan holds double identities of aid provider and aid receiver. Japan joined the Colombo Plan in 1954 and began providing foreign aid while still in the process of reconstruction after WWII. The Japanese government indicates that this was one of the earliest "south-to-south aid cooperation." Japan ended the repayment of all loans in 1990.

In 1975, Japan initiated a cooperation with Thailand to provide Japan's foreign aid to a third country, which was practically the first case of Japan's "triangular cooperation". As of 2020, Japan concluded an agreement for a triangular cooperation programme with 12 countries: Thailand, Singapore, Egypt, Jordan, Tunisia, Morocco, Chili, Brazil, etc. Triangular cooperation is an agenda of the "Global Partnership Initiative on Effective Triangular Cooperation (GPI)[7]" of the Organisation for Economic Cooperation and Development (OECD). Japan's Development Cooperation Charter, formulated in 2015, states that, "In implementing development cooperation, it is also important to take advantage of expertise, human resources and their networks, and other assets that have been accumulated in the recipient countries during the many years of Japan's development cooperation. Japan's triangular cooperation involving emerging and other countries capitalises on such assets. In view of the high regard held by the international community, Japan will continue to promote triangular cooperation".

All of the countries of type C concluded an official partnership with Japan, which indicates that Japan regards them with partners of key importance. It is worth noting that Jordan is the only country among type C countries to have concluded a defence MOU with Japan.

(D) Energy Security

The Arabian Gulf nations, Bahrain, Kuwait, Oman, Qatar, Saudi Arabia, and the UAE, can be understood as Japan's energy security partners. Their security has been stable and resilient in spite of uneasy crises. These nations collaborate with Japan to ensure a secure energy supply, and in exchange, and are recipients of technology transfer and investment from Japan. They are, however, classed as high-income countries, therefore

---

[7] OECD. The Global Partnership Initiative on Effective Triangular Cooperation (GPI). https://www.oecd.org/dac/triangular-cooperation/the-global-partnership-initiative-on-effective-triangular-co-operation.htm.

Japan is unable to assist them with ODA grants or loans. Japan has solely given ODA in the form of technical cooperation. Technical cooperation can be a low-budget component of ODA in contrast to loans and grants. This demonstrates that Japan has constraints when it comes to large-scale technology transfer to stable energy-producing nations through public sector. Japan's ODA to nations classified as category D is a "modest amount" (Table 7).

Japan's large-scale technical collaboration started after the first oil shock. Technological cooperation is classified into three subtypes: the deployment of Japanese specialists, the reception of trainees to Japan for training, and the dispatch of Japan's investigative team. In the instance of Saudi Arabia, the Japan International Cooperation Agency (JICA) has identified map-producing cooperation initiatives and electric standardisation projects as exemplary achievements (Komori 2011, 52–53). These are examples that private sector would not have achieved.

In contrast to lower-income group nations, technical collaboration has been conducted on a lesser scale with Arabian energy producers. From 1954 to 2018, cumulative data show that 9822 specialists and trainees were received and sent to Palestine, 7352 to Iran, and 9377 to Turkey. Saudi Arabia has 4076 technical cooperation agreements with reliable energy providers, Oman had 2113, and the UAE had 590. These records demonstrate unequivocally that the Japanese government has struggled to provide large-scale technological cooperation to energy-producing countries, despite the fact that the Japanese government may have desired to provide them with the most generous assistance possible, given that they are, of course, critical to Japan's energy security. Thus private sector and NPOs are expected to play larger role in technological transfer by governments of Japan and the Middle East.

The Japanese government has established a comprehensive relationship with the Gulf states, implying tight connections and mutual reliance between the two nations. The leaders of the Arabian Gulf nations have engaged with the Emperor of Japan, which underlines how a common royal character reinforces and deepens the relationship. Japan has approved defence memorandums of understanding with all Arabian Gulf states except Kuwait. Although the MOUs only specify extremely broad collaboration, they enable the Japanese government to act during regional crises.

(E) Emerging Cooperation

Israel is a nation whose ties with Japan have grown significantly since 2000. Israel received little ODA from Japan since its income level was comparatively high. In 2017, Japan and Israel established an innovative partnership. Instead of MOFA, Japan's Ministry of Economy, Trade, and Industry (METI) oversaw its completion. Israel has yet to sign a defence memorandum of understanding (MOU) with Japan. Japan's development assistance programme for Palestine, dubbed "Corridor for Peace and Prosperity", was launched in 2007 by then-Foreign Minister Taro Aso. It envisaged Israel, Palestine, Jordan, and Japan cooperating to create initiatives for the economic growth of Palestine, which would foster mutual trust. However, Israel's participation in this process of peacebuilding has been mostly inactive so far.

Japan–Middle East bilateral interdependence is categorised into five types, and the depth of interdependence varies based on security condition, ODA disbursement type, cooperation type, diplomatic partnership, and defence MOU. All five types of interdependence are also asymmetric.

5   UNIQUENESS OF MIDDLE EAST–JAPAN MULIFACETED COMPLEX INTERDEPENDENCE

Japan's energy policy shifted significantly in the aftermath of two major crises—the 1970s oil crisis and the 2011 Great East Japan Earthquake. Following the oil shock of the 1970s, Japan faced two types of diversification: energy source diversification and energy supplier diversification. Japan's energy business is split between upstream and downstream sectors, and the nation lacks a "big" energy firm, which essentially positions the country as a "weak negotiator". Furthermore, Japan's energy strategy is convoluted: 3E+S (Energy security, Economy, Environment, and Safety). Japan may not be able to compete financially with China if such severe competition takes place.

Nevertheless, energy-saving technologies are now widely used, and Japanese companies have shifted production to other countries, decreasing Japan's primary energy consumption dependence on oil to around 40%. Japan's oil consumption peaked in 1996 at about 5 million barrels per day and has been decreasing since then. Japan's economy has entered a phase of moderate growth.

Japan tried to diversify its oil supply by including some Asian countries, however, their net oil imports fell short. Additionally, Japan lacks compelling reasons to diversify its oil supply outside the Middle East region. Historically, Middle Eastern oil imports have been very cost-efficient, and Japan has relied on the US–Japan alliance to guarantee Middle Eastern security. Thus, building strategic relationships with world-class resource countries—Saudi Arabia and the United Arab Emirates—has resulted in energy security success. In the United Arab Emirates, Japan developed oil reserves. Sumitomo Chemical's Petro Rabigh in Saudi Arabia and Nghi Son projects in Vietnam represent a new strategy. The latter one is being developed in cooperation with multinational companies from the Middle East, Europe, Japan, and Vietnam.

Japan has been supplied with oil and gas by energy-producing countries, which has boosted Japan's confidence. They expect that Japan will remain a dependable consumer of large amounts of energy while also serving as a source of investment, technological transfer, and support for human resource development. They now expect their young to be entertained by Japan's technological transfer in the area of animation production. Japan must take all necessary precautions to guarantee its energy supply, since a future energy crisis may result in a decrease in energy expenditure required for the shift to renewable energy. Japan must provide more advantageous bidding conditions to energy suppliers than emerging oil consumers such as China, India, and South Korea in order to get oil concessions.

Japan's involvement in oil and LNG production has had a direct impact on interdependence and has proved to be a basis on which bilateral relations could be strengthened. Japan's sixth energy plan, launched in 2021, outlined a goal for raising the private sector's contribution of independent oil and gas field development to 50% of total oil consumption by 2030. Japan was awarded a new marine oil concession in the United Arab Emirates in 2018, bringing the country's share to 27.4%, and by July 2020, it had grown to 34.7%.[8]

---

[8] METI. Wagakoku no Sekiyu, Tennengasu no Jishukaihatsu Hiritsu (Reiwa Gannenn Do) wo Kouhyou Shimasu. July 22, 2020. https://www.meti.go.jp/press/2020/07/202 00722001/20200722001.html.

6 NON-ENERGY TRADE AND DIRECT INVESTMENT

Due to their financial strength and better governance systems, the Gulf Cooperation Council (GCC) states are more likely to attract international direct investment than other regional neighbors. Saudi Petrochemicals Development Company Limited (SHARQ) is an example in this regard. It was funded by 60 companies, including Mitsubishi Chemical, Mitsubishi Corporation, and the Japan Bank for International Cooperation. Mitsubishi Chemical started producing ethylene in 1987 via a joint venture with a local firm and expanded its capacity in the 2000s.

As of 1998, Saudi Arabia and Japan had 31 joint ventures totalling 5.7 billion Saudi riyals in investment (total investment including Saudi capital was 11.6 billion Saudi riyal). 26 of the projects were non-industrial joint ventures established in Saudi Arabia by a trading firm, a manufacturer of heavy electrics, a plant engineering company, and others with local partners. Japanese banks were the main source of GCC bank loans in the late 1980s and early 1990s. By the end of 1991, Japanese banks had provided GCC countries with $5.2 billion in loans, accounting for 30% of the total.

Additionally, lending rose from $3.8 billion in 1996–2000 to $4.4 billion in 2001–2005 and $16.8 billion in 2006–2010 by Japanese banks (averaged over a five-year period). Between 1996 and 2000, credit to GCC countries averaged $38.7 billion, but rapidly rose to $64.3 billion during the next five years (2001–2005) and to $235.2 billion between 2006 and 2010. Japan and the GCC countries achieved progress in the late 2000s in terms of foreign investment promotion policies, but the bilateral legal and institutional investment climate lags advanced economies and Southeast Asian countries. For further investment by Japan in the GCC, bilateral engagement rather than establishing a regional investment FTA appears to be more realistic especially given the political divisions between GCC member states.

Japan and the Middle East's interdependence has been uneven in terms of foreign direct investments (FDIs) and corporate engagement. Rentier state regimes, such as those seen in the GCC, are argued here to deter FDI from Japan. This has resulted in a clear disparity in FDI and this is reflected in the number of GCC firms operating in Japan being marginal in comparison to the number of Japanese businesses operating in the GCC countries. Nevertheless, the GCC has been a profitable market for Japanese companies to engage in and thus has underlined economic interests beyond the FDI disparity and energy trade.

It is clear that institutional issues may emerge as a consequence of FDI between industrialised and developing countries. Concluding new investment promotion laws that are "fair" to both countries would institutionally encourage FDI. Among the obstacles are high business costs, especially in the labour and tax domains, and difficulties acquiring qualified human resources. Language serves as an impediment to cultural interaction. Kuwait signed its first IPA with Japan in March 2012, making it the first GCC nation to do so. Following that, a legislative framework was created to improve the transparency, legal stability, and predictability of both countries' investment environments, as well as to protect bilateral investment and investor rights. A favourable tax system and human resource development are suggested to attract Middle Eastern investment to Japan.

7   Regime Security of the Middle East Countries

Japan's pragmatic internationalism embraces democracy, free markets, and multilateralism, but it also contributes to increasing interdependence with countries. In the Middle East, by embracing diverse political and economic rules and institutions, Japan holds flexibility in making foreign policy decisions based on context rather than ideology or dogma as has demonstrated in this volume. This pragmatism is the bedrock of asymmetric interdependence.

The governments of Middle Eastern countries pursue regime security through domestic governance and foreign relations, including interdependence with Japan. Japan's interdependence with the Middle East contributes to three channels: royal, governmental, and citizens, since Japan (i) maintains the principle of non-intervention in domestic affairs, even though Japan is a nation of democracy and human rights; (ii) provides income sources for their development and welfare through energy purchase payment, technological transfers, infrastructure building, service, and commodities (Japan is a stable energy security provider for energy suppliers); and (iii) sustains cultural and national legitimacy through multiple channels of civilisational dialogues and cultural exchanges. Royal diplomacy enhances the legitimacy of monarchies in the Middle East.

Japan, on the other hand, by 2015, did not export weaponry, police equipment, or domestic surveillance technologies that enhance regime's security and policing elements, while China and Israel provide exports in this area. Japan's Self-Defense Force (JSDF) participation in UNPKO deployments and multilateral marine missions in the Indian Ocean has proved to be limited to non-combat activities. While Japan's ODA seeks to avoid war, promote human security, and stabilise Middle Eastern nations, it is just one component of broader international assistance cooperation. Japan calls for triangular aid cooperation with Middle Eastern allies to offer technical assistance and refugee assistance to Middle Eastern refugees.

8   Protection and Security of Japanese in the Middle East

Japan's defence MOUs with Middle Eastern nations have not resulted in any tangible security cooperation. Due to this, it remains a dimension that has potential to be developed in the context of Japan's foreign policy. Military and law enforcement security remain critical in the Middle East, where armed conflicts and terrorism are real threats. As security and safety for Japanese citizens in the Middle East are first provided by local governments. Second, the Japanese have the option of contracting with private security firms operating lawfully in Middle Eastern nations. Third, the US is almost the only military force capable of executing large-scale invasion anywhere in the globe, despite the fact that the US's diplomatic and military actions often contribute to a regional war.

Japan is considered as a 'free rider' by some in international affairs, but a more accurate perspective is that Japan self-restricts its foreign policy with a focus on safeguarding its own citizens, but the Japanese government has never deployed planes or ships to rescue Japanese people during prior Middle East crises by summer 2021 for the evacuation from Afghanistan. As highlighted in this volume, during Iraq's 1990 invasion of Kuwait, Japanese people were taken captive in Iraq. Turkey used civilian planes to rescue Japanese citizens in Tehran during the 1985 Iran–Iraq War, bringing Japanese parliament member Inoki and the wives of Japanese prisoners to Amman in 1990 for talks with the Iraqi government.

An additional observation of note is that Japan's approach to regional issues is not always compatible with that of the US. In 1958, the Kishi cabinet opposed the United States dispatching forces to the Lebanon Crisis and attempted to mediate at the United Nations between the United Arab Republic (UAR) and the United States, proposing to the UN Security Council a reinforcement of the United Nations Interim Force in Lebanon (UNIFIL). Japan's foreign minister, Shintaro Abe, visited Iran and Iraq in 1983 to mediate the Iran–Iraq War for ceasefire. Japan provided logistical supports at the Gulf Crisis in 1990, but did not commit to multinational coalition force to liberate Kuwait from Iraqi occupation in 1991. Japan's "practical internationalism" is a convoluted concept that blends neoclassical realism (or realism oriented on defence and economic growth) with multilateralism. Article 9 of the Japanese constitution regulates it. The security viewpoint of the Japanese government is one of realism in the achievement of defence goals. Japan's post-1945 conduct has been dubbed neoclassical realism.

Japan's security mission should not be defined as militaristic, but encapsulating it within an adequate academic conceptualisation remains challenging. Japan's security role has included funding the coalition force, hostage rescue in Iraq, intelligence gathering in Iran, and minesweeping operations in the Gulf. Japan contributed money to 16 countries via the Gulf Peace Fund (GPF), including the United States and countries in Europe, the Middle East, Africa, and Asia. Japan's funding has not been slow; in fact, it has been faster than that of others, including the US Congress, and has been sufficient for US budgetary procedures.

Japan's participation in the rescue and relocation of Gulf War prisoners is noteworthy. Fifteen Americans were sheltered by the Japanese embassy in Kuwait. By arranging an international peace festival in Baghdad, Antonio Inoki contributed to the release of the United States', United Kingdom's, and Japan's last prisoners. Throughout the Gulf War, Japan supplied reliable intelligence on Iran's intentions, assisting in the stabilisation of relations between Iran and coalition soldiers and allowing coalition forces to concentrate on the battle on the Kuwaiti front. According to the Japan Maritime Self-Defense Force (JMSDF) mission commander overseeing minesweeping activities in the Gulf, he ordered the team to keep quiet after the mission. Japan's role in the Gulf Crisis deserves to be rehabilitated.

In 2015, the Japanese Act Establishing the National Security Council (NSC) was modified; it included provisions ensuring the security of

Japanese nationals. The amendment requires the Cabinet to consider on steps to protect and rescue Japanese nationals overseas. Additionally, the Self-Defense Forces Act was modified to include the protection of Japanese citizens abroad as a primary objective of the JSDF. The JSDF established a counterterrorism squad comprised of 300 elite soldiers (Seijibu 2015, 163).

9   CULTURAL UNDERSTANDING

It has also become clear from this volume's chapters that Japan and the Middle East have potential for greater interaction and knowledge exchange. In the case of Japan-Middle East relations, individuals and multinational companies have developed ties within Egypt, Turkey, Saudi Arabia, the United Arab Emirates, Qatar, Iran, and Israel, among other countries. Furthermore, there has been no major cultural conflicts between Japan and Middle Eastern countries. Thus, cultural exchanges between these countries, in addition to those conducted by scholars, teachers, independent non-governmental organisations, sister cities, artists, and the media, have promoted Middle East Japan interdependence.

It has been also been observed that certain cultural aspects have been entrenched in the daily lives of these countries. "Koshary", an Egyptian cuisine, is an example of a Japanese traditional food that has been naturalised, with sticky rice on Egyptian tables. In the Middle East, it is widely accepted that Japanese animations have a robust following. Another example is that of Marubeni who made a significant contribution by hosting an annual cultural festival for Qatar University to promote Japan-Qatar relations. Marubeni's example underlines how Japan's private sector involvement in local energy sector development has had a ripple effect, promoting bilateral cultural ties and political linkages. Japan's official development assistance (ODA) and building projects have also been aimed at fostering the development of cultural and symbolic infrastructure in the Middle East. Two such instances are Cairo's Opera House (National Cultural Center) and Istanbul's first Bosphorus Bridge. It is still necessary to use scientific methods to determine the depth, breadth, and nature of pro-Japan sentiments in the Middle East, as well as pro-Turkey, Arab, Iran, and Israel views in Japan.

Numerous scholars, among them Egyptian Professors Issam Hamza and Karam Khalil, as well as Japanese Professor Toshihiko Izutsu (1914–1993), established the standard for academic excellence in cross-cultural studies. Thus, the intermediary cultural responsibilities of governments, royals, and people are important as transmitters, interpreters, and stabilisers of society's understanding of other cultures.

10   Multilateralism

Japan's first step into more sophisticated diplomacy was during the 1973 oil crisis, when it combined strategic goals with tactical measures aimed at maximising national advantage. This is contrary to common belief, which believes that Japan prioritises its national economic interests above its relations with the US. Japan's diplomacy is conciliatory, in part because it bridges the gap between Western and developing nation values. Japan has two notable pillars: as a Western state, it is committed to stable democracy and capitalism; secondly, as a late-developed country, it has taken on the role as an advocate for developing nations and non-Western values.

The US and the European Union are proponents of liberty, democracy and human rights. China, as a developing country maintains that Western activities in the Middle East have been harmful, and the country maintains a policy of non-intervention in the area. Japan can be understood as proponent of both the developed and developing worlds, adhering to the values of "liberty, democracy, human rights and humanism" as well as developmentalism. Following the proclamation of the ODA Charter in 1992, Japan conducts electoral assistance missions to practically all elections in Arab nations and Afghanistan, but does not commit to forcing democratisation in any country. Thus, despite its seeming lack of aggression, Japan maintains "indirect multilateralism" with the West and the Middle East. Japan's engagement in the Middle East is steady and peaceful as a result of its democratic system and mutual cultural understanding. Japan's quiet diplomacy can be understood as motivated by a number of factors, but it is a technique used by the Japanese foreign policy establishment in order to maintain positive relations with two parties. Japan's diplomacy is devoted on building goodwill with the United States, a unilateral force in the Middle East that divides friends and adversaries. Japan's internationalists, or holders of conventional country and middle-power views are aware of Japan's complex diplomatic system.

Japan's low-key diplomacy is partly explained by the fact that the country is not a permanent member of the United Nations Security Council, and also lacks armed options in diplomatic crises due to constitutional constraints. Japan's regional involvement policy with developing countries, especially those in the Middle East, is based on triangular aid cooperation. Japan's establishment of the Gulf Peace Fund (GPF) during the Gulf War is another example of a regionally accommodative attitude to the US. Japan's stance on FDI through the GCC was likely influenced in part by the notion that the GCC offered a sufficiently big market for Japanese industry.

Japan has created a complicated web of interdependence with the United States, China, other OECD countries, and industrialised nations, including those in the Middle East. As a result, Japan maintains a healthy balance of competitiveness and collaboration within its foreign policy on a global basis. Japan actively analyses the politics, security, and economic affairs of major countries; nonetheless, Japan's contemporary foreign policy orientation is distinct in that it does not seek hegemony or impose political and cultural ideals on others. Foreign assistance is often regarded as Japan's most potent diplomatic instrument. Asia is rapidly developing, and Japan has chosen to focus its engagement in this key geopolitical area. Despite external pressures, it did not use the defence trade for diplomatic and economic goals by 2015. Japan has shown respect for Islamic culture in its domestic and foreign affairs. It has a low-profile foreign policy and yet balances this against a maintenance of its own identity.

Given this, Japan's efforts to adapt to external settings, traditional and popular cultural contents, has been best exhibited by a subtle and sophisticated "three-dimensional diplomacy". Nevertheless, in the final analysis it is possible to conclude that given the variations that exist, complex multifaceted interdependence provides the most convincing conceptualisation on Japan's relations with the Middle East and a typology can be advanced based on the specific bilateral relationship concerned. Given the differences, it is possible to conclude that complex multifaceted interdependence provides the most compelling conception of Japan's ties with the Middle East, and a typology depending on the particular bilateral relationship in question can also be proposed. It is based on this that this book seeks to offer a basis from which further academic enquiry can take place.

Bibliography

Hashimoto, Kohei. 1995. *Senryaku Enjo: Chuto Wahei Sien to ODA no Shourai.* Tokyo: PHP Kenkyujo.

Komori, Takeshi. 2011. *Tojoukoku kara Mita Nihon: Bunka ha Ibunka de Migakareru.* Tokyo: Bungeisha.

Seijibu, Yomiurishinbun. 2015. *Anzenhoshou Kanren Hō.* Tokyo: Shinzansha Publisher.

Glossary

Japanese and Other Non-European (Arabic and Turkish) Language

*al-ta*ʿ*āish (Arabic)*: Coexistence

*al-ta*ʿ*āun (Arabic)*: Collaboration

al-tasāmuh (Arabic): Tolerance

Asātīr (Arabic)/ Mirai no Mukashi Banashi (Japanese): *An animation film* "Future's Folktales" that Saudi manga producer, Manga Productions and Toei Animation, Japan, collaborated to produce, and was aired in the United States, Saudi Arabia and Japan in 2020.

Ayame: Iris

Bushido: Chivalry held by Japanese warriors, Bushi.

Captain Tsubasa: Japanese animation film on Soccer Player Boy named Tsubasa.

Cool Japan: Japan's soft power policy.

Dragon Ball: Japanese animation film on adventure story about a search for the treasure called "Dragon Ball".

Edo **period 1603–1868:** The era when Tokugawa family as Shogun (the commander of warriors) placed their government in Edo (Tokyo then) to rule Japan.

Edo **Shogunate:** Government by the Tokugawa ruling family as Shogun (the commander of warriors).

Enerugi anzen-hoshō: Energy security.

© The Editor(s) (if applicable) and The Author(s) 2023
S. Nakamura and S. Wright (eds.), *Japan and the Middle East*,
Contemporary Gulf Studies, https://doi.org/10.1007/978-981-19-3459-9

Ertuğrul (Turkish): The Ottoman Navy frigate which was dispatched to Japan.

Ertugrul 1890: Fictional movie aired in 2015, based on the non-fiction history of *Ertuğrul tragedy.*

Ertuğrul tragedy: A tragic incident that the Ottoman Navy frigate sunk off shore of Oshima island at Kushimoto town, Wakayama prefecture in Japan in 1890. 587 crews passed away and only 69 survived.

Gaiatsu: Force exerted from outside, or intervention from outside.

Gediz: Turkish frigate that visited Japan in 2015 on the occasion of the 125th year of the *Ertuğrul tragedy.*

Iwakura mission: A delegation mission led by Tomomi Iwakura visited the United States and Europe during 1872–73. The purpose of the mission was to amend unfair treaties with the West; as well as conclude a treaty of friendship (amity) with the Ottoman Empire.

iftar (Arabic): Meals eaten by Muslims after fasting.

Izokukai: Association of Bereaved Family (For the soldiers in the Second World War)

judo: A traditional combat sport in Japan.

judoka: Player of Judo.

juso teki na kankei: Multifaced relationship or multilevel relationship.

kado: A Japanese art of flower arrangement.

Kanz al-Hattab (Arabic) or *Kikori to Takaramono (Japanese)*: The first animation film "The Woodcutters' Treasure" produced together by Saudi Arabia and Japan, and aired by Tokyo TV in May 2018.

katana: Japanese swords.

karate: Japanese martial art.

Keidanren: Japan Business Federation. Japan's largest business organisation.

kimono: A traditional Japanese garment.

Koshary (Arabic): An Egyptian dish cooked with rice, noodle and vegetables.

Kumon Method: A tutoring programme, originating in Japan, in which children improve their skills in mathematics, reading, and languages.

Kurama Tengu: Tengu are humanoid monstrous creatures from ancient Japanese folklore whose faces are red and can fly. Kurama Tengu are the most well-known of the Japanese Tengu who were said to live in Mt. Kurama in Kyoto, Japan.

kyōran bukka: The hyper inflation that occurred in Japan in 1974.

Meiji era **1868–1912:** The era that Emperor Meiji (Mutsuhito) reigned in Japan.

Meiji Restoration (Meiji Ishin): The termination of feudalism by Tokugawa shogunate in 1867, and successive transition to Imperial rule in 1968, and political, economic and social modernisation in Japan to around 1890.

Namban trade: Trades flourished by *Nambanjin* (Portuguese and Spanish) traders who arrived in Japan during the sixteenth and seventeenth century.

Nara era **710–784:** The era that emperors placed capital in Nara (called *Heijokyo*).

NHK: Japan Broadcasting Corporation.

Nichi-Do Boeki Kyokai': Japan–Turkey Trade Association established in 1925.

Nichi-do Kyokai: Japan–Turkey Society (currently named Nihon Toruko Kyokai).

*Nihon Shohinka*n: Japanese products store opened in Turkey in1929.

Nihon Toruko Kyokai: Japan-Turkey Society established in 1926 (as Nichi-do Kyokai then).

Nihonkaigi: Japan Conference. A political organisation of new nationalists in Japan.

Rashomonesque: The Rashomon effect is a term related to the notorious unreliability of eyewitnesses. It describes a situation in which an event is given contradictory interpretations or descriptions by the individuals involved.

Renduku: A tradition of Japanese kite.

Sado: Japanese tea ceremony.

Sakhalin Island: The largest island at the far eastern end in Russia, located north of the Japanese archipelago.

Samurai: Japanese warriors or *Bushi in feudal periods.*

Seikei bunri: A foreign policy decoupling political conflicts from economic relations with a country.

Shakai kagaku: Social science.

Sogo-shosha: Japan's multinational trading companies that trades a wide range of goods and services.

Shigen gaikō: Resource diplomacy.

Shogunate: Government by Shogun (the commander of warriors) during feudal periods in Japan.

Siwār al-Dhahab (**Arabic**): "The Gold Ring", the first manga comic produced as Japan–UAE collaboration in 2008.

Sumo: A traditional Japanese style of wrestling rooted in Shintoism.

Taisho era **1912–26:** The era of the reign of the Emperor Taisho (Yoshihito) in Japan.

Tōakeizai Kenkyūsho: "East Asia Economic Institute". A research institute established by Imperial Japan in 1938.

Toei Animation: A Japanese animation production enterprise.

Tohoku: Northern area of Japan.

Tokkatsu: Spontaneous extracurricular activities by students in the educational curriculum.

Tsunami: Seismic sea wave.

Turgutreis (**Turkish**): A Turkish frigate that visited Japan in 1990 on the occasion's 100th year of the *Ertuğrul tragedy*.

Türk—Nippon Dostluğunun Sonsuz Hatıraları (**Turkish**): The book that the Turkish Embassy in Tokyo published both in Japanese and Turkish in 1938.

Wa: Moderate, tranquil, strifeless, be on good terms, settlement.

wasat (**Arabic**): Centre, middle way, moderation.

Yabani (**Arabic**): Japanese.

INDEX

© The Editor(s) (if applicable) and The Author(s) 2023
S. Nakamura and S. Wright (eds.), *Japan and the Middle East*,
Contemporary Gulf Studies, https://doi.org/10.1007/978-981-19-3459-9